Sociable Knowledge

Sociable Knowledge

*Natural History and the Nation
in Early Modern Britain*

Elizabeth Yale

PENN

UNIVERSITY OF PENNSYLVANIA PRESS

PHILADELPHIA

Published by
University of Pennsylvania Press
Philadelphia, Pennsylvania 19104-4112
www.upenn.edu/pennpress

Printed in the United States of America on acid-free paper
1 3 5 7 9 10 8 6 4 2

Library of Congress Cataloging-in-Publication Data

Yale, Elizabeth, author.
  Sociable knowledge : natural history and the nation in early
modern Britain / Elizabeth Yale.
      pages cm. — (Material texts)
    ISBN 978-0-8122-4781-7 (alk. paper)
    1. Natural history—Great Britain—History—17th century.
2. Natural history correspondence—Great Britain—
History—17th century. 3. Communication in learning and
scholarship—Great Britain—History—17th century.
4. Naturalists—Archives. 5. Topographical surveying—Great
Britain—History—17th century. 6. Topographical
surveying—Political aspects—Great Britain. 7. Natural
history—Great Britain—Historiography. 8. Natural history
literature—Great Britain. I. Title. II. Series: Material texts.
QH21.G7Y35 2016
508.4109′032—dc23
                                    2015022503

To my parents
Jane Louise Yale
Stephen Elon Yale

Contents

Note on Sources

All quotations from early modern papers observe the following conventions: Familiar abbreviations ("Dr.," "Mr.," and so on) have been left as is, while most abbreviations of names and words not now commonly abbreviated have been expanded in braces. Common abbreviations such as "wch," "ye," "yt," however, have been silently expanded to "which," "the," and "that." All superscripts have been lowered. Any text crossed out by an author, where legible, is shown with a line through it. Authorial insertions to the text are presented in angled brackets. Editorial comments and insertions are enclosed by braces (a practice necessitated by Aubrey's use of square brackets). Where dates are conjectural (as in dating of correspondence), they are enclosed by braces. These practices largely follow the recommendations of Michael Hunter as described in "How to Edit a Seventeenth-Century Manuscript: Principles and Practice," *Seventeenth Century* 10 (1995): 277–310; and *Editing Early Modern Texts: An Introduction to Principles and Practice* (Basingstoke: Palgrave Macmillan, 2007), with a few modifications to suit the complexities of the Aubrey manuscripts, particularly the *Naturall Historie of Wiltshire* (Bod MS 1 and Bod MS 2). Modifications for dealing with the Aubrey manuscripts are based in part on Kate Bennett's editorial practices in "Materials Towards a Critical Edition of John Aubrey's *Brief Lives*" (D.Phil. thesis, University of Oxford, 1993).

Dates prior to 1752, when Britain adopted the Gregorian calendar, are given in the "Old Style" (the old Julian calendar was eleven days behind the Gregorian calendar in the seventeenth century). The beginning of a new year is taken to be January 1, rather than March 25. When necessary for clarity, dates are given with the doubled year—for example, February 9, 1691/92.

Abbreviations

BL   British Library
Bod   Bodleian Library
EMLO   Early Modern Letters Online (emlo.bodleian.ox.ac.uk)
ESIO   Robert Gunther, ed., *Early Science in Oxford*
HO   Henry Oldenburg, *Correspondence*
Hooke, *Diary*   Robert Hooke, *The Diary of Robert Hooke, MA, MD, FRS, 1672–1680*
ODNB   *Oxford Dictionary of National Biography*
Pepys, *Diary*   Samuel Pepys, *The Diary of Samuel Pepys*
Phil. Trans.   *Philosophical Transactions*
RS   Royal Society Library

with topographical, chorographical, antiquarian, and natural historical works, many with "Britain" or "Britannia" in the title. These studies combined a fine-grained attention to the material descriptions of localities with a wide-angle vision of a national whole in which these localities were embedded. William Camden's *Britannia*, first published in Latin in 1586 and reprinted in English translation through the seventeenth and eighteenth centuries (it was serialized in a British newspaper as late as 1733), was the genre's ur-text.[3] Camden and those who followed him sought to frame a land-based vision of Britain that could serve as a foundation for political and cultural unity.[4] They did so amid the intense political upheaval that marked British history in the century before England's formal political union with Scotland in 1707. From the mid-sixteenth century they found ready support for their project among Tudor and later Stuart royalty and nobility. Creating Britain as a topographical object was a way of forging it as a political object.[5]

Natural history and antiquarian studies as produced by joining local studies together under a national vision offered an image of nation and nature as one. To paraphrase the naturalist Joshua Childrey, writing in *Britannia Baconica* (1660), topographical studies were mirrors that showed Britons themselves.[6] Sixteenth- and seventeenth-century scholars thus promoted new ways of thinking about localities and local identities as enmeshed within the nation and national identities. In effect they recast the national as the local.

Yet although many naturalists, antiquaries, and topographers agreed that "Britain" was their proper object of study, no two works defined "Britain" in the same way. There was much disagreement about where to set the topographical boundaries of the nation. Some books included within the orbit of Britannia only England and Wales; others included England, Scotland, and Wales; some included Ireland; and still others excluded England. Within these books further divisions were drawn, and it was made clearer on what terms constituents of the topographical Britain might be included as members of the political and cultural Britain. In the English translation of his *Britannia*, for example, published during the reign of James I, Camden adopted a position of equal fellowship with the Scots and deference to their knowledge about their land, surely more detailed and correct than his own. At the same time he held up Ireland as fit only for English colonization and domination. As Camden's treatment of Ireland implies, the significance of the landscape was hotly contested along religious lines.[7] Of course some authors were entirely unconcerned with putting the topographical pieces together into a British whole, each preferring to focus on his individual kingdom or some little corner of it. If an image of "Britain" emerged from topographical writing, it was a fractured and fragmented one, as riven by conflict as the British people themselves.

The Correspondence

Printed topographical writing, with its mix of natural and antiquarian particulars and national visions, required collaborations carried out over long distances. Although they could not agree on a single vision of Britain as a topographical and political object, naturalists and antiquaries increasingly joined together to construct and share their visions in a community distributed across the landscape and connected by correspondence. Correspondence was central to natural history and antiquarian studies, so much so that investigators often referred to the community in which they conducted their work as their "correspondence," sometimes with the definite or indefinite article. "The correspondence"—the sum of personal contacts between those engaged in scientific activity—was the foundation for the construction of natural historical and antiquarian knowledge. Through their correspondence, scholars scattered across Britain poured their stocks of local knowledge into a shared pot. The contacts that naturalists formed allowed them access to a perspective in which their own localities could be enmeshed with, and partially submerged in, an image of "Britain," however fractured or in dispute that image might be.

As intellectual fields, natural history and antiquarian studies were deeply and materially shaped by the possibilities (and constraints) of long-distance collaboration. Correspondence-based exchange encouraged scholars to think of their work as never fixed and never finished. Instability and incompleteness came to mark the production and consumption of natural knowledge in both print and manuscript. In their published works, naturalists and antiquaries sought to communicate to a broader audience the habits of thought and association that they had learned through working together in the medium of correspondence. Yet they were often speaking first and foremost to each other: when they entered into print, naturalists and antiquaries often did so through their correspondence, relying on their contacts to provide content and fund publication via subscription. Print also participated in the cycle of expanding and perpetuating their correspondence, with authors using the publication process as an opportunity to collect more correspondents. At the other end of the communications spectrum, naturalists and antiquaries increasingly sought to incorporate conversation into the written stream of knowledge. Whole systems of record keeping and paperwork, such as those of the early Royal Society, were established to impress permanence upon conversation and expand its reach through written channels. In integrating writing and conversation, these systems eased naturalists' anxieties about conversation as a source of credible knowledge. They also grafted the social and intellectual functions of face-to-face meetings, which were key for establishing the authority and credibility of natural knowledge, onto those of writing and correspondence, which allowed for individual investigators to be distributed across the landscape, a key requirement for topographical study.

The habits and forms of correspondence were even inscribed into the early modern archive. As they faced death, the Restoration-era generation of naturalists and antiquaries envisioned the papers they had amassed over the course of their lives as potential resources for those who continued their projects into the future. They established archives housing their papers and collections as means of fostering their preservation and continued use. These institutions instantiated a view of knowledge-making as an ongoing collaborative writing process.

Local Particulars, National Visions

Early modern naturalists and antiquaries united a boundless enthusiasm for local particularities—a hyperlocalism—with a desire to understand and represent Britain as a unified historical and geographical space, though they disagreed on the boundaries and configuration of that space. Topographical studies were often organized around counties or regions and were sometimes constructed narratively as journeys through the land. These studies set the scope of natural historical investigation by the political and cultural boundaries of counties, political administrative units hovering between local village society and the institutions of king, courts, and Parliament. Such studies included Robert Plot's *Natural History of Oxford-shire* (1677) and John Aubrey's *Naturall Historie of Wiltshire*. There were also county-based studies of antiquities, such as William Dugdale's *Antiquities of Warwickshire* (1656). These books were conceived of as components within an ideal "whole body and book" of British natural history and antiquities. Some books attempted to sum the components, aspiring to contain the entire field of counties in a single volume: these were the *Britannia*s. Childrey's *Britannia Baconica* was one such, as was Aubrey's *Monumenta Britannica,* a survey of ancient British monuments. Over the decades the "whole body and book" grew, as many scholars working over decades read, copied (sometimes with and sometimes without citations), and added to each other's work.

County and regional studies collected local particulars in more or less depth, depending on the patience and knowledge of their authors. Studies focused on single counties were often the most detailed, offering information on winds and water courses, plant and animal species, farming practices, local industries and inventions, antiquities, and noteworthy residents, such as those who had lived to extraordinarily great ages. Scholars writing in this tradition modeled their work on a number of different antecedents; one source was classical works in descriptive and mathematical geography and natural history, including those by Ptolemy, Strabo, and Pliny the Elder. Pliny's *Natural History,* known through the Middle Ages but available in a relatively complete version again only in the early modern period (it was printed in an English translation by Philemon Holland, who was also responsible for the 1610 translation of Camden's *Britannia*), was an encyclopedic review of nature, arts, and inventions. Though it had a broader scope than many seventeenth-century county natural histories, it shared with them a particular focus on human uses of plants, animals, minerals, and other natural resources. County and regional studies were also modeled on late medieval and Renaissance exemplars, such as Flavio Biondo's *Italia Illustrata* (1482), a humanist topographical survey of Italy.[8] As these examples make clear, early modern topographers working in these traditions did not share divisions that moderns make between the study of nature and that of culture. Rather, everything—human, animal, mineral, and plant—that was of, on, or involving the land was of interest to them, though some were more interested in some of these categories at the expense of others. Some authors focused more on antiquities and others more on nature, but all participated in a common scholarly community, as will be evident throughout this book.

Although this book focuses largely on county and regional studies, it also considers the adjacent, related genre of natural histories organized around natural kinds rather than political boundaries.[9] In the latter third of the seventeenth century, John Ray, working from his own notes and those he inherited from his friend Francis Willughby, produced a series of studies cataloging plant and animal life. In these works nature was increasingly, though not totally, abstracted from the land; Willughby's and Ray's catalogs were not organized as travelogues, though Ray was also known for his books of travels. Nature too was shorn of the classical and humanist literary framework in which fifteenth- and sixteenth-century naturalists had embedded it. Rather than list all previous references to a particular animal in earlier literature, as had continental scholars such as Conrad Gesner, Ray preferred to provide descriptions (and when finances allowed, images) of species based on his observations of them. Whereas the overriding focus of county and regional natural histories was the human presence in and human use of the natural world, these descriptions were less obviously linked to human needs. Despite these differences, however, the two genres of natural history were deeply related. Ray, for one, still corresponded widely with naturalists engaged in both kinds of studies, and he participated in joint projects organized around geographical principles.[10]

Both kinds of studies, those organized around political and cultural topography and those organized around natural categories, required intimate, detailed knowledge of human and natural landscapes and natural kinds, which was gained through travel and intercourse with others, whether in conversation, correspondence, or reading printed books. Scholars necessarily drew on each other's knowledge about particular places and particular subjects in order to build up British natural history and antiquities in both depth and breadth. Late seventeenth-century naturalists often credited Francis Bacon with inspiring and encouraging such collaboration.[11] In his *Great Instauration*, Bacon called upon men to "join in consultation for the common good; and being now freed and guarded by the securities and helps which I offer from the errors and impediments of the way, to come forward themselves and take part in that which remains to be done."[12] Restoring and expanding natural knowledge were massive tasks and would certainly take more than one generation, but investigators believed that if they worked together, they could be accomplished. Early in his career, for example, the botanist John Ray began to assemble a complete list of plants observed in counties across Britain, a project that resulted in his *Catalogue of English Plants* (1670), his *Synopsis methodica stirpium Britannicarum* (1690), and the county-by-county lists of plants in Edmund Gibson's 1695 revised edition of William Camden's *Britannia*. As a young man, Ray traveled widely to collect plants. But even in his younger days, before illness restricted his movements, he also worked collaboratively through his correspondence, engaging "friends and acquaintance[s] who are skilful in Herbary . . . to search diligently his country for plants, and to send me a catalogue of such as they find, together with the places where they grow."[13] In the prefaces to the second edition of the *Synopsis*, Ray acknowledged fifteen named contributors, among them Hans Sloane, Jacob Bobart, Robert Plot, and Edward Lhuyd.[14]

Bacon's writings were not the only origin point for collaboration, the use of which stretched back into the sixteenth century. Collaboration as well as observation, experiment, and fact gathering were long evident in the practices and writings of surveyors, antiquaries, artisans, natural historians, alchemists, physicians, humanists, gentlewomen, gardeners, and many others in England and abroad.[15] Although William Camden, writing at the turn of the seventeenth century, acknowledged few contributors to his popular *Britannia* by name, we know that he drew upon the works of many topographers and antiquaries, including William Lambarde, Sampson Erdeswicke, John Dee, George Owen, John Stow, and Richard Carew.[16] Likewise the absorption of the older topographical tradition into writing that was self-consciously "Baconian" indicates a fundamental sympathy between the two. In his *Britannia Baconica,* Joshua Childrey drew many of his remarks from earlier writers such as Camden and Carew.

Though this study focuses on the topographical disciplines, the formation of a widely dispersed correspondence was not unique to them; Bacon's injunctions were widely influential, as attested by the early history of the Royal Society and the correspondences developed by such figures as Samuel Hartlib and Henry Oldenburg, which touched on many scientific fields. There were also many similarities between the topographical correspondence and the sixteenth-century astronomical community visible in the letters of Tycho Brahe.[17] More broadly, topography and astronomy required geographically dispersed observers to collaborate with each other. Investigators distributed across different cities and countries cultivated connections with each other through travel and correspondence because developing knowledge in these fields required contributions from a wide geographical area. In the case of astronomy, this meant dispersal around the globe, as, for example, with the eighteenth-century effort to observe the transit of Venus. The more widespread observers were, the more accurately they could calculate the distance from the earth to the sun from transit data.

Correspondence and collaboration in natural history and antiquarian studies were shaped, however, by the particular priorities and demands of these fields. In the topographical disciplines, because investigators were dispersed across the landscape and the goal was to build up a complete understanding of that landscape, each one had a unique store of knowledge to contribute (even more so, perhaps, than in astronomy). This meant that priority—being scooped—was less of a concern. Though concerns related to priority and plagiarism were by no means unheard of in the topographical fields, they seem to have been more of a concern in the mathematical disciplines, natural philosophy, and mechanical philosophy, where practitioners' stores of knowledge were not unique and they were more often in competition to deliver scientific results. To take one example, Robert Hooke's career was peppered with priority feuds with Isaac Newton, Christian Huygens, and others.[18] Furthermore the topographical disciplines were also differentiated by their political resonances. The production of knowledge through correspondence was intimately connected to the national visions promoted in topographical works. Other scientific pursuits gained presence on the political and cultural stage; Newton's preeminence in the eighteenth century was such a source of national pride for the British, for example, that his name became a byword for British science and he was accorded a state funeral at Westminster Abbey.[19] However, no other disciplines took on as their object the formation of the "whole body and book" of the nation.

This was a distinction with a difference. There was a particularly tight connection between the construction of Britain as a scientific object and the medium of correspondence. The naturalists' Britain reflected the medium in which it was constructed. This is evident in Childrey's assertion that readers of his *Britannia Baconica* gained knowledge that made them neighbors to one another, though they might live at opposite ends of the island. It can be seen as well in naturalists' interest (even obsession) with the mechanics of travel and communication, especially the prominent places they accorded in their books to roads and waterways, the physical pathways that knit the country together. It is also visible in the divisions and inequalities that cut through these books, the social and intellectual hierarchies that they created between England, Scotland, Ireland, and Wales.

The medium of writing and the exchange of writing through correspondence defined the intellectual, political, and social contours of the topographical Britain. Collaboration was accomplished through the constant, everrenewing circulation of written material. "Papers" accumulated relentlessly as scholars collected and exchanged information. One could turn to the next empty page of a notebook and scribble another observation or copy a quotation. If a notebook was full, another sheet could be folded in or a new notebook started. Those who preferred to store their notes on slips in cabinets or closets could always hook in another piece of paper.[20] Letters piled up, gathered in bundles, bound in books, and stacked in presses, organized according to idiosyncratic personal filing systems. Papers could be continuously multiplied to accommodate the seemingly endless flow of new knowledge about nature and human history pouring through seventeenth-century Britain.[21]

Not so with print. Print seemed to impose a finality that did not always accord with the abundance flowing from nature and human history. In the summer of 1676, John Ray wrote to his young contemporary Martin Lister, "Your Notes and Observations in Natural History do very well deserve to be made publick . . . I have only this to object to you, and my self, against their speedy Publication, that the longer they lie by you, if still you prosecute the same Studies and Enquiries, the more perfect and full they will be, every day almost adding or correcting, or illustrating somewhat; but if you have quite given over those Researches, defer not to put them out."[22] Ray's words illustrate the paradox confronting all naturalists and antiquaries, indeed all collectors, in this period: they felt an imperative to make knowledge public, and yet any making public via printing was necessarily also a cutting off, an end to one's researches that invariably left some knowledge behind. According to Ray's letter to Lister, having already given up on the project was the only justification for publishing it as it was. Concerns about representing natural and human history fully and accurately ran so deep that they could even retard the progress of correspondence. In a letter to Edward Lhuyd containing some observations on fossils discovered in the cliffs of Harwich, just south of Ipswich on the North Sea, the apothecary Samuel Dale, a close associate of John Ray, apologized for taking so long to transmit his account. His excuse was that he was "desirous of making another <u>Tour</u> to <u>Harwich</u> <Cliff> before I wrote, that I might accompany this with some more fossils, and make my observations more perfect."[23]

Although "papers" were the primary medium in which natural historical and antiquarian knowledge was constructed, and print fell short in that any given printed book was an incomplete representation of natural and human history, transferring knowledge to print was a priority for most active investigators. They regarded printing with appreciation as one of the primary tools for prosecuting and disseminating natural history, though their esteem for it could be qualified under particular circumstances.[24] John Evelyn, in a phrase typical of the age, highlighted the "happy invention of that noble Art" in a treatise on collecting and interpreting ancient and medieval manuscripts (he was commenting on the ways in which scholars could use printed texts as aids in interpreting medieval manuscripts).[25] Properly managed, printing made an author's words visible to the learned world, entering them into the historical record as copies found their way into private and public libraries. Naturalists particularly valued printing as a guardian against plagiarism—a handwritten text shared with one or two people was more easily dissociated from its author than was a text made available to hundreds via the press. Printed texts also fed back into the production of scientific knowledge. By the eighteenth century printed botanical catalogs were the foundation for a globalized natural history. Far-flung investigators compared the images and textual descriptions in standardized texts with specimens discovered in the field, allowing them to determine with more accuracy whether a species had been previously identified.[26] It was just these kinds of catalogs, of plants, insects, fish, and birds, that John Ray spent his life compiling and publishing.

Printing one's writings was also one of the surest ways of preserving them for the future. In October 1691, after perusing the manuscript of John Aubrey's *Naturall Historie of Wiltshire*, John Ray wrote that he wished "that you would speed it to the Presse. It would be convenient to fill up the blanks, so far as you can; but I am afraid that will be a work of time, & retard this Edition."[27] As he composed the text, Aubrey had left blanks when he lacked concrete information; many, but not all, of these had been filled in by the time Ray read the manuscript. Aubrey, an old man, had written much over the course of his life but published little—in such a case, Ray felt, getting the book into print was more important than filling in its last few lacunae.[28] Aubrey regarded print as the surest fail-safe against misuse of his texts (including plagiarism) and the strongest platform on which to establish a scholarly reputation that would persist after his death.

Avoiding print was clearly neither possible nor desirable. But its perceived deficits could be at least partially remedied. Insofar as they could, naturalists and antiquaries sought to replicate the openness and endless expandability of scribal exchange in their printing projects. This contradicts often-assumed features (or effects) of early modern printing. Whereas Elizabeth Eisenstein has argued that the invention of the printing press allowed texts to be standardized, fixed, and widely disseminated, making the scientific revolution possible, Adrian Johns, in *The Nature of the Book,* argues that such features, rather than being properties inherent in printed texts by virtue of their being printed, were only painstakingly achieved over centuries as authors, printers, booksellers, and readers came to agree on a set of cultural and legal conventions governing the production and use of printed texts.[29]

Though not denying the important role that printing, or these values, played in the development of early modern science, I argue that the study of correspondence-based exchange reveals that fixity, standardization, and wide dissemination were not always naturalists' and antiquaries' primary textual or epistemic goals.

This is visible in projects that appeared in one or more substantially expanded or revised editions over the course of an author's lifetime. This phenomenon could be limited by booksellers' unwillingness to print second and third editions (they were reluctant to do so without the expectation of a ready market or some other source of financing) but not by writers' enthusiasm. However, when an initial edition of a book sold well, perhaps failing to meet the market's demand for it, the legal and economic incentives of the book market could coincide with the naturalists' ever-present desire to renew and expand their works.[30] Consider the four editions of John Evelyn's *Sylva* that appeared during his lifetime. Each edition was revised to include new information as well as minor textual changes. Between the third edition in 1679 and the fourth edition in 1706, Evelyn was still rethinking word choices. More strikingly, he incorporated more material culled from both reading and experience. Evelyn communicated these changes to his printer by annotating a copy of the third edition with additions, changes, and deletions, usually identifying where they should be inserted into the text with asterisks or other symbols.[31] The margins were marked with substantive additions every five to ten pages.[32] Print did not in this case imply finality. In subjecting the text to further revision, Evelyn treated his printed text more like a scribal collection. The successive revisions instantiated in print the idea that the investigation of nature was never complete. Evelyn was in the lucky position to be able to put such an attitude into practice: *Sylva* was popular enough that his printer was willing to invest in second, third, and fourth editions.

Readers also participated in appropriating the properties of scribal texts—revisability and expandability—to printed books. As historians of early modern reading have observed, readers rarely maintained their books in the state in which they left the bookseller's. At the very least they personalized them by binding them, but beyond that they added ownership marks, stray doodles, personal memorandums, and more focused marks of reading, including arrows, manicules, and stars labeling specific passages as well as more extensive reactions to the content.[33] To that list could be added annotations and other manipulations, such as interleaving new pages for additions, that reimagined (and reengineered) the print book into a print-manuscript hybrid that could be used to accumulate knowledge according to "scribal" methods. To take one example, the cleric William Turner, in *A Compleat History of the most Remarkable Providences, Both of Judgment and Mercy, which have Hapned in this Present Age* (a collection of stories and exempla demonstrating God's judgment and mercy in individual human lives, societies, and in nature), invited readers to treat his book as a framework for their own commonplace books.[34] Turner instructed the skillful reader to transform the book into a print-manuscript hybrid, an endlessly expandable collection of providences, by interleaving blank pages and adding new headings. Although it is unlikely that most—or even many—readers turned *A Compleat History of the most Remarkable Providences* into a commonplace book, his suggestion indicates that readers would be familiar with this way of repurposing certain kinds of printed books, particularly reference compendia, as personalized notebooks.[35] Readers also marked up printed books as part of collaborative intellectual projects. The Royal Society's copy of John Ray and Francis Willughby's *De historia piscium*, a catalog of fish species, includes annotations added in various hands through the eighteenth century. Readers treated the library copy as a collective commonplace book for piscine facts and observations.[36] As these examples show, for readers, the print book could be a foundation for their own writing. Like its manuscript counterpart, it was understood as customizable, revisable, and reconfigurable.

The Plan of the Book

In this book I argue that the scientific correspondence was the ground on which Britain was constructed as a topographical object. Though conversation, scribal treatises, and print were all vital to this process, in many ways they were channeled and refracted—even given body and substance— through their movement within naturalists' correspondence. The first chapter thus anchors the book with an exploration of what, precisely, is meant by the phrase "Britain as a topographical object." The printed topographical studies of Britain that appeared throughout the Stuart era form the basis of this exploration. I show that although these studies engaged in a common project of mapping and describing Britain's human and natural history, they reflected the political and cultural divisions of the age, with no two works defining Britain in the same way. This chapter explores in particular depth the push-pull relationships between the English (especially as concentrated in London and the university towns), on the one hand, and the Scots, Welsh,

Irish, and Cornish, on the other. Perhaps surprisingly, as an intellectual project the creation of a topographical Britain was by no means defined solely from the metropolitan center or even by the English; rather those on the "margins" played significant roles. Figures such as Edward Lhuyd, the Scottish physician Robert Sibbald, and the Anglo-Irish naturalist and political writer William Molyneux participated in projects that defined "Britain" from an English perspective, one that was conditioned by England's long history of pretensions to and possession of imperial power within Britain.[37] However, they also worked to develop their own images of Britain as a topographical object and often prioritized gathering and disseminating topographical knowledge about their own regions of Britain, which they saw as a path toward the economic improvement and political empowerment of those regions. Edward Lhuyd's invention of a pan-Celtic Britain that excluded the English and England entirely was particularly significant in this regard. Digging deeper into projects such as Lhuyd's, Chapter 1 builds on a broad historical literature on early modern Britain and Britishness, showing that though individual visions of the "topographical Britain" were contested, they were created within a shared cultural context, making topography a significant avenue for the development of "Britain" and "Britishness" in the seventeenth century.

Chapter 2 dives more deeply into the social and material realities of the scientific correspondence that linked British naturalists and antiquaries. In this chapter I track the movement of letters, objects (including natural specimens, books, and antiquities), and people across Britain, from urban lodgings to college rooms to remote mountaintops. This movement was accomplished via the state-run mails, which carried letters; a network of private carriers who transported larger packages by horse-drawn cart and boat; and the personal travel of individual scholars and their associates, who transmitted all of the above and conveyed personal messages, greetings, and news in their conversations with each other.

The scholarly project of documenting the topography, antiquities, and natural history of Britain developed alongside these networks, which provided the only way to unite far-flung observers in common projects. The Royal Mail was gradually established over the sixteenth and seventeenth centuries; previously those wishing to correspond with others—both domestically and abroad—had depended on willing merchants or friends traveling in the same direction, or access to diplomatic mail bags. Though civil war disrupted the mails, by the Restoration transporting private and government letters via horseback was a lucrative business. Starting in the late seventeenth century the government started to devote more funds to improving roads and building canals, allowing for speedier, more regular internal communication, transportation, and travel via horseback, cart, carriage, and boat. The topographical disciplines' reliance on correspondence is illustrated by scholars' attention to the materiality of correspondence and transport in their writings and published works. Scholars' letters from throughout the period are dotted with references to the necessity of an "active and large correspondencie" and the mechanics of sending and receiving letters. In *A Collection for Improvement of Husbandry and Trade*, a bimonthly newsletter published from 1692 to 1703, the apothecary John Houghton published informative essays on practical scientific developments alongside carrier and coaching timetables as well as lists comparing the prices of goods in various market towns.[38] Scientific and technical advancement was tightly connected to the practicalities of long-distance communication across Britain.

Each subsequent chapter examines a different aspect of early modern British scientific communication, situating it in relation to the correspondence. Chapter 3 turns to conversation as a medium through which knowledge was created and scientific community sustained. Conversation, like correspondence, was a social activity, undertaken for pleasure as much as for information. Naturalists and antiquaries sought out conversation with each other whenever possible; both scientific travel and the establishment of scientific and antiquarian societies, including the Royal Society and the Society of Antiquaries, were rationalized in terms of the opportunities they provided for conversation. London and the university towns of Oxford and Cambridge were the loci of scholarly conversation; many letters ring with happy remembrances of friendly meetings in these places and expressions of hope that such visits could be arranged again soon. When meeting face-to-face, scholars could also accomplish tasks that were difficult, if not impossible, to carry out through correspondence, such as cowitnessing of observations and experiments, studying the same specimen together, and delving into and resolving difficult questions that were too complicated or detailed to specify in writing.

Yet conversation also had its weaknesses: unless written down, it was quickly forgotten (or misremembered) and was necessarily confined to the people in the room or on the street corner where it occurred. Conversation made naturalists anxious: it was ephemeral, all too easily dissolving into empty talk, and it could persuade by rhetorical tricks rather than truth. They addressed these concerns by creating structures to capture conversation in writing and divert it into the stream of knowledge-making: the Royal Society was one such structure. At its inception, founding fellows instituted procedures for recording, archiving, and disseminating the fruits of conversations held at weekly meetings. As members of an exclusive society, they also controlled who could participate in those conversations. Though the criteria for participation were a subject of some controversy in the society's early years, in general they valorized gentlemanly, polite discussion that centered on "matters of fact" and that could, in principle, be witnessed by all (one might contrast here the more raucous, free-wheeling conversations of the London coffeehouses). Conversation was thus more fully incorporated into the production of natural knowledge: it was converted into paperwork.

Writing and conversation had a complex, back-and-forth relationship. The Royal Society did not always originate conversation; rather the fellows frequently used writing as fodder for conversation by reading those letters and discussing them and then turned that conversation back into writing in the form of meeting minutes and further correspondence. This system reflected the reality that naturalists and antiquaries were distributed across Britain, and indeed around the world, as well as, in the case of topography, the field's intellectual requirement of geographical distribution. In integrating conversation into an ongoing system of written communication and record keeping, the fellows of the Royal Society instantiated their Baconian vision of the creation of natural knowledge as an iterative, open-ended process. But they did something surprising as well: they turned conversation into a source of credible knowledge, even to the point where it was the conversation itself that gave written and printed texts, including the articles that appeared in the early *Philosophical Transactions,* their credibility.

Chapters 4 and 5 take on manuscript and print as modes for creating, exchanging, recording, and disseminating natural historical and antiquarian knowledge. Chapter 4 looks in more detail at a particular episode of scribal exchange. I explore the connections between early modern natural history and the media in which it was disseminated through a fine-grained examination of John Aubrey's *Naturall Historie of Wiltshire,* which Aubrey assembled and circulated to readers between 1665 and his death in 1697. Aubrey produced two copies of the text: the original, a rough working copy, now in the Bodleian Library; and a fair copy, now in the Royal Society Library. The major claims of this book are illustrated by Aubrey's manuscript, particularly through the ways in which it was studied, annotated, and excerpted by its readers. A close analysis of the two copies, and the history of how Aubrey assembled, used, and shared them, reveals that early modern naturalists worked through scribal exchange because papers could more easily be repeatedly revised and expanded as well as shared only among limited coteries of readers for comments and additions. The history of Aubrey's writings shows that fixity and standardization were not necessarily naturalists' primary textual or epistemic goals. It also illustrates how the particular affordances of manuscript made possible the characteristic early modern approach to natural and human history, in which new knowledge was continuously accreted through correspondence, conversation, observation, and reading.

Yet Aubrey's story also illustrates the limits of manuscript and the importance that naturalists placed on print as a mode for distributing knowledge, albeit from within the context of correspondence. Aubrey's *Naturall Historie* was read in the seventeenth century only in its manuscript form; it was never printed. This was not Aubrey's choice but was a strategy forced on him by his circumstances. Aubrey, born a gentleman, was ruined financially at mid-life and forced to sell his estates. For a time he frequently changed addresses in order to evade debt collectors. All this to-ing and fro-ing impeded his abilities to complete projects; he wrote *The Naturall Historie* over decades. As he entered his seventh decade, completing this and others of his works took on greater and greater urgency, and he devoted increasing amounts of time to filling in the gaps in his manuscripts and sharing them with readers. Yet Aubrey was unable to convince a bookseller to take a risk on one of his works; nor could he assemble the capital to finance printing them himself, with the exception of *Miscellanies* (1696), a collection of notices of seemingly supernatural events. In the case of *The Naturall Historie*, Aubrey—and his contemporaries, including John Ray—thought that circulating the manuscript should have been preparatory to printing. Knowledge was constructed through scribal exchange rooted in correspondence, but print was increasingly regarded as the proper output of that construction process. Aubrey saw his failure to print primarily as a failure to make his scientific contributions visible to posterity; his friends and readers saw it as a failure to make his contributions available to his contemporaries. Their attitudes suggest a certain emphasis on print as an organ for the dissemination and preservation of knowledge.

With these insights in mind, in Chapter 5 I consider print as a product of correspondence-based exchange, looking at scholars' use of subscription to finance publication and build readerships for their books. With subscription, authors and booksellers financed printing by signing up readers who paid a portion of the purchase price of the book in advance, with the rest to come at delivery. They assembled these readerships through their correspondence. Naturalists and antiquaries initially turned to subscription because their books were expensive to produce (engravings, in particular, came at a high cost) and drew limited audiences. Booksellers could be reluctant to take on such projects unless they were guaranteed in advance of selling copies and turning a profit. However, in the hands of late seventeenth- and early eighteenth-century naturalists and antiquaries and their readers, subscription publication was about more than financial contracts. In successful subscription publications, authors worked through their correspondence, developing their audience by building on existing personal contacts and inviting reader-correspondents to participate in shaping the content and material form of the books.

In Chapter 5 I focus in particular on the Welsh naturalist Edward Lhuyd's use of subscription to fund two projects, a 1699 fossil catalog (*Lithophylacii Britannici ichnographia*) and his *Archaeologia Britannica*, cut short by his death but planned as a multivolume survey of the antiquities, languages, and natural history of the Celtic regions of Britain. In the latter case, Lhuyd used subscription to accomplish what we might term eighteenth-century "crowd-sourcing" and "crowd-funding," with subscribers financing research and publication as well as producing some of the books' content. Lhuyd used printed tools to accomplish this, distributing subscription proposals through his correspondence as well as questionnaires that invited correspondents to contribute intellectual content according to a standardized form. Expanding his correspondence and creating a broad readership—that is, getting access to both information and financial support—were part and parcel of each other. His correspondence was his readership; his readership was his correspondence. Moreover printed books and readerships were constructed together, and the final publications, in their material, textual, and social aspects, were products of correspondence-based exchange. This chapter in particular illustrates the tight connections between the correspondence as a social formation and the "topographical Britain" that came out of that correspondence.

Chapter 6 examines naturalists' and antiquaries' attempts to ensure the survival of their papers, the products of lifetimes of scribal exchange, beyond their deaths. I return here to John Aubrey's story: his quest to ensure the survival of his papers by placing them in the Ashmolean Museum was all the more urgent because he had published very little. Many scholars regarded their papers as distinctly fragile, especially compared to printed books, because most of the materials they had amassed existed nowhere else but in the chests, presses, and cabinets where they were stored. Once the writers were dead, their papers were likely to be dispersed, destroyed, and recycled. Even if friends, relatives, and associates valued a dead man's papers for their intellectual content, these papers were unlikely to survive his death intact. Occasionally a collection of papers might be passed down through a family or to a friend who carried on the scholar's work.[39] If a family was well established and possessed an estate, papers stashed in the library might survive, whether through neglect or more active care and curation. More likely, though, a widow or a son, facing straitened financial circumstances, would recognize that a few pounds could be received for a collection, or a few treatises in it that were ready for the press, and sell it (or them) to a bookseller. Even if the bookseller purchased the whole collection, he was likely to break it up, auctioning off some pieces, publishing others, and junking the rest. In other cases former associates helped break up a collection, raiding it for materials that were either useful to them or potentially damaging to their reputations.

These were, from the dead man's perspective, the best-case scenarios. In fact, for many relatives and friends not engaged in scholarly activities (and even for some who were), the value of parchment and paper lay in the uses of the material itself, not the content. Used paper was recycled in any number of ways: sheets could be used to line pies during baking or be made into dress patterns, for example. Beyond these more mundane threats, scholars also had to consider Britain's recent history as an inhospitable home for books, manuscripts, and papers of all kinds. During the Reformation the monastic and university libraries had been destroyed or practically emptied of their books, and untold texts had been dispersed. Through the seventeenth century, numerous religious and civil disturbances, including a civil war, the Popish Plot, and the revolution of 1688–1689, continued to threaten the security of books and papers in both private and public hands.

British naturalists and antiquaries thus lived in a world profoundly hostile to the survival of their intellectual patrimony. To remedy this, they established and stocked with materials institutions that, as part of their mission of promoting experimental philosophy and natural knowledge, preserved books, manuscripts, and personal papers. In the seventeenth century these included the Ashmolean Museum and the Royal Society. This movement continued in the eighteenth century with the physician Hans Sloane's collecting activities and the founding of the British Museum.[40] Naturalists' and antiquaries' efforts to preserve their papers within these institutions tell us much about their understanding of science as a cultural enterprise and their own hopes and expectations regarding their place in history. In establishing these archives within institutions devoted to scientific research, they signaled their hope that future scholars would use their materials to continue building Baconian accounts of natural history and antiquities. They were determined to exert ongoing influence over future scientists by making it possible for them to appreciate and make use of their forbears' contributions as authors, collectors, and investigators. Their efforts also suggest a presumption that scientific activity would continue to be a cumulative endeavor and that they were future scholars' collaborators. In inventing the archive, naturalists and antiquaries attempted to build correspondence-based methods of scribal exchange into the foundations of the new science.

This book plaits together strands in the history of science, the history of the book, and the history of Britain. It deconstructs the interrelated systems of writing, print, and conversation that naturalists and antiquaries built as they sought to develop knowledge of natural and human history in Britain along Baconian lines. These chapters show how writing and correspondence, as open-ended, iterative modes of communication, drove those systems. Brought to the fore are the relationships between correspondence and the intellectual and political project in which naturalists and antiquaries were engaged. This shows how complicated and often vexed topographical images of Britain emerged out of naturalists' and antiquaries' correspondence, shedding light on their roles in the formation of a shared national culture within Britain as well as on the development of "Britain" as an idea. Ultimately, this book not only demonstrates new ways of reading the intertwined development of science and nation in early modern Britain but also serves as a model for grounding our understanding of the construction of scientific knowledge and the formation of scientific communities in the material and social realities of communication, which, taken together, constitute "sociable knowledge."

Chapter 1

"This Book Doth Not Shew You a Telescope, but a Mirror": The Topographical Britain in Print

What sort of thing was Britain? This is a difficult enough question to answer in the here and now, when Scotland, Wales, Northern Ireland, and England, though for the present still bound together in the United Kingdom, are being driven apart by regional desires for self-governance. In September 2014 another referendum on Scottish independence seemed so likely to pass that in the week before the vote, a jittery Westminster promised the Scots maximum devolution of powers if they rejected independence.[1] Though independence was voted down, as of this writing (October 2014) it remains to be seen whether, and how, those promises will be carried out. The trend is certainly toward a looser union rather than a closer one. In this context, what makes for "Britain" as a nation, a geographical object, a historical entity, a people?

The question of what Britain was was difficult to answer in the seventeenth century, as well. Political, cultural, religious, and linguistic differences divided the peoples of the North Atlantic islands that now comprise Ireland and the United Kingdom. Wales had come under English domination in the early fifteenth century, but the Welsh long maintained a distinctive culture and language. In 1603 Scotland came to share a sovereign with England and Wales, but this did not lead immediately to a more thoroughgoing union of either cultures or political and administrative structures. Throughout the century Ireland remained partially occupied, though neither completely controlled by the English nor integrated into Britain. Tensions between England, Scotland, and Ireland were one of the causes of the British civil war. In 1707, with the union of Scotland and England, it became proper to speak of "Great Britain" existing as a political entity. However, in many ways—not the least of which was the continuing subordinate status of Ireland—this process of union was incomplete, at best.

Before political union became even a partial reality, topographical writers wrestled with the question of exactly what sort of thing Britain was. In his 1675 *Britannia,* the first British road atlas, John Ogilby listed the various methods according to which the "geographers" organized their books: some followed "the Natural Traduction of Rivers and Mountains, Others the Distinction of People and Inhabitants, Others again more frequently, the Politique Division of Princes." There was, additionally, the "Itinerary Way," which Ogilby followed, arranging his survey along the principal roads of England and Wales.[2] Though topographers recognized the books produced through these diverse methods as kin to each other, part of the same family of inquiry, each book generated a different "Britain."

Many topographers took the route of defining Britain by geographical contiguity. This included England, Wales, and Scotland but excluded Ireland. Additionally this definition tended to suggest that England, Wales, and Scotland were more unified, both politically and culturally, than they were. Works that followed this path, such as Joshua Childrey's *Britannia Baconica,* displayed an ever-present tension between conceiving of individual regions, or kingdoms, as separate objects of study (as attested by numerous internal references to England, Wales, and Scotland) versus envisioning Britain as a whole. They were perhaps most successful at the latter when viewing Britain from an "oceanic" perspective, that is, as an island. This perspective suggests the deep continuities between the topographers' project and the formation of the British Empire in the seventeenth and eighteenth centuries, which bore intimate discursive and ideological connections to this image of Britain as an island and seafaring nation.

Was it defined by shared language? This too was unwieldy: by the seventeenth century, English was the dominant language in England and Cornwall and among portions of the Irish, Scots, and Welsh elites, but Welsh, Scottish Gaelic, and Irish Gaelic were still spoken by majorities in Wales, Scotland, and Ireland. In the West Country a few even still spoke Cornish. Looked at through the prism of language, Britain might also include the French territory of Brittany, where the residents spoke Breton, a Celtic language. The diversity of English dialects and accents spoken even within England was a barrier to the formation of a broader English national identity, not to mention a British one, as naturalists recognized.

Shared descent, which topographers attempted to trace through their reconstructions of linguistic history, did not offer an easy solution either. The myth that Britain owed its founding to the wandering Trojan hero Brutus was increasingly being understood as just that, a myth.[3] As Colin Kidd has observed, history (as seventeenth-century antiquaries understood it) increasingly suggested that the various peoples of Britain descended from different waves of invaders: Celtic peoples, Romans, Anglo-Saxons, Vikings, and Normans, to name a few of the groups who arrived over the millennia and left their mark on the cultural, linguistic, natural, and built landscape of Britain.[4] Edward Lhuyd, mapping the descent of the peoples of Britain from the histories of their languages, eliminated England entirely and created a Britain defined wholly by relationships between the Celtic peoples.

Beyond these options, Britain might also be defined by commerce and trade ties: topographies of trade held in productive tension local particulars and national visions. Topographers both observed and promoted trade connections, participating in a long process by which local markets across Britain became more interconnected.[5] Each region of Britain, each county and each nation, had its distinctive products, but these were traded around the islands as a whole and even internationally. In their work on trade, topographers constructed an image of the local as enmeshed in the national.

In addition there was Ogilby's "politique division of princes," which in practice often meant defining "Britain" by the extension of English political hegemony and the incorporation (willingly and unwillingly) of Wales, Scotland, and Ireland into the project of building a "British" Empire.[6] Camden's *Britannia*, which was published in six revised and enlarged editions within its author's lifetime (1551–1623), led the way in this regard. Pitching his work directly at James I in the 1610 English translation, he wrote that "the glory of my country encouraged me to undertake" to "restore antiquity to Britaine, and Britain to his antiquity."[7] A century later Edmund Gibson's revised *Britannia* (1695) covered the same territory.[8] In the dedicatory letter to John Somers, a counselor to William III, Gibson proclaimed that "Descriptions of Countries" were among the most pleasing of scholarly endeavors, as they allowed one to express "one's Love for his Native Country."[9] In using the name *Britannia*, a word whose origins lay deep in the classical past, Camden and later authors attempted to proclaim the unity of the peoples and lands of the "Atlantic archipelago."[10] But from Camden's perspective, Britain was not a fraternity of equals; Camden's was an Anglo-centric unity. The 1695 revision, like the original, largely constructed Britain from an English perspective, devoting more attention to England than Ireland, Scotland, and Wales combined.

Bookended by the first English translation of *Britannia* and its revision were a number of projected and completed natural historical, antiquarian, and topographical studies with "Britannia" or "Britain" featured prominently in their titles.[11] Although the publication dates of these books spanned a century, they represented an interconnected corpus in that earlier works continued to be read and were often extensively quoted or paraphrased in later works. Most prominently Camden served later writers as both a source of information and a foundation upon which to build. Through the century, the replication (with variations) of Camden's text across different "authors" helped to establish it as a somewhat stable version of the topographical Britain, one oriented toward an English readership.[12] Regional writers with a narrower focus, such as Richard Carew, author of a 1602 study of Cornwall, continued to be cited as well. In his *Britannia Baconica* (1660) Joshua Childrey quoted both Camden and Carew for material beyond his own sphere of local knowledge. Indeed, Childrey quoted the thirteenth-century topographer Gerald of Wales, hinting at the deep historical continuities between early modern writings and medieval, as well as classical, precedents.

This chapter maps the lineaments of the topographical Britain. Natural historical and antiquarian writing offered a range of possibilities for conceptualizing Britain as an object of learned inquiry. It also drew on and intervened in contemporaneous debates about Britain as a political object, both explicitly and implicitly. The two, in fact, were not separate projects: because naturalists and antiquaries took into their remit languages, settlement patterns, trade, the distribution of natural resources, and local customs, in defining Britain as an object of topographical inquiry, they sketched its political and cultural outlines as well. Though topographers may have had dreams of a comprehensive, unified account of British nature and antiquities—a "whole body and book" that could serve as the foundation for a unified country—their works presented a more mixed picture, reflecting the political and social discourses of the day.

In particular, in their work topographers writing in the *Britannia* tradition attempted to hold in productive tension the competing forces that bound and drove apart England, Wales, Scotland, and Ireland. Their ideal was a national vision composed of local particulars, rather than national visions that regularized or stamped out local particulars. Though regional diversity could function to stymie the formation of "Britain," topographers attempted to understand it as a source of unity, whether that meant mapping local contributions to the national economy or looking for the hidden connections between the Celtic languages and peoples. This did not mean that topographers were univocal in their concept of Britain. Some chose loyalty to their individual region, or even county, over loyalty to "Britain," never mind England, Scotland, Wales, or Ireland. In some cases English naturalists wrote about Wales, Scotland, and Ireland without knowing much about local particulars in those places. In some cases they were aware of this and apologetic about it—in the 1610 English translation of *Britannia,* dedicated to James I, Camden was reluctant to hold forth on Scottish antiquities—out of respect, he claimed, for those whose knowledge was deeper and more detailed. In other cases they were ignorant and hostile, often within the same book—Camden's attitude toward Catholic Ireland reflected this combination.

Part of the work of this chapter is thus parsing out what "national" and "local" meant to topographical writers of diverse backgrounds following diverse lines of inquiry. In doing so, I hope this chapter complicates a tempting narrative: that the formation of "Britain" as a nation was a process driven solely by the English, or perhaps the English in concert with the Scots.[13] Certainly the English took the largest role in defining the topographical Britain and liked to see themselves as the driving imperial power behind the creation of Great Britain.[14] Latter-day historical scholarship on early modern topographical and antiquarian scholarship has also tended both to privilege the English perspective and isolate the English, Welsh, Irish, and Scottish traditions from each other, deemphasizing connections between them and perhaps unintentionally reinforcing a narrative of English dominance.[15] What this chapter argues, however, is that Welsh, Scottish, and Anglo-Irish naturalists were by no means passive bystanders in the debates about the topographical Britain; rather they were crucial contributors (though the Catholic Irish and Highland Scots were largely, though not entirely, shut out of the process).

Ultimately, I argue that the images of Britain that these topographers created, in both their unity and their disunity, were grounded in the dispersed collaborative medium in which they worked, their correspondence. The quotation of this chapter's title speaks to this relationship between printed visions and topographical investigators joined in correspondence. As explored in greater detail below, Joshua Childrey, in his *Britannia Baconica,* argued that his book reflected to Britons an image of themselves: "This book," he wrote, "doth not shew you a Telescope, but a Mirror."[16] Visions of Britain such as Childrey's were reflections of the correspondence through which they came into being. In the mirror of print, naturalists' and antiquaries' correspondence was made visible.

A Shared Landscape

One seemingly straightforward path to defining Britain led along the seashore, the idea being that the geographically contiguous lands of Wales, England, and Scotland could be considered "Britain." This approach had the advantage of seeming natural: the limits of Britain were those set by the sea. Yet it faced several complications, including political tensions between Scotland and England and English topographers' limited knowledge of Scotland and Wales. Digging into these works, we also see tension between the national definition of the topographical object of study and the natural historian's project of collecting information about nature in order to theorize about the causes of natural phenomena. Naturalists hailed Britain as a microcosm of the world, offering in itself versions of all the rarities of nature that could be found abroad. Yet, as this description implies, natural phenomena (and their causes) were not necessarily unique to Britain. Naturalists found themselves adducing supporting examples from outside their texts' declared geographical boundaries. Britain, as represented in these texts, was never a stable topographical object.

Defining "Britain" as a contiguous geographical unit involved both drawing links between the various regions of Britain and distinguishing Britain from other countries, particularly those in Europe: topographers looked both inward and outward. Joshua Childrey took this approach in his 1660 *Britannia Baconica.* Childrey encouraged readers to open their eyes to the wonders in their own country. Addressing gentle readers, he asked, "And what is there worth wonder abroad in the world whereof Nature hath not written a Copy in our Island? I would have those that know other Countreys so well, not to be strangers to their own, which is a compendium of all others."[17] He promoted his book in terms that appealed to his fellow Britons' pride. Why travel abroad when Britain offered everything one might want in the way of natural curiosities and rarities? Childrey's metaphor—Britain was a "compendium of all others"—suggests an image of Britain's landscape as a book in which knowledge that was otherwise scattered was brought together and summed up. He offered his "Portable-book" as a guide to those wonders, a take-along index to the landscape-as-compendium.[18]

In contrasting the wonders of Britain with those on offer in other countries, Childrey defined Britain as a geographical unit in opposition to those countries, and he projected an alliance, based on shared geography, between Britons scattered across that land. This alliance included not just the gentry but also the "vulgar," to whom Childrey also recommended the book. *Britannia Baconica* would broaden their minds by showing them how many strange and wonderful things could be found at their own doorsteps: as noted in the introduction, the book was not a "Telescope, but a Mirror," Childrey wrote, "not about to put a delightful cheat upon you, with objects at a great distance, but shews you your selves."[19]

Childrey so deeply identified Britons with their topography that his book was a mirror that showed them not their land but themselves. This identification of Britons with Britain is not wholly surprising coming from someone writing from within a chorographical tradition, as Childrey was. Chorographers sought to draw links between the characteristics of the land and the people living on it. However, Childrey expanded this chorographical mode of thinking beyond the local, applying it in a national context. It was not just that the Welsh were products of Wales or Northumbrians products of Northumbria: all were products of Britain.

Reflecting these aims, Childrey described natural rarities across England, Scotland, and Wales. He organized his *Britannia Baconica* regionally: England and Wales were broken up by counties; and Scotland was treated on its own. Yet he also drew links between similar natural phenomena that occurred in different regions, suggesting the ways in which people scattered across Britain might see each other as neighbors. These links were part of Childrey's efforts to theorize about the causes of natural phenomena. As he passed through Kent, Childrey proposed that medicinal springs and iron mines (and hot springs and silver and tin mines) were causally linked, bringing as supporting evidence mines and springs in near propinquity to each other in Bath, Devonshire, Cornwall, Wales, Bristol, and Gloucestershire.[20] He also offered descriptions of natural phenomena that encouraged readers to visualize Scotland, Wales, and England as a unified geographical space. Often these had to do with the seas surrounding Britain. Ocean tides reached notoriously far up the Thames, for example, because the "floods" (currents) that ran east from Cornwall and south from Scotland met at the mouth of the Thames "with very great noise and rippling," and the sea swelled into the river.[21] Elsewhere, several times in the book, Childrey mentioned the great schools of herring that circuited "our Island" and "round about *Britain*."[22]

Imagined from the outside, as an island, England, Scotland, and Wales were unified as "Britain." Yet viewed from within, Childrey's Britain was variegated, particularized terrain. His description of Scotland clocked in at just six pages, much less extensive than his account of England and Wales, and it was not broken down into counties.[23] He also tended to refer to "England" and "Scotland," rather than Britain, as the national backdrop against which he illuminated the distinctive features of each county. For example, he noted that the quality of the air in Suffolk was "so good, that it is by some Physicians thought to be the best in England."[24] Similarly in his description of Northumberland he observed that "by Bywell Castle is a great store of Salmons: As indeed there is in most of the North of England, and in Scotland."[25] That Childrey described the individual nations as the relevant context for comparison, rather than, say, "Northern Britain," suggests an ongoing disunity within his conception of Britain.

For all that Childrey attempted to draw national boundaries around his subject, the world beyond those boundaries kept seeping in. The nationalist aim of presenting a guidebook to Britain's wonders was in conflict with the Baconian injunction to collect local particulars as broadly as possible. In adducing supporting evidence for the relationship between medicinal springs and iron mines, Childrey reached beyond British boundaries, including examples from Saxony on his list. Similarly when discussing a town that had been swallowed by the sea in Sussex, he mentioned further examples not only from Scotland but also from the Low Countries.[26] Inspired by Bacon, Childrey hoped to theorize from individual instances to "universal maxims."[27] For that purpose non-British examples were also useful. *Britannia Baconica*, defined as a portable guidebook to Britain's natural wonders, constantly escaped the limits of the first word of its title in service of the aims suggested by the second. At the same time, these non-British examples had the effect of reinforcing Childrey's claim to the reader that there was no need to seek abroad for wonders, as they could all be found in England, Scotland, and Wales.

Trade

Topographers, especially those more focused on natural history, took a strong interest in trade. They mapped regional contributions to the broader national economy and helped to promote regional resources that they saw as under-exploited. Indeed trade was one of the ways in which national and local could be held in productive tension, as goods were produced locally but circulated nationally, and even internationally, contributing to the overall economy of Britain. Comprehensive natural histories, such as Childrey's *Britannia Baconica*, and regional histories, such as Carew's earlier *Survey of Cornwall*, devoted considerable space to the distinctive natural resources, and natural products, that each region supplied. This interest in trade was front and center in the conceptualization and research of such works: in 1682 the Scottish physician Robert Sibbald circulated a set of queries for a natural history and description of Scotland in which the first questions were, "What the Nature of the County or place is? And what are the chief products thereof?"[28] In fore-grounding economic activity, naturalists such as Childrey, Carew, and Sibbald did not merely participate in ongoing processes of regional and national integration that characterized the early modern British economy; they attempted to use natural history to help guide and spur forward those processes.

The improvement of trade was a fundamental justification for the pursuit of natural history because nature was the foundation of trade. Nature, rightly husbanded, was the source of the goods that men traded. A good understanding of natural history was fundamental to economic prosperity. Samuel Hartlib, writing at mid-century, espoused one version of this belief, linking Protestantism, prosperity, and natural history in a unified millennial vision that all prosperity derived ultimately from nature:

> Now to advance Husbandry either in the production and perfection
> of earthly benefits, or in the management thereof by way of Trading,
> I know nothing more usefull, than to have the knowledg of the
> Natural History of each Nation advanced & perfected: For as it is
> evident, that except the benefits which God by Nature hath
> bestowed upon each Country bee known, there can be no Industrie
> used towards the improvement and Husbandry thereof; so except

> Husbandry be improved, the industrie of Trading, whereof a Nation
> is capable, can neither be advanced or profitably upheld.[29]

Trade was linked to nature through husbandry. The improvement of husbandry required an accurate, detailed knowledge of nature, that is, in Hartlib's words, of the providential distribution of God's "benefits" across a
nation. From that foundation of knowledge, industry could be applied to
the improvement of husbandry and the production of goods from nature
increased.[30] Profitable increase in trade would follow.

Following the Restoration, many topographical writers and publishers
maintained Hartlib's link between natural history, husbandry, and trade,
though they may have eschewed his millenarian Protestantism.[31] John
Aubrey, in the preface to his *Naturall Historie of Wiltshire*, bundled together
"scrutinie into the waies of Nature" and "Improvement in Husbandry." He
saw interest in both of these as recent developments. Before the civil war, he
wrote, both had been regarded as presumptuous and ill-mannered—even
sinful, in the case of "scrutinie into Nature"—even when improvements
increased profits, because the improver was setting himself up as "more
knowing than his Neighbors and forefathers."[32] When John Ogilby published his *Britannia, or, an illustration of the Kingdom of England and dominion of Wales* (1675), he justified it in terms of how it reflected and enhanced
British imperial power and (not unrelatedly) encouraged domestic trade in
Britain. Ogilby dedicated his *Britannia* to Charles II, proudly proclaiming
that it had been the practice of peoples of all great empires—the Persians,
the Greeks, the Romans, and the Assyrians—to survey and document their
principal thoroughfares. Britain likewise, to improve its "Commerce and
Correspondency at Home," required such a survey.[33]

Ogilby's book was an exercise in nation-making: he linked trade, communication, and empire to each other and predicated their expansion on the
diffusion of accurate knowledge of the roads.[34] Just as Childrey did in *Britannia Baconica,* Ogilby yoked the oceanic and the national. Ogilby placed this
survey squarely in the context of broader British imperial and commercial
ventures, noting that his efforts to "Improve Our Commerce and Correspondency at Home" paralleled Charles's efforts to ensure that Britons would
have open to them "all those Maritin Itineraries, Whereby We Trade and
Traffique to the several Parts and Ports of the World, through the Two and
Thirty Points or Bearings of the Universe"[35] (a mariner's compass had thirty-
two bearings marked on it). His ambition was to provide tools that made

roadways navigable and opened them to commerce and correspondence on a national scale, to match Britain's trade beyond its shores.

Trade linked the local and the national: natural resources and the goods they were fashioned into may have had local origins, but they circulated in national and international economies. Childrey discussed numerous goods in these terms. Stroud, in Gloucestershire, was a center for scarlet-dyed cloth because the water there was peculiarly suited to the dying process. Walfleet in Essex sent oysters to London, while Suffolk "yields much Butter and Cheese," though the Cheshire cheese made all other cheese seem inferior by comparison. Great numbers of herring were fished every year in September along the shores of Norfolk, and Leicestershire produced "the best Limestone in England."[36]

Topographers took an active role in encouraging the integration of local and national economies. They sought to identify and promote local resources that could be mined, processed, or in some way improved upon and offered up for consumption across Britain. In a letter written while on his Welsh progress, Lhuyd noted the discovery in Merionethshire in northwestern Wales of a new kind of marble "which when polished represents a number of small Oranges cut across; the reason whereof is an infinite quantity of *Porus* or *Alcynoium* stuck through the stone."[37] The stone was strikingly attractive and "might serve very well for inlaying work, as tables, windows, cabinets, closets etc and would make curious salt cellars."[38] Lhuyd went on to close this letter with a request that if his correspondent knew any merchants who dealt in alum or copper ore, he would let them know that the counties of western Wales were rich in both.[39] Lhuyd sought to bring these natural resources to the attention of those with the expertise and financial resources to exploit them.

Language: Uniting and Dividing

Naturalists and antiquaries were intensely interested in the linguistic topography of Britain. They cataloged place names, variations in local dialects and local slang, the vocabulary and grammar of Celtic languages, and the historical relationships between Celtic languages, which could be established by studying surviving Celtic-language manuscripts. Most basically they sought to map linguistic difference and similarity across Britain, both historically and in the seventeenth-century present. In this section I focus on linguistic differences in seventeenth-century Britain, and in the next I turn to the connections between linguistic topography, history, and descent.

Linguistic differences were observed as both causes and markers of social and cultural disunity. In *The survey of Cornwall* (1602), Richard Carew noted that by the late sixteenth century, knowledge of Cornish was in precipitous decline: "English speach doth still encroche vpon it, and hath driuen {Cornish} into the outermost skirts of the shire."[40] Most everyone, Carew wrote, knew some English, and fewer and fewer knew any Cornish. However, when approached by an outsider—an English person—the Cornish were likely to pretend total ignorance of English: "and yet some so affect their owne, as to a stranger they will not speake it: for if meeting them by chance, you inquire the way or any such matter your answere shalbe, *Meea nanidua cowz asawzneck,* I can speake no Saxonage."[41] In Carew's telling, the Cornish pretended ignorance of English in order to maintain boundaries between themselves and perceived outsiders.

Naturalists were interested in linguistic difference in part because they recognized it as an impediment to national commerce and correspondence. Indeed in the preface to his comparative dictionary of Celtic languages, the first volume of his *Archaeologia Britannica*, Edward Lhuyd felt the need to begin with an apology for even attending to such a subject because "Diversity of Languages is Generally granted to be rather an Inconveniency than the Contrary."[42] Naturalists sought ways to bridge these gaps, or at least make the various local dialects and languages legible to travelers, particularly those who went from the orbit of London, Cambridge, and Oxford to more remote parts of Britain. In 1674 John Ray published *A collection of English words, not generally used*, a compendium of words peculiar to the north, south, and east of England. This collection offered definitions of local dialect words that Ray had collected in his travels around Britain in the 1660s with his fellow naturalists Francis Willughby, Nathaniel Bacon, and Phillip Skippon. It was published with catalogs of English fish and bird species and some notes on mining, ore processing, metal work, and alum- and salt-making that had been similarly gathered from conversations with miners and craftspeople during their travels.

In the letter to the reader that prefaced the volume, Ray focused on the northern dialects' unintelligibility to southerners: "in many places, especially of the North, the Language of the common people, is to a stranger very difficult to be understood."[43] He believed that his collection therefore would be of some use to travelers in the north of England. Ray's publication of this dictionary, and his justification for it, suggested that regional differences within England were sharply felt. It also implied that his ideal reader was someone from the center (for example, London, Cambridge, Oxford) traveling in the north. Yet Ray also included southern and eastern dialect words, indicating on some level that this was also a project designed to encourage mutual intelligibility and was not just about making the periphery intelligible to the center—or that even in the home counties the "language of the common people" contained dialect words unfamiliar to the educated.

Ultimately such aids would help naturalists see past the accidents of local linguistic variation (which might assign one species a diversity of names) to the underlying reality of nature, allowing them to classify species rationally and universally according to an agreed-upon set of characteristics.[44] Naturalists across Europe were thus interested in documenting and understanding local vernaculars.[45] One might see a similar motivation in Ray's *Dictionariolum trilingue* (1675), which listed words, broken down by category, in English, Greek, and Latin. The categories were not unlike those found in county natural histories—Ray began with words related to the heavens and worked his way through words related to plants and animals, human bodies and human health, and culture, society, and the built environment (the main difference was that Ray included a section listing words related to God and religion). When collecting words in the Celtic regions of Britain, Edward Lhuyd used the lists in the *Dictionariolum trilingue* as his standard vocabulary.[46]

Ray's focus on regional English dialects suggests two insights about the nature of the project of fashioning Britain as a scientific object. First, naturalists were not universally (or always) interested in Britain as a whole. In their work they frequently privileged one region over another. Because many of these naturalists were English first, England was of course the privileged region. There was more at work here, however. In Ray's presentation of England as a linguistically diverse space, we see that it is not necessarily appropriate to read seventeenth-century England as unified—politically, linguistically, scientifically, or otherwise.

Furthermore, insofar as one reads the formation of Britain as a colonial process—one in which the English extended their hegemony over Wales, Scotland, and Ireland—it is in some cases more appropriate to identify the northern counties (and the West Country, which included Cornwall, though Ray did not discuss their dialects) with Wales, Scotland, and Ireland. Cultural and political hegemony was extended from London and its environs to the rest of England: although Ray included in *A collection of English words* dialect words from southern and eastern England, in the letter to the reader he framed his project as an aid to southerners attempting to understand northern dialects, and not the other way around.[47]

Language, History, and Descent: Britain Without England

Tracing human descent through history was another way of mapping the boundaries of the British "nation." Naturalists-antiquaries started from the proposition that relics of human relations lay strewn across the languages of Britain, and therefore linguistic topography offered a key to the history of human descent and settlement in Britain. For example, ancient Celtic place names suggested a history of Celtic peoples in a location, whereas Scandinavian place names—or regional dialect words with Scandinavian origins—suggested a history of Viking settlements. Getting more deeply into the structure of the languages could show historical and contemporary similarities between the grammars of Welsh, Scots and Irish Gaelic, and Cornish that could be used to define the historical connections between present-day speakers of those languages. In his *Villare Anglicanum*, a dictionary of English place names, John Aubrey proposed that if it were possible to trace the etymology of some Welsh words to Greek, this would be "good Evidence (without being beholding to Historie) that there was a time, when the Greeks had Colonies here."[48] Such an effort was doomed, but it does indicate what the naturalists hoped to gain from the study of language: evidence for the movement and settlement of peoples that was somehow independent of conventional historical evidence. The topography of languages promised to escape history, to provide an independent check on the chronicles and myths that Britons had been living with since the Middle Ages. In this section I trace topographers' efforts to map the history of the people they referred to as the ancient "British," often understood (at the time) as the ancestors of the modern Welsh, largely through the study of the Celtic languages.

The relationship between historic inhabitants of Britain and the then modern-day composition of its population was a subject of active debate among naturalists, antiquaries, political writers, and historians. This question had crucial implications for relations between the various kingdoms and regions and each group's understanding of itself (this continues to be true into the present).[49] Political writers, in particular, sought to shore up the foundations of the English constitution—and the liberties enshrined therein—by locating its origins in the histories of the peoples of Britain. Common descent could be used to unite the various peoples of Britain: where established, it provided the basis of a common cultural and national identity. However, awareness of differences in origins tended to divide the peoples of Britain—each individual group made strides, perhaps, toward "a more or less coherent" sense of a history that defined them as a nation, but it was difficult, if not impossible (and may or may not have been desirable, depending on one's perspective), to spin a unified historical narrative about the peoples of the British Isles and Ireland.[50]

Topographical writers' understandings of the ancient British and estimations of their contributions to the formation of Britain and the British landscape ranged from utterly dismissive to proudly appreciative. In *The most notable antiquity of Great Britain vulgarly called Stone-Heng* (1655), the first printed treatise on Stonehenge, the architect Inigo Jones argued that the ancient British peoples were entirely too rude and barbarous to have constructed a monument as complex as Stonehenge. Jones's book offered a particularly striking example of the link between English estimations of the ancient Britons and English prejudices against the "Celtic" peoples of early modern Britain.[51] According to Jones, the ancient Britons were utterly devoid of the understanding of art, science, or mathematics that would have equipped them to build Stonehenge.[52] Instead, Jones contended (totally wrongheadedly) that the Romans constructed Stonehenge according to classical architectural principles. John Aubrey, on the other hand, writing at roughly the same time, identified Stonehenge as a Druid temple, defining his Druids as "the most eminent Priests [or Order of Priests] among the Britaines."[53] Aubrey, who claimed Welsh ancestry, saw affiliations between similar ruins scattered across Britain. He sought out and where possible incorporated accounts of ancient British monuments in North Wales and Scotland into *Monumenta Britannica*, his study of British antiquities.[54] Aubrey's interpretation of stone circles as Druid temples became immensely popular through the eighteenth century when it was promoted by the antiquaries William Stukeley and William Borlase.[55]

In political history as well, opinions of the ancient British were neither wholly negative nor wholly positive, though over time this field turned more decisively away from them as progenitors of the English constitution. Earlier writers had made the argument that Britain's foundations could be located among the ancient Britons, shrouded in time immemorial. However, by the

late seventeenth century, historians, especially those of the proparliamentary
and Whiggish type, came to believe that the Saxons were the true progenitors
of English liberties. This argument, which was founded in a century of
increasingly sophisticated antiquarian scholarship on Saxon England, had
been popularly made in Nathaniel Bacon's oft-reprinted *An historicall discourse of the uniformity of the government of England*, which was first published
in 1647.[56] Those on the Royalist side of things, on the other hand, tended to
emphasize more the inheritance from the Normans. Even those who still
sought to locate the foundations of English liberties in ancient Britain argued
that little could be known about their governance, given the lack of surviving
written documents. Regardless of which side one took, the shift to seeing the
transfer of power from Saxons to Normans as a key moment in the history
of the English constitutions led English writers to minimize the contribution
that the Welsh made to the national polity, both as a people in the then
present day and in their past incarnation as the ancient British.[57] Not coinci-
dentally, these arguments had a topographical basis: the boundaries of the
medieval Saxon and Norman territories mostly mapped onto present-day
England, which meant that the English claimed a direct line of descent from
these peoples, but not the ancient Britons, whose descendants lived in Wales,
Ireland, and Scotland.[58]

Working amid this complex backdrop, Edward Lhuyd took the option
of defining Britain from its geographical edges. In 1695 he issued proposals
for a "British Dictionary, historical and geographical."[59] Partly inspired by
his work on the 1695 revised edition of Camden's *Britannia*, he proposed a
study of the natural history, antiquities, languages, and customs of Wales,
Cornwall, Scotland, Ireland, and Brittany. This project consumed the last
fifteen years of Lhuyd's life and was built around extensive travel—he was on
the road for four years—and a questionnaire that he issued to the clergy and
gentry in an edition of four thousand copies. He planned a multivolume
treatise but in the end finished only the first volume, a comparative study of
"British" languages, before death cut his labors short in 1709. Based on the
strength of this treatise, Lhuyd has come to be regarded as one of the originators of the modern study of these languages, now more commonly identified
as "Celtic" languages.[60]

Lhuyd's definition of "Britain" was complex and shifting. In his 1695
prospectus, he focused primarily on Wales.[61] In these proposals Lhuyd defined "British" as the Welsh, Cornish, and Armorican, or Breton, peoples.
Yet his project had implications for understanding British history beyond the

early modern geographical boundaries within which those peoples lived. As was not uncommon, Lhuyd believed that these were the descendants of one group present on the isle at the time of Julius Caesar, that is to say, prior to the Romans' arrival in Britain. Roman and early medieval Saxon invaders drove the "British" to the more remote margins of the "Atlantic archipelago." Their language was likeliest to be preserved uncorrupted in Wales, which had been less exposed to "Foreign Languages introduc'd by Conquest."[62] Yet Lhuyd did not necessarily believe that the ancient "British" were the only original inhabitants of Britain. In the proposals Lhuyd maintained a separation between the "British" and the peoples of Scotland and Ireland, though he did see them as historically and linguistically related.

Lhuyd's conception of "Britain" and "British" as objects of historical and topographical study continued to develop over the course of his research and seems to have expanded by the time he published the linguistic component of the *Archaeologia Britannica* in 1707. The title page proclaimed that the *Archaeologia Britannica* was a study of the "languages, histories, and customs of the original inhabitants of Great Britain" based on travels in "Wales, Cornwal, Bas-Bretagne, Ireland and Scotland."[63] The book was a compilation of comparative dictionaries and grammars of Welsh, Cornish, Breton, and Irish, which Lhuyd regarded as very similar, if not identical, to Highland Scots. Even within this volume, however, "Britain" and "British" were shifting signifiers. He sometimes glossed "Ancient Scots" as "Northern British." Yet at the same time he maintained a separation between the "British" language as spoken in the south—in Wales, Cornwall, and Brittany—and the "Scotish" spoken in the north and west—in Scotland and Ireland. He tended to associate "Scotish" with the Picts, the ancient inhabitants of Britain who had been pushed aside by the "Britans" just as the "Britans" were pushed aside by the Romans and the Saxons.

Yet despite these fractures in Lhuyd's concept of "Britain" and "British," one thing was clear: the only way to understand the history of these languages and, through the languages, the history of the various peoples inhabiting Great Britain was by studying all of them; they had spent centuries jostling along together, pushing each other about, and borrowing from each other's languages, and their histories were intimately connected.[64] Lhuyd mapped the geography of languages in order to elucidate these historical relationships. In a letter written while traveling through the Highlands of Scotland, Lhuyd noted that "most names of places throughout the kingdoms of Ireland and Scotland relish much of a British origin; though I suspect that upon a diligent comparison . . . we shall find that the antient Scots of Ireland were distinct from the Britains of the same kingdom."[65]

Lhuyd's comment, with its suggestion that language groups affiliated with both the "antient Scots" and the "Britains" were present in Ireland, hints at the complexities involved in tracing the movements of ancient peoples, not to mention in trying to link those peoples to present-day groups. In the vocabulary notebooks he kept while traveling in Scotland, he logged common words in at least two Scottish dialects; he also hoped to capture key words in at least three different Irish dialects.[66] Lhuyd systematically analyzed these data in order to deduce the relationships between the languages, requiring at least five to six specific examples using "core vocabulary" (that is, the words from Ray's *Dictionariolum trilingue*) to show that any given difference between the languages was a consistent rule.[67] Following this method, Lhuyd first established the division between the "P-Celtic" and "Q-Celtic" language families broadly recognized today.[68] P-Celtic includes Breton, Cornish, Welsh; Q-Celtic, Scots and Irish Gaelic. Extensive comparative study was the only way to uncover relationships such as this.

Lhuyd cast the "Britains" spread across Great Britain and Ireland as people with deep connections to each other. Yet this was not a group whose shared identity was already widely recognized, either by the English or by each other. Relationships between and among the Scottish, Welsh, and Irish veered from contentious to nonexistent. Little in the way of a shared sense of identity united "Britains" in Wales, Scotland, Ireland, and Cornwall.[69] The word "Celtic" as a collective term for these peoples was only beginning to gain currency in the late seventeenth and early eighteenth centuries, in part because of Lhuyd's work. For many of the "Celtic" gentry and nobility, culture and a sense of identity were rooted in local topography and history.[70] If they looked beyond the local, it was to England, especially London and Westminster, rather than toward each other. This can be seen in a political context—for example, in the process of negotiation that led to the union of Scotland and England in the very year that Lhuyd published the first volume of the *Archaeologia Britannica*.[71] Leading Scottish politicians looked to the relationship between England and Ireland not in solidarity but primarily as an example of unwelcome colonial dependency. The orientation toward England was also visible in the histories of Britain that emerged from both Wales and Scotland: to the extent that they argued for any sort of historical connections between the parts of Great Britain, it was either between Wales and England or between Scotland and England.

Among the "vulgar," those whose horizons were encompassed by parish and village society and who spoke English either not at all or as a second language, local identities and local relationships were even more paramount.[72] In addition, while the Welsh, Scottish, and Irish gentry and clergy displayed enthusiastic interest in local antiquities, natural history, and languages, they did not generally see local topography (or their own identity) as a component of a "British" whole.[73] Lhuyd, in seeking to trace the relationships between the "British," actively constructed that shared identity through the creation of linguistic, cultural, natural, and material histories that could serve as its foundation. He created his "Britain" as both a topographical object and a political object.

Lhuyd further articulated in his 1707 *Archaeologia Britannia* a vision of the Welsh/British as the "First Planters of the Three Kingdoms," the first founders of colonies, in the British Isles.[74] Latching onto this language of planters and colonies, he crafted a vision of Celtic history appropriate to the dawn of a British imperial age. In this he echoed John Speed, who referred to the ancient Britains as the "first Planters and Possessors" of the island of Britain.[75] Such a phrase was redolent with rich associations to projects for imperial expansion and the crafting of the British Empire. Lhuyd's use of the word "planters" suggests something of the political overtones his work carried. Planters were those who established colonies—another word Lhuyd used, as a label for the earliest human settlements in Britain.[76] In the wake of rebellions in Ireland, led first during Elizabeth I's reign and then again at mid-century during the War of the Three Kingdoms, the English established plantations in Ireland. Land was transferred from rebellious Irish subjects, both native Irish and Old English, Catholic descendants of Norman invaders who were mostly settled in the southeast around Dublin.[77] English colonists in the Americas, from Massachusetts Bay to Virginia, were planters.

Planting implied control of territory and settled cultivation of the land, at least partly in the image of Adam and Eve, the first planters; its associations were agricultural, political, and biblical. Planters fixed themselves firmly in the land. Not all of the peoples who had visited Britain had done this, in Lhuyd's view. In his additions to the 1695 edition of Camden, he firmly rejected the possibility that medieval Vikings had constructed the massive stone circles that could be found across Britain: they were but "roving Pirats," roaming from place to place rather than establishing the communities that could build such monuments.[78] Planting implied civilization: seventeenth-century English planters in Ireland and in the Americas went forth to tame "wild" lands and gradually remake local populations, environments, and culture in England's image.[79] In Ireland this included importing the structures of English governance and English Protestantism.[80] Land was divided by counties, replacing traditional lordships; courts of assize were instituted; and Gaelic inheritance laws were replaced by English ones.[81] English and Irish were encouraged to blend, but only on English terms: under Cromwell's leadership the Catholic Irish were made to worship in Protestant churches.[82] The virtuoso William Petty's numerous schemes for "civilizing" the Irish by encouraging marriage between English planters and Irish women were meant to transmute the Irish into English.[83]

Lhuyd's description of the ancient Britons as "planters" and their dominions as "colonies" implied that the Celtic peoples—Welsh, Scottish, and Irish—had a natural role to play in the eighteenth-century expansion of the British Empire. Statements such as this were historically used to promote the contribution of the Celts, specifically the Welsh, to the expansion of the "British" Empire; in the sixteenth century, for example, John Dee argued for the legitimacy of Elizabeth I's claims to possessions in the Americas by tying them to the lands supposedly discovered by the twelfth-century Prince Madoc, who, according to legend, crossed the Atlantic.[84] In this reading, the English owed the Welsh thanks for the "British Empire." Lhuyd went even further, raising up not only the Welsh but also the Celts of Ireland and Scotland (as well as Cornwall and Brittany, though to a lesser degree). Yet this position was one that Lhuyd arrived at only after direct study of the remains of the past, as he prepared his contributions to the revised *Britannia*. He initially found it difficult to overcome the notion that any antiquities that appeared to reflect a sophisticated culture could be attributed to the ancient Britons, and not, say, the Romans.[85] This is not surprising, given Lhuyd's immersion in English antiquarian and natural historical culture, and the widespread English image of the Celts, especially the Catholic Irish, as barbaric and uncivilized. But awareness of the climate in which he worked renders Lhuyd's reference to the ancient Britons as "planters" all the more striking as a statement of fellowship.

Lhuyd's *Archaeologia Britannica* was not universally well received when it was finally published in 1707. The critiques spoke to divisions between England and the rest of Britain and, possibly, to divisions between the Celtic regions. Wits laughed that the fruit of so many years of study, and so much expense by Lhuyd's subscribers, should be an etymological dictionary of Celtic languages. The sniping, which echoed traditional English attacks on the Celtic languages, particularly Welsh, started before the book was officially published. Lhuyd, though he acknowledged that few agreed with him, argued that Welsh was a comparatively ancient language and that certain words in ancient Latin and even Greek could be traced back to the original British (John Aubrey, had he still been alive, would have been sympathetic to this claim).[86] Lhuyd addressed the critiques defensively in his introduction, claiming that his detractors' invidious partiality clouded their judgment. They claimed that only "half a dozen" or "half a score" individuals in the nation could possibly be interested in the subject of Celtic antiquities and languages. Lhuyd observed that if their critique were serious and impartial, they would have to admit that there were closer to "Three or Four Hundred" such individuals: still a small number, but enough to support the production of a book such as Lhuyd's *Glossography*.[87] Lhuyd was silent as to broader motives fueling his unnamed critics' censures, but a defense orchestrated by the Royal Society revealed that questions of national partisanship were an issue. In a letter published by Hans Sloane in the *Philosophical Transactions* shortly after the book's publication, the antiquary William Baxter gave an account of the book and then turned to a defense of Lhuyd as a scholar: "I cannot conclude without taking notice of one Calumny that has been whisper'd about by Men of Passion or Intreague, *viz*. That this Book is design'd to serve a certain Interest. I therefore think my self oblig'd in Justice, to certifie to the Publick, that after a careful perusal of all the Parts of this Work, I cannot discern a Syllable any where that in the least tends to favour any Party, or is any way concern'd in any National Distinction."[88] Baxter, who corresponded with Lhuyd on antiquarian matters, defended his impartiality and attempted to distance his work from the political context of the early eighteenth century, in which questions of "national distinction" and the relationships among England, Scotland, Ireland, and Wales were very much at issue. In his correspondence Lhuyd carefully tracked the publication of Baxter's review, hoping that, by providing a good character for his book, Baxter would help him move more copies of it.[89]

However, devoting serious attention to the "British" languages and antiquities was a political act, and it was interpreted as such by Lhuyd's critics as well as his admirers. Whether they offered praise or critique, correspondents, some of whom had been contributing to the project since Lhuyd first canvassed for subscription over ten years prior, spoke to the questions of what bound and what divided the Celtic regions of Britain. The Irish antiquary Roderic O'Flaherty questioned whether Lhuyd was right to include

England's Britain was defined not by shared ethnicity but by the exercise of power. Britain was those territories that the English government—either king, Parliament, or some combination of the two—controlled or sought to control. The Britain thus produced was shot through with conflict and compromise. It heavily emphasized a Protestant vision, which meant that Ireland's status within the topographical Britain was particularly problematic. Yet by no means was England's Britain constructed solely by the English: in various ways and under various terms, Welsh, Scottish, and Anglo-Irish scholars contributed to the construction of England's Britain. When these works ventured onto Irish territory, though, the native Catholic Irish figured largely as objects of study and scorn, rather than as participants in the topographical project.[93]

Given his genre-defining power, Camden is a fit starting point for an exploration of the topographical Britain as it developed from an English perspective.[94] The title page of Philemon Holland's 1610 English translation of *Britannia* indicated that it was a "chorographicall description of the most flourishing Kingdoms, England, Scotland, and Ireland."[95] However, "England" appeared in larger type than "Scotland" and "Ireland," and Wales (not to mention Cornwall) was subsumed into England, appearing nowhere on the title page. This structure aligned with the era's political reality, in which the English monarch was king of the kingdoms of England, Scotland, and Ireland but Wales was a dominion, for political purposes, considered part of England. In certain respects Camden's *Britannia* emphasized the geographical unity of Britain, particularly the three nations of the main island. In part because Camden treated Wales almost as a part of England, Wales received more extensive coverage than Scotland and Ireland. Wales was physically integrated as well: Camden organized his book as a trip around Britain, taking the reader through Wales on his way from western to northern England.

Camden's approach to Scotland (repeated in both the 1610 translation and Gibson's 1695 revised edition) suggested a view of the Scots as respected equals, rather than subordinate partners, in the project of Britain. As a relative stranger to Scotland, Camden began by apologizing for even attempting to discuss the topography of that nation. Yet "Scotland also ioieth in the name of Britaine," and so he hoped that the Scots might give him leave to include their nation in his book. What was more, England and Scotland were now united under one "most sacred and happie Monarch," James VI and I.[96] Camden hoped that his *Britannia* could provide a foundation for their further political unity and help contribute to ending any discord that persisted between the two "otherwise invincible" nations.[97] Camden's statement came at a time when the Crown had only recently been unified, and James I had pushed for but failed to secure a more thoroughgoing political union from Parliament in 1606–1607. England and Scotland shared a head but not a body, and in promoting Anglo-Scottish union, Camden's proclamation reflected a hope rather than a firm reality.

In bringing together the human and natural histories of the diverse peoples and landscapes of Britain into one book, English naturalists and antiquaries implicitly (and sometimes explicitly, as in Camden's case) made the case for a unified British polity. In the revised 1695 edition, Edmund Gibson altogether dropped from the title page any divisions between the realms of Britain: his *Britannia* was a survey of Britain, full stop.[98] Within the book Gibson's English contributors represented British cultural, ethnic, and linguistic identities, especially as expressed at the borders between regions, as products of the historical mixing and mingling of different peoples. In the additions for Cumberland, in the north of England, Hugh Todd reproduced a letter from William Nicolson to the antiquary William Dugdale. In the letter Nicolson, who was born in Cumberland and went on to become the Anglican bishop in the northern Irish town of Derry, explicated an inscription on a baptismal font that had been written in "Danish" runes. He wrote, "Only the Language of the whole seems a mixture of the Danish and Saxon Tongues; but that can be no other than the natural effect of the two Nations being jumbled together in this part of the World. Our Borderers, to this day, speak a leash of Languages (British, Saxon, and Danish) in one; and 'tis hard to determine which of those three Nations has the greatest share in the Motly Breed."[99] Though evidence for it could be found across Britain, historical contact between peoples was especially visible in the border zones, where it produced "motley breeds" who clearly could not trace their ancestry back to a single group.

Yet divisions and tensions remained. The continued Anglo-centrism of the 1695 *Britannia* was visible in its coverage: each English shire received an extensive description, while the treatments of Wales, Scotland, and Ireland were often brief, even cursory, by comparison. Remarks on these three regions were sourced from one individual each, while remarks on English counties were supplied by upward of twenty local gentlemen and clerics.[100] On the other hand, Edward Lhuyd and Robert Sibbald, who provided most, if not all, of the remarks on Wales and Scotland, were welcome, respected contributors to the revised *Britannia*. Getting their contributions right was important to them, as evidenced by the pains they took in their labors. Their work illustrates the complexities faced by Welsh and Scottish naturalists who participated in Anglo-centric topographical projects.

In their work Lhuyd and Sibbald displayed a kind of dual national consciousness, giving voice to allegiances to both Wales and Scotland, respectively, as well as to Britain. Lhuyd invested himself deeply in the construction of a British identity that tended to exclude the English. Yet he also expended enormous effort in fulfilling his obligations to Gibson, undertaking a special summer tour through Wales to collect material for the project and providing additions more extensive than those given by any other individual contributor.[101] He also undertook to retranslate the entire section on Wales from Camden's 1607 Latin edition.[102] This double labor of translation and supplementation was a heavier burden than that shouldered by most of Gibson's contributors.[103] Lhuyd's efforts made a difference: it was not a given that Wales would be included on his terms. In July 1694, with printing under way, the English printer Awnsham Churchill, who worked with Gibson as a co-undertaker for the project, threatened to cut some of the material on Wales from the finished volume. (In seventeenth-century book parlance, undertakers managed the production of books by subscription, overseeing both financial and editorial aspects of the process.) Lhuyd sought the help of Martin Lister in persuading Churchill not to do so.[104] Through his enthusiastic participation in the *Britannia* project, Lhuyd promoted Wales to a broader British readership, one that included the English, and worked to elevate its status as part of a broader Britain. Gibson, in his introduction to the revised *Britannia,* praised Lhuyd's diligence, suggesting that given competent encouragement (that is, funds), he could do a fine job with any county in England.[105] Perhaps this was the highest form of praise Gibson could offer.

Sibbald, similarly, held allegiances to both Scotland and Britain. In 1682 Charles II appointed Sibbald geographer royal for Scotland (he also served Charles and his brother James as a royal physician). Sibbald was charged with producing maps, a natural history, and a study of the antiquities of Scotland. The warrant for his appointment emphasized the contribution that accurate, detailed geographical knowledge would make to husbandry and trade.[106] The warrant's emphasis, however, was very much on His Majesty's kingdom of Scotland, not on Scotland within a broader British context. Yet Sibbald, like Lhuyd, was enmeshed in a pan-British correspondence: at various periods in his life he lived in London, and he corresponded with virtuosi in England

and Scotland who shared his interests.[107] As an Episcopalian for most of his life (with the exception of a brief period during which he identified as Catholic), Sibbald, unlike many Scots, was generally aligned with rather than opposed to the Anglican Church.[108] Sibbald also collaborated with Gibson on the 1695 *Britannia*, providing new material for the sections on Scotland and the outer British Isles. In his additions Sibbald documented the cross-border links between England and Scotland, noting, for example, that in the shire of Teviotdale, people supported themselves by trading cattle, sheep, and wool with the English across the border.[109]

Sibbald's engagement in the project of constructing the topographical Britain can be seen in his promotion of a newer etymology for "Britain," one in keeping with the fundamental precept of natural history, that knowledge of nature was the foundation of trade, economic improvement, and British political and cultural identity. The medieval Brutus myth, which suggested that the British were descended from a hero of the Trojan War, had been dying even in Camden's day. Camden had promoted an etymology that traced Britain to the ancient British word for "blue" because some of the ancient inhabitants of Britain—the Picts—had painted their bodies blue with plant-based dyes.[110] This derivation was reprinted in the 1695 *Britannia* (much of the 1695 copy was taken from Holland's 1610 translation, rather than being retranslated).[111] Later in the book, however, Sibbald discussed an alternative etymology of Britain in his essay on the "Thule of the Ancients." This was included near the end of the 1695 *Britannia* in the section that dealt with Britain's outer northwestern islands. In this essay Sibbald attempted to pin down the physical island that corresponded to "Thule," an island that, for classical Greek and Roman writers, marked the northwestern edge of the known world. Toward the end Sibbald repeated a claim, which he credited to the seventeenth-century French biblical scholar Samuel Bochart, that Britain was derived (via Greek) from the ancient Phoenician word for "Land of Tinn," on the theory that tin was the most important product that Mediterranean civilizations would have obtained from Britain through trade.[112]

One might see Sibbald's etymology as a descendant of the Brutus myth, in the sense that it retained a whiff of the prestige of the classical origins story while updating it to make it plausible for a late seventeenth-century audience. Sibbald was not the only one to link the ancient British to the ancient Phoenicians, who were, like the early modern British, seagoing traders: the disreputable antiquary Aylett Sammes went him one better in his *Britannia antiqua illustrata* (1676), claiming that the customs and language of the early British were deeply shaped by commercial contact with the Phoenicians.[113] Aubrey's and Lhuyd's attempts to read ancient British as a species of ancient Greek and Inigo Jones's to impute Roman origins to Stonehenge also come to mind as efforts to create a lineage in which the British were linked to, if not descended from, ancient Mediterranean peoples.

But Sibbald's story about linguistic history and national identity put trade, specifically trade in products derived from the land, center stage as a defining feature of British identity.[114] Sibbald's etymology sidestepped complicated questions about descent and relationships between historical and present-day British peoples—early modern discussions of the Brutus myth inevitably led to questions about which of the British peoples were the descendants of Brutus, with the result that some were excluded from the national mythology. Neither did this etymology denigrate the past inhabitants of Britain, as did Camden's story about the blue-painted Britons. Though Sibbald well knew that tin was chiefly a product of one region of Britain, Cornwall, in this etymology, through the alchemy of international trade, all of Britain became identified with it.

Sibbald and Lhuyd's work demonstrates that English, Scottish, and Welsh naturalists-antiquaries were capable of defining Britain as common ground. Ireland's relationship to Britain, as represented in English topographical studies, was more vexed, as it was in life. Britain-as-projection-of-English-hegemony was most visible when English naturalists came to Ireland. On a most basic level, Ireland was divided from England, Scotland, and Wales by the sea; though the latter three could be defined "naturally" as one nation, it was more difficult to include Ireland in this way. The English had a long historical tradition of viewing the Irish as the other—the barbarians—against which they defined their own civility. In the early modern era, as this othering took on religious overtones with the rise of intense anti-Catholicism in Protestant Britain, it was increasingly taken up by the Welsh and the Scots as well.[115]

When Camden came to describe Ireland in detail, he depicted it as an island with a unique human and natural history that could not be fully covered by the label of Britain, as Scotland and England were, much less subsumed into England, as Wales sometimes was. In both the 1610 translation of Camden and its 1695 revision, discussion of Ireland was set off from the rest of the book by an interlude that represented the sea crossing to Ireland. At this point the name "Britain" was used to refer exclusively to England and Scotland. Furthermore, Ireland was never depicted as a potential equal,

England's partner in the matter of Britain, as Scotland was. Camden did not open the section on Ireland with a grand proclamation about the strength and peace to be found in political unity between England and Ireland. Instead he emphasized the wildness and incivility of the native Irish (as opposed to the "English-Irish," settled in the Pale): contradictorily, they "love idlenesse and withal hate quitnes."[116] In Holland's translation, Camden mourned that the Romans had never conquered Ireland, for surely they would have brought civility with them. He marveled at the contrast between the Irish medieval past, when Ireland boasted a vibrant, learned monastic culture (they had taught the English their letters), and now, when it was "rude, halfe-barbarous, and altogether voide of any polite and exquisite literature."[117] Other writers were even more extreme in their descriptions of the ancient Irish. Speed, in *The theatre of the empire of Great Britain*, touched on the diet of the ancient Britons. Based on descriptions collected from ancient writers, including Strabo, Solinus, and Pliny, he emphasized their "temperance of diet." This he contrasted with the ancient Irish, who were cannibals. Accusations of cannibalism were commonly bandied about in the early modern European world as a way of marking off boundaries between civilized and uncivilized; in this particular case, Speed attributed the claim to St. Jerome.[118]

Overall, Camden's history of Ireland put forward the argument that the conditions and actions of the native Catholic Irish easily justified their subordination to English rulers. Though Camden saw some bright spots in the Irish past, for him, the island began and ended in barbarousness, which he consistently opposed to the civility of the Romans and the English. Touching on more recent history, Camden devoted an entire chapter to the sixteenth-century conflict between the Irish Earl of Tyrone and the English.[119] He characterized the conflict as a "rebellion . . . begun upon private grudges and quarrels intermedled with ambition" that spread across Ireland under the "pretense of restoring libertie and Romish religion."[120] He regarded its English suppression as the basis for "firme peace, as we hope, for ever established."[121]

These kinds of prejudices were replicated, and even more closely linked to projects for English imperial control of Ireland, in subsequent English topographical writings. In Gerard Boate's 1652 *Irelands Naturall History*, published by Samuel Hartlib and dedicated to Oliver Cromwell, the native Irish hardly figured at all. According to the title page, the book was published "For the Common Good of Ireland, and more especially, for the benefit of the

Adventurers and Planters therein."[122] In the dedication Hartlib expounded enthusiastically on the promise of the title page: a natural history of Ireland would be the greatest aid to the planters, soldiers, and adventurers colonizing Ireland in the wake of Cromwell's conquests. Hartlib represented Ireland as a realm cleared for the free settlement of not only the Protestant English but Protestants from the Continent as well—exiled Bohemians and other refugees from the Thirty Years' War.[123] Neither the native Irish nor the Catholic Old English had a role to play in this new Ireland—in Hartlib's Protestant vision, they were not even subordinate; they were invisible. Natural history, prosperity, and Protestant English colonization of Ireland were further linked in the Down Survey of Irish land, which William Petty conducted for Cromwell. Petty surveyed landownership as well as the quality and productivity of the land county by county in preparation for the transfer of much of that land from its Irish Catholic owners to soldiers in Cromwell's army.[124] Petty, though less anti-Catholic in theological terms than Hartlib, nonetheless saw Roman Catholicism as an impediment to the increase of trade in Ireland, as Adam Fox has observed.[125] Petty also maintained the link between topographical knowledge, the improvement of trade, and English imperial dominance in Ireland (and elsewhere).[126] Through the Restoration he plied Charles II and other influential members of the court with reports, grounded in his new methods of "political arithmetic," encouraging the Crown to take a strong hand in displacing Irish Catholics with Protestant English planters.[127]

However, the story of the establishment of Ireland's place within England's Britain cannot be told solely in terms of English efforts to establish imperial dominance. The case of William Molyneux indicates that further complexities inhered in the production of topographical studies of Ireland. Molyneux was from a wealthy, Protestant Anglo-Irish family with roots in Calais. As a student at Trinity College Dublin, he became interested in natural philosophy and mathematics. After a stint in London studying law at the Middle Temple, he returned home, where he founded the Dublin Philosophical Society, modeled on the Royal Society, in 1683. Like Sibbald and Lhuyd, Molyneux maintained an extensive correspondence with British naturalists. As secretary of the Dublin Philosophical Society, he exchanged letters and meeting minutes with the Royal Society and the Oxford Philosophical Society.[128]

Topography was one of Molyneux's many scientific interests. He served for a time as surveyor-general and chief engineer for Dublin, and he took responsibility for the Irish sections of the bookseller Moses Pitt's *English Atlas*.[129] Pitt's *Atlas* was to be a luxury product, a complete, up-to-date atlas of the world in eleven volumes, but only four volumes were ever published. Expected to include six hundred plates, the project failed on account of exorbitant production costs of as much as one thousand pounds per volume, compounded by financial losses Pitt incurred through his misadventures in real estate development.[130] In promoting the project, Pitt advertised the support of Charles II, his brother the Duke of York, Prince Rupert, the Royal Society, and the universities of Oxford and Cambridge. The maps, made from plates that had been engraved earlier in the century for Dutch cartographer Johannes Janssonius's *Atlas major* but partially recut based on the latest available knowledge, were to be accompanied by reams of historical and topographical information, at least some of it newly collected. Leading scholars, including Christopher Wren, John Pell, Robert Hooke, Thomas Gale, and Isaac Vossius, signed on to advise Pitt and monitor his progress.[131]

Though it fell far short of Pitt's projections, this was intended as a prestige product, meant to demonstrate the heights to which English knowledge of the world, and English printing, had ascended by the late seventeenth century. In participating in this project, then, Molyneux worked in concert with English mapmakers, virtuosi, and printers. In the early 1680s he issued a set of queries requesting information for the account of Ireland.[132] Respondents were largely Anglo-Irish and Protestant, reflecting the makeup of Molyneux's correspondence. Molyneux did work with at least one Catholic Irish, rather than Anglo-Irish, antiquary, Roderic O'Flaherty of County Galway, author of a 1685 treatise on Irish history. O'Flaherty's involvement in the project spawned an ongoing correspondence; O'Flaherty also worked closely with Lhuyd on the Irish Gaelic portions of the *Glossography*, mailing him printed sheets of the dictionary heavily annotated with his remarks and offering extended critiques of the entire book in his letters.[133] Nevertheless, Molyneux and most of his respondents saw themselves as participants in a Protestant, Anglo-centric "Britain," an allegiance reflected in the questionnaire that Molyneux circulated. As noted on the questionnaire, interested persons could pick up their free copies at the bookshop belonging to Dudley Davis in Dublin. A brief advertisement followed: patrons could also purchase at Davis's shop William Dugdale's *Antient usage in bearing of such ensignes of honour as are commonly call'd arms* (1682), which was published with a "Catalogue of the Present Nobility and Baronets of England, Scotland, and

Ireland."[134] Given a small space to insert an advertisement for other books he carried, the bookseller chose this one, suggesting he presumed a readership who saw, either in actuality or aspirationally, the British nobility as their appropriate social context.

Yet how much was a shared culture worth, when it came down to it? In the 1690s the English Parliament handed down a series of laws and judgments restricting Irish trade. Among other things, the English sought to limit Ireland's woolen exports to England in order to protect the English trade in woolen fabrics. The Irish Parliament, which was in a weakened state following the revolution of 1689 and subsequent warfare in Ireland, refused to approve the new statutes, but their rejection of them did not halt their implementation.[135]

Molyneux registered vocal opposition to these laws in *The case of Ireland's being bound by acts of parliament in England, stated*, published in 1698. He marshaled historical precedent to support the argument that though subjects of the same king, England and Ireland possessed independent representative institutions, and the English Parliament had no jurisdiction over Ireland. He argued that Ireland was not a colony of England but, like Scotland, an independent kingdom with whom England shared a king, properly governed by the king in concert with a Protestant Anglo-Irish Parliament.[136]

Molyneux's claims to coequality with England were founded on the sort of arguments about human descent and the definition of Britain that featured prominently in topographical works. By no means did Molyneux argue that the majority Catholic Irish should have any part in governing Ireland: though Molyneux had corresponded with Irish antiquaries such as O'Flaherty, he nevertheless wrote strictly in defense of the "Protestant Interest of Ireland."[137] The Protestant Anglo-Irish were descended from "English and Britains" who had "from time to time" crossed the Irish Sea and seized power over the Irish.[138] Molyneux argued that the Anglo-Irish, therefore, as the descendants of the English conquerors of Ireland, could claim the same rights and liberties maintained by the English in England.[139] The Anglo-Irish were no less English than the English, no less British than the British. Indeed, Molyneux was not averse to a closer political union with England, one that would admit Anglo-Irish representatives to the English Parliament, though he thought it unlikely.[140] He was correct in this assumption. His arguments for Anglo-Irish liberty were condemned in England: the English were by no means willing to grant that liberties flowed from shared descent, especially when Anglo-Irish liberties conflicted with English trade.[141]

Conclusion

In both its unities and its divisions, topographical writing was a mirror in which Britons could see themselves reflected. It attempted to instill in readers a sense of "Britain" as a shared political, linguistic, cultural, and geographical space. However, collectively topographical works displayed a profound uncertainty as to who and what should be included in Britain and Britishness. This was not merely a result of the different methods that topographers followed, as per Ogilby. No matter which method one followed—linguistic, historical, economic, geographical—topographical studies exposed competing forces uniting and dividing Britons. Topography may have been a cracked mirror, but the Britain it reflected came prefractured.

Topographical writers revealed the Scots, Welsh, Anglo-Irish, Catholic Irish, and English as peoples with deeply rooted independent cultural, linguistic, and political traditions. Yet, as topographical writings also recognized, Ireland, England, Scotland, and Wales shared equally long histories of political, commercial, and cultural contact, even integration. Connection and contact—through trade, conquest, intermarriage, or the kind of social and educational mingling that occurred in London and the university towns—only intensified in the latter half of the seventeenth century. Many naturalists and antiquaries were at the forefront of this movement, getting into contact with each other through travel, correspondence, and the reading of each other's books.

In some ways topographical writers participated in a "colonial" dynamic, in which the non-English British affiliated themselves both with English versions of Britain and their own "native" traditions (while some English writers felt free to pay minimal or no attention to the non-English parts of Britain). Molyneux, Sibbald, and Lhuyd participated in the project of constructing Britain from an English perspective. Yet they also resisted it, or at least maintained strong ties to their own piece of Britain, however they defined it.[142] Their national visions—and identities—were neither strictly in concert with English versions of the same nor wholly oppositional. Neither were they consistent across projects, as can be seen particularly in Lhuyd's career. So too were their identities and practices as scholars hybrid, fluid, and contextual. This can be seen, again, in Lhuyd's career in his dual use of English and Welsh in his correspondence. One might compare the complex, shifting colonial identities and national visions expressed by Spanish Creole clerics-scholars in New Spain in the eighteenth century, described by Jorge

Cañizares-Esguerra, as they worked to define the history of the New World with and against Enlightenment historians of empire writing in Spain.[143]

Molyneux's work as a topographical investigator and as a defender of Anglo-Irish liberties highlights the complexity of "British" identities and loyalties. It also shows how histories of human descent in the British Isles, a familiar concern in topographical writing, could be deployed in attempts to negotiate national relationships in the late seventeenth century. Like Sibbald and Lhuyd, Molyneux collaborated with London-based scholars, making points of contact with England and Englishness and even with Britishness. So too did others in his Anglo-Irish milieu—Dugdale's catalog of the nobility, advertised on Molyneux's questionnaire for the English atlas, was, after all, a register of the English, Irish, and Scottish nobility. Yet it was these points of contact, these engagements, that were, for Molyneux, arguments for why Ireland could not be fully ruled by England and subsumed within Britain. The distinctiveness of Ireland as a kingdom within Britain, coequal with England, was rooted, for Molyneux, in Anglo-Irish claims to being fully English. As such, the Anglo-Irish, Molyneux believed, were subjects of the British king but were not bound by a Parliament in which they had no representation.

Both Molyneux and Lhuyd met with resistance to their attempts to graft their parts of the "British" nation into relationship with England and empire. This resistance was symptomatic of the limits, set largely though not entirely by the English, that Welsh, Anglo-Irish, and Scottish naturalists met when they participated in the project of defining Britain. Lhuyd, although he had his supporters in the Royal Society, was mocked when he spent his scholarly energies (and his subscribers' money) on writing into being a Britain without England.

The failure of Molyneux's arguments is particularly striking given the overall aims of topographical writing. Molyneux's statement that shared liberties flowed from common descent foundered in the face of the English Parliament's insistence on protecting English trade. In their books seventeenth-century naturalists often rhetorically depicted a Britain knit together by trade ties that crisscrossed regional and national boundaries. Many of them set natural history as the chief cornerstone of the improvement of trade—and thus of Britain as a nation and of British identity. Yet when it came down to it, local particulars could not be nationalized quite so easily. Topographical writing was inevitably deployed in the service of particular arguments and political visions that imagined (and enacted) allegiances that included some "Britons" and excluded others. The political equality and economic freedoms that Molyneux sought for the Anglo-Irish depended on the total subordination of the Catholic Irish. There was no master vision of the land that could serve as unified and unifying ground, the basis for an economy that would knit together a Britain in which the local and the national were held in tension to the satisfaction of all. Nor could there be.

Printed topographical works were deeply marked by the scientific correspondence that was the context of their creation. Britons spread across Ireland, England, Wales, and Scotland came in contact with each other through correspondence. They created a shared forum for assembling and debating topographical knowledge, one that, though largely populated by English scholars, was by no means totally dominated by them. Neither was this a shared forum in which individuals were encouraged to abandon their locally rooted perspectives. In fact topography, which presented national visions amalgamated out of local particulars, demanded that individuals maintain their local and regional allegiances, their pride in knowing their land. The tensions in topographical writing—its dream of producing a whole "body and book," a national vision of Britain, its production in reality of many different, though sometimes overlapping, visions—were present in its necessarily collaborative mode of construction.

Chapter 2

Putting Texts, Things, and People in Motion: Learned Correspondence in Action

The construction of Britain in printed topographical works went hand in hand with the rise of correspondence as the forum for creating knowledge about British nature and antiquities. In promoting new ways of thinking about national identity, topographers, naturalists, and antiquaries communicated habits of thought and being that they had learned by working together via correspondence. Through correspondence, each individual interwove his local knowledge with that possessed by others scattered across Britain. They debated shared questions, though they did not always arrive at shared answers. Travel and letters allowed naturalists to understand the national as the local: to echo Joshua Childrey, mutual correspondence made it possible for each scholar to feel that all of Britain was at his "own door."

In practice, this correspondence was a complicated dance, the steps of which were the constant movement of letters, books, papers, and specimens by post and carrier and people by horse, foot, carriage, and boat. In a 1692 letter to Anthony à Wood, John Aubrey, describing his travel plans and the locations and destinations of various sets of his papers, summed up these exchanges: "I have here sent II of my volumnes which I intend to print: and desire your perusall, and castigation; as also Mr Collins of Magd{alene} Coll{ege}: to whom pray remember me. {manicule in margin} I desire to heare of your receipt of ~~the~~ my MSS. that they may not miscarry. Tomorrow I goe to Mr Ray {into?} Essex for a weeke. About the middle of Aug: I am for Chalke & Wilton: and thence to Oxford about the beginning of

Septemb{er}./ My <u>Surrey</u> is now in Dr Gales hands, before it goes to Mr
Ch{arles} Howard & Mr Jo{hn} Evelyn. Pray let me heare from you."[1]
Aubrey's letter illustrates different ways of transporting information, things,
and people. First, there was his letter to Wood, probably enclosed with his
manuscripts and sent to Oxford via carrier (though letters mailed alone usually traveled by post). Next were the manuscripts. One manuscript had been
sent by carrier to Wood; another, Aubrey's *Perambulation of Surrey*, went to
Thomas Gale, the headmaster of St. Paul's School in London, with whom
Aubrey sometimes lodged. The latter manuscript would make its way, by
either carrier or a personal messenger, to Howard and then Evelyn, both of
whom had family connections to Surrey. Third, Aubrey himself traveled: first
to John Ray, in Essex, and then on to Wiltshire, where he would stop at
Broad Chalke, his brother's farm, and Wilton, the estate of the Earl of Pembroke, until finally he would come to Oxford. At each stop along their paths,
letters, manuscripts, and man would be drawn into conversations with both
old and new friends and readers. These conversations, in turn, would be
reinscribed into new letters as Aubrey and others drew on them as sources
for new observations to communicate to correspondents. Through personal
travel and the circulation of letters and books, knowledge was collected and
inscribed into the books of nature, old friendships maintained, and new ones
forged.

The material goods of early modern knowledge making—which
included plant and animal specimens as well as letters and papers such as
Aubrey's—were fragile and difficult to transport. Indeed in the days before
well-developed systems of regular mail coaches and sound roads, *people* could
be difficult to transport. The travel diaries of Celia Fiennes (1662–1741),
for example, testify to the muddy, often impassible roads and draughty,
pestilence-ridden inns that greeted travelers across Britain, and it was only in
the late eighteenth and early nineteenth centuries that a truly national road
system was built.[2] Yet naturalists (and their materials) were scattered across
Britain from Dublin to Aberdeen; from the high mountains of northern
Wales to the basement of the Ashmolean Museum in Oxford; from estates in
Wiltshire to villages in Essex; from the naval yards at Deptford to the Royal
Society's meeting rooms in Gresham College. To make natural history and
antiquarian studies, people and things had to travel. The threading of correspondence across Britain was necessary to the realization naturalists' and antiquaries' intellectual ambition, the construction of "the whole body and
book" of British natural history and antiquities.

This chapter reconstructs the ways in which naturalists moved books, papers, specimens, and themselves, creating an image of a seventeenth-century British scientific correspondence. I consider naturalists' and antiquaries' communications with each other from both material (how and why did things and people move around?) and social (how and why did naturalists maintain relationships across great distances?) perspectives. I show how naturalists and antiquaries circulated not just information but also material goods, estimates of each other, and "service" (favors and promises of favors).

While some of the social and intellectual aspects of the diffusion of knowledge in early modern Europe have been elaborated by historians of science, they have rarely been coupled to the material realities of communication.[3] In particular, this chapter grounds the "diffusion" of ideas and information in the movement of letters, books, packages, and people between towns, cities, and countries by horseback, horse- or ox-drawn carts, and riverboats and sailing ships.[4] The main sources for this reconstruction are naturalists' letters, which eloquently express their frustrations and anxieties regarding long-distance communication and travel but also (by their very being) demonstrate the successes of their efforts. Their letters offer a wealth of information on the social links—no less vital than the material ones—along which information, goods, and favors traveled.

These links spanned England, Wales, Scotland, and Ireland, connecting naturalists in city, town, and country. Indeed, though the wider world defined by burgeoning British imperial and commercial ties is not the focus of this book, correspondence extended wherever British merchants and colonists traveled. Naturalists built their correspondences within the context of a wider world of British communication and information exchange, a world in which polite correspondents kept each other up to date on the latest news as a way of maintaining social ties and circumventing purveyors of printed news, which they regarded with some suspicion.[5] Naturalists sought long-distance contacts as a way of stitching together their individual patches of local topographical knowledge. The quilt they formed was necessarily incomplete and partial, with some of the pieces quite loosely joined together. Each individual, with his own particular interests within the larger field and his own collection of correspondents, held a different section of it. But each section overlapped with others, in terms of the connections between their interests and the connections between their sets of correspondents. As we saw in Chapter 1, these connections did not, of course, prevent dissension about exactly what constituted "Britain" as a topographical object of study. However, these connections were the medium through which naturalists and antiquaries articulated their visions of Britain as a scientific object. They may have sometimes differed on how they defined the nation, but they shared the goal of uniting local particulars under a national vision of the land. Furthermore a naturalist's or antiquary's correspondence as a material and social formation was at the heart of the vision of the nation that he projected in his printed works.

"An Active and Large Correspondence"

Rich material, social, and intellectual links made up a scientific correspondence. Naturalists identified a correspondence as the sum of these links. More than just an exchange of one or two letters, a correspondence was a fruitful relationship that persisted over time. As early as 1643 Samuel Hartlib, in a pamphlet addressed to Parliament, called for a "Correspondencie for the advancement of the Protestant Cause."[6] In the late 1690s Edward Lhuyd's star had risen high enough that he received an offer of "correspondence" from August Quirinus Rivinus in Leipzig, who offered to give him news of German fossil discoveries.[7] Their exchange was to be founded on material, not just intellectual, exchange: the Leipzig naturalist opened his offer with a gift of "3 or 4 books and some Formd Stones."[8] Though he was concerned that Rivinus had not behaved well by John Ray, Lhuyd accepted the offer; given the opportunities opened by such an exchange, it was worth navigating potential social difficulties, including the possibility that a correspondent would not deal frankly or fairly with one. Like this one, a correspondence could be between two people, but more often it referred to the sum of interactions between many people linked to one another through the exchange of letters. Elsewhere, Lhuyd referred to John Woodward's "boast" of a "correspondence with five hundred persons . . . beyond the seas."[9]

An "active and large correspondence" was a necessity, both for the gathering and production of knowledge that went into books and for selling those books. Martin Lister, for example, relied heavily on a broad correspondence to send him material—specimens as well as information—for his landmark *Historiae conchyliorum*, a multivolume natural history of shelled animals (including mollusks and gastropods) published between 1685 and 1692. Correspondents, including Hans Sloane, Edward Lhuyd, John Ray, Samuel Dale, and Thomas Townes, the latter a physician posted in the Caribbean, sent him species from across Britain and the British Atlantic world.[10] Success in print too required an extensive correspondence. Henry Oldenburg ran into trouble when he contracted to print the *Philosophical Transactions* with an Oxford printer who had an insufficient correspondence. Richard Davies took over the job from Royal Society printers John Martyn and James Allestrey when plague closed London printing shops in 1665. But in his first go, Davies sold only three hundred of one thousand copies printed. Oldenburg's profit was based on sales, so a failure to sell seven hundred issues represented a serious loss.[11] A chastened Oldenburg wrote, "If he not be a man of an active and large correspondence, I had done much better, never to have committed it to him."[12] The possession of an "active and large correspondence" was crucial for booksellers and others seeking to move books because print was distributed through the social links of correspondence.

In some ways, as Lhuyd, Oldenburg, and Lister's experiences demonstrate, the correspondence was akin to our "social network." But it was not identical to it. Neither can "correspondence" or "the correspondence" be simplified down to one thing (of course neither can the social network; the term has many different valences). There was "a correspondence," in the sense of letters passed back and forth primarily between two persons; there was a bookseller's commercial correspondence, the "active and large correspondence" described by Oldenburg; and there was the naturalist's correspondence, the connections from which he collected information. The correspondence could encompass both weak and strong ties, as described by David S. Lux and Harold J. Cook.[13] Weaker ties might predominate more with international correspondence or with commercial correspondence.

However, the connections that made up the British correspondence were tighter and more personal, differentiating it from some (though not all) modern-day social networking and the broader early modern international scientific correspondence, of which it was, in some sense, a subset. It depended more on face-to-face interaction and the frequent exchange of long letters. The elite class was smaller and more compressed, and naturalists and antiquaries played multiple roles within it. In addition they were gentry, clergy, nobility, and advisers to the monarch and his ministers. For example, John Aubrey, Samuel Pepys, and John Evelyn had intimate audiences with Charles II and his advisers; Pepys, as a naval administrator, met with them regularly. Others played leading roles in their counties. Additionally for British naturalists, scholarly correspondence was at least sometimes "commercial" correspondence, in the sense that naturalists gathered information, financed books, and exchanged specimens for money through their correspondence.

Among British naturalists, face-to-face interaction was usually the basis for correspondence. That is, correspondence began between two or more people who knew each other, initially at least, through local, face-to-face relationships. "Weak ties" were still important for the communication of topographical knowledge of Britain, especially when it came to information exchange between the metropolitan center and Wales, Scotland, and Ireland. Yet even these kinds of ties often got their start when Scottish, Irish, and Welsh naturalists traveled to London, Oxford, and Cambridge and then met in person. The Aberdeen naturalist George Garden opened his first letter to Henry Oldenburg by fondly recalling their meeting in London the summer before: "I am very sensible," Garden wrote, "of the great civility, wherewith you were pleased to entertain Master Scougall and me, when we waited on you last Summer; and shall be ready on all occasions to give you that account you then desired of things philosophical that may occur here, to promote that noble design you have in hand." Garden went on to give an account of a man with something "peculiar in his temper, that inclines him to imitate unawares all the gestures and motions of those with whom he converseth," whom he and Oldenburg had discussed when they first met.[14]

Naturalists regarded correspondence as a poor substitute for direct interaction, especially when it came to establishing a relationship. Introducing oneself by letter to someone whom one had not met in person was generally regarded as rude. In 1676 John Aubrey recommended to Robert Plot that he consult with Sir Jonas Moore on some matter. Plot, however, begged off: "As for S{i}r Jonas Moore's assistanse in my affaire," he wrote to Aubrey, "as I doubt not but it will be very considerable, so I take it as a very great Honour that He will bee pleased to afford it me: but to write to Him in my owne behalfe, especially being altogether unknown to Him too, I must confesse I have not the confidense: I must therefore only begg of you, that you would be pleased to preserve some memory of me in Him till opportunity shall give me leave to waite on Him in London which I hope may be within a little time."[15] It was preferable to approach a potential patron first in person rather than through a letter, though an intermediary might make one known, or "preserve some memory of" one in the person one sought to meet, before that meeting took place.

Despite this preference for face-to-face relationships, gentlemen "personally unknown" to each other could be united through correspondence, after a fashion. Correspondents distinguished, though, between personal acquaintances made face-to-face and those made through letters. Robert Plot and

John Ray corresponded in 1691, yet in a letter to Edward Lhuyd, Ray disclaimed acquaintance with Plot's character, writing in response to Lhuyd's negative report, "He is a Gentlema{n} personally unknown to me."[16] Because he so trusted Lhuyd's "judgmt & Charity" (and because Lhuyd's judgment confirmed Ray's experience), Ray was inclined to trust Lhuyd's estimation of Plot, which was generally negative. (To his former assistant curator, Plot was a tight-fisted, grasping creature, eager for preferment but stingy toward those below him.) Letters between two gentlemen personally unknown to each other might be transmitted by a third person acquainted with both parties. Sometimes this occurred even when two people ran in the same circles but were perhaps not great friends. For example, in February and March 1680/81 Aubrey funneled multiple requests for stacks of Robert Plot's natural history queries through Edward Tyson, who acted at the time as Plot's informant on the goings-on of the London scientific virtuosi.[17]

Correspondence was also a means of creating or maintaining "virtual" face-to-face presence. Writing to Lhuyd in the fall of 1692, John Ray noted, "I presume Mr Aubrey is by this time returned to London, though I have not as yet received any notice thereof from him."[18] Recall also Robert Plot's request to John Aubrey to "preserve some memory of me in" Sir Jonas Moore until such time as he was capable of introducing himself. In this way letter writers attempted to insert themselves as virtual presences in others' in-person interactions.

They also used their correspondence to spark and frame further conversations. With an extensive correspondence, a naturalist could multiply his presence by gaining access to other people's connections, which might be very distant from him in geographical or social terms (or both). Edward Lhuyd disseminated the printed proposals for his study of British languages, natural history, and antiquities through his correspondence, asking that his friends personally distribute proposals among their acquaintances, both in face-to-face meetings and in their correspondence. To Martin Lister, he wrote, "I'll send you more papers to morrow, but I would have them onely put into such hands as are proper. For my Paper is not calculated for a bookseller's shop, nor to lye in a Coffee; because people that understand not the matter, will think it unreasonable."[19] Because the project was so large (in the end there were almost two hundred subscribers distributed across Wales and England), Lhuyd was unable to seek out and talk with each and every potential supporter; however, he still felt it important that proposals be disseminated via personal contacts. If encountered by the general run of customers in a coffee shop or a bookstore, his project might be misunderstood and its chances for success damaged. Working through individuals, one was surer of approaching someone who would already be kindly disposed to the undertaking. Lhuyd's associate could appropriately frame it and its value (both to the individual subscriber and to the larger community of the learned) in a conversation or a letter. In this case building financial support for the project was as much about limiting the wrong kinds of conversations, such as the mocking and dismissive kind one often saw in coffee shops, as it was about fostering the right kinds.

Lhuyd's example also suggests that when seeking support for a project, naturalists worked through textual and conversational channels simultaneously. This may have been particularly important when working through intermediaries, as they might forget or misstate the details of a project. The presence of the printed or written text had the potential to communicate the original author's meaning more clearly and accurately. But it would not do for potential patrons to encounter the text unless it was appropriately framed in a conversation or a letter: establishing the right social context for the reading of a text was just as important as clearly conveying information in that text.

Going Postal

The material foundation of "an active and large correspondence" was the government-run postal system. This system, which allowed naturalists to send and receive letters in a regular and timely manner and with reasonable confidence that they would arrive at their destinations, developed over the sixteenth and seventeenth centuries.[20] Although the royal post was established early in the reign of Henry VIII, it was primarily designed to carry official correspondence until 1635, when Charles I opened the royal mailbags to private communications. Under Henry VIII postal routes were laid along major thoroughfares, such as the road from London to Dover, with horses and riders ready at intervals to relay the mail.[21] The precise routes that were laid fluctuated, however, with the needs of the Crown; posts along the road to Ireland were more carefully staffed during times of political trouble and rebellion, for example.[22] The royal mail sometimes carried private letters, especially toward the end of the sixteenth century, but official correspondence was always prioritized.[23] Private postal services were established as well; for example, English merchants organized the Merchant Adventurers post in the mid-sixteenth century. London immigrant or "Stranger" communities organized their own posts for communication with friends and associates on the Continent.[24] Much letter carrying, however, went on according to no organized system, as servants, family members, private carriers, and even travelers headed in the right direction would be pressed into service to deliver letters. There was no unified postal system to which all had access. Correspondence could easily miscarry and be opened by someone other than the intended recipient(s), for good or for ill. Correspondents carefully crafted the missives they sent through this insecure, patchwork system with these expectations in mind. Individuals relied on personal relationships to secure delivery of letters: the name and identity of the individual letter carrier—say, a trusted servant—could be an important guarantor of a letter's transmission and, to its recipient, its authenticity.[25]

Although none of these issues was eliminated by Charles I's reforms, conditions for sending and receiving correspondence within Britain did become increasingly uniform. As a means of private communication, mail became somewhat more accessible, more trusted, and more impersonal. Posts were laid according to regular, well-maintained routes from London to the north and west, and they ran all day and all night. Spurs led off the main roads to connect provincial towns.[26] Although the speed of the post continued to vary somewhat, depending on the weather, the quality of the horses kept at each postal station along the route, and the diligence of individual postmasters, round trip from London to Edinburgh was supposed to be six days.[27] The carriage of foreign letters was assimilated into the national post by a 1657 act of Parliament that also incorporated Ireland into the British postal system.[28] By the late seventeenth century the British post was a well-established royal bureaucracy, a valuable state monopoly.

On a practical level, how did an individual send and receive letters? What kind of knowledge did one need? At the very least, in order for a letter to reach a correspondent, one had to know where to send it. This may seem a trivial thing; after all, in the twenty-first-century world we have a multitude of options for communicating across distances: we can send a letter, an e-mail, a fax, or a telegram; we can pick up the phone or dial through our personal computer to reach a friend on her land line, mobile phone, or computer. In early modern Britain, by contrast, in order to communicate with someone, one had to know his or her physical location or at the very least where that person received letters (which might not always be a home). In the days before public directory listings, phone books, or Google searches, the only way to get an address was to ask someone, either the person directly or someone who knew that person. The act of communication entailed a minimum degree of acquaintance with the recipient of one's letter. No seventeenth-century letter was directed to "the resident" or "current occupant" of a house.

Compared to their twenty-first-century counterparts, the addresses on seventeenth-century letters varied wildly. They only sometimes included street names. There were no street numbers; in cities and towns lodgings or businesses were identified by the signs hanging outside buildings (and a sign did not necessarily bear any intrinsic connection to the trade carried on inside the building—for example, booksellers Abel Swall and Awnsham Churchill operated shops under the signs of the unicorn and the black swan, respectively).[29] In the country an address might simply be the name of an estate or a house. After the Restoration even London coffeehouses served as points for sending and receiving mail (though no one guaranteed the privacy of letters sent and received therefrom).[30] John Aubrey variously received letters addressed "For John Aubrey Esq fellow of the Royall Society, to be left with Mr Bridgeman, at Mr Gregorys in Linco{l}ns Inne fields, next dore to little Turne Style the Diall house / London" (all that in one address); "These to John Aubrey Esqr at Mr White's house Chymist in Holywell Parish in Oxford"; and "To his verie lovinge friende Mr John Awbrey at his fathers howse in Broad-chalke close to / WILTSHIRE. Leave these at the holly Lambe in {Sarum}."[31] According to the latter, the letter was to be left at the "holly Lambe," a public house in Salisbury (with the city referred to in the address by its Latin name). Rather than using numbers, such addresses defined the recipients' locations in reference to local establishments and landmarks and the people who lived in and owned those places. Not even Aubrey's name was stable but rather fluctuated from Aubrey to Awbrey and back again depending on his correspondent's whim. Letter carriers were expected to have, or acquire, a minimum degree of personal knowledge about the people sending and receiving letters. Who took the letters at the inn at the sign of the Holy Lamb in Salisbury? Where in Holywell Parish, an area of Oxford just west of the Bodleian Library and Ashmolean Museum buildings, did Mr White, the chemist, keep his shop? Restoration letter carriers needed to know these things.

Correspondents were not particularly surprised when letters failed to reach their destinations. To hedge against this possibility, many letters opened with a summary of the sender's last letter. An exchange between Aubrey and the Aberdeen antiquary and professor James Garden illustrated the balance that correspondents struck. Between June 1694 and March 1695 a number of letters Aubrey sent to Garden failed to reach their destination. In the letter that finally reached Garden, dated 9 March 1694/95, Aubrey expressed a fear, not that his letters had been misdirected, but that Garden might be dead since he had failed to respond to any of the previous letters. Since Aubrey sent this last letter, his hopes and fears must have been balanced somewhere between the possibility that none of his previous letters had arrived and that his correspondent was dead. The postal system was reliable but not so reliable that multiple letters sent from London to Aberdeen could not go missing, as Garden confirmed was the case in his reply to Aubrey.[32]

Despite advances over the course of the seventeenth century, in the 1690s there were still reaches of Britain that remained unconnected to the postal system, especially in the dark and stormy months of winter. For months at a time in his travels through the wilds of Wales and Ireland and the Scottish Highlands, Edward Lhuyd was unable to post letters detailing his progress to his patrons and friends back home in Oxford and London. Lhuyd's solution was to save up material for less frequent but fatter letters home. In December 1699, six months after his last letter, he wrote to Martin Lister, "This comes heartily to beg your pardon for so seldome writing; the chief occasion whereof was my rambles of late through countreys so retir'd, that they affoarded neither post nor carrier; as not having much communication (this time of the year especially) with the cultivated parts of the kingdome."[33] Lhuyd wrote from Bathgate, a town near Edinburgh, after some months' sojourn in the Highlands. His correspondence with the physician Tancred Robinson had been similarly impeded.[34]

International correspondence operated according to different rules. While naturalists' correspondence within Britain tended to travel point to point (that is, between individuals), international correspondence was typically funneled through "intelligencers," such as Henry Oldenburg and Samuel Hartlib. Intelligencers were individuals possessed of a particularly "active and large correspondence." They occupied a privileged position within the community of naturalists. Acting as information brokers, they transmitted letters from one person to another, and when they received a letter that they judged to be of broad interest, they copied and shared it with a wider audience (a generally accepted practice at the time). They could negotiate for naturalists the practical difficulties of sending mail internationally, the primary one being that there were no stable, public international systems for mail delivery. The main international mail delivery systems were privately run by business concerns; as early as the sixteenth century the Fugger family, for example, ran regular mails connecting their various offices, delivering private mail as well as business correspondence.[35] Intelligencing on an international scale was thus close kin to commerce, relying on similar protocols. Naturalists contracted out to intelligencers a certain kind of "local knowledge." If correspondence was funneled through an intelligencer, correspondents needed to keep track of only one address rather than many. When Oldenburg accompanied Robert Boyle's nephew on his Grand Tour in 1657–1658, all of his correspondence with Boyle and the boy's mother, Lady Ranelagh, was sent and received through Samuel Hartlib.[36] Famously, Oldenburg acted as a conduit for communication between Isaac Newton and Gottfried Wilhelm Leibniz and Robert Hooke and Christiaan Huygens.[37] Intelligencers seized on opportunities to become more than just relay stations. Oldenburg, for example, used his position as middleman to attempt to smooth over differences and mediate between naturalists locked in fierce disputes. Some intelligencers attempted to transform their work into a source of income, though these plans tended to come to naught. Hartlib sought to formalize his role through the creation of the "Office of Address," a Parliament-funded bureau for the exchange of information about new mechanical inventions, improvements in husbandry and agriculture, and employment opportunities. Parliament promised a stipend but was not forthcoming with the money. The Royal Society once promised to cover the "Expence of letters" and even provide "something of an honorarium besides" for John Aubrey "to keepe a Correspondence with my numerous company of ingeniose Virtuosi in severall Counties."[38] But these promises seem to have been castles in the air. Although an intelligencer's services were essential to the functioning of the learned correspondence, it was a challenge to make them pay.

The Carrier's Trade: Moving Books and Papers

While letters traveled by post, packages were sent by carrier.[39] Carriers traveled many of the same routes as the Royal Mail but were organized and managed privately. Although some carriers were solely devoted to the business, it could also be a side occupation. Farmers, for example, seeking profitable employment for themselves, their horses, and their wagons turned to

carrying in the off-season. In some parts of England, wagons came into fashion only in the first half of the seventeenth century; before that goods were
moved over land in two-wheeled carts.[40] In the farther reaches of Britain—
the Welsh Marches or Derbyshire, for example—carrier wagons were likely
to be replaced by packhorses, which could better navigate treacherous, narrow roads.[41] Rates were regulated by local authorities. In the early 1690s
Parliament passed an act specifically obligating justices of the peace, also
responsible for overseeing local road maintenance, to regulate carrier fees in
their domain.[42] In 1692 justices of the peace in the West Riding of Yorkshire
set rates from London to towns no farther north than Leeds (a distance of
about two hundred miles) at one pence per pound.[43] Typically each town
had a carrier who waited one day a week (or more, depending on how many
packages a particular area generated each week) at a local public house to
accept packages for delivery.[44] Carriers typically had a fixed route connecting
a provincial town with London or another urban center. A guide published
in 1637, *The carriers cosmographie*, listed all the carriers in inns near and in
London, what days of the week they could be found at the inns, and where
they carried goods.[45] In the 1690s the apothecary John Houghton regularly
published a table of carrier routes, drop-off points, and charges in his weekly
periodical, *A Collection for Improvement of Husbandry and Trade*. Destinations
from London were primarily market towns and regional centers such as Not-
tingham, Colchester, Cambridge, Derby, and Warwick.[46] Coaches, which
carried people, were differentiated from carriers, who transported goods. One
issue of Houghton's *Collection* lists fifty-six different carriers and twenty-nine
coaches; perhaps there was more of a need to move goods than people in the
late seventeenth century.[47]

Carriers were plagued with the same problems that affected the mail.
Detailed local knowledge was required to send and receive packages by carrier. Such information was neither reliably nor regularly made known beyond
localities (as the publication dates of *The carriers cosmographie* and Houghton's *Collection* attest). In a letter to William Musgrave requesting back issues
of *Philosophical Transactions*, the physician Robert Peirce gave Musgrave
detailed instructions for sending them by the Oxford-Bristol carrier, who
passed through the village of Marshfield once or twice a week. Packages and
letters would reach Peirce via "a foote man" who delivered letters that had
been left at the post inn in Marshfield.[48] Peirce's instructions make it clear
that one could not assume that one's correspondent possessed basic knowledge about how to send a package between two towns less than one hundred

miles apart. This was so because carrier routes, as well as correspondents'
addresses, were often vague, ill-publicized, or unstable. This was so even in
Peirce's instructions: he thought the post inn was called "the Starre," but he
was not sure.[49] Local, personal knowledge of how packages were delivered in
a particular community was paramount, and the system could tolerate a fair
degree of fuzziness.

Naturalists were sometimes suspicious of their carriers, not trusting them
to transmit precious books and boxes safely. On 18 November 1691 the botanist John Ray received a jarring letter from his friend John Aubrey. Aubrey
inquired after the manuscripts of *The Naturall Historie of Wiltshire* he had
sent to Ray for his perusal in September of that year. By the time Ray read
the letter, he had already read and annotated his friend's book in the comfort
of his home in the village of Black Notley in Essex and had remitted it to the
local carrier—who made the round trip between Essex and London once a
week—with careful instructions to return it to Aubrey. Somehow, however,
the package failed to make it into Aubrey's hands, as an alarmed Aubrey
informed Ray by letter. One can imagine Aubrey's state when the autograph
manuscripts representing over thirty years' work went missing on the road
from Essex to London. Ray responded in haste:

> Sir, Your Letter dated Novemb. 12 came not to my hands till this
> day noon. Had you sent it by Post I had received it last Friday.
> Upon reading of it, finding that you had <not> received your
> Manuscripts I was much surprised & startled. I sent them inscribed
> according to your Directions this day fortnight, & inclosed therein
> an open Letter to you. Such an Accident as this never yet befell
> me, & 'tis too soon now. The Carrier is now gone up to London,
> so that I cannot examine him about it. . . . If it be not casually
> drop't out of the wagon, I doubt not but we shall retrieve it. The
> losse of it would be inestimable.[50]

Although Ray was correct that the manuscripts had simply been delayed
rather than lost, both Ray and Aubrey were deeply alarmed. The two books
Aubrey lent to Ray were unique and irreplaceable manuscript texts containing annotations, drawings, and botanical samples not included in the only
other extant copy, an autograph copy that Aubrey deposited in the library of
the Royal Society in 1691.[51]

Naturalists and antiquaries were occasionally cheated by their carriers. The most common stratagem was to claim upon delivery that the recipient needed to pay more postage even though the sender had paid the posted fee. Aubrey opened a 1679 letter to Wood with a screed against a lying carrier: "I recd your welcome ltr of Dec. 23. and this day the pacquet. but the Carrier is a knave. the carriage that you payd for was blotted-out and 4d more was inserted for me to pay. I grudge not the money, for the gladness of the ltr; but am vex't at the abuse."[52] Aubrey, though vexed, had little choice but to pay the four pence if he wanted to receive his letter.

Another problem that sometimes cropped up was a lack of local knowledge on the part of a carrier. When a carrier did not know the addressee of a package, he would hold on to it until someone came to pick it up. Edward Lhuyd at times ran into this problem in Oxford: packages addressed solely to him sometimes failed to arrive. He wrote to John Aubrey, "for the generality of the people at Oxford doe not yet know, what the Musaeum is; for they call the whole Buylding the Labradary <or Knackatory> & distinguish no farther. That nothing miscarried soe directed to Dr Plot was because the person was known better than the place, but things directed to me or Mr Higgins commonly stay'd at the carriers till we fetch'd them."[53] In this instance, the carrier's knowledge was more personal than institutional: he knew Plot, the old keeper, well enough but not Lhuyd or where to send a package addressed to the museum. So that a recipient would know to look out for a delivery, naturalists usually sent word by post when a package was on its way. Correspondents hoped that carriers would know enough to deliver packages, but they had strategies for keeping the system functioning when carriers lacked that knowledge.

To get around the problems that plagued shipments by carriers, naturalists sometimes sent important packages by trusted friends rather than unnamed carriers. In a letter to Aubrey, Robert Plot promised, "And as for the booke that I have {one of Aubrey's manuscripts}, I will take care to send it not by any Carrier, but some faithfull friend, that knows how to value so great a treasure."[54] The book that Aubrey loaned Plot—in which Plot found "many things in it much to my purpose, though not <very> many in Oxfordshire"—probably contained notes that Aubrey had made as a natural historical and antiquarian surveyor for John Ogilby's projected *Britannia*.[55] Naturalists also bargained with carriers. In their correspondence regarding Royal Society matters in the early 1680s, Francis Aston and Robert Plot watched carrier charges carefully, and with good reason. After being charged an exorbitant eighteen pence for the delivery of the shipment of "the earth in the little box," Aston asked Robert Plot to "bargain for the carriage, and set it down on the Bundle for a direction" before sending anything to him from Oxford by carrier.[56] They could also work through existing commercial networks. William Molyneux worked out an arrangement with a Dublin bookseller to ensure regular delivery of issues of *Philosophical Transactions* to the Dublin virtuosi. It would have been "difficult to supply some few single persons with this book by itself."[57] But issues could be included in the four or five "parcells of books" the bookseller received each year.

Despite frustrations with knavish carriers and worries that papers could be lost, naturalists depended on their carriers. Notes and asides in their letters indicate just how much. In 1683 and 1684 many of the letters that Aston wrote to William Musgrave and Plot contained some reference to a packet of books or papers being sent by carrier. During these years, the three served overlapping tenures as secretaries of the Royal Society.[58] Their correspondence dealt largely in the official business of the society. This included determining the contents of each issue of *Philosophical Transactions*, then printing in Oxford, as well as exchanging scientific news garnered from all over Britain and the Continent, giving accounts of each society's meetings, and distributing sets of queries for large-scale demographic and natural historical projects that required hundreds of informants, such as William Petty's demographic study of parish christenings, marriages, and deaths.[59] Almost invariably each of Aston's letters included a postscript saying that he was also sending a bundle, or a roll, or a parcel of papers by the next carrier.[60]

Movers and Shakers: Making Things Travel

Sometimes circulating the material goods of knowledge was as easy as crossing the street. One day in 1683 John Aubrey decided to show his friend Elias Ashmole a "Barberian Lyon" skin given him by Edmond Wyld, a merchant acquaintance with business in northern Africa ("Barberian" is a reference to "Barbary," or present-day North Africa):

> I obtained some time since of my worthy friend Edmond Wyld Esq.
> a Barberian Lyon's skin. . . . When I carried [it] in my hand from
> my Lodging to Mr. Ashmole's office (a crosse-alley between the 2
> streets) there was a great mastiffe belonging to that alley (that I did

not presently see), that came smelling after it with great astonish-
ment, the people of the alley called to me, and told me of it: and
asked what it was, for they never saw the dog doe so {that is, follow
anyone down the street} before, though they (sc. Coach-makers)
bring in quantities of tanned skinnes for their use.[61]

Aubrey stepped out to show a rare lion's pelt to his friend Ashmole, a collector of such things, and a large dog followed him down the alley between his
rooms and Ashmole's office: just another day in the life of the virtuoso, but
an incident Aubrey felt worth sharing in a letter to his Oxford-based friend
William Musgrave, then a secretary of the Royal Society.[62] The ease with
which Aubrey could step down the alleyway to Ashmole's office suggests
why so many naturalists and so much scientific activity were concentrated in
London. Though an experience could be retailed in a letter, collaboration
was much easier when people and resources were short walks away from each
other.

The impulse driving naturalists to collect and move massive amounts of
Yet not all collaboration could happen in London. Natural history and
antiquarian studies took place in farm and field and provincial town; learned
activity was distributed across Britain. In addition it required natural and
antiquarian materials, such as Aubrey's lion skin, as well as books and papers.
The stuff of natural history included living plants, seeds, dried and pressed
leaves, flowers, and roots; formed stones and other mineral specimens; and
dead and preserved animals or animal parts, such as pelts and bones. Antiquaries picked up in the course of their travels old coins, fragments of ruined
buildings (ancient Roman as well as more recent monastic varieties), urns,
Saxon weaponry and jewelry, and sketches of ruined buildings, monuments,
and ancient earthworks. As explored in this section, naturalists and antiquaries had to find ways to move all this stuff through their correspondence.

The impulse driving naturalists to collect and move massive amounts of
materials was twofold. In the first place, naturalists were increasingly interested in both systematization and understanding the regional distributions of
naturalia. Some gentlemen collectors still built their collections primarily for
show, filling them with the rarest and most unusual specimens. Ashmole, for
example, sought to highlight objects "extraordinary in their Fabrick" as well
as those that might prove useful to medicine, manufacturing, or trade.[63]
However, naturalists increasingly prioritized systematic collecting.[64] In order
to develop systematic, complete accounts of nature, they needed to collect

not only extraordinary natural specimens but also a multitude of more run-of-the-mill specimens. To understand regional distributions, they also needed to know where these specimens came from. These priorities can be seen in the great catalogs of plants, insects, fishes, and birds produced by John Ray, in part from notes and drafts left by Francis Willughby.[65] Edward Lhuyd assembled a collection of formed stones in order to produce a systematic field guide to British formed stones for the use of other naturalists.[66] In instructions to plant collectors in northern Wales (discussed more extensively below), Lhuyd requested ten to twelve samples each of herbs of ordinary size and fifteen to twenty of very small species (possibly because small plants were more easily damaged in transit).[67] The queries Lhuyd sent out before his natural history collecting expedition through the Celtic regions of Britain and France indicated the range of systematization. Lhuyd distributed about four thousand query sheets, blanketing every Welsh parish and parts of Cornwall, Scotland, Ireland, and Brittany.[68] Lhuyd asked his respondents in every parish to identify for him antiquities, fish, animals, plants, formed stones, rocks, and manuscripts. Lhuyd asked not for the most notable specimens but for representative specimens from *every single parish*. Only then could nature be mapped across the nation.

Lhuyd, in fact, regarded the "exotics" that filled some gentlemen's cabinets of curiosity with disdain because systematic accounts of nature could not be made from them—nor could they be used to map regional distributions of plants and animals. They were surprisingly uniform across different collections. They were also sourced from a more international market. For example, Lhuyd wrote in 1699 of a collection recently purchased by the University of Edinburgh that it contained relatively few specimens representing the natural production of the individual collector's "own country."[69] In order to differentiate kinds of organisms and go about the project of constructing a British natural history, it was necessary to collect as many specimens as possible and, if possible, multiple specimens of each kind, from within Britain, and to document where they were collected.

Although naturalists collected as broadly as possible, their collections were inevitably imbalanced. As he became more homebound, Ray's collection of insects, for example, tilted toward species he and his daughters could collect within walking distance of his home in Essex. This imbalance was the second term of the equation regulating the exchange and circulation of specimens. By collecting multiple specimens of individual species, naturalists ensured that they had extras on hand to trade with fellow naturalists.[70] In addition, naturalists sometimes circulated unique specimens with the expectation that the originals would be returned. Through exchange, naturalists built the kinds of collections upon which systematic treatises could be built. Through circulation, naturalists at least gained the sight of various specimens, though not permanent ownership of them.

In the late seventeenth century Lhuyd drafted a set of instructions for collecting plants from the mountain and coastal areas of northern Wales. The instructions requested that plants be collected along the streams and rivulets at the top of Cader Idris and specified that a "trusty fellow" who could navigate the treacherous upper reaches of the mountain while "observing punctually" an exacting set of directions for what to collect and how to collect it should be chosen for the job.[71] This person was unlikely to be Lhuyd's literate correspondent; as Lhuyd observed elsewhere, an "illiterate shepheard" was more likely to have the necessary familiarity with mountain tops.[72] Notably, though Lhuyd's instructions for collecting plants were largely written in English, plant names were given in Welsh (in which Lhuyd was fluent). Lhuyd used the terminology with which his readers, and the "trusty fellow" chosen to scale the mountain, would have been familiar. Collecting plant specimens across Britain required moving across languages, using the names familiar to the places in which those plants could be found. In other words, doing natural history on a national scale required familiarity with regional linguistic topographies.

The "trusty fellow" was specifically instructed to "gather nothing that grows lower than a quarter of a mile of the Top." Given the changeability of Welsh weather and the precariousness of the footing at the top of the mountain, his task was not without some danger. The collector was warned to go only "as high as he can with Safety" but to push that limit as far as possible. Collectors were also to "be directed to a baich or sandy place where Môr-gelyn grows" ("Môr-gelyn" was a "Tea-plant") as well as the interior of Harlech Castle, a Norman castle that by the seventeenth century was "a place much talkd of" not for its defensive capabilities but on account of the plants growing in its ruins. At each place the collector gathered multiple samples of the roots, leaves, and branches of all the plants, being "cautious in picking up the very least thing his eyes can discover." The collectors were paid one farthing for each distinct species collected. The plants collected from Cader Idris alone "can not amount to less than 2 shillings."[73]

Once the collector had returned with the specimens, he handed them off to a packer, who prepared them for shipment by carrier. The packer was addressed throughout the instructions in the second person, and it was he who was to select and supervise the collector and the carrier. The instructions to the packer and carrier were as follows:

> You must get a box of an indifferent size; such as you might guesse would scarce contain them; then lay in some mosse at the bottom of it lightly besprinkle'd with water. Soe lay in the shrubs & greater plants first, pressing them down with your hands pretty close; then a little mosse lightly wetted; & soe the rest of the plants, putting here & there a little mosse upon them as you lay 'm in. When all are put in fill up the box with Mosse: that they may have noe room to be dishevld in the Carriage & besprinkle it lightly with water: Soe nayle it up securely, boreing some small holes in several parts of the cover, wherein the Carrier must besprinkle a handful or two of water every night; & see the box layd in a sellar or some cool place. They should be gather'd one or two or at farthest 3 days before the Carrier sets out.[74]

These directions for packing and shipping the plants were based on procedures developed by Jacob Bobart, the Younger, the head gardener at the Oxford Physic Garden, and had been used to transport plants to Oxford from France, Italy, and Germany.[75] For the plants to be shipped successfully—that is, for them to be more alive than dead when they arrived at the Physic Garden—the carrier had to follow pretty specific instructions. To the carrier, who was used to transporting less finicky goods such as wool, grain, manufactured items, and perhaps books, these requirements may have taken some getting used to, especially the request to "besprinkle a handful or two of water every night; & see the box layd in a sellar or some cool place."[76] Thus preserved and cared for, nestled in their beds of damp moss, the plants would safely make their way from Cader Idris to the sheltered beds and glass houses of the Oxford Physic Garden. Similar procedures could be used to transplant live snails as well: Lhuyd sent some via carrier to Martin Lister, at work on his *Historiae conchyliorum*, in a "small strawberry basket" packed with wet moss.[77]

As these examples show, collecting and sending specimens were more complex than sending and receiving a letter or a packet of papers. First of all, more people were involved—in addition to the carrier, collectors and packers were needed. Furthermore those people needed to follow specialized, carefully elaborated procedures in order to ensure that the plants were successfully transported. When carrying a packet of papers, a carrier needed to know only the address of the recipient. When delivering plants, a carrier also needed to know how to care for his living freight. He had to take on some of the knowledge of the naturalists and become skilled in tasks that gardeners and botanists took for granted.

Naturalists expended much effort managing exchanges such as these because writing was insufficient as a means of conveying information. They had to see and physically handle specimens. This was evident in a 1691–1692 exchange between John Ray, Lhuyd, and Jacob Bobart, who had gathered a collection of Oxfordshire insects. Lhuyd, as one of Ray's contacts, served as an intermediary between Bobart and Ray. Ray wanted to see the insects in order to determine if there were any species found in Oxfordshire that he had not seen in Essex—this would add to the completeness of the natural history of insects on which he was working (published posthumously in 1710 as *Historia insectorum*). Ray was frustrated by efforts to describe the insects in letters, writing to Lhuyd that "by Descriptions I doubt we shall hardly scarce come to a right understanding of one another."[78] Ray was unable to travel so far as Oxford to see the specimens because of chronic illness, one of the symptoms of which was painful sores on his legs. In response to these concerns, Bobart devised a way of securing the insects in a case such that they might travel without being harmed. Although we do not know exactly how the insects were transported unharmed, Ray's correspondence provides us with a wealth of affective information that gives us insight into the importance and difficulty of transporting specimens over long distances. In his correspondence with Lhuyd, Ray freely expressed both his worries about transporting the insects and his joy when he opened the box and viewed the collection.

For over a year Lhuyd and Ray wrote back and forth about Bobart's collection of insects, worrying about and working out the particulars of transport. Ray fretted that the collection would be damaged in transport by wagon. The insects would fare well enough on the first leg of the trip, by boat down the Thames from Oxford to London. But, Ray wrote, "I fear they cannot be so fixt & put up but they must receive some damage in carrying & recarrying by the jotting of the Wagon" that would take them from London to Black Notley, near Braintree in Essex.[79] Bobart, however, devised a method for securing the individual insects and, through Lhuyd, insisted on sending them. Ray acquiesced, requesting that Lhuyd send them through his London bookseller, Samuel Smith.[80]

The box of insects arrived at Christmas, a timely gift. To Lhuyd, Ray wrote,

> That very day that your L{ette}r came to hand, the Box of Insects was also brought me, so that you were not out in y{ou}r conjecture. The several insects were so well fixt, that, to my admiration, there was not one of them stirred by the shaking & jolting of the wagon, but came as entire as they were sent out. I wish I may have as good successe in remitting them. Upon opening of the box I was mightily taken, I might say enravished, with the beauty of the spectacle, such a multitude of rare creatures, & so curiously conserved. Truly the ingenuity & industry of the Collector Mr Bobert is highly to be commended, & he encouraged to proceed.[81]

One phrase in Ray's description hints at how the insects were preserved: they "were so well fixt" that the "shaking & jolting of the wagon" had not disturbed them. The use of the word "fixt" suggests that the insects were pinned in place or attached to some kind of backing, but it is difficult to glean more precise information from Ray's description. Ray wrote most volubly about his emotional response to the collection. "Admiration," "taken," "enravished," "beauty," "spectacle," "curiously": as Ray tried to describe the experience of opening the box and seeing, and studying, the insects, his vocabulary soared above its usual restrained tones. It was almost as if the successful transport of the collection was a miracle in itself, one due solely to "the ingenuity & industry of the Collector Mr Bobert." Ray's emotions here might be thought of as the inverse of Aubrey's when Aubrey contemplated having lost the manuscripts of *The Naturall Historie of Wiltshire.* Ray, doubtful that the collection would survive transport, must have opened the box with some trepidation. His trepidation was erased as he was "taken" and "enravished" by the sight of the preserved insects. Here was a transportation success of the highest order. Even in success we see how fragile the material links between naturalists were: because Ray never quite expected the insects to arrive intact, his admiration—his enravishment—at the sight of the collection was all the more overwhelming.

These examples, the instructions to plant collectors on Cader Idris and the successful shipment of Bobart's collection of insects, provide a view of the individual, material links that made seventeenth-century natural history possible. The successful prosecution of seventeenth-century natural history required certain systems to be in place. These were both structural—the national road and river network on which packages traveled—and personal—the carrier and his team of horses; the river pilot; Samuel Smith, Ray's bookseller and agent in London; and Bobart, whose personal expertise guided the safe shipment of the cases of plants and insects. The national network developed largely for commercial use, to bear loads of raw and finished materials (food, such as butter, eggs, and grain; raw wool and finished cloth; fuel, such as coal and wood) around the country, but once in place, it could just as well support the collecting games of curious naturalists.

Moving People

In the seventeenth century, travel, even within Britain, was no small matter. In his Celtic travels Edward Lhuyd was more than once mistaken for a spy or a tax collector, handled roughly, and thrown in jail; in the remoter reaches of Britain, he was unable to reach friends through the mail. John Ray, incapacitated by old age and painful sores on his legs, was unable to make the journey from Essex to Oxford.

Despite these difficulties, though, naturalists and antiquaries traveled avidly and planned prospective trips even more avidly. They did so for two reasons. The first motive was similar to that driving the exchange and circulation of specimens and objects. Naturalists traveled in order to observe nature firsthand and build the comprehensive collections of plant, animal, and mineral specimens upon which their work was based. Antiquarians also traveled with the aim of developing their collections. They gathered descriptions and sketches of ancient monuments, transcribed chronicles and other texts in out-of-the-way libraries, and dug up such relics as Roman coins and long-buried bones. But travel was not just about collecting specimens and observing nature. It had a second, social, raison d'être: naturalists and antiquarians also journeyed to talk with each other, to establish and renew the bonds of friendship and correspondence.

Edward Lhuyd, in subscription proposals for his study of the natural history, antiquities, and languages of the Celtic regions of Britain, best summed up naturalists' intellectual reasons for travel: "It's well known, no kind of Writing requires more Expences and Fatigue, than that of Natural History and Antiquities: it being impossible to perform any thing accurately in those Studies, without much Travelling, and diligent Searching, as well the most desert Rocks and Mountains, as the more frequented Valleys and Plains. The Caves, Mines, and Quarries must be pry'd into, as well as the outward Surface of the Earth; nor must we have less regard to the Creatures of the Sea, Lakes, and Rivers, than those of the Air and Dry Land."[82] Lhuyd described the difficulties (and the joys, quite possibly) of natural historical travel: the naturalist traveled all the most arduous roads, over rocks, mountains, and deserts, and into caves, mines, and quarries.

Antiquarian research also required substantial travel. Lhuyd's linkage of natural history and antiquities led the way here, in that the firsthand research increasingly prized in both natural history and antiquarian circles was accomplished only through travel.[83] Lhuyd's predecessor at the Ashmolean, Robert Plot, in proposing a journey through Wales and England in search of "curiosities of both Art and Nature," wrote,

> And first, whereas it was a considerable part of the Business of John Leland with all imaginable Care to collect and preserve the ancient MSS. Books of the Abbeys and Monasteries then upon their Dissolution, and that notwithstanding his industrious Performances great numbers there were that never came to his Hands; and such as did, quickly after his Death, through the Iniquity of the Times, being dispers'd again, great part of the MSS. in England are, as it were, lost to the World, lying secretly in Corners and in private Hands, no Man knowing either what MSS. there be, or where to find them: it shall be one of the principal Ends of my Journey to search all the Publick Libraries of Cathedral and Collegiate Churches, of the Colleges in each University, and other Publick Libraries wheresoever, and make distinct Catalogues of them all. And as for such MSS. as shall be found in private Hands, it would not be amiss if the University of Oxford would imploy me to buy up (if they cannot be begg'd) as many as can be purchas'd for the Bodlejan Library; and where they will by no means be parted with to procure leave (if worth while) that an Amanuensis may transcribe the whole, or at least have the Perusal and Liberty to make Abridgements, as Leland did of many. But if neither of these will be admitted, 'twill be some

satisfaction that they are added to the Catalogues of the rest, to inform Men that there are such Books, and in what libraries and in whose Hands they are.[84]

As Plot's description of his plan indicated, travel, for natural historians and antiquarians, required a certain willingness to be invasive. Not only did they peer into quarries and trek to the tops of mountains; they also invited themselves into the private libraries of gentlemen and the public libraries of bishops. Plot anticipated difficulty from the gentlemen (though not the bishops): he hoped to buy up or transcribe manuscripts in private hands but realized that he might be granted neither sufficient funds nor access to the manuscripts and would have to content himself with simply making note of them in a catalog.

Given the material and social obstacles facing the traveler, how did natural historians and antiquaries manage their expeditions? Realizing that they were likely to encounter suspicion and resistance, travelers sought credentials that would encourage those they met to accept and assist them. Letters of recommendation were the typical remedy. Plot, noting that John Leland traveled as an official emissary of Henry VIII, desired a similar commission from Charles II: "And as for such MSS. or other Curiosities that shall be found in private Hands, a Recommendation from his Majesty must needs prove so effectual, that I shall surely be admitted to the perusal or making an Abridgement of any MSS. and of having a Sight and Examination of all other Rarities either of Art or Nature."[85] The king's word, though, was not sufficient for Plot; he also planned a sort of letters-of-reference pyramid scheme. He obtained a general letter of recommendation (it might as well have been addressed "To whom it may concern") signed by Ralph Bathurst, Oxford's vice chancellor; John Wallis, professor of geometry; and James Hyde, one of Charles II's personal physicians, among others.[86] He planned to take this letter and other, more personalized letters of recommendation to the most ingenious people in every county and ask them in turn for letters to the next level of ingeniosity that the counties offered.[87] Plot's general letter of commendation was handwritten on parchment, which was more durable than paper and so better able to withstand the rigor of travel.

Through their correspondence traveling naturalists smoothed the path before them by cultivating local connections in advance of trips. In one letter to Martin Lister, Edward Lhuyd sought several different letters of introduction in preparation for his travels in Ireland and Scotland. Lhuyd wrote from

Wales six weeks before embarking to Ireland. He asked Lister to point him toward "some acquaintance there who may direct us to make the best of our time" as well as particular introductions to a Dr. Wellase, mentioned in Lister's previous letters, "and any other particular friend in Ireland." He further recalled that John Campbell, the second Earl Breadalbane (1662–1752), had promised letters of introduction to Lister if he ever traveled to the Scottish Highlands. As that was the next leg of Lhuyd's trip after Ireland, he begged Lister to see if that promise could be extended to him.[88]

In order to make the most of their travels and win access to private lands and private libraries, naturalists such as Lhuyd had to win the confidence of people who were not naturalists. The average landowner in the Scottish Highlands was unlikely to be impressed with Edward Lhuyd himself or a letter of introduction bearing Martin Lister's signature. But the signature of John Campbell, as Lhuyd recognized, could easily open doors. Campbell's value lay in both his stature and his local renown. He was not just any lord but one known locally in the Highlands. A naturalist's connections, no matter how prominent, were worthless if they were not recognized by the locals to whose libraries and resources he sought access.

Other letters of Lhuyd's confirm the importance of cultivating prominent local connections above all else. In preparation for sailing to Brittany, the last leg of his trip through Celtic-speaking regions of Britain and France, Lhuyd wrote to his friend Thomas Tonkin.[89] Lhuyd had heard that Tonkin's father-in-law corresponded with a gentleman at the port of Morlaix, where Lhuyd planned to land. Lhuyd specifically asked "his favour therefore, in getting me recommended to some scholar well acquainted with the British language, and antiquities; and then I hope to shift for myself."[90] Lhuyd had letters of introduction to two abbots in Paris, but these, he recognized, would be nearly useless in Brittany.

Sometimes even quality letters of introduction could not protect a traveler. After only three weeks in Brittany, which he spent hard at work collecting notes on the Breton language ("Armorican" to Lhuyd), his studies were interrupted by the *intendant des marines* of Brest. The intendant sent a messenger to Lhuyd's lodgings to arrest him on suspicion of treason:

> The messenger found me busy in adding the Armoric words to Mr
> Rays *Dictionariolum Trilingue* with a great many letters and small
> manuscripts about the table, which he immediately secured, and
> then proceeded to search our pockets for more. All these papers he

ty'd up in a napkin, and requiring me to put three seals thereon, added three more of his own. I told him I had brought letters of recommendation to the Theologal of the City, who is the third person in the Diocese; upon which he went with me to him. The gentleman own'd it, and deliver'd him the letter, adding another in our behalf to his master, the Intendant, and a third to a captain of a man of war at Brest. Having secur'd our papers, he granted us the favour of going to Brest before them, a-part, that the country might not take notice of our being prisoners.[91]

By Lhuyd's account, the messenger found him busy catching up on his philological note taking. He used the vocabulary lists in Ray's trilingual dictionary as a basis for his own collections of Celtic words and compiled his vocabularies in a copy of Ray's book, working from notes taken over the course of his travels. In that moment he was working on adding the Breton words to his master copy. This activity of writing, which required a profusion of "letters and small manuscripts," was immediately suspicious as spy work. Despite letters from a high-ranking cleric (the "Theologal"), Lhuyd was held on suspicion of being a spy for just under two weeks in the jail in the castle at Brest. Initially refused an allowance for food and having only letters of credit with local merchants rather than cash to pay for his own, Lhuyd bargained with some Irish soldiers at the castle to pass him viands through the ground-floor window of his jail cell.[92] He was released after an interpreter studied the papers that had been seized—many of which were written in Welsh and Cornish—and determined that "they contain'd nothing of Treason." Lhuyd was aided in part by the interpreter's vanity. Though unable to read Welsh and Cornish, he was "loath to own himself puzl'd; so told {the French officials} in general, without any exception, none of my papers related to State-matters" (which they did not, being primarily Welsh and Cornish poetry, word lists, and other philological resources, but how could the translator know that?).[93] Lhuyd was released, and his papers were given back to him, but he was ordered to return immediately to England. Although he had originally intended to travel on to Paris, where his patron Martin Lister had important contacts, Lhuyd turned around and took the next boat back to England.[94]

As Lhuyd's experience indicates, the difficulties facing the naturalist and antiquarian traveler were often social in nature. When traveling, naturalists and antiquarians frequently dealt with officials and other locals who had little knowledge of or respect for their credentials. Compared to these problems, bad roads and terrible weather seem hardly to have been worth remarking upon. Lhuyd rarely mentioned these inconveniences, instead dwelling on the negotiations and introductions that ensured access and assistance from local landowners. Letters of introduction to or from local notables were necessary but sometimes not sufficient to ensure access and protect them against harassment. The traveling naturalists and antiquarians struggled to gain access to private land and private libraries. Once access was granted, they had to convince private gentlemen to permit them to copy, take away, or buy samples of what they found on those gentlemen's land and in their libraries. Beyond access to things, there was also access to information. Lhuyd noted this in his proposals for the natural history of Wales, when he spoke of the necessity of carrying money along to pay small sums to local workers, particularly miners, for information, such as details surrounding the collection of specimens.

For the traveling naturalist, such as Lhuyd, patronage was dispersed across many correspondents, acquaintances, informants, and subscribers, and yet he still had to find ways to align his interests with patrons who were not, at heart, naturalists. This made his situation both like and unlike that described in many classic studies of patronage in science and the arts, which focused on court patronage and the absolute (or would-be absolute) ruler.[95] At the court all energy was focused on the ruler, and status and power were measured in one's distance therefrom. The concentration of patronage in the absolute ruler meant that clients sought to align their interests with the ruler at all times in order to maintain patronage, which could create courts devoted to specific sciences or areas of investigation. Driven by the interests of the *Landgraf*, for example, the court of Hesse-Kassel under Prince Moritz (1572–1632) was a center of research into alchemy, Paracelsian thought and practice, chemical medicine, and the associated hermetic arts.[96] Courtly patronage could also lead to the cultivation of certain styles of doing science: according to William Eamon, curiosity and virtuosity emerged in this period as scientific virtues precisely because they were the virtues that the learned prince sought to display in encouraging scientific activity at his court.[97]

Lhuyd's situation was like that of the client of an absolute ruler in that he had to find ways to align his interests with those of his patrons, that is, his subscribers and those who assisted him as he traveled. This is reflected in the way he framed his appeals to subscribers, both in the initial subscription proposals for his research and in the questionnaires he issued. However, with over two hundred subscribers, he was not beholden to any one individual.

The dispersal of patronage thus set Lhuyd on a somewhat more equal footing with his patrons than, say, the average alchemist in the court of Hesse-Kassel. He was not free from the necessity of designing and promoting his research to appeal to the shared interests of his subscribers. But, because Lhuyd needed no one of his subscribers in particular, he was free not to tailor his research to any of their individual needs. If one gentleman would not give his shilling, within limits, Lhuyd could find another.

In contrast, as a traveler Lhuyd very much depended on each individual who assisted him: without them, he would be unable to gain access to the materials that formed the foundation of his project. Any one individual's power was restricted both geographically and temporally and was far from absolute. But because what Lhuyd sought was detailed knowledge about localities, he was no less dependent on those individuals. Because each patron had only local power, the traveling naturalist needed many patrons. For his trip to France, for example, Lhuyd needed two sets of letters: one set that might gain him introductions in Brittany and another that would admit him to Parisian circles. Even then the usefulness of these letters was limited; for example, his letter from a local merchant was no help when the messenger sent by the *intendant des marines* knocked on his door.

Passing Favors: Exchanging Services Through the Correspondence

Much as correspondents exchanged specimens, letters, papers and manuscripts, and observations, they also traded "service," promises of favors and assistance in each other's projects. Service was immaterial but provided tangible benefits nonetheless and, like letters, papers, and specimens, was a unit of natural historical and antiquarian exchange. Through the exchange of service, naturalists engaged others in collaborative work. The exchange and fulfillment of promises of service enabled fruitful research travel and the collection and exchange of specimens beyond a particular naturalist's geographical reach. Offering and performing services were also ways for peripheral members of a correspondence to participate in and gain access to the work of others. It appears, for example, to have been one of the main ways John Aubrey maintained any status within the community of naturalists and antiquarians after the definitive collapse of his financial affairs in the 1670s.

"Service" was usually offered at the close of a letter with the sender's regards to his correspondent. James Long concluded a letter to Aubrey by asking him "to present my humble services to all my Humaine Friends of the Royall Society and particular to my lord and President Mr Hillard and Mr Hooke."[98] Long's use of "service" here was vague and rather general, but effectively he asked Aubrey to "say hello" or give his regards to their mutual friends. Correspondents also presented their services directly to each other, frequently closing letters with the phrase "Your humble servant." The phrase conveyed a polite—and often formulaic—willingness to be of service without promising anything in particular.

Service could also be linked to more concrete promises of help. In a letter to John Aubrey, Plot sent his service to Robert Hooke, with whom Aubrey lodged. However, Plot presented

> pray not only my servise, but excuse that I have not yet provided him a servant, which I should be very gladd to be my selfe, were I now at fourteen: but pray acquaint Him the true reason of it, that it has not been for want, but perhaps, my too much care that has occasiond this delay, for there are no less than two now that profess themselves, whereof one indeed is a very pretty boy, honestly bred, and very forwardly, but has not got any insight, or shewed . . . any naturall inclination to Mechanicks: However if Mr Hook please to trye him for a month or more whether he may be for his turne . . . or no, pray send me word as soon as you please, and He shall imme-diately be sent up, to you.[99]

Plot linked the presentation of service to an apology for a failure to perform a favor: that of identifying a boy to serve as Hooke's servant and assistant in London. In this linkage of service to actual favors, one sees that "service," like facts, a book, or a plant or insect specimen, was not just a formulaic letter closing but another unit that naturalists exchanged between each other. Fulfilling promises of service could take considerable time and effort—as searching for a servant for Hooke seems to have taken Plot—but was worth it because it engendered reciprocal promises from one's correspondents.

These letters, with their presentations of service and their apologies, also illustrate the ways in which naturalists used correspondence to prompt and direct conversations. In both Long's and Plot's letters, "service" was pre-sented indirectly: both writers asked Aubrey to convey their messages to third parties in the context of conversations. Long used his letters to Aubrey to "broadcast" his wishes to a wider group of friends. Though distant from the center of scientific activity and sociability, the absent Long could be present in his friends' conversations and thoughts when Aubrey invoked his name and offers of services. Plot preferred not to tell Hooke directly that he had not found him a suitable servant, as he had promised to do—the likeliest candidate was a "very pretty boy" who displayed no "naturall inclination to Mechanicks." Instead he asked Aubrey to convey the bad news to Hooke for him. Aubrey and Hooke were close friends, close enough that Aubrey frequently lodged with Hooke and received mail and stored some of his books and papers in Hooke's rooms at Gresham College. In breaking this news to Hooke, Aubrey could perform an important service for Plot, suggesting something of his value as a go-between in the community of virtuosi.

Although correspondence was sometimes regarded as a stopgap or inferior substitute for face-to-face interaction, a large correspondence conferred some definite advantages on the naturalist or antiquarian. The presentation of service highlighted one of these "technical advantages." Through the exchange of services, one built up a correspondence of geographically dispersed friends and helpers. When a naturalist was unable or disinclined to travel, he could draw upon members of his correspondence to gather and send facts and specimens from beyond his local orbit, as when Lhuyd shipped Ray boxes of insects, dried and pinned, and sent Lister live snails packed in wet moss. Similarly, John Aubrey tapped Dr. James Garden of the university at Aberdeen (elder brother to George, who corresponded with Henry Oldenburg) for accounts of stone circles in Scotland to include in his *Monumenta Britannica*, a comprehensive survey of ancient British monuments.[100] Aubrey had personally studied a number of British monuments in England—particularly Stonehenge and the massive stone circle and barrows near Avebury, both in Wiltshire—but was unable to travel through Scotland. Garden, whose knowledge of Scotland's ancient monuments derived from reading, study of the artifacts, and reports made by judicious persons, was eager to assist. In his letter of 15 June 1692, he provided Aubrey with an extended account and promised him that if any more information came to his attention, he would send it straight on. If he could be of any help, he wrote in closing, "you may freely employ / Your faithfull friend and humble servant / Ja: Garden."[101]

As useful as Aubrey's contact with Garden was for Aubrey, Garden perhaps benefited even more from the exchange. For participants far from the central hubs of scientific activity—London primarily and Oxford and Cambridge secondarily—correspondence provided opportunities for participating in natural history and antiquarian exchange that were difficult to obtain locally, where individuals interested in these subjects were thinner on the ground. One might compare the historian Lisbet Koerner's study of Baltic natural history a few decades later, during the Enlightenment, in order to understand the dynamics at work.[102] Like Garden, Baltic natural historians (typically German or Scandinavian in origin) were far from the centers of scientific action. One way they dealt with this problem was to make the peculiarities of their "peripheral" locations objects of study, turning living on the edge into a virtue.[103] Like these Baltic natural historians, Garden gained access to the wider natural historical and antiquarian community because he possessed knowledge about the periphery not available to the scientific center. Garden's example also shows, however, that interest in the periphery did not have to come from the periphery. Garden's information was valuable because of the way it fitted in with Aubrey's concept of Britain and its history. Aubrey believed that the standing stones he studied at Avebury and Stonehenge had been produced by a pan-British pre-Roman people. Thus his own antiquarian theories, along with his ideas about the extent of pre-Roman British culture, generated his interest in seeking out evidence of similar stone constructions across Britain.

Through correspondence, and the provision of services in the form of facts and specimens, scholars such as Garden could meaningfully participate in the work of natural history and the study of antiquities.[104] Indeed, Garden's contact with Aubrey led to further opportunities for service: on the basis of Aubrey's correspondence with Garden, Lhuyd singled him out as a "great lover and a competent judge" of antiquarian studies, as well as one with "great acquaintance" in the Highlands. Lhuyd's comment showed that it was not just knowledge that was at stake when a naturalist at the heart of things sought the aid of one at the geographical margins. Garden was useful also (possibly even primarily) because he was connected socially in the Scottish Highlands, where Lhuyd and Aubrey had few contacts. Edward Lhuyd put Garden's natural and social knowledge to work, inviting him to fill out and distribute query sheets for his *Archaeologia Britannica* project on the comparative natural histories, languages, and antiquities of Celtic Britain.[105]

Scholars in England and Ireland linked up with each other through their correspondence as well. In 1685 the scholar Phillip Mathew, based at Trinity College Dublin, prepared the way for Lhuyd and Plot to make a "Philosophical progress" through Ireland. Mathew went to great lengths on his correspondents' behalf. In expectation of their visit, he made "a most exact enquiry in all the four Provinces. I have employ'd my friendds in most of the South & West parts of Ireland, & have obtained the favour of most of the Clergy in the North coasts (by the interest of the Archdeacon of Downe) to procure for you all the variety of shells &c this Island will afford."[106] Through Mathew, Plot and Lhuyd gained access to the Irish gentry and clergy, a social world beyond their ken. Notably it was an Anglo-Irish world, the "Archdeacon of Downe" being a chief administrator (ranking just below the bishop) of a northern Irish diocese of the English church in Ireland. The rest of Mathew's letter hinted at the reciprocity involved in such provisions of service: he requested from Plot and Lhuyd copies of issues of *Philosophical Transactions* as well as miscellaneous natural philosophical items, such as a lodestone and some phosphorus.

Ultimately, Phillip Mathew's and Garden's importance as correspondents resided largely in their social connections in and local knowledge of regions that were at once peripheral and central from the perspective of Oxford and London—peripheral, in that metropolitan naturalists had few social contacts there, and central, in that knowledge about them was key to the intellectual project of natural history and antiquarian studies, that of forming Britain as a topographical object.

Conclusion

This chapter began as a study of the "rich intellectual, social, and material links" that made up seventeenth-century naturalists' and antiquaries' correspondence. As the analysis has made clear, these categories of exchange were related to each other in complex ways. In a correspondence the smallest fact had to be written down on a sheet of paper, folded up, addressed, sealed with melted wax, and sent through the post. Sometimes—as when one traveled through the Highlands of Scotland—sending a letter was impossible. Intellectual exchange was blocked by the material limits of the post. The materiality of intellectual exchange becomes clearer when we consider Lhuyd's instructions for collecting, packing, and transporting live plants or Ray's wonder when he opened Bobart's box of insects. The movement of information—the construction of knowledge—was necessarily also the movement of things.

Social information always traveled in letters alongside intellectual information. As we see in Lhuyd's preparation for his travels in Scotland and Ireland, as well as in his removal from Brittany, the right connections were a precondition for useful natural historical work. Yet social relations were also determined by material and intellectual exchange: naturalists' estimations of each other, as expressed in their correspondence, grew out of their experiences with each other's generosity (or lack thereof) in exchanging service, natural specimens, and facts and observations. Recall how Rivinus, the Leipzig naturalist, opened his correspondence with Lhuyd with a gift of books and fossils. In another example, Ray promised Lhuyd a copy of the second edition of his *Miscellaneous discourses concerning the dissolution and changes of the world* (1692) after Lhuyd sent Ray some observations he added to that work.[107] Good relations between naturalists were founded on balanced material, social, and intellectual exchanges.

Moreover, British naturalists and antiquaries articulated their conception of Britain, not just England, as a topographical object of study through their correspondence. This interest in the "periphery"—from James Garden's Scottish Highlands, to the northern mountains of Wales investigated by Lhuyd, to Phillip Mathew's Ireland—meant that denizens of the "periphery" had concrete information, material goods, and social favors to offer naturalists in the "center" in exchange for inclusion in their correspondence. In particular, the increasing emphasis on travel and personal investigation gave the periphery a valuable hand to play: only naturalists on the fringe had the personal connections and local knowledge that would gain their correspondents access to the kinds of goods and information for which they traveled.[108] Knowing this, naturalists at the center developed relationships with naturalists at the fringes and called upon them for information and access in times of need. Recent work on science, commerce, and empire in the early modern world has elaborated the important role of such local contacts, which included "creole" settlers as well as non-Europeans, when naturalists traveled across oceans seeking botanical, zoological, and geographical knowledge.[109] As this chapter has shown, they were necessary to bridge the distances locally too. For the English in particular, "Britain" was unknown territory. Mapping, inventorying, and economically integrating an empire was a process that began at home.

Chapter 3

Natural History "Hardly Can Bee Done by Letters": Conversation, Writing, and the Making of Natural Knowledge

Writing to Robert Boyle in 1659, John Evelyn put forth his plan for an ideal natural philosophical research institute: he suggested that "some gentlemen, whose geniuses are greatly suitable, and who desire nothing more than to give a good example, preserve science, and cultivate themselves, join together in society, and resolve upon some orders and œconomy, to be mutually observed."[1] Evelyn imagined the gentlemen (and their wives) living together in a setting that was part working country estate, part Oxbridge college, and part monastery. Thirty or forty acres of land, a mix of "tall wood" and "upland pastures or downs," would be sufficient. A large, central building would house the library, dining hall, drawing rooms, guest rooms, and kitchens and servants' rooms. They could have this built or modify an existing structure if one were available. The fellows would live in cottages closer to the woods. Wives and husbands would take up separate cottages. The fellows would share facilities for scientific experimentation and observation, built to their requirements: "There should likewise be one laboratory, with a repository for rarities and things of nature; aviary, dovehouse, physic garden, kitchen garden, and a plantation of orchard fruit, &c. all uniform buildings, but of single stories, or a little elevated. As a convenient distance towards the olitory garden should be a stable for two or three horses, and a lodging for a servant or two. Lastly, a garden house, and conservatory for tender plants."[2]

Evelyn's list of the facilities required for scientific investigation overlapped considerably with what would have been (or soon would become) available at a modernizing, well-to-do country estate.

In these orders for an imagined society, Evelyn structured opportunities for conversation into the daily routine. Fellows were to meet in the refectory at noon and four for food and fellowship, and Evelyn specifically set aside the hours from four to seven as "conversation hours." In good weather the fellows might talk outside as they walked the grounds. In the winter the conversation hours were even more important, "because the nights are tedious, and the evening's conversation more agreeable." On Thursdays they would play music together during discussion hours. Fellows would be allowed to take their meals privately no more than twice a week and were required to give weekly public accounts of their progress in their studies.[3] Properly communicating the plan to Boyle required a conversation about it: in closing his letter, Evelyn proposed to visit Boyle in town to show him a "rude plot" of the college building.[4]

Whatever else it may have represented (including a desire to retreat from the "uncharitable and perverse" times, when Oliver Cromwell's son Richard ruled as lord protector and the public peace was scarcely guaranteed), Evelyn's proposal signaled a desire for daily conversation with like-minded investigators.[5] Distance would be removed as a barrier to conversation for the fellows resident in the scientific college. They would be able to talk directly with each other, examine natural specimens together, and conduct experiments and read books side by side. Though Evelyn's plan had something of the monastery about it, it also departed from that model and was more like a college in emphasizing both conversation and contemplation as interrelated activities that led to the development of knowledge about the world.

Plans such as Evelyn's captured something fundamental about the desires and aims of early modern British naturalists and how they planned to achieve them. The schemes that naturalists, virtuosi, and intelligencers drew up for the reform of natural knowledge (real, imagined, and even sometimes enacted) all emphasized advancing scientific knowledge by creating more venues for conversation. In *New Atlantis*, published posthumously in 1627 with his *Sylva sylvarum*, Francis Bacon imagined Solomon's House as a retreat from the wider world in which researchers were to live together, gather information, and perform experiments and then discuss them together.[6] At mid-century the Protestant reformer Samuel Hartlib, a German immigrant to London, proposed to establish an office of address, to which men interested in employment (or finding workers) as well as the latest in inventions, curiosities, and scientific advances might repair to share information, though not necessarily freely—Hartlib envisioned himself and his trusted associates as the keepers of information that flowed in by conversation, disseminating it more broadly only as they saw fit, for the public good.[7] During the 1640s and 1650s, as Hartlib attempted to establish himself as a Protestant clearinghouse for scientific news, shifting groups of those interested in the new mechanical philosophy, astronomy, alchemy, practical arts and inventions, and natural history met in Oxford and London to experiment, observe, and discuss their findings and theories.[8] The vogue for conversational meeting places was not confined to England. Theophraste Renaudot, with the support of Jean-Baptiste Colbert, established a *bureau d'addresse* in Paris: every Monday afternoon from 1633 to 1642, Renaudot opened his home for wide-ranging discussions on scientific, natural, and cultural topics.[9] Throughout the century others, such as Evelyn, imagined plans for natural philosophical colleges at which conversation among investigators would be encouraged or even, as in Evelyn's plan, demanded by the "rule" of the place. Robert Boyle proposed one such plan; another had Robert Hooke's initials attached to it. Similar plans were proposed or considered by Thomas Henshaw, Thomas Bushell, Kenelm Digby, William Petty, Henry Hammand, and Abraham Cowley.[10] When the Royal Society was founded after the Restoration of Charles II, weekly group conversations were a centerpiece of its activities.

In addition to creating conversational centers, naturalists sought out conversation in their travels. Indeed a large part of the point of traveling as a topographer was engaging knowledgeable individuals in discussions. Conversations with all sorts and kinds of people—husbandmen, shepherds, scholars, housewives, gamekeepers, groundskeepers, miners, scholars, and gentlemen—figured heavily in the production of natural historical and antiquarian knowledge. Conversation was regularly noted as a source of knowledge as early as the late sixteenth and early seventeenth centuries. In the preface to the 1610 English edition of his *Britannia*, William Camden noted, "I have travailed over all England for the most part, I have conferred with most skillfull observers in each country."[11] Verbal exchanges were also hospitable: given the importance of face-to-face interaction in the correspondence (an importance that also spoke to the premium placed on hospitality as a value in early modern Britain), by engaging knowledgeable locals in conversation and developing relationships with them, traveling naturalists thus incorporated them into their correspondence.

But conversation did not stand alone. What was characteristic of the virtuosi's treatment of conversation, and distinctive from that of earlier eras, was the way they incorporated it into systems of writing and print. They sought to archive and disseminate conversation, to make it useful to naturalists and antiquaries beyond those who just happened to be in the room where a verbal exchange took place. For late seventeenth-century scientific virtuosi, conversation and correspondence—indeed conversation and writing more generally—stood in intimate relation to each other.[12] Reports of discussions—who was present, what was said, why it was significant—circulated through correspondence and were recorded in diaries. Much of the information that naturalists collected and circulated through their correspondence was originally gleaned from conversations. At the Royal Society, as well as other institutions that privileged group discussions, conversation was integrated into a knowledge production process built around writing, correspondence, and print. In the society's meeting rooms, a space was created for a body composed primarily of gentlemen to conduct verbal exchanges according to canons that they felt would be most likely to produce scientific knowledge. They were to be open-minded, to avoid discussion of religion, to entertain all hypotheses and suggestions, to be plainspoken, and to avoid being imposed upon by those of superior rank.[13] As detailed in the Royal Society's founding statutes, the fruits of these interactions were "registered" in writing by secretaries and clerks hired for that purpose. These materials were archived for the future, transmitted to others through correspondence, and put into print, as the fellows saw fit.

The Royal Society can be seen as an institution devoted to making conversation productive. Their activities in this regard were motivated as much by fears that conversation was all too likely to devolve into airy, idle pleasures as by their conviction of conversation's promise. Furthermore, although writing captured some conversational particulars, both writers and readers felt that it failed to communicate discussions fully. Sometimes this gap was productive. As Mario Biagioli has argued, the distance between correspondents, and the necessary incompleteness of the information that could be transmitted across the gap, allowed the Royal Society to project an image abroad of a fellowship that was more active and authoritative than it seemed when viewed from a local perspective.[14] But sometimes the gap was frustrating. In the winter of 1687 Sir James Long wrote to John Aubrey from Draycot Cerne, his Wiltshire estate. Long began his letter with a lament that Aubrey had not come to visit him in some time: "I have had hopes (it now seemes ill grounded) that I should have had your company herre long before this time that wee {might} have conversed about the naturall history of this county: which hardly can bee done by letters of what length so ever they bee."[15] Long desired Aubrey's presence so that they might enjoy each other's company and conversation. But he did more than this: in fact he rejected letters as fit vehicles for natural historical exchange, suggesting that such exchange could be fully accomplished only in conversation. Long was far from the only one to observe that writing was inadequate to the task of communicating scientific matters. Despite the frequency with which they exchanged letters, naturalists often felt them to be second-best replacements for face-to-face conversations.

The irony inherent in Long's desire was that natural history was done by letters (as Chapter 2 made clear). In the same letter that opened with his lament that correspondence was not a fit venue for natural history, Long went on to transmit detailed answers to a round of queries that Aubrey had communicated in his last letter. For the virtuosi, writing and conversation were intertwined: writing archived conversations, transforming the pleasures of the moment into reliable and durable contributions to natural knowledge. Were it not for writing, particularly correspondence, even the tenuous record of early modern scientific conversation that we do have would not have been preserved. Yet writing could never equal conversation: not all that could be said could be reproduced with the pen.

In the Field: Natural Historical Travel, Country Hospitality, and Conversation

Good company and good conversation were the foundations of an individual's moral and spiritual development, the advancement of natural knowledge, and the improvement of trade on a national level. These three things were not unrelated. In a brief manuscript tract titled "Admonitions and directions of a good parent to his Child, especially a Son," Henry Oldenburg presented scientific and philosophical conversation as a moral and spiritual duty: the child was charged to seek out the company of "those, with whom you may converse profitably in acquiring knowledge of the works and creatures of God, I mean, of Natural good things, as Physick and Natural philosophy; or in Artificial good things and Mechanical Ingenuities."[16] Here and elsewhere in this letter, Oldenburg highlighted the conditions under which he believed natural philosophical conversation to be "profitable": it must always be focused on knowing God through his works, and the individual must not approach it (or anything else in life) without first engaging in serious examination of his soul and his relationship with God. Every day was to begin and end in prayer, figured by Oldenburg as "converse" with the Lord.[17] Oldenburg further ranked good conversation in "Physick and Natural philosophy" as third on the list of things one should seek in one's company: above all, they should be "Lovers of God" and those "with whom you may converse in Moral good things."[18] Oldenburg was not alone in these sentiments. Samuel Hartlib, representative of the larger field of correspondence that he superintended, similarly related and similarly hierarchized spiritual, moral, and natural philosophical conversation, including conversation within the (Reformed) Christian virtuoso's broader responsibilities for communion and communication with those who shared his godly values and natural philosophical interests.[19]

A great deal of the value of scientific conversation lay in the opportunity not just to talk together—to trade in information—but also to *look* and *point* together. This was quite literally true, for example, when it came to making accurate drawings of specimens, as Martin Lister indicated in the preface to his 1678 *Historiae animalium Angliae* (*History of English Animals*). In describing the process by which the book's engravings were created, he noted that he had asked the artist William Lodge to draw specimens in his presence: "My aim," Lister wrote, "was to see that the excellent artist did not merely . . . express his own personal conception. To facilitate this I first of all indicated with my finger the characteristics of each species that I most particularly wished to have depicted."[20] When Lister and the artist were together before the specimen and the paper, one barrier to understanding was removed. With the objects and the people present, it became possible to discuss and resolve disputes and discrepancies as they arose, and for Lister to direct the artist to see as he saw.[21]

It was nearly impossible to convey all the relevant details of an object, apparatus, or experimental procedure via correspondence, and when confusion or disagreement arose, it was difficult and tedious to seek clarification. Printed botanical and zoological reference books could help; if correspondents each possessed a copy of the same volume, they might identify plants and animals by folio and page numbers.[22] But this practice of identification presumed that the first correspondent, who possessed or desired a specific specimen, knew what it was he had or wanted. What if a naturalist said not

"I have *this*" or "I want *this*" but "What *is* this?" In this case a correspondent might include drawings with his letter. In addition specimens could be shipped via carrier. The desire to replicate visual and tactile possibilities available when investigators were together also drove the development of detailed, precise scientific illustrations in printed works (at least when authors or publishers could afford such things), as with the engravings of the air pump in Robert Boyle's *New experiments physico-mechanicall, touching the spring of the air and its effects*; such visual aids, combined with writing, made the experience of reading more like "being there."[23]

But not all naturalists were accomplished draftsmen (Ray's and Aubrey's correspondence, for example, rarely included drawings), and (as discussed in Chapter 2) shipping specimens could be an onerous business, and not everything could be put in the mail. Furthermore two individuals might not see or represent natural specimens in the same way; this was why Lister felt the need to stand over William Lodge as he drew. In attempting to communicate a thing's qualities in absence of the thing itself, writing, even when supplemented by drawing, always fell short; hence James Long's assertion that natural history could not be done by letters, "of what length so ever they bee." No matter how many lines one devoted to describing a thing, one could not be sure of capturing it fully. John Ray alternated between attempting to identify animal and plant specimens based on written descriptions and throwing up his hands in frustration. In one letter to Aubrey, Ray offered probable identifications for a "strange bird" (he called it a "Garrulus Bohomicus, or a Silktail" and pointed Aubrey toward Lister's description of it in *Philosophical Transactions*) and "a sort of large mosse-berry" described by Aubrey but gave up on a "little yellow Insect, as yellow as Gold" that lived in soil impregnated with saltpeter.[24]

Within topographical fields, conversation and travel went hand in hand as modes of gathering and exchanging knowledge. Travel opened up opportunities for conversations with those who bore specialized knowledge of an area of nature or a geographical area.[25] Naturalists used topographical query lists to seek out knowledgeable persons with whom they might converse while traveling.[26] In his "Quar's to be propounded to the most ingenious of each County in my Travels through England," Robert Plot asked after specific kinds of people: mathematicians, inventors, those engaged in the study of insects (particularly bees and silkworms), and husbandmen engaged in experiments in improving methods of cultivation. Plot used his queries to find experts with whom to converse. Lhuyd, similarly, asked after those in each county in Wales most knowledgeable about Welsh names for plants, fish, insects, birds, and stones.[27]

Naturalists also used topographical query lists to encourage and systematize conversation, to make it part of a cycle for the production of natural knowledge. In his queries Plot asked respondents to remember, "whatever you meet with (worthy notice) in your reading, or converse in the World, upon any of these subjects, to take notice of it" and report it back to him.[28] Edward Lhuyd too hoped that his "Parochial Queries," issued in 1696, would generate further natural historical conversation between neighbors, exchanges that would also be reported back to him. Lhuyd entreated "the favourable Assistance of the Gentry and Clergy in those other Countries mention'd in the former Proposals: And that in all Places, they who are dispos'd to further the Design, would please to communicate this Paper where they think fit, amongst their Neighbours; interpreting some *Queries* to those of the Vulgar, whom they judge Men of Veracity, and capable of giving any the least Information towards it, that may be pertinent and instructive."[29] Through the queries, Plot and Lhuyd encouraged others to approach conversation more systematically and when they encountered information that might be useful to the natural historical project, to write it down and send it on.

In some ways topographical travel, with its emphasis on conversation, was a variant on learned travel more generally. Some advice given by "a Learned man," recorded by John Evelyn in a commonplace book, was typical: the traveler profited not by sitting alone in his "chamber, or Inn; but by habitudes with & acquaintance with able & conversable persons; therefore above all get the knowledge of some of those, & some person to introduce you amongst the good company, which I esteeme above all other advantages whatsoever for a Traveller."[30] In topographical travel there was an extra imperative to converse with those whose knowledge was unlikely to have entered a written record available in Oxford or London. Individuals with whom one sought conversations while traveling often operated outside the bounds of a naturalist's correspondence. These people were miners, shepherds, gardeners, farmers: those whom Edward Lhuyd termed "the vulgar." In *Archaeologia Britannica*, Lhuyd specifically mentioned the importance of conversation with "those whose Education or Natural Talent disposed them to ridicule."[31] Lhuyd, by his own account, thoroughly enjoyed conversing with "Shepheards and Colliers," much preferring such exchanges to academic debate in Oxford and London. He characterized the latter, conducted via the back and forth of printed pamphlets, as so much "pompous jarring."[32]

When naturalists traveled to conduct research, the country home was as important a site of conversation as the field. At their country homes and parsonages gentry, nobility, physicians, and clergy offered hospitality and conversation that was crucial to completing natural historical and antiquarian studies. Early modern country homes—particularly grand estates—were more or less porous spaces open to friends, visitors, and supplicants. The English ideal of hospitality dictated that homes and, especially, tables be kept open to guests.[33] Advice manuals and other proscriptive literature particularly emphasized their readers' Christian duties to the poor, but it was understood that entertainment and hospitality should be offered to friends, neighbors, and acquaintances of all social levels. The landowning elites, who were capable of maintaining extravagantly laden tables, their fruits drawn from estates stocked with produce, game, fish, and livestock, bore this responsibility of hospitality as their particular burden.[34] Generous displays of hospitality (particularly to the poor) were not only recommended by Scripture; they also offered the landowner opportunities to remind his neighbors of his position of wealth and authority within the county and in some cases the nation.[35] Women played crucial roles in ordering the houses to make this hospitality possible and in welcoming and entertaining guests.[36] Though beginning to fade by Long's time (due to a combination of social dislocation, population expansion, and the state taking on a greater role in providing for the poor over the previous two centuries), this ideal maintained a powerful hold over English imagination and behavior, remaining prominent in proscriptive literature through the end of the century.

Robert Plot relied on the hospitality of those he encountered as he traveled through Oxfordshire collecting material for *The natural history of Oxford-shire* (1677). Armed with nothing but a letter of recommendation signed by a selection of prominent Oxford scholars (including John Wallis and Ralph Bathurst), Plot introduced himself into one gentle home after another.[37] He kept a clear record of the conversations he had in those homes in his book: throughout the book he described natural specimens (often but not always geological) that were given him by the gentlemen he visited or which he viewed in their homes. Visiting with a Mr. Read of Ipsden, Plot made special note of his host's dining table: the graining of the wood naturally formed the shape of a jack fish, an oddity Plot reported in his chapter on plants.[38] In 1682 Aubrey secured from James Long an invitation for Nehemiah Grew to stay at Draycot Cerne while conducting experiments testing the properties of the local waters.[39] Long offered to assist in the experiments himself.[40]

While traveling through Wales, Scotland, Ireland, Cornwall, and Brittany, Lhuyd relied heavily on country house hospitality, lodging with and receiving mail at the homes of friends and subscribers.[41] Some gentlemen also opened their libraries to him, a particular boon as many contained rare Celtic language manuscripts.[42] When Edward Lhuyd first began publishing the results of his investigations, he framed his acknowledgments to those who had assisted him during his research travel in terms of the ideals of hospitality: "I have in general throughout *Wales*, receiv'd the utmost Civility from Persons of all Qualities; not only as to Hospitality . . . but also in their Readiness in Communicating any Manuscript; and in mentioning or shewing any thing in their Neighborhood, whether Inscriptions or other Particulars, that might seem to deserve Notice."[43]

Yet Lhuyd also ran up against the limits of country house hospitality. Publicly—that is, in print, where these acknowledgments appeared—Lhuyd was all smiles, praising the generosity, hospitality, and openness of those he met. In more private venues, such as his correspondence, however, he acknowledged that there were limits to his contacts' hospitality; for example, some of the gentry insisted that Lhuyd peruse their books only in their libraries, refusing to lend out books once Lhuyd was back in Oxford or even to allow Lhuyd or others to make transcripts. Sir William Williams wrote to Lhuyd,

> You are heartily welcome to see and read any of my Books usefull to
> your design at Llanforda; but I'll not by any means lend any book
> out of my house nor admit {there} or in my other place coppies to
> be taken of any of them; if I should comply therein the Books now
> only in the custody of Cosen Vaughan and myself would be dispersed; which I hope to prevent; and I suppose no reasonable person
> will blame my rejecting your request being (as I hinted before) very
> willing you should read any of them in my house: you promising on
> your word not to transcribe any part of them &ce.[44]

There was a disjunct between the priorities of the scholar and those of the gentleman, who was concerned primarily for the integrity of his library. Lhuyd was frustrated, but Williams felt that the limits he set were completely reasonable: he was only doing his best to protect his books and manuscripts, rightly fearing that if they were loaned out, they would never be returned. It was possible that Lhuyd could be trusted to return books, but it was a fact of life that people who borrowed books frequently failed to return them. The reasoning behind the opposition to transcription is less clear, but perhaps Williams was worried about readers marking up his books or copying material that turned out to be sensitive.

Local informants valued hospitality as much as traveling researchers did. Correspondents looked forward to visits and opportunities for conversation and company. They eagerly anticipated extending hospitality and paying their respects to travelers. Ingenious gentlemen and clergy living in the country often felt isolated. For those living outside the metropolis and the universities, scientific conversation could be hard to come by—scientific correspondence emanating from the countryside was populated with dismissive references to the intellectual poverty of the writers' neighborhoods. Sayes Court, Evelyn's home in Deptford, was only a few miles out of the city, but this was far enough out to place it thoroughly in the "country," at least in the imaginations of its residents, despite the naval dockyards right next door. This sense of isolation partly explained Long's desire for Aubrey's company and conversation; it was a rarer feature of his life than he would like. In a country village, the visit of a virtuoso was an event. When Aubrey stayed with John Ray in Essex in 1692, the botanist introduced Aubrey around to other locals, fellow travelers in the investigation of nature.[45] Though topographical studies were difficult to prosecute without country house hospitality, country living itself could be an obstacle to the pursuit of scientific conversation.

This problem was not uniquely scientific. Thomas Sprat, in an aside in *The history of the Royal Society of London*, pointedly singled out the English nobility's historical attraction to the country—they were "for the most part scattered in their Country Houses," rather than concentrated in cities—as an obstacle to the development of English arts and letters, both spoken and written. It was in "frequent conversations in Cities, that the Humour, and Wit, and Variety, and Elegance of Language, are chiefly to be fetch'd."[46] Sprat argued that in the peace following the civil war and the Interregnum, the time was ripe to bring forward more concerted efforts to develop the English language as a medium for conversation, rhetoric, and literature. This could best be done in London and the university towns of Oxford and Cambridge, where the density of people interested in scientific topics meant that one could have a scientific conversation any day of the week if one wished, as attested by the diaries and correspondence of virtuosi- and scholars-about-town such as Robert Hooke, Samuel Pepys, Edward Lhuyd, and Robert Plot.

Country virtuosi looked forward to visits from traveling naturalists, in some cases even regarding them as their due. These expectations became visible when researchers flouted them. When he traveled, Lhuyd received reports, both directly and through intermediaries, that he was missed when he failed to make time to visit with correspondents while traveling through their neighborhoods. One of Lhuyd's contacts in Swansea, in southwest Wales, the Oxford-educated clergyman and merchant John Williams, was sad to have just missed Lhuyd when he traveled through the region in 1693 as he was preparing the Welsh material for Gibson's revised edition of Camden's *Britannia*: "When you were in this Countrey; the first time I heard it from Mr Franklyn you were past retrieving, having quitted it some daies before. I bemoane my misfortune in it; for by an earlier informacion (besides the chief satisfaction of your company & convers) I could have <waited on you, &> had from your selfe an exact account of your designe in this new edition of Cambden."[47] Similarly, when collecting material for his own *Archaeologia Britannica* later in the decade, Lhuyd heard from his correspondent Isaac Hamon that a John Watkins, who had expressed interest in subscribing to Lhuyd's scheme and had a few Roman coins to show him, was "much troubled because he had not your company when you were in Gower."[48]

Williams and Lhuyd eventually fell out when Lhuyd pressured Williams to support him in a dispute over the nature of fossils with the naturalist John Woodward. Here too hospitality was key. The question was whether fossils were the remains of plants and animals or generated by seeds in the earth; Woodward was entirely on the side of their being organic remains. Williams refused his support to Lhuyd and returned to him unsigned letters against Woodward to which Lhuyd had asked him to put his name. Prominent in his letter to Lhuyd explaining why he continued in good relations with Woodward was a description of Woodward's personal kindness in visiting with him and extending hospitality to him. As he wrote to Lhuyd, when Williams met Woodward in London in 1696, Woodward prevented him from forming "any sowre opinion concerning him . . . by kindly comeing to see me twice; and a third time I was entertain'd by him att Gresham Coll with greate fairness & a very obligeing view of some of his collections."[49] Williams advised Lhuyd of his wish that Lhuyd and Woodward would be reconciled, so that they could continue their investigations as friends. His judgment of Woodward depended crucially on the "excellent candid temper" that he displayed in these conversations and the kindness he showed in visiting with Williams, especially in inviting him to Gresham.[50]

Doubts About Conversation

If conversation was a crucial element of learned natural history and antiquarian studies, it was also deeply troublesome, as naturalists feared that it could just as easily be an unproductive dead end as a path to new knowledge and new relationships. Naturalists' suspicion of conversation partly had to do with their experience of it: it was often just as much about pleasure as it was about knowledge making. Naturalists appreciated this—they emphasized the pleasure of conversation in their letters and diaries—but it also made them wary of conversation's value. There was also the "easie vanity of fine speaking" to consider; in his history of the Royal Society, Sprat warned that one of the dangers in forming a scientific assembly founded on generating knowledge through conversation was that artful rhetoric could persuade a man to give his assent to falsehoods, stymieing scientific progress.[51] Additionally there were questions about access, control, and codes of conduct, also treated extensively by Sprat: who was conversing, and how? At the wrong times, in the wrong places, with the wrong people, conducted according to the wrong rules, conversation could be actively detrimental to the furthering of natural knowledge, naturalists feared.

Pleasure mingled with utility in naturalists' comments on conversation and company. In their letters correspondents entreated, even demanded, the pleasure of each other's company. In some cases these laments were probably formulaic offerings. However, in many other cases they seemed to express sincere regret, even longing. Scientific collaborations were often rooted in friendship, and the demands of friendship could be fully satisfied only in fellowship. After a particularly good week with him in Oxford, Aubrey wrote to Anthony à Wood, "I can not expresse what a wonderfull refreshing 'tis to my soule to spend a weeke at Oxon, among so many good & ingeniose acquaintance."[52] In 1669 Aubrey wrote to Wood that he "should be the happiest man to see you in Wilts{hire}," closing with an effusive, exclamation-pointed "Dear Anthony!"[53] In a letter to Aubrey, Edmond Gibson, writing from Oxford, confessed that he was prejudiced as to whether Aubrey should print his *Monumenta Britannica* in Oxford or London: "The prospect of your company and conversation would tempt me to pass over all the inconveniences that might obstruct your printing" in Oxford.[54] In 1663, as a young naval administrator, Samuel Pepys found great pleasure, and developed expertise in his professional domain, in conversing with shipbuilders. In June of that year he spent an afternoon with the Woolwich shipwright Anthony

Dean learning "the method of drawing the lines of a ship, to my great satisfaction."[55] That same month he spent a morning with Sir William Warren examining the various kinds of timber used in ship construction, "whereby," he wrote, "I have encreased my knowledge and with great pleasure."[56] Of course conversation could also be tedious; for example, Pepys's office mate Sir John Mennes bored Pepys to distraction with his chatter on scientific subjects, including anatomy and chemistry.[57] At times it could offer pleasure's inverse: angry words might be exchanged, or a public conversation (say, at a coffeehouse) could become a contest for social and intellectual dominance (though that provided its own kind of pleasure, at least for winners and onlookers).

London's coffeehouses and taverns were popular sites for animated conversation on scientific topics. Emerging first at Oxford in the 1650s, coffeehouses rapidly proliferated after the Restoration of Charles II.[58] By 1663 there were over eighty in London alone.[59] The young Pepys often stopped for a dish of coffee at Will's Coffeehouse or Grant's Coffeehouse between visits to the Royal Exchange, White Hall, and his bookseller's. The conversations drifted from court gossip to naval affairs to the latest books and plays. Scientific topics on occasion became the focus of the discourse, especially if Robert Hooke or William Petty happened to drop in. In November 1663 Pepys witnessed a raging argument between rival parties of physicians and apothecaries as to the merits of the ancient Galenic versus the newer chemical medical traditions. Pepys did not take a firm side in the intellectual debate. He noted that one of the apothecaries spoke "very prettily, that is, his language and sense good, though perhaps he might not be so knowing a physician as to offer to contest with them."[60] Pepys weighed pretty rhetoric against professional qualifications, but he took pleasure in such conversations without necessarily making firm judgments about their truth.

The city streets too offered opportunities for pleasurable conversations. One August morning, standing outside Temple Inn about to catch a coach to St. James, Pepys ran into Robert Hooke. They talked for a while about the nature of sound: Hooke correlated the musical notes made by string instruments with the rate of vibration of the strings and claimed to be able to tell how fast a fly beat its wings by the "note that it answers to in Musique during their flying."[61] Pepys was skeptical of the details of Hooke's ideas but recorded that "his discourse in general of sound was mighty fine"; he communicated his ideas "mighty prettily."[62] "Pretty," in addition to its familiar modern meaning, could describe for Pepys something that was cleverly or artfully done, praise that Hooke would have appreciated.[63] In describing this encounter, Pepys emphasized the quality of the rhetoric and the pleasure that he found in it, while reserving judgment on its truth.

Though most virtuosi, such as Pepys, appreciated the pleasure of a good conversation, they did not necessarily make that pleasure their primary index of a conversation's value. Those who sought to make face-to-face exchanges lead to new knowledge were more worried about the potential of those exchanges—especially the pleasant ones—for veering off into unproductive dead ends. Conversation might be pleasurable, but it also needed to lead to practical results—improved manufacturing processes, new methods for finding longitude, new ways to enhance the fertility of the soil, to name a few of the projects that preoccupied the early Royal Society.

This was one of the dangers of coffeehouses. Coffeehouse conversations could be free-wheeling, combative, and raucous. Individuals could use this to their advantage, but it could also work against them. Robert Hooke advanced his career through his performances in the coffeehouses, settings in which he fiercely attacked opponents and made ambitious, even grandiose, claims about experiments planned and completed.[64] Some rejected the coffeehouse altogether as a fit venue for philosophical conversation; John Flamsteed, astronomer royal and one of Hooke's erstwhile victims, was one such.[65] In coffeehouses the Royal Society as an institution could all too easily become the butt of jokes—as when Arthur Coga, who the society hired to be the human subject in an experiment in the transfusion of blood between sheep and humans, turned out to be a drunk. Phillip Skippon wrote to John Ray, "The Effects of the Transfusion are not seen, the Coffee-Houses having endeavoured to debauch the Fellow, and so consequently discredit the Royal Society, and make the Experiment ridiculous."[66] Though Coga may have taken his own initiative in spending the fee he received for the experiment on alcohol, Skippon blamed the coffeehouses for inducing Coga to drink: they "endeavoured to debauch" him.[67] In Thomas St. Serfe's *Tarugo's wiles; or, The coffee-House* (1668), as well as Thomas Shadwell's 1676 satire *The virtuoso*, the episode was parodied as an example of the foolishness of the virtuosi.[68] One of Shadwell's characters, skeptical of a virtuoso's claim that blood transfusion transferred physical and mental traits from the "emittent" to the "recipient," observes, "I believe if the blood of an Ass were transfused into a Virtuoso, you would not know the emittent Ass from the Recipient Philosopher, by the Mass."[69] Though the coffeehouses and the streets were fertile sites for plans and projects, fellows acting as a corporate body could not control or channel the conversations there as they could in the Royal Society meeting rooms.

Concerns about conversation were reflected back at the Royal Society by the wider culture, in which their project was mocked as so much talk—grandiose, extravagant talk that produced little in terms of practical results. In *The virtuoso*, the street is the stage for a violent confrontation between a crowd of ribbon weavers and the foppish natural philosophers who the weavers believe have invented a ribbon-weaving machine that threatens their jobs.[70] This scene was inspired by real-life events: in August 1675 ribbon weavers rioted in the streets of London, destroying "engine-looms." These looms, which had been invented on the Continent and were thus associated with non-English, or "Stranger," weavers, allowed operators to manage multiple shuttles at once.[71] A man operating an "engine-loom" could do in one day the work of seven to ten men working with hand looms.[72] In the play Sir Formal, one of the virtuosi, tries to calm the "Rabble of People" with the power of his oratory.[73] Some are pacified, but others interrupt him, dismissing his words and threatening violence. One says, "His Tongue's well hung, but I know not what he means by all this stuff"; a second continues, "Pox on you, you shall say no more. What's this to the invention of the Loom?"[74] The crowd shouts him down with cries of "a Rogue, a Villain! A damned Vert{u}oso!" and falls upon him. Another one of the virtuosos, Sir Nicholas Gimcrack, trying to calm the crowds, admits that he "never invented an Engine in my life. . . . We Vertuoso's never find out anything of use; 'tis not our way."[75] The crowd disperses only after shots are fired.[76] Throughout the play, but particularly in this scene, Shadwell cast the virtuosi as fatuous and bombastic—their rhetoric is as empty as air, incapable of moving crowds or even, it turns out, leading to the invention of anything so useful (and as threatening to the interests of artisans) as a ribbon-weaving machine.

In this scene Shadwell played with historical events in order to sharpen the satire against the natural philosophers. Shadwell first attributed the engine-looms to the natural philosophers, when in reality the ones responsible for bringing them into widespread use in England were the "Stranger" or immigrant communities as well as the more prosperous English ribbon weavers, who could afford to invest in such looms.[77] Not that natural philosophers were not interested in advancing such machines; they just were not the prime force driving the trade toward them. Aubrey, for example, recorded a story in which Christopher Wren tried to sell London's silk stocking weavers on a new, more efficient loom, which he offered to them for four hundred pounds.

They refused, saying that "it would spoile their Trade."[78] Likewise in the actual protests in the summer of 1675, ribbon weavers burned engine-looms because they saw them as a very real threat to their livelihoods.[79] But Shadwell's satire depicts the virtuosi as incapable of actually building mechanical devices: there is no economic threat here. In rendering the natural philosophers' machine imaginary, Shadwell limned the limits of their discourse. The ribbon weavers are frustrated by Sir Formal's words; they want him to stop talking and bring out the machine that threatens their livelihoods so they can destroy it, and possibly him. Sir Nicholas Gimcrack admits that the virtuosi have made no such machine; indeed they are incapable of it because they are incapable of inventing anything useful.

The satire bit deep; the character of Gimcrack persisted through the century as a defining image of the natural philosopher. Robert Hooke attended a performance of the play in June 1676 at Dorset Garden and was not pleased at what he viewed as a pointed attack at him. He wrote in his diary, "Damned Doggs. *Vindica me Deus.* People almost pointed."[80] John Evelyn, who also in 1676 attended a satire that was probably *The virtuoso,* took it as a direct attack on the activities of men such as him.[81] Twenty years later William Wotton wrote of "the sly Insinuations of the Men of Wit, That no great Things have ever, or are ever like to be perform'd by the *Men of Gresham*, and, That every Man whom they call a *Virtuoso*, must needs be a *Sir Nicholas Gimcrack*."[82] Shadwell's satire spoke to the virtuosi's fears about themselves and their work: namely that though talk was necessary to circulating information, evaluating evidentiary claims, developing and advancing particular projects, and gaining patrons, it always threatened to degenerate into idle pleasure and empty words.

This was fine under some circumstances. Though Shadwell's play derided scientific conversation as so much empty talk, Pepys's judgments of his conversations, whether at the coffeehouse or in the street, typically focused on the pleasure he took in them and in the rhetorical quality of the arguments on offer. Hooke's rhetoric on sound, delivered on a street corner, was "mighty fine." At the other end of the spectrum, John Mennes wearied Pepys by reading anatomy to him "like a fool." The particulars of any given conversation might or might not be true; Pepys readily admitted when he was not qualified to judge their truth. While Pepys was riding home in a coach with Mennes after a pleasant Sunday with various members of Sir William Batten's family, Mennes talked "all the way of Chymistry, wherein he doth know something; at least, seems to me, that cannot correct him."[83]

The conversations that Pepys recorded in his diary, and the judgments he applied to them, were often a more positive version of *The virtuoso*'s presentation of scientific conversation as a frivolous dead end.

By contrast, when the Royal Society met as a corporate body, it was more focused on securing conversation as a source of credible contributions to natural knowledge. The difference between the society's attitude and Pepys's stemmed from the uses to which the information was being put. We can see this in the way Pepys's attitude toward conversation fluctuated. Pepys frequently treated scientific conversation as speculation and as pleasure; however, when a conversation had direct bearing on his job, his ability to do it well and advance in his career at the Naval Office, he took it more seriously (though he might have still taken pleasure in it, as he did in his sessions learning about shipbuilding with Anthony Dean). Similarly, in their meetings the fellows of the Royal Society were attempting to increase the store of natural knowledge. The Royal Society worked to make conversation productive by incorporating it into a system of writing and printing. It could not be an independent instrument in the construction of natural knowledge but was used in tandem with, and integrated into, various forms of writing and print, particularly correspondence but also meeting minutes and the Royal Society's journal. Wary of examples of feckless virtuosi such as those presented in Shadwell's play, naturalists were leery of empty words.

Paperwork: Incorporating Conversation into Systems of Writing and Print

As in Evelyn's plans for a philosophical college, conversation was a cornerstone of the Royal Society's methodology for developing natural philosophical knowledge. According to Thomas Sprat, whose history of the society served as one of its key promotional documents in its first decade, conversation and debate among gentlemanly equals were far superior to individual labors as means of getting at natural philosophical truths. Though experiments might be completed away from the society, Sprat wrote, jointly probing the causes of the phenomena exhibited in the experiment was the key business of the society. Sprat attacked the lone natural philosopher as too prone to fixing on attractive but ultimately wrong conceits and allowing his judgment to be clouded by his own fancy. It happened even to an observer with the best intentions of rigor. He might begin well, Sprat wrote, but "the delight of his success swells him: he triumphs and applauds himself, for having found out some important Truth: But now his Trial begins to slacken: now impatience and security creeps upon him," and he becomes sloppy in his work, seeing confirmatory evidence everywhere.[84] "Such," Sprat wrote, "is the universal inclination of mankind, to be misled by themselves."[85] Assembled together, on the other hand, the fellows could entertain speculative hypotheses and raise questions and objections until all bad ideas had been filed away, as if talk were sandpaper. In conversation, "every rubb is here to be smooth'd; every scruple to be plain'd."[86] It might take time, Sprat wrote, but in natural philosophy the race was not to the swift.

Furthermore, in fellows' conversations with each other, Sprat wrote, distinctions of rank could not be made the basis for authority, and neither could fancy rhetoric.[87] The English, with their natural plainspokenness—"an universal modesty . . . proper to our Soil"—had a leg up in this regard.[88] Of course this antirhetoric rhetoric was not the same as no rhetoric. As a generation of historical scholarship has shown, the Royal Society developed a rhetoric of experience and experiment that served to ground the authority of their natural philosophical claims. This discourse emphasized facticity and the role of the individual observer, as well as his social credentials (especially if he was a gentleman) or his experiential knowledge (this might be leaned on more heavily by a tradesman or an artisan).[89] These conversational protocols (both as described by Sprat and as analyzed and, in some ways, restated by historians of science) were key: without them, speech was just as likely to lead one astray as it was to contribute to the production of natural knowledge. With them, the Royal Society offered a place where solitary laborers could meet for structured, well-regulated conversations in which experiments and matters of fact could be debated.[90]

The actual practice of the Royal Society did not precisely match Sprat's idealized depiction of it. As Daniel Carey has observed, the minutes of early Royal Society meetings show that the fellows often had to take information as it came to them, and given that they had only a limited ability to command the labor of others, they were not always choosy about rejecting factual accounts that came to them from distant observers.[91] However, the society did integrate conversation into a systematic process of knowledge production and dissemination in which conversation was transferred into writing and print. In its earliest years the society's face-to-face activities were augmented by Henry Oldenburg's work as secretary and editor of the *Philosophical Transactions*: through correspondence and print he recorded, transmitted, and archived the results of their conversations.[92]

The system for registering, circulating, and making information permanent involved several layers of writing and print and the movement of information from writing into conversation and back. Individual fellows presented discourses they had composed on experimental matters of fact, sometimes accompanied with demonstrations and images. These became the fodder for discussion. Presenting, reading, and discussing correspondence sent by those outside of London took up a significant chunk of meeting time as well. Discourses and correspondence received and read were entered into the society's letter books, register books, and books of classified papers, sometimes with copies of letters multiplying across these archival registers. During meetings, the secretary recorded rough minutes; the clerks used these as the basis for the official minutes that they copied into the journal books.[93] Oldenburg took it upon himself to follow up with those whose correspondence had been presented, letting them know that the society appreciated their contributions. Correspondence and conversation ramified beyond official channels as well, as individual fellows continued to record and discuss events at meetings in multiple venues, including in their personal notes, their correspondence, and in conversation at other venues, such as coffee shops and homes. Oldenburg, in particular, reported what was discussed in Royal Society meetings to his correspondents as a way of encouraging them to share information that might be presented at future meetings.[94]

The journal books sometimes named individual fellows, noting who presented a discourse, read correspondence, or offered a particular point in response to what was read. In one example, in May 1672, Oldenburg read aloud a letter from Martin Lister describing an operation in which a stone was cut from under his tongue after it had been forming for eight years.[95] The letter had been communicated by Robert Moray, who had it from the Archbishop of Canterbury, who had it from the Archbishop of York, who had it from Lister. Both Robert Boyle and Dr. Edmund King were recorded as having spoken in response to this account, both to say that they had seen similar stones grow in other bodies. King offered a second, more elaborate experience as well. In the course of autopsying the body of a man who died of "strange swowning fits," he found a small stone in the "Arteria Venosa" (the pulmonary veins), which he believed had caused the man's death by blocking the circulation of his blood. King was asked to produce "this Relation in writing, for the Register book."[96] Despite this request, King's account does not appear to have entered the register book.

In this exchange we see the ways in which the Royal Society protocols encouraged the conversion of writing into speech and speech into writing. Yet it also shows that though the Royal Society attempted to set up a secure pipeline for the production of natural knowledge, there were leaks, as individual contributors failed to follow up with requests that were made to them. These leaks were, in some sense, just as natural to the process as successful transmission of information from conversation, through writing, and into print. The Royal Society was able to offer contributors a certain degree of fellowship, prestige, and international notice, particularly through publishing their letters in *Philosophical Transactions*; however, the livelihoods of most contributors did not depend on any single contribution made (or not made) to the society's archives or Oldenburg's journal, and they might withdraw their cooperation at any moment, either because they did not feel sufficiently honored or because they simply forgot amid the pressing business of life. The fragility of the economy of credit underlying the publication of *Philosophical Transactions* became apparent in the late 1660s when unauthorized Latin translations circulated in Europe. The translators bungled the titles of respect due to certain contributors, such as Christian Huygens. Oldenburg feared that such discourtesy might lead individuals to cease corresponding with the society.[97] It took a great deal of labor on Oldenburg's part to keep this fragile economy of credit functioning.

Conversation was rarely transcribed exactly in the journal books; rather it was summarized, and more often than not without attributions to specific people. Individuals formally presenting material—whether it was the curator offering a demonstration, a fellow reading a discourse, or the secretary reading a letter—were named, but the responses were usually expressed in terms of the corporate will of the society. Appearing frequently were the words "it was ordered" and "it was desired," as in "it was desired" that the contributor be thanked and his letter registered by being copied into the letter book. As this formulaic language indicates, the minutes by no means accurately represented individual speech; rather, as with early modern legal records, such as depositions, the minutes represented a collaboration between the fellows present at any given meeting and the clerks and secretaries responsible for keeping the records, the latter of whom used their customary forms of language to express the statements of individuals and the will of the group.[98]

The way in which the minutes translated speech into writing put the focus on writing rather than on conversation. What was most important was not the discussion that followed a contribution but the further actions of observing, experimenting, writing, and printing that were recommended in the course of the discussion. This was evident in an episode from 1672 involving Martin Lister, Nehemiah Grew, Henry Oldenburg, and the fellowship of the society, represented in the minutes and Oldenburg's correspondence as a united corporate voice. For example, when Oldenburg in December 1672 read aloud Martin Lister's letter on the structure and function of the veins of plants, the company responded by ordering it circulated to Nehemiah Grew, an expert on the subject. At the next meeting, Grew, who resided in London, presented a set of comments on Lister's observations. These the society ordered to be cast into queries and transmitted in a letter to Lister. Lister, receiving them from Oldenburg, revised his original piece, and Oldenburg printed the revised letter in *Philosophical Transactions* some weeks later.[99] These revisions, however, happened without further comment from the Royal Society as a corporate body. Lister wrote to Oldenburg to ask that the revised letter not be read again to the society, as "what I have added anew, is soe little that I thinke it will be but crambe bis cocta," or "twice-cooked cabbage."[100] Conversation was neither the starting nor the ending point in this example; however, in its face-to-face meetings, the Royal Society provided crucial direction to Lister, Oldenburg, and Grew, forwarding the production of written and printed discourse.

The journal books thus represent the conversation, the face-to-face interaction of fellows in the weekly meetings, as one step in a process of knowledge production. Any one conversation in and of itself could not advance the progress of useful knowledge; however, it could be a tool for putting the society's corporate stamp of approval on an individual's contribution (his letter or discourse). As an authority-creating process, it bore some resemblance to modern academic peer review procedures, though it was far from identical to them.[101] Presenting a letter or a discourse at a meeting enrolled that submission in a system in which it was further preserved and disseminated by being copied into a register book or letter book or printed in *Philosophical Transactions*. By rewarding them with attention, this recognition also encouraged individuals to produce more such submissions. Correspondents often opened their responses to Oldenburg by commenting on how gratified they were to have their letters receive the notice of the society. Luke Hodgson, a Newcastle physician, remarked in a letter to Oldenburg how honored he was that his submissions on a fire burning in a coal pit received the attention of not only the Royal Society but also of "so worthy a person" as Robert Boyle.[102] The further letters that such attentions encouraged became yet more fodder for the society's conversations, more things that could be printed in *Philosophical Transactions.*

Yet this system was by no means fully secure.[103] In addition to the problem of correspondents and fellows dropping the ball, there were regular breakdowns in record keeping, with minutes not always being kept carefully, as, for example, toward the end of Oldenburg's life when he was without a clerk to copy the rough minutes into the journal books.[104] Oldenburg was also at this time dealing with financial difficulties and Robert Hooke's antagonism, which further scattered his attention and energies. Early secretaries, including Oldenburg and Hooke, also transferred society records back and forth between the society premises and their own residences, in part because they lacked adequate work space at the Royal Society. The boundaries between "public" and "private," between "official" and "personal," were at best fuzzy. At times the society even used Hooke's chambers in Gresham College for its meeting space, library, and repository. Gradually the Royal Society sought to enforce stricter boundaries between official and personal business, requiring in 1677 that "all papers and books concerning the Society be kept in the Repository or Library of the said Society; and that if any thing be to be transcribed, it be done there."[105] However, these proscriptions were not regularly followed. As late as 1699 Richard Waller wrote to Hans Sloane, upon a request of Sloane's for information from the Royal Society records, "as to what you write about the bookes I have none of the Journals nor Registers here, only the booke that the foul minits are entered in . . . I believe Dr Hooke may have one of the Registers."[106] The "Hooke Folio," which includes extracts from the journal books and rough meeting minutes taken by Hooke when he was secretary, disappeared from view for many years precisely because it had been separated from the "official" body of records, though it was recently rediscovered.[107] The volume of rough minutes of meetings of the council (the Royal Society's executive body) from 1699 to 1712, when Hans Sloane was secretary, can be found not in the Royal Society Library but with Sloane's other manuscripts at the British Library.[108]

In part, the boundary between public and private was so porous because it was impractical to construct a high wall between them. However idealized the rhetoric of recording every small detail (in Sprat's *History*, for example), processes of inscription and records management depended on the labor and designs of a handful of individuals, rather than fully elaborated bureaucracies. It was impossible for those individuals to keep up with the constant flood of speech and correspondence.

However, this porosity was not necessarily a failure of the society's processes; it was instead characteristic of those processes. Though it may not have matched the society's idealized vision of itself, as embodied in statutes and in Sprat's history, it served the aims of individual members as they sought precedence against each other, as in the case of the conflicts between Oldenburg and Hooke, which were in part disputes about the control of the society's records.[109] Moreover it was characteristic of the ways in which early modern Britons dealt with paperwork: two late seventeenth-century ambassadors to Turkey, for example, James Brydges, Lord Chandos and William Trumbull, regarded the correspondence and papers they produced and collected in the course of their official duties to be their own personal property.[110] They wielded papers against each other, rather than considering them common possessions of their office. When Trumbull arrived in Istanbul to take over from Chandos in 1687, Chandos, reluctant to give up the post, attempted to thwart Trumbull by absconding with the embassy's register of diplomatic correspondence.[111] Trumbull had to develop his own sources of information in order to build up for himself an archive of intelligence, the foundation of an ambassador's work, which largely consisted of promoting British trade.[112]

In some ways printing was the least secure—and least formalized in terms of its place in the early Royal Society's institutional procedures—link in the natural philosophical knowledge supply chain. Though the Royal Society had obtained the power to license printing as part of its original charter, it did not regularly supervise and fund printing itself. Rather it approved to be printed materials brought forward by fellows. The Royal Society as a corporate body shied away from taking a firmer hand in directing and financing printing because in doing so it exposed itself to heavy financial risk (as the society experienced with Ray and Willughby's *De historia piscium* [1686]) discussed in Chapter 5. In its early years *Philosophical Transactions* was very much Oldenburg's enterprise. The Royal Society as a corporate body had a hand in it; Oldenburg often selected pieces for the journal after they had been read and approved at one of the society's meetings, and the council read issues before licensing and occasionally suggested changes. Both Oldenburg and the Royal Society were content to give the impression to outsiders that the journal bore the full natural philosophical authority of the society. However, during the years in which *Philosophical Transactions* was published and edited by Oldenburg, the society's journal books frequently recommended that letters be entered in the register book, but they rarely recommended that letters be inserted in the journal. Oldenburg chose material for inclusion and made financial arrangements with the printers himself. In the early years the journal's stability and continuance depended on Oldenburg's attention to it, as became clear when the journal ceased production upon Oldenburg's death in 1677, to be revived only in the 1680s by Robert Plot, Edmond Halley, and Richard Waller. In the interim Hooke's attempt at a replacement journal, titled *Philosophical Collections*, failed miserably.[113]

The journal's fragility as well as its successes speak to the central place of correspondence in the production of natural knowledge in the second half of the seventeenth century. As Adrian Johns has argued, the journal form, as adapted by Oldenburg, was a printed version of Oldenburg's correspondence: its seriality was a print expression of the way in which information and knowledge emerged over time through the exchange of letters.[114] Thus, in addition to offering an opening to print publication to individuals who did not have a full treatise in them, it reflected the manuscript sensibility of the age. A journal was not a finished tome, a final word; instead it promised an endless stream of information. This sense of endless continuity was captured in Robert Plot's decision to start the revival of *Philosophical Transactions* with the page number at which Oldenburg left off before his death.[115] On the other hand, printing the journal addressed the weaknesses to which both correspondence and conversation were prone: writing and speech failed to serve as a basis for publicizing discoveries and inventions such that individuals received public credit for them. Martin Lister, in thanking Oldenburg for his work on *Philosophical Transactions,* captured nicely the limits of correspondence and conversation and the way in which print blew past these limits. He thanked Oldenburg for "the benefit & favour of your monthly Tracts. Your indefatigable Industrie having given us the opportunity of a register, which if it had been on foot some yeares agoe, the English had not lost the Credit of soe many new discoveries, which did more properly belong to them, than the first Publishers."[116] Like the Royal Society's manuscript instruments, *Philosophical Transactions* was a "register"; however, unlike them and crucially, it was a public register. Through it both natural philosophy and the reputation of the English were enhanced.

Conclusion

To return to the proposal with which this chapter began, plans such as Evelyn's for an ideal natural philosophical research institute proved difficult to implement. For one thing, they required substantial funds. Evelyn estimated that purchasing and setting up an estate would cost sixteen hundred pounds, and annual expenses for nine persons, including servants, would run to four hundred pounds. Who had that kind of money and a sufficiently ardent desire to use it to advance the progress of natural knowledge? A Robert Boyle, perhaps. Evelyn offered to contribute furnishings for the cottages, but little besides. He would have committed more of his fortune but was concerned about supporting his family. Neither could state funding be counted on. Just a few years earlier the Puritan reformer Samuel Hartlib had pinned his hopes on Parliament to fund his office of address, only to be disappointed. At the Restoration of Charles II, the virtuosi who founded the Royal Society received the monarch's royal imprimatur, but though free with his name, the king was not forthcoming with funds. In these early years the Royal Society grew and expanded, establishing routines that helped to secure the passage of information and knowledge through conversation, writing, and print. Yet it always operated on tighter financial margins than its fellows would have liked, preventing them from establishing a natural philosophical college like the one proposed by Evelyn and thwarting, or stalling, corporate and individual plans for the print publication of their works.

The difficulty with such schemes was more than monetary, however. As attractive as schemes such as Evelyn's were, ultimately early modern naturalists could not accomplish their aims by sequestering themselves on a forty-acre patch of ground. Natural history and antiquarian studies aspired to cover all of Britain, and as this chapter has shown, this required extensive travel and conversation with individuals across the domains about which naturalists wrote. There were also the social imperatives to consider: though epistolary relationships were all well and good, they were initiated and renewed through face-to-face contact. These conversations often occurred within homes, which, as James Secord has shown, continued to be important sites of conversation on science (especially scientific books) into the nineteenth century. As in the seventeenth century, the ideals of hospitality in polite society were crucial to shaping conversational practice.[117]

The insufficiency of a localized, face-to-face operation was also illustrated by the dynamics of the early Royal Society and the procedures it set in place for processing conversation and paperwork. Face-to-face meetings were a central component of the society's work: through these meetings correspondence and discourses were processed. Sometimes, as in Sprat's idealized vision, these submissions were subjected to criticism and questioning, and every rub was smoothed and every scruple planed. More often, though, society fellows gave these materials their stamp of approval without recording any particular bits of criticism or praise. The correspondence and discourses were then copied into the society's records and, if Oldenburg was so moved, printed in *Philosophical Transactions*. Face-to-face conversation as formalized in the society's meetings thus often functioned to impress the society's authority on the materials submitted to it. Keeping records of these face-to-face conversations was key to producing that authority: without these records, both in writing and in print, all this talk was no better than Sir Formal's and Sir Nicholas Gimcrack's empty words. But the meetings and their records were insufficient in and of themselves for producing natural philosophical knowledge: without the correspondence sent to society fellows from across Britain and abroad, they would have had relatively little on which to put their stamp of approval.

To create the whole "body and book" of the topography, natural history, and antiquities of Britain, information had to be pooled from many naturalists located across Britain, and investigators had to travel across each county collecting, talking, and writing as they went. Accomplishing this project thus necessarily required collaboration at a distance through writing and print. The next chapter, in turning to an episode in the history of long-distance collaborations, will show, at a material level, how through collaborations conducted in writing naturalists developed topographical, antiquarian, and natural histories that pushed beyond local boundaries.

Chapter 4

John Aubrey's *Naturall Historie* *of Wiltshire*: A Case Study in Scribal Collaboration

In the mid-1680s John Aubrey started *The Naturall Historie of Wiltshire*, two manuscript volumes that were the product of thirty years' observing and collecting in his home county, on a journey to at least six different readers.[1] Over the next ten years the manuscripts traveled from reader to reader. Sometimes they passed back through his hands between readers, sometimes not. On occasion he traveled with them. In horse-drawn carts they jounced along rough country roads, arriving at one reader's house in Somersetshire with the wooden box they traveled in "all broken to Splinters."[2] In the fall of 1691 Aubrey and John Ray exchanged frantic letters when it appeared—briefly— that the manuscripts had fallen off the back of a carrier's cart while in transit to London from Ray's home in Essex.[3] Late in life Aubrey dropped them off with a carrier who waited weekly at the Saracen's Head, a London public house, to be taken to Oxford, where they would be added to the collection of Aubrey's papers in the library of the newly founded Ashmolean Museum.[4]

This chapter, through an analysis of the travels and travails of Aubrey's *Naturall Historie,* develops the themes of the first chapter, articulating how naturalists constructed images of Britain as a topographical object through collaborative writing in their correspondence.[5] Over the course of four decades, as Aubrey stitched it together from loose notes and fragments and sent it from reader to reader, his *Naturall Historie* continuously accreted new writing. Through this process the manuscript came to reflect the knowledge and expertise of its many writers. By the time it came to the Ashmolean, it had become the product not only of Aubrey's pen but also of the pens and pencils of all those who read and wrote in it as well as those of Aubrey's friends and acquaintances whose letters and pamphlets he copied or inserted into the text.

I argue that the topographical object that emerged in the "finished" manuscript of *The Naturall Historie* mirrored the social organism, Aubrey's correspondence, that produced it (to echo Joshua Childrey once again). Although Aubrey initially wrote his *Naturall Historie* as a county natural history, with restricted geographical boundaries, through the process of collaborative reading and writing, it expanded beyond those boundaries to encompass natural knowledge about Britain and even the Continent. Part of this was down to Aubrey himself: he bound into the manuscript a range of materials on British natural history and antiquities, such as notes comparing Scottish and English folk customs.[6] Aubrey's collaborators' comments expanded the manuscript further, in that they provided annotations reflecting their interests and expertise. These readers, including John Ray, John Evelyn, Thomas Tanner, and Thomas Gale, added information to Aubrey's stock of natural knowledge. The readers based their comments largely on their experiences of the natural world in their home counties in England and during travels on the Continent. In doing so, they further wrote *The Naturall Historie* out of the local context and toward a national and even international one.

Both internally and externally *The Naturall Historie* illustrated the instability of Britain as a topographical object. It did this internally because it was a product of years of accumulation on Aubrey's part and it harbored a host of different writers, each of whom tugged it in a different direction, with some of their annotations, for example, extending the book beyond English borders and into continental Europe. Even Aubrey was unable to keep the text within its ostensible geographical boundaries. The book did this externally because it was one among many natural historical and antiquarian works that each offered its own construction of Britain (or pieces of it) as a topographical object. *The Naturall Historie of Wiltshire* was one book in a crowded field of works offering visions of British, Scottish, English, Welsh, and Irish topography in which local and national stood in productive rather than destructive tension, in which the local was not lost in the national, but in which the national was constituted by the sum total of all its local particulars. Yet collectively naturalists and antiquaries could not make the sums agree: each of their books offered a different way to work the topographical arithmetic.

In this chapter I first explore how Aubrey created *The Naturall Historie* over time, starting in the 1660s with loose notes, jottings, and papers and ending in the 1690s with two bound manuscript volumes. Over the course of thirty years, he built up a detailed study of the flora, fauna, and natural and social geography of his home county. I next consider the manuscripts' travels to readers, examining what they added in the form of annotations as well as took away by copying Aubrey's text into their own commonplace books.

Working in the medium of manuscript, Aubrey's readers became his collaborators.[7] Yet the history of Aubrey's *Naturall Historie*, and readers' interactions with it, also displays the limitations of scribal exchange and suggests how it functioned in comparison to printed and face-to-face communication.[8] Two episodes illustrate these limitations. In the first instance, I examine Aubrey's deep fear of plagiarism, expressed through accusations leveled at the naturalist John Ray, who read several of Aubrey's treatises in manuscript. Fears of plagiarism were endemic to scribal exchange and represented the reverse of the personal trust on which this particular form of intellectual intercourse depended. Next, I explore how the virtuoso and diarist John Evelyn commonplaced *The Naturall Historie*. Evelyn's use of *The Naturall Historie*—especially the ways in which he altered the fragments he excerpted—shows how naturalists built knowledge through writing, rewriting, augmenting, copying, and recopying each other's papers. It also offers another view on questions of trust and credit, and how credit was assigned in both manuscript and print, as Evelyn copied Aubrey's text without attaching his name to it.

The material history of Aubrey's manuscripts demonstrates the complexity that inhered in individuals' attempts to use scribal technologies to construct natural knowledge. Scribal technologies (pen and paper) fostered a collaborative approach to natural history in which knowledge was always incomplete, never finished or final. Yet with printing available as a means for exchanging information and making it public, they were not sufficient in themselves for producing natural knowledge. Early modern naturalists were acutely aware of the possibilities, and shortcomings, of scribal modes of communication and print, especially in relation to each other. In addition, as Aubrey's story shows, naturalists' decisions as to whether to print their finished works or to share them with readers in manuscript were not made in a vacuum.[9] When it came to printing especially, much depended on a naturalist's access to financial and social capital, as well as the time to polish and perfect the work for the press. In many ways Aubrey's decision to restrict himself to circulating his papers rather than instead (or also) printing them was the decision of someone who was a marginal player. An analysis of the texts and textual community that this decision brought into being thus offers a way into the landscape of late seventeenth-century scientific communications. It allows us to map not only the relations between writing, long-distance collaboration, and the construction of local and national topography, but also those that obtained between authority, money, and community.

The Naturall Historie of Wiltshire as a County Natural History

The Naturall Historie of Wiltshire was a county natural history, an encyclopedic survey of the natural, social, and economic history of the county of Wiltshire in western England, in which Aubrey was born and which remained his home base off and on for much of his life. The first volume was an inventory of the soils, waters, airs, flora, fauna, agricultural practices, and notable human arts and inventions of Wiltshire. The second volume branched out into what a twenty-first-century reader might consider cultural, social, and economic history; chapter titles in this volume included "Agriculture & Improvements," "The History of Cloathing & Cloathiers of Wiltshire," "Faires & Markets, their Rise & decay," and "Antiquities & Coines."[10]

As a county natural history, *The Naturall Historie of Wiltshire* was supposed to be one chapter in the "whole body and book" of the *Britannia* tradition of natural historical, chorographical, and antiquarian writing discussed in Chapter 1. County natural histories were limited in their geographical reach but detailed and wide-ranging in their subject matter.[11] Robert Plot, author of popular natural histories of Oxfordshire and Staffordshire, undertook his subject precisely because it was "of so great variety."[12] Plot's studies, like Aubrey's, encompassed the heavens, beasts, birds, stones, men and women, arts (that is, mechanical arts), and antiquities. Plot, unlike Aubrey, did not cover cultural and social history more broadly; this was a distinguishing mark of Aubrey's county natural histories that hearkened more directly back to one of the genre's origin points, the writings of figures such as John Leland.[13] County natural histories tended to eschew the marvelous and the strange, focusing instead on useful arts and inventions and natural knowledge that would advance husbandry and other local economic enterprises.[14] In focusing on agricultural improvement, writers drew from classical models. Gentle and noble agricultural "improvers" turned to classical literary texts to rediscover how to manage their estates, and they wrote their own manuals and guides drawing on both their own experiences and the classical tradition.[15] But county histories' avoidance of monsters and the marvelous, though pronounced, was by no means complete. Each history's requisite chapter on "men and women," which covered accidents of birth and death, including examples of multiple births, conjoined twins, and deaths by fright and haunting, delved into that category.

British county and regional natural histories as a genre embodied a turn to the local as the foundation of the national, and Aubrey's interest therein was replicated across the ranks of the Royal Society. In particular, county natural history offered a framework for understanding people—their culture, their psychology, and their physical constitution—as products of local environments. According to the chorographic tradition in which Aubrey wrote, the characteristics of a people were determined by the airs, soils, and waters where they lived.[16] The natural categories that offered the keys to understanding human psychology, physical makeup, and health were reflected in the chapter divisions according to which Plot and Aubrey structured their natural histories. Airs, waters, and earths took up positions at the beginnings of their books, laying the foundations for later chapters on beasts, fish, birds, plants, insects, reptiles, and people.

One aim of county natural histories was to promote the health of local populations. Galenic medical tradition, on which chorographical beliefs drew, linked health to one's locality.[17] One's body was naturally suited to remain healthy in the environment in which one had long lived; trouble ensued if one moved out of that climate.[18] If a person did fall ill, the best remedies might also be found nearby—not only because body and environment were tuned to each other, but also because foreign remedies were often expensive and the purity of their ingredients was impossible to verify.[19] In his *Naturall Historie*, for example, Aubrey encouraged systematic county surveys of botanical resources—such as that performed by John Ray for Cambridgeshire—as means of discovering "Plants to cure us, that grow (perhaps) within 5, or 10, miles of our abodes."[20] These could be undertaken by apothecaries; Aubrey made an effort to offer one for Wiltshire. Aubrey's concern to promote such surveys more broadly indicated his national frame of mind. Yet his statement also suggested that local particulars might not be in all cases a foundation for national unity: the Galenic localism on display in this passage suggested that the botany of each region would primarily be of interest in that region, as each region would source its botanical remedies locally.

County natural histories oscillated between the local and the national. Aubrey set his local study in a national context while remaining vague on exactly how he defined his "Nation," a word which at the time carried connotations of a people united by common ancestry as well as language and culture. To be part of a nation was to be part of a kin group; hence the importance of descent as a category of analysis in topographical constructions of Britain. Explaining his interest in local natural history, Aubrey wrote, "There is no Nation abounds with greater varietie of Soiles, Plants, & Mineralls, than ours: and therefore it very well deserves to be surveyed . . . and to take no notice at all of what is dayly offered before our Eyes is <grosse> stupidity."[21] In this passage Aubrey implicitly contrasted his "Nation" with foreign ones; his comment echoed Joshua Childrey's notion that Britain offered a compendium of the world's natural diversity. But by "Nation," Aubrey may have meant Britain, England, or possibly, in oscillating fashion, both. Elsewhere in the preface, listing studies comparable to his, he mentioned only natural histories of other English counties.[22] However, the book made multiple references to British natural history and antiquities: on one of the book's title pages he made a note that Edward Lhuyd had told him there were fossil shells in North and South Wales (see Figure 1 below).[23] In the preface he made note of William Camden, whose *Britannia* encompassed England, Scotland, Wales, and Ireland, as a writer working the same ground as he was.[24] These references suggest a more expansive view of the British "Nation." But even to the extent that Aubrey had "England" in mind, he may not have objected to something broader: then as now, the English had a habit of saying "England" when they meant "Britain."[25]

Aubrey engaged in yet more productive blurring in using the word "Nation" to refer to both the people and the land, writing "no Nation abounds with greater varietie of Soiles, Plants, & Mineralls, than ours" and also, on the next page, "I am the first that ever made an Essay of this kind for Wiltshire, and (for ought I know) in the Nation."[26] The former identified "nation" with land; the latter affiliated it more with people. This back and forth between nation as land and nation as people thoroughly identified the land with the people and the people with the land, all the while remaining vague about who the people were and where the boundaries of their land lay. Overall, Aubrey's lack of specificity allowed readers to imagine the nation as "English" or "British" as they wished. Aubrey's readers-commentators, for example, relying on their own personal experiences, generally confined themselves to adding information with an English provenance. Not only a creation of its writers, the topographical Britain was what readers imagined it to be as well.

Collaboration, Status, and the Production of Natural History

The Naturall Historie emerged gradually, taking shape first as a collection of research notes and then as a bound manuscript book, over a period of about forty years. Its life in Aubrey's correspondence ebbed and flowed with Aubrey's own fortunes. Looking back in 1685, Aubrey recalled that he had first begun taking notes on the natural history of Wiltshire in 1656. Aubrey portrayed these earliest jottings on Wiltshire's natural history, made when his status as a propertied gentleman was still intact, as casual observations set down as he traveled between his estates. Over the years Aubrey "augmented" this collection regularly and often—"daily," according to his own account—and it grew into "a good Penus natu{ra}lis of my <owne> Collecting."[27] (The Latin *penus* means "store of food, provisions, victuals.") Through the 1660s and 1670s his notes were most likely a collection of loose papers covered with jottings and notes. They were not yet the manuscript book they would become but rather research notes that could (Aubrey hoped) find a place in the making of a printed book. He did not necessarily intend to publish them himself; he hoped to find a collaborator who could make use of them. In the mid-1670s Aubrey fixed on Robert Plot, then working on the natural history of Oxfordshire that he would publish in 1676, as the man who could make his vision a reality.[28] Having collected "many fine things" in Oxfordshire in addition to his collections for Wiltshire, Aubrey offered his notes and further assistance to Plot, getting in touch with him via Anthony à Wood, their mutual Oxford acquaintance.[29]

Aubrey hoped initially to enter into an arrangement in which he would supply Plot with research notes for incorporation into published natural histories. But even before Plot agreed to look at what Aubrey had collected, Aubrey's plans for their collaboration burgeoned. He began to see the natural history of Oxfordshire as one in a projected series of county natural histories.[30] The material that Aubrey thought Plot might be interested in reading kept multiplying: "I have written," he informed Wood, "of Naturall history (for Dr Plotts) of Wilts and Surrey besides pieces of other Counties Ten sheets closely written and shall send him more."[31] This vision was encouraged by the work he performed for John Ogilby in the early 1670s, researching the topography and history of Surrey and other counties for Ogilby's projected historical and geographical survey of England and Wales.[32] Aubrey seems almost to have attempted to use sheer force of will to bring into being a collaboration with Plot, in the process illustrating how naturalists working together through their correspondence generated natural historical knowledge on a national scale. Aubrey enlisted others in this project, putting his social connections to work for Plot. He wrote to his Welsh cousin Henry Vaughan (the metaphysical poet) to collect notes on Brecknockshire and "other circumjacent Counties."[33] Working through friends at the Court of Chancery, he enlisted attorneys "in every county of England and Wales" to collect information on "Husbandry and Huswifry."[34] At times Aubrey imagined himself as the lead partner in their collaboration, such as when he suggested that Plot could "assist for Oxfordshire" while Aubrey superintended the project at the national level.[35]

However, Aubrey's enthusiasm for collaboration outran Plot's own, and though the doctor studied Aubrey's notes on Surrey and Wiltshire, he otherwise kept his distance and ultimately rejected further collaboration.[36] Although the two remained in contact through the 1670s and the early part of the 1680s, they did not become close friends. Aubrey tended to work through mutual friends rather than approach Plot directly with requests, even after gaining his acquaintance, indicating a coolness in their relationship.[37] A decisive break, signaling the end of any hope of collaboration, came in 1684. Aubrey again offered to share his notes, but Plot, by then keeper at the Ashmolean, demurred that he would not write natural histories again, "unless it were for his Native Country of Kent."[38]

By comparison, Aubrey collaborated somewhat more successfully with Anthony à Wood. He conducted biographical research for Wood, traveling around the country writing down inscriptions on tombstones and ferreting out biographical facts and stories from old acquaintances of his subjects. Anthony Powell, in his biography of Aubrey, suggests that Wood, who gained access to Aubrey's contacts and Aubrey's writing style, got a better end of the deal than Aubrey, though Aubrey did sometimes borrow money from Wood.[39] The editor responsible for the posthumous publication of *The natural history and antiquities of the county of Surrey* thought the same thing: the collaboration was "beneficial to both, particularly the latter {that is, Wood}, to whom {Aubrey} communicated large Materials towards his noble Designs since published, so highly to the Credit of the University of Oxford."[40] A list in Wood's diary of "Queries to be sent to Mr. John Aubrey," written in winter 1679/80, suggested the ways in which Aubrey served Wood. In the note Wood tasked Aubrey to research a multitude of biographical details, the uncovering of which must have been tedious. These included epitaphs, birth and death dates, and birth, death, and burial places of a range of individuals, including the lawyer John Godolphin, William Petty, the clerics Vavasor Powell and Francis Potter, and the parliamentarian pamphleteer Marchamont Needham.[41] In some cases Wood also sought the titles of all books written by his subjects. Information such as this was scattered across not just London but also the counties where these men had lived and died; in order to find it, Aubrey had to visit the individuals' burial monuments, inspect parish registries, question booksellers, and track down the surviving friends and relatives of the dead.

The great lengths to which Aubrey went to secure a collaboration with Plot, and the approach to collaboration that he took in his work with Wood—in which he went dogsbodying around southern England—reflected the precariousness of his financial situation and of his position within the learned correspondence. When his father died in 1652, Aubrey inherited estates in both Wiltshire and Herefordshire as well as substantial debts. In 1661–1662 he sold the Herefordshire lands to settle some of his debts. He hoped to solidify his financial position through a marriage to Joan Sumner in 1666, but that plan failed. In 1671 Aubrey was forced to sell his Wiltshire estate and boyhood home, Easton Piers, in order to settle the legal and economic disputes that arose from the broken engagement.[42] He felt the loss acutely. In 1670, as the lawsuit was concluding, he wrote to Wood, in one of his last letters from Easton Piers, "I am now taking my leave of this beloved place, where I first drew breathe."[43] He was reduced to a nomadic existence and was even driven at various points in the 1670s to sell his books to get by.[44] During the remainder of his life, he was intermittently pursued by lawsuits and debt collectors and received his mail at as many as seventeen different addresses, changing residences so often partly to elude the debt collectors. At the height of his panic in the early 1670s, he even spread false rumors that he had traveled abroad to Italy and France, and he asked Wood to direct his letters to "Thomas Awbrey" rather than John.[45] Thomas Tufton, Earl of Thanet, whom Aubrey served as a secretary and London business agent partly in exchange for Tufton's protection from debt collectors, once wrote to him, "Your lodging like an enchanted castle, being never to be found out, I shall in the future direct my letters to Mr. Hookes chamber in Gressam Colledge."[46]

Deprived of estates and income, Aubrey pursued service to his natural historical correspondents, and the work his friends and patrons could throw his way, as a means of keeping together body and soul. The kind of work he undertook, which involved fairly frequent travel in search of information, was well suited to the nomadism imposed by his financial and legal circumstances. His friends and patrons, including Tufton, Wood, Robert Hooke, John Ogilby, and his friend the Wiltshire gentleman James Long, with whom he consulted on *The Naturall Historie,* provided him with meat and drink and a roof over his head as he traveled. At the time of Aubrey's death, he was being supported by the goodwill, and bread and board, supplied him by Lady Long, James's widow.[47]

Aubrey's friends and patrons offered him more than just food and a place to sleep. A seat at their tables also admitted him to conversation and fellowship and a meaningful role as a contributor to the production of natural historical knowledge. As he was a gentleman, his natural historical collections had been but the by-products of his attentive custodianship of the welfare of his estates and his county. But with the loss of one self, one place within the community, he had to fashion a new one.[48] For Aubrey, pursuing collaborations was a way of maintaining a place in the community and even developing a new persona, once the comfortable role of "country squire" was no longer his.

Manuscript, Print, and the Decision (Not) to Publish

In 1684 Plot decisively rejected Aubrey's offers of collaboration, suggesting that Aubrey should edit and publish his notes on his own. Aubrey then took matters into his own hands. But instead of following Plot's advice to print the *Naturall Historie,* he collected his notes into a manuscript book and added title pages, a table of contents, and a dedication. Around this time Aubrey stopped thinking of his collection as something to be printed and instead saw it as a book in its own right. In the dedicatory letter to Thomas, Earl of Pembroke (dated June 1685), Aubrey wrote, "Considering wherefore, that if I should not doe this myselfe my papers might either perish; or be sold in an Auction, and somebody else (as is not uncommon) put his name to my Paines: and not knowing any one that would undertake this Designe while I live, I have tumultuarily stitch't up, what I have many years since collected."[49] Though others had encouraged Aubrey to print his notes (and would do so again in the coming years), Aubrey did not seek to print his *Naturall Historie*. His primary concerns, as he said, were that his papers would survive after his death and that he would receive credit for the knowledge contained therein. Interestingly, he seems to have believed that this was unlikely if the collected notes remained papers but more likely if they were "tumultuarily stitch't up." Loose papers were less secure than bound manuscripts, more open to misappropriation, more likely to be lost. In being bound into a book, papers took on a formal coherence and became recognizable, and respected, as the finished product of a particular author (or at least their author hoped they did).

As his phrase "tumultuarily stitch't up" indicates, Aubrey was aware that *The Naturall Historie* was more a rough draft than a finished treatise: the contemporary meaning of the word "tumultuarily" was "hastily and without order; irregularly, confusedly, unsystematically, at random." Interestingly, one of the *OED*'s examples for this meaning is a letter from John Evelyn to Aubrey, in which Evelyn presented his comments on Aubrey's collections for Surrey, apologizing that they were set down "tumultuarily, as they came into my sudden Thoughts."[50] Aubrey used the word to describe the (lack of) order in his materials for Surrey as well: "I now set Things down tumultuarily, as if tumbled out of a Sack, as they come to my Hand, mixing Antiquities and Natural Things together, as I have here done them."[51] In the last fifteen to twenty years of his life, Aubrey was interested in the information itself, in piling it up and preserving it for the future. He hoped, at the same time, to save his historical reputation. For his purposes, a "tumultuarily stitch't up" manuscript book was just fine. The cost of publication was also a factor. Aubrey does not seem to have sought print publication for *The Naturall Historie*, though publication costs did thwart his plans for publishing other treatises, including his *Monumenta Britannica* (as discussed in the next chapter).

Circulating and preserving texts in manuscript, rather than printing them, was not an unusual step for an author of antiquarian studies and county natural histories. This may have been in part because authors in these fields relied on older manuscript records as sources; these included church, city, and corporation records, charters, and personal manuscripts held at estates.[52] Topographical, antiquarian, and natural history texts were copied and recopied throughout the early modern period, in some cases many years

after their writers' deaths.[53] The distinction between the sources of topographical writing and topographical writing itself was something of a rough
one, in fact, because these texts became sources for later writers. John Leland's
descriptions of Tudor England, compiled from observations he made while
surveying the dissolving monasteries for books for Henry VIII's library, were
famous among sixteenth- and seventeenth-century antiquaries. The eight
manuscript volumes had been donated to the Bodleian beginning in 1632 and
were widely consulted throughout the seventeenth century. Yet they did not
start to appear in print until 1710.[54] Other scribal authors whose works were
printed only after initial circulation in manuscript, if at all, included the
surveyor John Norden, the Tudor antiquary Laurence Nowell, and the Devon
antiquaries Sampson Erdeswicke, Thomas Westcote, and Tristram Risdon.[55]
While many of these authors were long dead by the late seventeenth century,
their papers were still actively sought and used by scholars, providing models
for the continuing preservation and circulation of antiquarian and natural
history texts in handwritten form. Aubrey painstakingly tracked the existence
of such manuscript treatises and notes and used them in his own research.[56]

Yet despite this legacy of scribal copying and circulation in antiquarian
communities, ultimately Aubrey felt that tumultuarily stitching up his notes
was something of a stop-gap measure. He held out hope that his work still
might appear in the press after his death. In the dedicatory letter to Pembroke, he wrote that he hoped for an editor, "some ingeniose and publique
spirited <Wiltshire> young man, to polish and compleat, what I have here
delivered rough hewen."[57] Binding up his notes, sharing them with readers,
and depositing them in the Ashmolean would preserve them until the editor
appeared.

The longed-for editor was a recurring figure for Aubrey; many of his
manuscript books, he felt, could be set in order for publication only by the
hand of another. In a letter now bound with his *Idea of Education of Young
Gentlemen*, for example, Aubrey identified his friend Anthony Henley as
someone who might take on that volume.[58] Aubrey often referred to the
hoped-for editor as his "Aristarchus," a reference to Aristarchus of Samoth-
race (c. 216–144 B.C.). One of the first literary critics and editors in the
Hellenic world, he was cited as the archetypal critic by Horace and Cicero.[59]
In the case of *The Naturall Historie*, Aubrey thought that he had found his
Aristarchus in Thomas Tanner, a "publique spirited young Wiltshire man,"
who, at the time of Aubrey's death, was a student at Queen's College, Oxford
increasingly known for his interest in antiquities and natural history.[60]

Aubrey chose Tanner as one of his readers and annotators. Aubrey's decision not to focus on shepherding his texts into print and his admission that he required an editor to prepare them for the press illustrated how he and his contemporaries understood the differences between print, manuscript, and papers. Loose papers were unfit for circulation and were likely to be destroyed upon their creator's death. In a "rough-hewen" but bound manuscript, information could be disseminated to a limited coterie and preserved for the use of future researchers. The press, which offered enhanced opportunities for dissemination and preservation, required polishing and editing, which included filling in gaps in the text and choosing between various ways of wording a passage.

Aubrey's longing for an Aristarchus revealed a tension in his attitudes toward manuscript and print, and their relative value. He sought access to print publication and understood print publication, for at least some of his texts, as the goal of writing. However much natural history might be collaboratively constructed in writing, ultimately it was further disseminated and preserved in print (though this process was mediated through correspondence, as discussed in the next chapter). This was not always the case; for example, Aubrey explicitly decided not to print his *Brief Lives* out of a concern that the material it contained was too sensitive to expose to the public, especially while some of his biographical subjects were still alive.

Aubrey and his contemporaries recognized numerous drawbacks to not printing one's works (at least where concerns about the sensitivity of information were not present). In writing, Aubrey missed the instant recognition that print publication bestowed. In letters to Wood and others, he lamented the obscurity that would attend his failure to attach his name to a printed book. Scribal circulation exposed him to the threat of plagiarism—what he called the "wrong" of "putting out anothers Labours under your own name."[61] As Adrian Johns and Deborah Harkness have noted, and Aubrey recognized in his own time, a printed text was better than a handwritten text when it came to establishing claims of priority.[62] Printing a text by no means necessarily put a stop to the misuse and plagiarism of one's words. Nor can we make a black and white definition of what constituted plagiarism in the early modern period—as Johns has argued, this was always a contested category. However, print had the greater potential to provide a public record of an author's claims because it preserved texts in a multitude of copies. Manuscripts, including those shared with friends, such as Aubrey's *Naturall Historie*, existed in at most a few copies. Given this, the textual record represented by such papers and manuscripts was more easily destroyed or muddled and more readily altered or falsified (though bound manuscripts were more secure than loose papers). As a result, private manuscripts were felt to be a less solid foundation for priority claims.

To get around these difficulties, contemporaries tried creating institutional manuscripts, such as central records, registers, or repositories, but this practice was not foolproof. Institutional manuscripts, such as the Royal Society's register book, in which discoveries and inventions were recorded, allowing claims of priority to be marked and inventions to be shared with others, fared slightly better. Secured by the Royal Society's authority, the register book was perceived to be at least partially protected against tampering and the accidents of time. Yet individual fellows and Royal Society employees, such as Robert Boyle and Robert Hooke, still rejected the register book in favor of print publication because print offered them wider publicity.[63] Hooke also suspected that Henry Oldenburg, who bore the responsibility for maintaining the register and the society's other paper instruments, was not an impartial guardian thereof.[64] In the keeping of manuscript registers, a set of practices developed (shakily at first) to demarcate that which was supposed to be institutional, public, and trustworthy from that which was personal, private, and open to manipulation.

Ultimately, Aubrey's decision to tumultuarily stitch up his papers, rather than print them, suggested that there were no absolutes in the early modern communications field. Rather, one made a series of choices about when and in what medium to communicate one's work, strategizing across the field, acting in response to moves made by one's friends and fellows, and hoping for the best. For Aubrey, these decisions were deeply conditioned by economic, social, and temporal realities. In an ideal world, he likely would have preferred to see his *Naturall Historie* in print. Furthermore, although Aubrey's contemporaries clearly valued collaborative writing as a tool for producing natural histories, they assumed that print was the ultimate destination for a collection of materials such as those contained between the covers of Aubrey's *Naturall Historie*. Yet once it became clear to him that printing the text was beyond his means, that he was running out of time and money, Aubrey made the best of the situation and sought to share and preserve his work as a bound manuscript, "tumultuarily stitch't up" from his loose papers.

The Material Text: The Working Draft of *The Naturall Historie*

Aubrey's working draft of *The Naturall Historie*, painstakingly assembled over many years, is the copy that he shared with readers. It offers a view of natural history under construction. This is true on both intellectual and the material levels. In terms of both intellectual organization and content, the two volumes are something like early modern commonplace books. For the most part, information is not presented as narrative; the chapters are collections of notes and observations jotted down and arranged by subject. Like many commonplace books, *The Naturall Historie* was a product of a lifetime of research and reading. Materially this is evident in the very construction of the pages, which might be termed "cut and paste." Each folio is layered with Aubrey's notes, additions, and queries to himself, written both on the original pages of the book and on slips inserted between pages or pasted down on them. Initially, Aubrey wrote the main text on the rectos of each page, leaving the versos open for revision and additions. Over time he filled the versos. The Latin word *quaere,* Aubrey's command to himself to probe something further, is sprinkled liberally throughout the text.[65] Blank spaces were left throughout the text for facts, names, and dates that he expected to fill in later.

A closer examination of the front matter of the first volume of *The Naturall Historie* reveals the material form that natural history took while under construction. There are three title pages, between which are interspersed various notes, letters, and the pages of the opening chapter of the book, a chorographical survey that is not listed in the table of contents. The first title page describes the text as "The Naturall Historie of Wiltshire, 1685."[66] Aubrey used this page as a space for memorandums to himself and his readers, reminding himself, among other things, to "Insert Dr Listers paper of Clays."[67] (See Figure 1.) The second title page—written on the verso of the first—gives the title of the work as "Memoires of Naturall Remarques in the County of Wilts." Below this line Aubrey wrote and then later crossed out "To which are annexed Observables of the same kind in the County of Surrey, and Flynt-shire."[68] (See Figure 2.) The third title page is on the recto of folio 12; it announces the book as "The Naturall Historie of *Wiltshire.*" This title page is also dated to 1685; as on the others, Aubrey listed himself as a fellow of the Royal Society.[69] Inserted before and between the three title pages, the reader finds family trees mapping Aubrey's paternal and maternal ancestry; notes on ways to determine the cardinal direction of east for theologically correct church construction; comparisons of English and Scottish folk traditions to pagan customs described in Greek and Roman literature; a dedicatory letter to Thomas, Earl of Pembroke; and a chorographical survey of British soils and the relationship between their properties and those of the

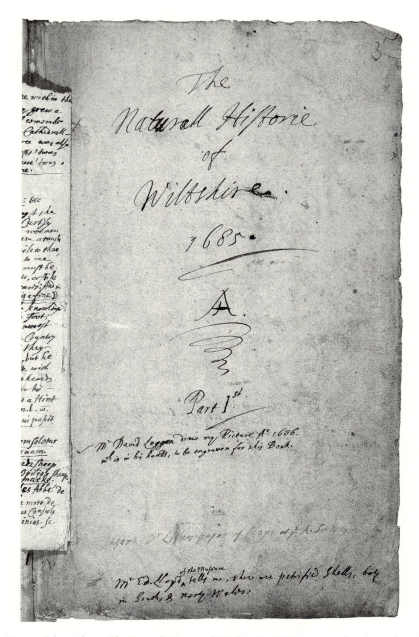

Figure 1. John Aubrey, *The Naturall Historie of Wiltshire,* Bod MS Aubrey 1, f. 3r. Reproduced by permission of the Bodleian Library, Oxford. This is the first of three title pages in Aubrey's working draft. Note Aubrey's memorandums to himself, including at the bottom, "Mr Ed. Lloyd <of the Musaeum> tells me, there are petrified shells, both in South, & North-Wales." Even on the title page Aubrey leaped the bounds of the shire, incorporating British natural history more broadly.

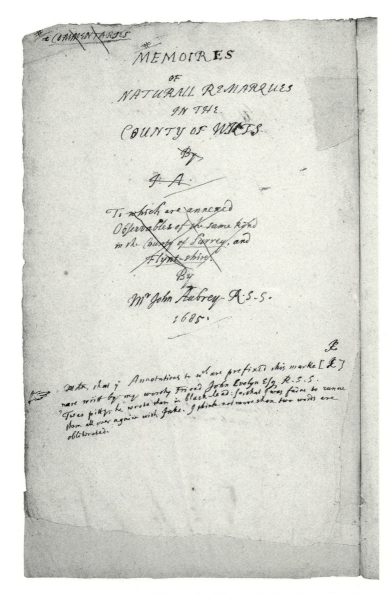

Figure 2. John Aubrey, *The Naturall History of Wiltshire*, Bod MS Aubrey 1, f. 3v. Reproduced by permission of the Bodleian Library, Oxford. This page shows an alternative title, "Memoires of Naturall Remarques in the County of Wilts," which Aubrey used for the fair copy of the manuscript deposited in the Royal Society Library in 1692. Note that references to natural histories of Surrey and Flintshire are crossed out. Aubrey separated these notes out before sending the manuscript to the Ashmolean; throughout Aubrey's lifetime, the contents this and other of his works were in flux. Also on this page is Aubrey's note that he had traced John Evelyn's penciled annotations in pen and marked them with his initials, preserving and elevating them as a mark of his special esteem for Evelyn.

plants, animals, and people that drew sustenance from them.[70] Following the third title page, there is a commendatory letter from John Ray recommending that Aubrey "speed {the manuscript} to the Presse."[71] The rest of the chorographical survey continues after this letter.[72] The "front matter" is brought to an end by a table of contents.

The eclectic organization of the front matter is representative of the general state of the manuscript. For example, the section on "Air" (listed in the table of contents as the first chapter) begins with a transcription of an "Account of an Echo in Scotland" by the royally well-connected Scotsman Robert Moray, one of the founding fellows of the Royal Society.[73] Aubrey went on in this chapter to include notes on aural phenomena from Gloucester and Oxford, more examples of the text jumping its Wiltshire fences and escaping for British pastures.[74] Inserted throughout the text are numerous letters, printed pamphlets, slips of paper with Aubrey's notes and corrections, and botanical samples (pressed and dried leaves and flowers).[75] Some of the slips had been pasted onto pages such that the reader could lift the slips to see the text (if any) underneath them; others had been pasted down completely. A few of the slips were intended as anchors for botanical samples.

The use of these slips tells us something about the process by which Aubrey wrote *The Naturall Historie*. It seems likely that when he came across relevant information but did not have the manuscript at hand to record it in, he took notes on slips of paper and then pasted or inserted them in the appropriate places sometime later. They appear to be placed now as they were when Aubrey deposited the manuscript in the Ashmolean Museum. This can be seen from cross-references tying text written on pasted-down slips to that on the underlying pages. The integration of text across slips and the underlying pages indicates that Aubrey placed many, though probably not all, of the slips in their current locations. For example, Aubrey copied the text of an advertisement for a medicinal spring near the Devizes, a Wiltshire village, that had been printed in Henry Coley's almanac "about 1681."[76] Below the slip, on the page itself, Aubrey labeled and explained the advertisement, which he had asked Dr. Richard Blackbourne, a physician with a practice at Tunbridge Wells, to write. Further illustrating themes from Chapter 1 of this book, this slip, and Aubrey's explanation of it, gives a concrete example of how collaboration resulted in local sites and resources being promoted to broader British audiences. Aubrey identified the spring as a site to be promoted to the health-conscious, corralled Blackbourne to write the ad, and got it into Coley's almanac.

With Aubrey's use of slips, the material construction of the book reflects his circumstances, especially the nomadism enforced upon him by penury, which sometimes separated him from his papers as he could not always travel with them. For example, a discussion of elder trees and the uses of products made from elder wood and elderberries begins on the page and then continues on a slip.[77] The slip consists of a quote from William Coles's *The art of simpling* (London, 1656) discussing the use of elder sticks to prevent the formation of galls while riding a horse. The presence of the slip and Aubrey's use of it to record a reference suggest that he took down the quote from *The Art of Simpling* when he did not have access to *The Naturall Historie* (perhaps while perusing someone else's library while staying in their house?). When he could, he pasted the slip into the appropriate section of his papers.

The Naturall Historie bears witness to a long history of use, rewriting, and reworking by its author, and yet it was never brought into a fixed, finished state. This was no accident. By initially leaving the versos of each folio blank, Aubrey built spaces for revision and addition into the manuscript. He also left white space on the rectos: generous margins that were filled, over time, with both Aubrey's and his readers' notes. There are also blanks within the main text on the rectos. Whenever he did not know a name, date, or fact, Aubrey left a space to fill in later. As time passed and work on the project continued, he used the white space he had granted himself to rewrite, expand, and correct the text, crossing out or pasting over some original text and rewriting and adding between the lines, in the margins, on the versos, and on slips that he partly or wholly pasted to the pages (see Figures 4 and 5 below for examples). Sometimes he revised the text without choosing between two different wordings, writing an alternate phrase above the line without crossing out the original. When he assembled the text as a bound manuscript, rather than rewrite it to cover the gaps in his knowledge—which he might have done had he privileged the physical appearance of completeness above obtaining a full natural history—he left the text incomplete and continued to work on it. When Aubrey sent the manuscript to readers, the remaining blanks spaces functioned as invitations to them to collaborate with him by filling in the gaps, invitations that they eagerly accepted.

The Naturall Historie was very much a working draft. Its final form was produced through accretion and collection over a lifetime, and it entered the archive still unfinished. There is underlying order to the manuscript—title pages, a dedicatory letter, a table of contents, chapter headings, topical entries within chapters, ruled margins—but it has been overlaid by insertions, deletions, and annotations that sometimes threaten to overwhelm that order. Aubrey made some attempts to organize the manuscript along the lines of a printed book, and yet the book kept escaping those bounds.

To a modern eye trained in the regularities of the printed page, the untidiness of Aubrey's work can seem a deficit, a barrier to digesting the information contained therein. Yet for Aubrey and his readers, it was a productive force, key to the text's function as a repository of observations and facts about nature, arts, and antiquities. Within its basic chapter structure, which laid out the categories according to which information was collected and organized, its messiness and openness to revision reflected the fact that it was an ever-growing, living collection of natural knowledge. Notably, Aubrey did not generate a clean copy of the text to share with readers, as he had done for the Royal Society. This decision, like his decision not to print the text, may have been at least partially conditioned by exigencies of time and money. However, as we shall see below, in adding their own stores of facts and observations to the text, Aubrey's readers recognized the working draft's productive, messy open-endedness. Rather than protesting against the text's irregularity and failure to conform to "print standards," they contributed to the project on its own terms.

The Social Text: Building a Community of Readers Around *The Naturall Historie*

The tumultuary stitching up of *The Naturall Historie* seems to have marked a turning point for Aubrey. After assembling his notes into a book, he seems no longer to have thought of it in preprint terms but decided instead to exploit the affordances of the manuscript medium. It was at this time that he began sending *The Naturall Historie* out for readers' perusal and annotation. In this section I trace the manuscript's travels in the early 1690s, considering how readers responded to and participated in the text. Readers' marks reveal a shared understanding of the manuscript text as a repository of information about nature and antiquities. In their annotations readers largely transmitted local knowledge they had gained through long experience, indicating that they saw county natural histories not as ends in themselves but as foundations for broader comparative studies of nature, agriculture, and topography, in which localized studies were integrated into national and even international contexts.

Circulating *The Naturall Historie* in order to obtain annotations and comments from readers was, for Aubrey, a step in securing his papers' survival after his death. Readers' commentaries, in the form of their annotations as well as letters that Aubrey inserted, gave the text a history of readership. In the early 1690s he sent the manuscript to Ray, Evelyn, Tanner, and Gale, each of whom annotated it. These were not the first people to read *The Naturall Historie* (Andrew Paschall had read it in 1685), but they were the first to annotate it, and Aubrey sent it to them in quick succession, as part of a broader, deliberate program to engage particular readers and obtain their comments on his works.[78] The Bodleian *Naturall Historie* manuscript was one of several that Aubrey shared around this time. He also circulated *Monumenta Britannica, The Idea of Education*, and *Adversaria Physica* at about the same time. These activities coincided with his growing awareness that he was "not very young, & a mortall man."[79] As he approached death, Aubrey felt a need to create a historical legacy for himself. In the late 1680s he began work on preparing his papers for their final resting places, the libraries of the Ashmolean Museum and the Royal Society. This project occupied him during the last ten or so years of his life. For Aubrey, getting and preserving evidence of readers and their favorable reactions to the text were ways of demonstrating to history that he and his achievements were valued by the natural history and antiquarian community he had spent much of his life struggling to serve.

It was also about this time that the Royal Society requested a fair copy of the manuscript, which was made and deposited in the society's library before Aubrey shared the working draft with Ray, Evelyn, Tanner, and Gale.[80] This further helped to mitigate the possibility that the text would be lost to posterity. The society paid the cost of the transcriptions (seven pounds).[81] Aubrey was gratified and surprised by the society's attention to him; he "did not expect so great honour from them."[82] From the Royal Society's perspective, sponsoring a transcription meant getting a text on the cheap, as funding a printed edition of a work required a much higher outlay.

Aubrey gave the fair copy the title *Memoires of Naturall Remarques in the County of Wilts.* (See Figure 3.) With the word "Memoires," which conveys something like "memorandums," this title suggests a more modest, and realistic, assessment of what the text actually was: a collection of notes rather than a full-fledged treatise. He also cleaned the text up considerably, as one

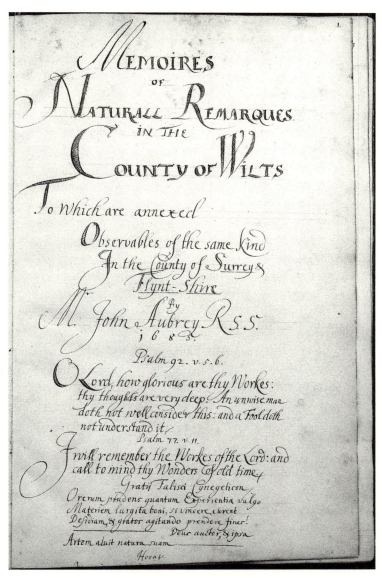

Figure 3. John Aubrey, *Memoires of Naturall Remarques in the County of Wilts*, RS MS 92, title page. Reproduced by permission of the Royal Society. This is the fair copy of *The Naturall History of Wiltshire* made at the request of the Royal Society in 1691. Aubrey retained 1685 as a "publication date" for this manuscript, a choice that highlights the identity of the working draft and the fair copy as an edition and confirms the mid-1680s as the point at which Aubrey's notes on Wiltshire stabilized into a relatively fixed text. Note also the quotations from Psalms and *Cynegeticon*, a poem on hunting composed by the Latin poet Gratius, a contemporary of Ovid. In the translation by Aubrey's friend (and annotator) Christopher Wase, published in 1654, the first excerpt reads, "O what great gifts doth wise experience throw / On the rude world, would they but sloth forgoe, / And reach their wishes with industrious hands!" (sig. B5 + 5v); and the second reads, "God first descry'd / The cure, which constant nature doth provide" (sig. B5 + 6v).

would when producing a fair copy for a printer, though he retained 1685 as a "publication date" on the title page. For the most part, the Royal Society copy lacks the inserts, botanical samples, and pastedowns scattered throughout the working draft. There are many fewer blank spaces, crossings-out, and deletions, and alternative wordings are almost entirely absent as well.

There are marginal notes in the Royal Society's fair copy, but they are almost exclusively notes written for the reader—such as apposite literary references—rather than notes and queries written by Aubrey to himself or notes written by readers. (The exceptions, discussed in Chapter 6, are marginal notes written by readers who encountered the text in the Royal Society Library in the eighteenth century.) Once the fair copy was in the library, Aubrey seems to have regarded it as finished. Though he updated the fair copy to reflect some of the additions later made to the working draft, he did not copy in his readers' marginalia.[83] In a sense, Aubrey "published" the text by depositing the fair copy in the Royal Society Library, where it was available to readers in a fixed version that closely resembled how it might have looked had it been printed.

Aubrey's continued pursuit of the circulation and preservation of the working draft, even once the fair copy was secure in the Royal Society Library, suggests the value he placed in his raw materials and in his friends' commentaries on them, as well as the incommensurability of the working draft and the fair copy. Moreover, that Aubrey's commentators invested their time and energy in the project suggests that they valued it as a contribution to topographical knowledge as well. Aubrey sent the entire manuscript to the botanist John Ray in the fall of 1691. Ray annotated it and returned it to Aubrey by the end of the year. This was the occasion on which both Ray and Aubrey feared it had fallen off the back of the cart on its way back to London and been lost forever. Thomas Gale, master of St. Paul's School in London, probably read the manuscript next.[84] Gale was one of Aubrey's close friends; in 1693 Aubrey often received his London mail at Gale's house. The manuscript next passed to the diarist and virtuoso John Evelyn, most likely in the spring or summer of 1692.[85] Ultimately, in the mid-1690s, *The Naturall Historie* wended its way to Oxford with Aubrey's other books and papers, and yet it did not come to rest. Once in Oxford, as happened with the other manuscripts Aubrey sent to the Ashmolean, it was read by various scholars, fellows, and students. Thomas Tanner, Aubrey's "Ingeniouse and publique spirited young Wiltshire man," was one such reader.[86]

Aubrey carefully selected the readers to annotate the manuscript. Not every reader wrote in its pages, and evidence survives that readers who did leave annotations were explicitly invited to do so. Andrew Paschall, who read the manuscript in 1685, did not leave marginal comments. In the chapter on hawks and hawking, Aubrey set himself a reminder to ask his friend James Long to "write marginal notes" in that chapter "for he understands it as well as any Gent. in this Nation!" [87] In the end Aubrey transcribed into the text a note that Long had written about hawking, but he did not get him to annotate the text.[88] Such comments reveal that Aubrey painstakingly curated his manuscript as a repository of knowledge, collecting natural historical and antiquarian observations, and the contributions of particular readers, much as an early modern virtuoso might place human and natural objects in a cabinet of curiosities. These objects were significant not only for their beauty and curiosity. Because many were gifts, they also bore social meanings, representing the relationships between givers and receivers. Aubrey's readers' contributions had a similar dual function. He chose particular readers for their expertise, even desiring to invite them to annotate specific chapters in which their knowledge was greatest. But controlling access to the manuscript was only partly about controlling the quality of information that ended up in it. He also selected his readers and preserved their annotations as loving memorials of his friendships (lifelong in some cases) and conversations with them. One might compare *The Naturall Historie*, as annotated by its readers, to the popular humanist genre of the *album amicorum*, or friendship album. Friends wrote poetry, drew pictures, and otherwise decorated pages in each other's albums.[89] The entries in a friendship album—and the marginal comments in *The Naturall Historie*—testified to its owner's and author's relationships within the community of the learned.

Aubrey's attention to preserving his readers' notes further indicates that he valued them both as contributions to his intellectual project and as memorials to his relationships with their authors. Aubrey marked some of the marginal notes with their authors' initials; he was particularly careful to preserve and identify Evelyn's comments. Before depositing the manuscript at the Ashmolean, he traced over with a pen each of Evelyn's penciled comments. He announced this on the verso of the book's first title page: "Note, that the Annotations to which are prefixed this marke [JE] were writt by my worthy Friend John Evelyn Esq R.S.S. 'Twas pitty, he wrote them in black lead: so, that I was faine to runne them all over againe with Inke. I thinke not more than two words are obliterated"[90] (see Figure 2 above).

Evelyn generally used pencil to annotate books and write first drafts of commonplace notes, transcribing (or possibly retracing) these notes in pen once he was confident that he wanted to preserve them. Evelyn's standard method can be extracted from advice he gave his grandson and heir on how to dispose of his (the elder Evelyn's) loose papers, notes, and half-finished and finished treatises. Evelyn lamented that among his papers were "innumerable Insignificant Collections & Atempts, desultory & undigested, cast into no method some hundred of Authors marked with my blak-lead Crayon, also I intended to have transcribed into Adversaria; But had never leisure{.} In short—most if not all, mere Embrios, or Trifles, the marks of Time Indiscreetly lost, & fit onely to be abolished, and {surely?} not seriously Repented of."[91] In writing marginal notes in pencil in *The Naturall Historie*, Evelyn may have been absent-mindedly following his customary practice. He may also have been leaving to Aubrey the decision as to whether his remarks were worth permanent inclusion in the manuscript.

Perhaps Evelyn wrote his notes in pencil because he was also using the pencil to prepare *The Naturall Historie* for commonplacing. Each of the passages that Evelyn eventually transferred to his commonplace book is marked in the margin of *The Naturall Historie* with a small pencil slash or cross. Many passages that were not transferred to the commonplace book are also marked in this way, suggesting that Evelyn read through the text once and marked passages he might want to copy, and then culled from among those on a second pass through the text, copying them into his notes. One wonders why Evelyn left these pencil marks in the text, rather than erasing them, and what Aubrey thought of them, if he noticed, but it is difficult to say.

In tracing over the pencil annotations in pen—and in marking that he had done so on the reverse of the title page of his book—Aubrey reaffirmed his commitment to their inclusion in his book. Aubrey could have erased the annotations entirely or, if he valued the information but not Evelyn's presence in the book, recopied them in his own hand and then erased them. By labeling them and making them permanent, he signaled that the annotations were welcome additions and that he approved, as author, of the inclusion of Evelyn's voice in his book. That this was an actively made, well-considered choice is further emphasized by one of the cases in which Aubrey did not trace an entire annotation of Evelyn's. In response to a passage in which Aubrey discussed the relationship between professional occupation and religious fanaticism (Aubrey said that anchor-smiths were less likely to be fanatics because their work tired them out), Evelyn wrote, "Yet we have one in

Deptford an Extraordinary Rash Anabaptist" (Deptford, where Evelyn lived, was also the site of one of the royal dockyards). Aubrey copied over every word except "Rash," which may be clearly, though faintly, read in pencil.[92] Perhaps Aubrey sympathized with extraordinary Anabaptists? Regardless, in giving Evelyn a place on a title page, Aubrey elevated him above the other contributors and granted him an authorial status comparable to his own. In preserving and labeling the annotations, Aubrey indicated a particular stance toward history: the annotations were not only for his own personal use but should be just as accessible to future readers as the text he had written.[93] Aubrey's efforts to preserve Evelyn's annotations indicated his wish that the author of *Sylva*, of all the annotators, be clearly recognized by future readers as his "worthy friend."

Readers Writing in Books: Annotation as Collaborative Writing

The annotations that Aubrey's readers added to *The Naturall Historie* illustrate the ways in which any particular national topography—the landscape as a "topographical object" demarcated by political boundaries—reflected the correspondence from which it emerged. Their notes pushed *The Naturall Historie* further toward being a comparative, county-by-county study of natural history, arts, and antiquities in England and beyond. The readers' vision was notably English and continental, rather than British (in contrast to Aubrey's). They offered up descriptions of flora, fauna, husbandry, and human arts and inventions in many places, including Cambridgeshire, Lincolnshire, Essex, Yorkshire, Somerset, Surrey, Deptford, Paris, the Alps, and Italy. Their own experiences, gained through residence and travel in these places, were the primary sources of the comments, but they also drew upon their reading, conversation, and correspondence. Aubrey's readers all assumed that the thing to do with a local natural history was to augment it by adding to it the same kinds of information from other locales, to generate something somewhat more universal in scope. Just how universal it became, though, depended on readers' particular interests and experiences. If Aubrey had chosen the Welshman Edward Lhuyd and the Scottish James Garden as annotators, he likely would have had a wealth of notes relating comparative facts and anecdotes from Wales and Scotland. The boundaries of the "body and book" of nature were set by the correspondents involved in a particular project. In this case, though Aubrey encompassed Scotland and Wales within his notion of the "Nation," his readers populated the margins with information of English and continental, rather than British, origins.

Much of what Aubrey's readers wrote does not seem to have reflected specialist natural knowledge; rather they offered the sort of knowledge about nature that was spread broadly across social classes in Britain, at least in the country, if for no other reason than most people needed to farm, forage, fish, trap and shoot birds, and raise domestic animals (or employ others to do so for them) in order to eat.[94] Beyond these commonalities, each annotator had a slightly different focus. Ray, of all the commentators, tended to offer comments that reflected a more general or systematic perspective. Evelyn kept his annotations pointed and particular. He drew the most extensively on reading, conversation, and correspondence, in addition to personal experience, as warrants for his comments. Gale supplemented Aubrey's text with supporting evidence from other counties. Tanner, the only reader who had lived for any extended period of time in Wiltshire, was the only one to describe things and people in that county.

In general the readers supplemented Aubrey's text with more information, rather than venturing to correct it. This tendency reflected a general sympathy with the Baconian ideals inspiring Aubrey's project: the goal of *The Naturall Historie* was to pile up information that might serve later naturalists. It also suggested that the readers understood that they, for the most part, had no stock of personal knowledge upon which to base corrections of Aubrey; therefore they could add to the book but not criticize it. The exceptions in this case proved the rule: Ray, who freely contradicted Aubrey, and Tanner, who occasionally stepped in to make adjustments on the finer points of Wiltshire topography, did possess a solid foundation upon which to base amendments and corrections.

Judging by their comments, all of Aubrey's readers were much more interested in natural history than social, cultural, and economic history, which was the primary focus of the second volume. Topics in the second volume included histories of artists and learned men given pensions by the Earls of Pembroke, noted gardens, nonagricultural trades, and strange accidents, such as multiple births and deaths by fright, that had befallen men and women living in Wiltshire. This volume was much more sparsely annotated than the first. Only Evelyn and Gale left any comments in it, and these were few and far between. Gale's one comment had an agricultural bent, making it more of a piece with natural history than social or cultural history, as Aubrey and his readers would have understood those terms.[95] Tanner may not have read the second volume, and Ray at least had it in his possession, though he left no comments in it.[96]

Ray left the most annotations in the text. Unlike the other readers, his comments were not rooted only in the particular experience of particular places; they reflected a broader, more generalized knowledge of nature (see Figure 4 below for an example). He frequently supplied information where Aubrey had left blank spaces and corrected Aubrey's misidentifications of plant species. He responded tetchily to Aubrey's enthusiasm for modish words, philosophical speculation, and peculiar local customs. On several occasions, in his conviction that some species did not grow in England, he flatly contradicted sightings of particular plants.[97] Most of his comments focused on the correct identification of plants; the difficulties he faced in this respect hint at one of the very real barriers facing the construction of a systematic account of British natural history in the seventeenth century. Given the variations in local dialects, there were no one-to-one links between names and species of plants. Ray, who helped develop and attempted to use the "universal character," an ideal rational language whose purpose was to restore the natural links between names and things, was particularly concerned with determining the Latin names of plants for which Aubrey provided only colloquial names.[98]

In identifying plants by their Latin names, Ray attempted to restore the true relationship between nature and language, ensuring that there was one name for each kind of plant. For example, he corrected Aubrey's spelling of the Latin names of plants, lest a difference in spelling lead to a misidentification.[99] More frequently, however, Aubrey used colloquial plant names. Yet these names could not be trusted for the purpose of plant identification, as they varied from place to place. For example, Aubrey wondered if a plant called "naked boys," the juice of which was said to kill lice in children's hair, was a variety of wild saffron. Ray could clarify Aubrey's question only so far: "'Naked boys' is I suppose Meadow Saffron or Colchicum—for I do not remember ever to have seene any <other> sort of Saffron growing wild in England." Ray could only suppose in this case because the charming colloquiality of the name "naked boys" precluded any certainty.[100] Aubrey's reliance on colloquial names caused genuine difficulty for Ray. In response to Aubrey's list of plants growing around St. Mary's Priory, for example, Ray wrote, "Calver-keys, Haresparseley, Mayden honesty are Countrey names unknown to me."[101]

Ray's critical comments, in devaluing local expertise, ran counter to the general rule in topographical studies that individuals were presumed to be authorities on their localities. In addition to his corrections of Aubrey's plant misidentifications, Ray responded severely to Aubrey's reports of what he regarded as superstitions. When Aubrey noted that "in South Wiltshire they observe, that if dropps doe hang on the Hedges on Candlemas day {2 February}: it will be a good Pease yeare," Ray responded in the margin that "this is a generall Observation: we have it in Essex. I reject as superstitious all prognosticks from the weather on particular days."[102] In a letter giving more general comments on *The Naturall Historie*, Ray's primary substantial criticism was that Aubrey was "a little too inclinable to credit strange relations."[103] This was a serious (and possibly insulting) criticism, as indicated by the fact that Ray prefaced his words with a request to Aubrey to give him leave to speak freely. Concerns for politeness did not prevent Ray from offering the criticism, however. Ray was clear about what belonged in a proper natural history and what did not.

The liberties he took were rooted in his more systematic knowledge of British natural history, gained through the years he had spent observing and cataloging British fish, birds, and insects. The breadth of his knowledge of British natural history led him to feel freer than other readers to criticize and correct Aubrey's text: Ray's more systematic knowledge overrode Aubrey's local knowledge. Aubrey, and many of his contemporaries, sought a balance between the local and the national, in which local was contextualized in the national but not subsumed by it. In contrast, Ray practiced a brand of natural history in which broader knowledge of national flora and fauna gave one the license to suppress, reframe, and deny local knowledge: recall Ray's flat denial that Aubrey had seen certain plants he claimed to have seen. The presumption that knowledge of nature on a national or even universal scale overrode local knowledge, which became more characteristic of natural history and biology in the eighteenth and nineteenth centuries, threatened to upset the delicate balance between local and national that defined the seventeenth-century topographical vision of Britain.

John Evelyn's comments, in reflecting his interests and expertise as a landowner, a gardener, and a traveler, did the most to destabilize *The Naturall Historie*'s presentation of Britain as a topographical object. He related stories and facts drawn from his travels in Europe, his reading in natural philosophy and natural history, conversations and correspondence with others, and his experience as a gardener and a landowner in Surrey and at Deptford. Evelyn made fewer comments than Ray, but those he did make tended to supplement Aubrey's text instead of correct it. He did not copyedit, nor did he fill in blanks in Aubrey's sentences. In comments based on his experiences at Deptford and Surrey (eight of his thirty comments), Evelyn offered up vignettes of country life. In chapter 10, "Beasts," Aubrey commented, "We have no Wild Boares in England, yet it may be the right that ~~that~~ heretofore we had, and did not thinke it convenient to preserve that Game."[104] Evelyn wrote in the nearby margin, "There were wild Boares in a forest in Essex formerly. I sent a Portugal Boar & sow to Wotton in Surry which greatly increas'd, but they digged the earth so up & did such spoyle {the} County would not indure it. but they made incomparable Bacon."[105] (See Figure 6 below.) Elsewhere, Aubrey described a particular kind of "soft white stone, betwixt chalk and freestone" that was found at a quarry at Compton Basses and was notable for its fire-resistant properties. In the margin Evelyn wrote about a similar kind of stone—relatively soft, yet wear- and fire-resistant—found "in Galton rear Rygate in Surrey" (Rygate was about ten miles east of the Evelyn family home in Wotton).[106] Other examples included mention of a spring on his estate in Deptford and the excavation of his family's mausoleum at his Surrey estate.[107]

Evelyn's annotations, grounded in his experience of country life, highlighted one of the central features of the county natural history: works in the genre were often about what happened and what was found on the country estates of the gentry and the nobility. Aubrey began taking natural history notes as a young man as he traveled back and forth between his two estates (maternal and paternal) in Wiltshire. The chapters of *The Naturall Historie* were peppered with letters from Sir James Long, Aubrey's friend and the proprietor of the estate of Draycot-Cerne, as well as notes drawn from their conversations. In *The natural history of Oxford-shire*, Robert Plot dedicated each table to a different Oxfordshire noble (both men and ladies). In ten of sixteen plates, patrons sponsored depictions of specimens, antiquities, and engineering works (such as fancy water fountains) found or constructed on their land.[108] In *The natural history of Stafford-shire* (1686), Plot dispensed with engravings of natural objects and simply depicted the estates of the noble and gentle patrons who paid for the plates and the publication of the edition. Natural history's audience was made up of those who owned land in that area.

Evelyn's comments reflected not only life on his estates but also his experiences in Europe, where he traveled in the 1640s–1650s; his own reading; and conversation and correspondence with others. Five of his thirty comments were drawn from his travels. Sometimes he combined in the same comment knowledge gained from travel and from books (eight comments pointed to books; two of these overlapped with the travel comments). For example, when Evelyn was in Paris, there was "an Artificial phonocamptic in the Garden of Thuilleries a scheme whereof I took, & such may be made in any flat plaine, & reflects the voice very perfectly. The Ladys used to sing at a certain place & distance from it." (A "phonocamptic" is a surface or apparatus designed to reflect sound and produce pleasing echoes.) He further directed Aubrey to Kircher's *Musurgia*, which contained "several diagrams etc" of the phonocamptic.[109] In a comment that may have been drawn from either correspondence or conversation, Evelyn reported the Countess of Clarendon's advice for turning "the harshest waters . . . phlegmatic" (soak fir shavings in them).[110] Another comment reflected both conversation and travel. Opposite the opening page of the chapter in which Aubrey related his theory of the geological formation of the earth, Evelyn wrote, "Mr <Edmund> Waller as we were traveling over the Alps fancied that at the Creation, these mountains were the Sweepings & Rubbish of the World heap'd-up together."[111]

Thomas Gale sourced his comments from local, personal experience and a wider knowledge of British natural history and topography. Gale had experience in Yorkshire and Cambridgeshire, in particular. He popped into the text now and then with nifty little details (see Figure 5 below for an example). Many of his comments can easily be identified by his name or initials, which were probably written in by Aubrey.[112] He confirmed Aubrey's observation that hazel trees were a "signature of Freestone, as well as Mineralls" with a notice of a quarry in Cambridgeshire "near Hazeling field."[113] He filled in two of the blanks in Aubrey's county-by-county list of local breeds of cows with descriptions of the cows of Lincolnshire and Yorkshire. The cows of Yorkshire were "black large headed. They will not bear a pyed calf." In Lincolnshire cows were "red, very large, long legged," and had "bad hornes."[114] Straying even farther from Yorkshire and Cambridgeshire, Gale worked from common prejudice in defining "Cornish" as "chuff, rough, abrupt, clownish, rustic."[115] (The words were all roughly synonyms for each other.) He also backed up one comment with a reference to the historical record, noting that he had checked a ledger book to clarify the history of a marl pit west of Salisbury.[116] (Marl, a chalky, white, mineral-rich earth, was used to enrich soil for farming.) Here, a record book stood in for local experience.

Of Aubrey's four contemporary annotators, Tanner alone focused primarily on natural history and antiquities in Wiltshire, the ostensible topic of the book. This very fact illustrates how important personal, local knowledge and experience were as bases for readers' annotations. Born in the village of Market-Lavington and educated in Salisbury, Tanner lived the first sixteen years of his life in Wiltshire and retained an interest in its antiquities and natural history. Although they brought to the text facts and observations based on their diverse local experiences, the other readers could not speak directly to Wiltshire particulars in the way that Tanner could. All seven of Tanner's comments referred back to that county. He marked each with a distinctive cross with a dot in each quadrant. His annotations corrected, supplemented, and added to Aubrey's text and were supported with examples that appear to have been drawn from direct observation as well as the reports of other local witnesses whom he considered credible. Although Aubrey denied that wild oats grew in Wilts, for example, Tanner could point to wild oats growing in "the West Clay of Market-Lavington field."[117]

Like Aubrey, Tanner drew on local memory as evidence. Where Aubrey asserted, based on evidence from Camden's *Britannia*, that the town of Deverill was so called because a stream or "rill" ran underground nearby, Tanner replied, "I am informed by the minister of Deverill-Longbridge and another Gentleman that lived at Maiden-Bradley {near Deverill} 30 years, that they never knew or heard of this River Deverill that runs underground."[118] Both the comment and the original text stand in the final manuscript—Aubrey did not judge between Camden's words and the minister's memory.[119] Tanner also sometimes extended Aubrey's lists of Wiltshire *naturalia* (these comments seem to have been based on personal witness). Alongside Aubrey's own entry on yew trees, he listed three other Wiltshire locations where the trees grew.[120] This comment included an additional, non-Wiltshire geographic reference: in a note about yew trees, Tanner mentioned that Leland observed "39 vast Eugh trees in the Churchyard belonging to Stratfleur Abbey in Wales" when he traveled there in the mid-sixteenth century. But this came from reading the Leland manuscripts in the Bodleian Library (volume 5, Tanner noted), not travel or personal experience.[121]

Aubrey and his readers used the margins as spaces for conversations, illustrating the collaborative possibilities of scribal exchange. Interactions occurred between readers as well as between the author and his readers. Aubrey, Ray, and Evelyn, in particular, used the margins to engage with each other. Aubrey's and Ray's marginal conversations began with the "queries" with which Aubrey littered his manuscripts. These queries, Aubrey's notes for further research, usually took the form of questions addressed to individuals with relevant expertise. Ray, having the opportunity to read the manuscript, answered queries addressed to him (as well as some that were not).[122] In one case Ray left a query for Aubrey asking him to clarify the name of a plant that he (Ray) was unable to identify precisely.[123] Evelyn and Ray commented on a yellow flowering herb that Aubrey described as having covered the ruins of London after the fire of 1666: "and on the south side of St Paul's Church, it grew as thick as could be: nay on the very top of the Tower." Ray observed that "it grows abundantly by the waysides between London & Kensington," and Evelyn further directed Aubrey to Robert Morison's *Plantarum historiae universalis Oxoniensis*, published in the 1670s and 1680s by subscription.[124] One might compare these uses of the various spaces on the written page to the early twenty-first-century digital genre of blogging. Comments sections on blogs function similarly to the margins of the page, allowing readers and writers to discuss the issues and questions raised by a writer's original post. As on the manuscript page, so on the Internet: blog readers are writers as well.

With its readers' annotations, Aubrey's *Wiltshire* was as interconnected with other counties and lands as he was with other people. Indeed, Aubrey's local natural history extended beyond county borders *because* his correspondence did: his textual vision was a product, and a reflection, of the connections between a group of people distributed across the land. This was visible in the text even before readers got their hands into it, as Aubrey himself incorporated a multitude of insights and observations explicitly drawn from correspondence and conversation, many of which touched on English, Scottish, and Welsh—rather than Wiltshire—natural history and antiquities.

If Aubrey's textual vision of Britain never quite stabilized, neither did the material text (or texts) in which it was inscribed. Aubrey's open-ended, never quite finished construction of British natural history and antiquities also reflected the media in which he worked, the loose papers on which he collected his observations and which he eventually bound together for sharing with readers. As loose papers, his *Naturall Historie* was always open to one more fact, one more addition. One more letter could always be filed with the papers or transcribed into them. This is not to employ any technological determinism, to suggest that working with papers required these particular working habits. Rather, it is to suggest that Aubrey found papers a congenial medium for his project, and the material state of his papers, and eventually his bound *Naturall Historie* mirrored—even embodied—the intellectual vision he created.

In not restricting themselves to building up information about Wiltshire and in freely annotating the text, Aubrey's readers took their cues from him, building on what he had already created, both materially and intellectually. Rather than pretend an intimate knowledge of Wiltshire, Evelyn and Gale supplemented and criticized the text based primarily on their experiences and knowledge of the places with which they were familiar, and Ray offered comments and criticisms that reflected a systematic knowledge of British natural history developed over a lifetime, one that threatened to overwhelm the more locally rooted perspectives brought by Aubrey and his many contributors. The manuscript natural history became a collaborative, comparative project, one that ranged more widely than the particular expertise of any one author or commentator could have allowed. In this way Aubrey pursued the project that he had once hoped Plot would undertake: an encyclopedic natural history of every British county.[125] By responding in the way they did, his readers indicated that they shared his conviction that the ultimate goal of the county natural history was not simply to pile up information about individual counties but to compare and synthesize that information across counties.

The Downside of Collaborative Writing: Fear of Plagiarism

If scribal texts offered sites for productive collaboration, they also threatened its opposite. Fears of misuse and plagiarism—what Aubrey called the "wrong" of "putting out anothers Labours under your own name"— bedeviled early modern naturalists.[126] They struggled to identify what constituted plagiarism and to seek redress when they perceived that their texts were misused, especially as those texts transitioned from script to print. Aubrey reserved his harshest words for those who interfered with an author's text and the public credit that authors were due. John Fell, bishop of Oxford and the superintendent of the university press, became a target of his ire for altering the text of Wood's *History and Antiquities of the University of Oxford* before its publication.[127] In a 1679 letter to Wood, he wrote, "I say could one have thought that this good exemplar {'Practiser' above 'exemplar'} of Piety, & walking Common prayer–booke, could have made such a breach in the Moralls <& Justice>? & to have such a pruritus (or what worse shall I call it) in the Tyranny of the Presse, & in scratching out authors {'authors' above something scratched out} due prayses, and expunging & interposing? that have made the Universitys worse thought of than ever they were before? Who can pardon such a dry bone? A stalking, consecrated engine of Hypocrisy."[128] Aubrey was quick to attack Fell, who he felt had wronged his friends. He strongly contrasted Fell's appearance of piety—the bishop was supposed to be a "walking Common prayer-booke"—with the dark moral villainy of "scratching out authors due prayses," for which he called Fell a "pruritus," which meant an annoying itching of the skin, particularly in the nether parts.

Aubrey was just as quick to attack when he felt his own work was threatened. His suspicions even landed on some whom he valued as readers and collaborators. In the winter of 1692, a few months after Ray had read *The Naturall Historie*, he published *Miscellaneous discourses concerning the dissolution and changes of the world*. The book discussed the age and formation of the earth, a subject treated in chapter 8 of *The Naturall Historie*, "An Hypothesis of the terraqueous globe." According to Aubrey, this chapter, which he labeled a "digression," was an exposition of ideas first presented by Robert Hooke in the early 1660s. While Aubrey awarded Hooke the credit for the "Hypothesis," Aubrey was the author of the text, a patchwork assemblage of excerpts from Ovid's *Metamorphosis*, pamphlets and letters relating news of earthquakes around the globe, scriptural texts, and theorizing about the origin of hot springs and formed stones.[129] In the "Hypothesis," Aubrey attributed to Hooke only the basic idea that the world is ancient and that the "ruins" that tell its history are visible all around; according to Aubrey, Hooke first described the idea at a lecture given to the Royal Society "in 1663, or 1664."[130] In the "Hypothesis," Aubrey tacked together the data that he believed supported this idea. The digression is short, only twenty pages or so, and is less a coherent treatise and more a collection of evidence Aubrey thought relevant to the question of the age and formation of the world.

Ray's *Miscellaneous discourses*, on the other hand, was a lengthy treatise on the dissolution of the world that drew heavily on scripture as a framework for interpreting the earth's geological history and future. Nevertheless, in a letter to Wood, Aubrey complained,

> Your advice to me was prophetique, *viz* not to lend my MSS. You remember Mr J. Ray sent me a very kind letter concerning my *Naturall history of Wilts:* only he misliked my Digression, which is Mr Hooke's Hypothesis of the Terraquious Globe whom I name with respect. Mr Ray would have me (in the letter) leave it out. And now lately is come forth a booke of his in 8vo {*Miscellaneous discourses*}

which all Mr Hooke's hypothesis in my letter is published without
any mention of Mr Hooke or my booke. Mr Hooke is much troubled about it. 'Tis a right Presbyterian trick.[131]

Long sensitive to writers who consulted his manuscripts only to slight him
in print, Aubrey suspected that someone who had recently read his work on
the history of the earth and then published his own book on it must have
stolen from his manuscript.

In fact, throughout the text Ray liberally sourced his work, not just
crediting other printed books but also noting when an insight, incident, or
fact came to him through his correspondence, even to the point of reprinting
whole letters.[132] Nowhere did *Miscellaneous discourses* replicate the exact
words or sense of Aubrey's digression.[133] Ray referred to Robert Hooke's
theories regarding the origins of fossils with praise, acclaiming him, "Hook,
whom, for his learning and deep Insight into the Mysteries of Nature, I
deservedly honour."[134] While Ray may have read "An Hypothesis of the
terraqueous globe" before composing certain parts of his own book, he does
not seem to have copied it or withheld credit. One might compare the well-
known antagonisms between Hooke and Newton, particularly the episode in
which Hooke demanded that Newton publicly award Hooke credit for his
contributions to the discovery and working-out of the inverse-square law of
gravitational force in the *Principia*.[135] In that case Aubrey wrote to Wood on
Hooke's behalf, defending Hooke's prior claim to the discovery of the law;
perhaps Hooke pushed him to write here as well.[136]

The important thing in this episode is not plagiarism itself but the fear
of plagiarism. Ray attempted to manage the fear his correspondents might
feel, and maintain good relations with them, by crediting them when he used
the information they sent him. Yet upon the publication of *Miscellaneous
discourses*, Aubrey immediately (and angrily) concluded that Ray had misap-
propriated *The Naturall Historie*—suspicion and fear were at the forefront of
his thoughts. Despite his fears, however, Aubrey continued to share material
with Ray. In the summer of 1692 he traveled to visit Ray at his home in Essex
and loaned him the manuscript of his *Adversaria physica*.[137] As Aubrey could
not afford to fund his own natural historical investigations or publications,
his access to and participation in natural history and antiquarian circles
depended on his willingness to share information with others. The marginal
nature of his own position, as well as a closer perusal of *Miscellaneous discourses,* may have encouraged him quietly to drop his accusations against Ray.

In this regard it is telling that Aubrey reserved his attacks on both Fell and Ray for letters to Wood, rather than expressing them directly or publicly. He vented his anger and frustration privately instead of risking a confrontation with those he suspected of wrongdoing. Ray's expertise, visibility, and publishing record in natural history; their cordial relationship; and his approval of *The Naturall Historie* were markers of status and prestige not to be lightly tossed aside.[138] Perhaps in writing to Wood, Aubrey was doing a favor for Hooke and never meant it to affect his relationship with Ray. On the other hand, in writing to a biographer, he did get the accusation into the historical record.

Ray took steps to secure papers as a collaborative technology and was generally Aubrey's close and trusted friend. Yet Aubrey was still unable to dismiss entirely his fears that Ray would misappropriate his writings. This fear was the flip side of the very virtues that naturalists tapped into when they shared texts scribally. Limited scribal readerships could foster productive collaborations and texts that memorialized them. Manuscript exchange also allowed Aubrey to share his work without having to assemble the capital to pay for print publication. But by forgoing the public record that print offered, he exposed his work to potential misuse. For naturalists such as Aubrey, with limited financial means and a sometimes marginal social position, scribal exchange could be a particularly attractive and particularly dangerous mode of communication.

Commonplacing and Copying: John Evelyn's Appropriation of *The Naturall Historie*

As with print, knowledge shared in scribal copies was never static. Readers augmented, transformed, and otherwise appropriated what they read within their own contexts and for their own uses.[139] No one reader used a book in the same way as another. Appropriating a text was both an intellectual and a material process. As we have seen with *The Naturall Historie*, readers could be invited into a scribal text and their appropriations could transform the text itself. But the process did not necessarily stop there, as readers made copies of texts and portions of them for their own stocks of notes. This process of appropriation could appear in the historical record when it led to authorially unauthorized publication of a work, whether in print or scribally—what Harold Love has termed "user publication."[140] The first edition of Thomas Browne's *Religio medici*, for example, was an unauthorized printing based on a scribal (and, according to Browne, imperfect) copy of the text.[141]

Authors tended to cast such appropriations as misappropriations. But once an author released a copy of a text to readers, it was impossible to prevent the reuse and recontextualization of one's writing. Yet the reader's appropriation of the text was central to the production of new knowledge through collaboration (as even a jealous author such as Aubrey seems to have acknowledged by inviting readers to annotate the text). As Aubrey keenly recognized, a writer who never shared anything, and thus never opened his texts up to appropriation, was a writer who died destined to be forgotten by history.

The transformations that knowledge could undergo as it passed from collaborator to collaborator are illustrated by Evelyn's use of *The Naturall Historie*. When Evelyn read the manuscript, in addition to annotating it he extracted thirteen pages of closely written notes from it, apparently without Aubrey's knowledge.[142] These thirteen pages included eighty-seven passages extracted from *The Naturall Historie*. Evelyn's commonplace notes, though ostensibly transcriptions from *The Naturall Historie*, actually diverge from that text in both subtle and overt ways. These changes range from relatively minor scribal slips, such as the substitution of one synonym for another, to more extensive alterations, including interpolations of entire paragraphs not present in the original.[143]

The ways in which Evelyn altered and added to Aubrey's text, both in his own notes and in the original manuscript, illustrate the productive incompleteness of scribal texts. For example, as he transcribed from *The Naturall Historie,* Evelyn interpolated relevant information based on his own experiences. When Evelyn copied Aubrey's description of some experiments with honeybees undertaken by a Wiltshire country parson, he added an account of Italian beekeepers who kept their hives on boats. "They set stocks of Bees on benches in Boates," Evelyn wrote in his notebook, "which lie at Anchor neere the shore, & when the Bees have ben some time gathering, they move the boate to a fresh station, & so row from place to place, & as they observe the Vessel to sinke, guesse at the fittest season to take the Hony."[144] Evelyn added a similar though not identical version of this anecdote to *The Naturall Historie*. He wrote it in next to Aubrey's original description of the honeybee experiments, which involved weighing the bees several times a day to determine how much nectar they collected.[145] The two naturalists profited equally from this trade of facts: both gained a new nugget of information that helped them build a more complete understanding of a natural phenomenon, in this case the production of honey. The medium of manuscript, ever expandable and never finalized, facilitated the extensive collaboration required by the Baconian approach to natural history.

Printed texts were also extended collaboratively through annotation. Annotations were shared between authors and readers as well as between readers. In 1736 William Oldys, for example, produced custom copies of his biography of Sir Walter Raleigh, adding seven handwritten pages filled with information compiled after the book went to press. He sent these copies to friends to thank them for their assistance in sharing materials that went into the biography and inspire them to continue in helping him to correct and augment it.[146] Ann Blair, Owen Gingerich, and H. J. Jackson have observed cases in which readers shared marginal notes with other readers, but these activities seem to have been more directed toward aiding the reading of others, rather than collaborating with a book's original author.[147]

As he took notes, Evelyn subtracted sources and citations. Although Aubrey carefully noted when, where, and from whom he learned information, Evelyn removed these sources as he transcribed. Aubrey identified not just fellow gentlemen and naturalists but also farmers, laborers, clergy, and women, including his own mother, as sources of particular facts. Evelyn replaced these sources with anonymous pronouns and phrases such as "a friend of mine." For example, the following is how Aubrey recorded how a group of miners discovered a way of flushing bad airs from coal mines:

> Sir Paul Neale sayd, that in the Bishoprick of Durham is a Coalery belonging to one Mr . . . . . . which by reason of the damps, that did so frequently kill the Workmen (sometimes 3, or four in a moneth) that he could make little or nothing of it. It happened one time, that the Workmen being merry with Drinke, fell to play with fire-brands, and to throw live-coales at one another, by the head of the Pitt where they usually have fires. It fortuned that a fire-brand fell in to the bottome of the Pitt; whereat there proceeded such a noise as if it had been a Gun: they, likeing the sport, threwe downe more firebrands, and then followed the like noise, for severall times, <&> at length it ceased. They went to worke after, and were free from Damps. So having by good chance found out this Experiment, they doe now, every morning, throw down some coales, and they work as securely as in any other mines.[148]

Aubrey related not only the incident, which he called an "Experiment," but also the name of the man who told him about it (Sir Paul Neale), the year in which their conversation took place (1655), and where the "experiment" occurred (Durham). Aubrey did not know the name of the man who owned the mine, but regarding that as a key piece of information, he left a blank space in his text so that he could fill it in later. When Evelyn copied the story of this discovery into his commonplace book, he retained the location of the mine but neither the source nor the date of the report.[149] Neither did he leave a blank for the name of the mine's owner. In his transcriptions Evelyn retained the information from the text while eliminating the conditions of its collection.

Such a cavalier attitude toward the names of minor country gentry might lead one to suspect that Evelyn eliminated witnesses based on criteria such as social class or prominence among naturalists. However, even eminent witnesses could be cut out by Evelyn's habit of separating stories and facts from the circumstances of their discovery. For example, in the course of describing the lackluster response that he felt often greeted those who attempted to improve and innovate in the study of nature, Aubrey described the reaction that the English physician William Harvey received when he first published his discovery of the circulation of blood: "he told me himself, upon his publishing that Booke, he fell in his practice extremely."[150] Aubrey reported Harvey's experience as if he learned of it from Harvey in a personal conversation or a letter: "he told me himself." Evelyn's version reads, "the famous Dr. Ha{r}vey (who found out the Circulations of the Blood,) was so discountenanc'd, that he soone fell mightily in his practise, upon his first brotching that Opinion."[151] Dr. Harvey's name remained—without it the story would have little meaning. But Evelyn stripped the source from the fact, and it is no longer clear where the anecdote came from.

Evelyn eliminated even Aubrey as the author of *The Naturall Historie*. Contrary to his usual practice, he did not preface the notes he took from *The Naturall Historie* with the book's title and the author's name. But Evelyn did not simply forget to include Aubrey's name at the beginning of the notes. There are several points in the text at which Evelyn could have easily mentioned Aubrey by name, and yet he chose not to. In one instance, for example, Aubrey described an unusual technique he used to measure the proportion of uplands to valleys in Wiltshire: "To find the proportion of the Downes of this County, to the Vales, I did divide Speeds mappe of Wiltshire with a paire of cizars, according to the respective Hundreds of Downes &

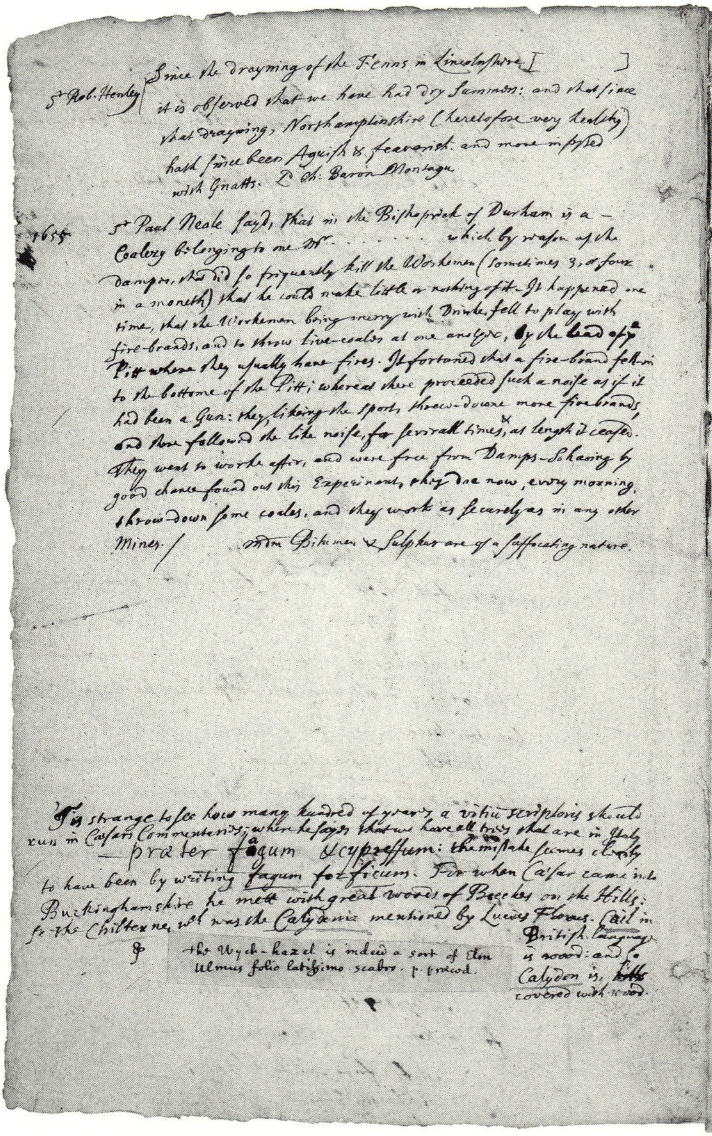
Sr Rob. Henley | Since the drayning of the Fenns in Lincolnshire [ ]
it is observed that we have had dry Summers: and that since
that drayning, Northamptonshire (heretofore very healthy)
hath since been Aguish & feaverish. and more infested
with Gnatts. Ld Ch: Baron Montague

1655 Sr Paul Neale sayd, that in the Bishoprick of Durham is a Coalery belonging to one Mr. . . . . . . which by reason of the damps, that did so frequently kill the Workemen (sometimes 3, or foure in a moneth) that he could make little or nothing of it. It happened one time, that the Workeman being merry with Drinke, fell to play with fire-brands, and to throw live-coales at one another, by the head of ye Pitt where they usually have fires. It fortuned that a fire-brand fell in to the bottome of the Pitt; whereat there proceeded such a noise as if it had been a Gun: they liking the sport, threw-downe more fire-brands, and there followed the like noise, for severall times, at length it ceased. They went to worke after, and were free from Damps—So having by good chance found out this Experiment, they doe now, every morning, throw-downe some coales. and they worke as securely as in any other Mines. / Item Bitumen & Sulphur are of a suffocating nature.

'Tis strange to see how many hundred of yeares a vitiu scriptoris should run in Caesars Commentaries; where he sayes that we have all trees that are in Italy — praeter fagum & cypressum: the mistake seemes clearly to have been by writing fagum for ficum. For when Caesar came into Buckinghamshire he mett with great woods of Beeches on the Hills: sc. the Chilterne, wch was the Calydonia mentioned by Lucius Florus. Cail in British language is wood: and Calydon is, hills covered with wood.

the Wych-hazel is indeed a sort of Elm Ulmus folio latissimo scabro. p. praecod.

Figure 4. John Aubrey, *The Naturall Historie of Wiltshire*, Bod MS Aubrey 1, f. 15v. Reproduced by permission of the Bodleian Library, Oxford. This image displays several distinctive features of the working draft of *The Naturall Historie.* First, Aubrey credited the source of information where possible—this can be seen in the anecdote that begins "Sr Paul Neale sayd"—and left spaces for information he did not currently have, as with the blank space for the name of the mine owner in the second line of the same passage. This can be contrasted with John Evelyn's practice of eliding sources, for example in his note recording the contents of this passage, which he marked with a light pencil slash visible in the left margin. This page also shows an example of John Ray's annotations, a comment on "wych-hazel" trees pasted in at the bottom of the page. This slip is marked with a small flower, which keys it to a spot on the facing page of the text (f. 16r). Aubrey used versos to add additional notes to the main text, which was recorded on the rectos.

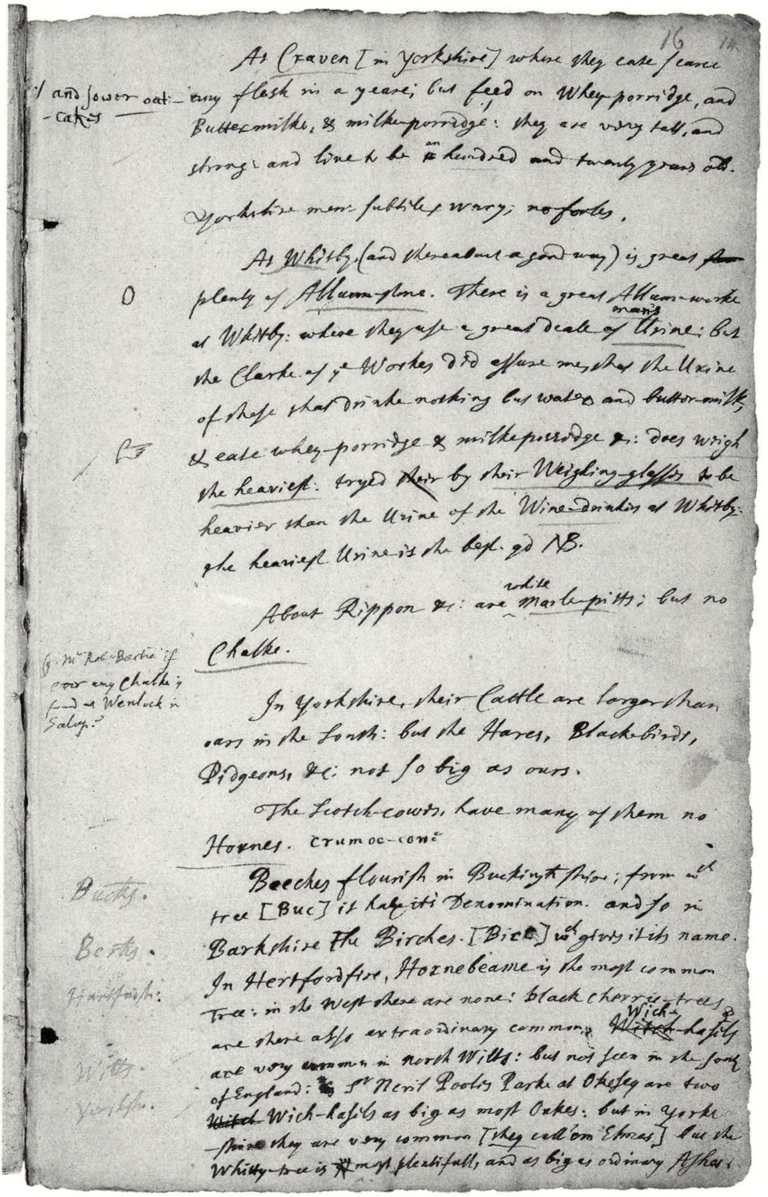

Figure 5. John Aubrey, *The Naturall Historie of Wiltshire*, Bod MS Aubrey 1, f. 16r. Reproduced by permission of the Bodleian Library, Oxford. This image shows the small flower mark, in the lower right-hand corner of the page, that links back to John Ray's comment on "wych-hazel" trees on f. 15v. There is another pencil slash of John Evelyn's, next to the manicule in the left margin. Two notes, "sower oat cakes" in the upper left-hand corner and "crumoc cow" about two-thirds of the way down, were probably contributed by Thomas Gale.

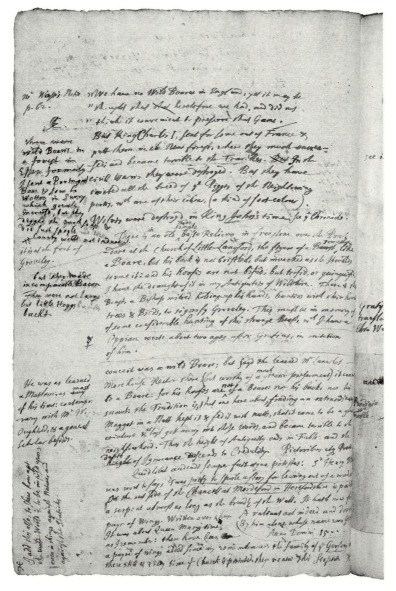

Figure 6. John Aubrey, *The Naturall Historie of Wiltshire*, Bod MS Aubrey 1, 132v. Reproduced by permission of the Bodleian Library, Oxford. On this page Aubrey preserved John Evelyn's penciled annotations by tracing over them in ink. The conversational features of the text, in which various voices engage each other, are also apparent. Aubrey, quoting some notes lent him by Christopher Wase, observed that there were no wild boars in England, though there may once have been. Evelyn, in the margins, related that there were once some in Essex. Aubrey also added antiquarian evidence in support of the idea that there were once wild boars in Britain, describing a stone relief in a church in Little Langford, Wilts, a village outside Salisbury, showing a boar.

Vales, and I weighed them in a curious balance of a Goldsmith."[152] Evelyn's copy of this passage was almost identical to the original except that Aubrey's "I" was converted to "a friend of mine" and "Wiltshire" was changed to "a County."[153] The closeness of the transcription in all other respects suggests the deliberate omission of Aubrey's name and any identifying detail.

Evelyn seems to have followed a similar, though not identical, pattern in notes taken from Aubrey's *Idea of Education of Young Gentlemen*, likely in the spring of 1692.[154] Evelyn recorded these notes on two loose sheets of scratch paper folded in half, to be filed in a bundle with his other notes on education gathered for a planned, but in the end never written, treatise on the subject.[155] Some of the material in these pages was drawn from Aubrey's *Idea*; some, possibly, was from other readings on the same subject; and some was material of Evelyn's own composition, including the start of a draft letter to Sidney Godolphin, the widower of Margaret Blagge, Evelyn's "spiritual friend," advising him on his son's education after Eton. In excerpting *Idea of Education of Young Gentleman*, Evelyn did not entirely erase Aubrey in the process of appropriating his work. He labeled his notes from the *Idea* with Aubrey's name and an abbreviated title of the work. On the outside of one of the folded sheets, Evelyn wrote "Aubery" at the top of the page and "Aubery Educatio" at the bottom of the page, each accompanied by a symbol consisting of two overlapping triangles.[156] Evelyn used these symbols and positioned them on the sheets so that it would be easy to file the notes in a bundle of related notes and retrieve them once they were filed. The label at the bottom is upside down when the paper is unfolded, implying that the paper was filed folded, and might be accessed from either direction. On the back (which is the outside when the sheet is folded) is another label: "Education / To Direct Young Scholars how to proceede in their study: / remember to add these loose sheetes to the Bundle marked {overlapping triangle symbol}."[157]

These notes on education are somewhat difficult to interpret, given that Evelyn wrote them in a small hand there are many abbreviation and crossings-out, and they were later damaged by dampness and moved around Evelyn's archive and refiled in different places at various points in their history. However, the notes that can be traced to Aubrey's *Idea* seem to show Evelyn appropriating, and recasting, his reading material roughly according to the pattern laid down in his notes on Aubrey's *Naturall Historie*. In some cases Evelyn paraphrased Aubrey's text while offering his own spin on it, writing more negatively than Aubrey, for example, of young gentlemen being taught card games, gambling, and chess. Aubrey argued that such schooling encouraged numerical literacy as well as "a <u>foresight</u> in the management of their Affaires."[158] Evelyn agreed and noted Aubrey's observation that "politicians are generally Gamesters," rendering it in his notebook as "Greate politicians are apt Gamblers."[159] However, he sounded a note of moral caution that was absent from Aubrey's discussion, writing that he was against the "love and excesse" of gaming.[160]

Although Evelyn did label the pages of notes from Aubrey's *Idea* with Aubrey's name, he followed the general pattern of eliminating sources within individual notes. Evelyn copied some of the recommended authors and books on Aubrey's reading list for law students and some references to anecdotes involving celebrated people (Queen Elizabeth and Cardinal Mazarin, chief adviser to Louis XIV and his mother, Anne, for example), but he did not attribute any of the information to particular persons. For example, in an anecdote relating Elizabeth I's habit of training up men to be ministers of state by sending them to travel abroad, he began, "'Tis said of Q. Eliz{abeth} . . ."[161] Aubrey's original opened, "I have heard my old Friend <Mr> Fabian Philips . . . say, that Queen Elizabeth did . . ."[162] As in Evelyn's notes from *The Naturall Historie,* this contrasted with Aubrey's pattern of citing individuals as sources for particular pieces of information, whether they came to him through print, manuscript, correspondence, or conversation.

In appropriating Aubrey's manuscripts, Evelyn immediately began transforming the information they contained. He selected particular details over others; he rewrote and paraphrased, sometimes retaining whole passages or sentences, sometimes retaining just an idea; and he added and interpolated, recontextualizing what he read against his own stock of information and his moral and ethical beliefs. As an author, Evelyn took notes such as these avowedly for the purpose of feeding them into his own writing projects. The process of recasting others' words into his own began with the first reading of a text: in addition to penciling annotations into *The Naturall Historie,* Evelyn lightly penciled a slash or an x next to many of the passages that he eventually commonplaced (see Figures 4 and 5 above for examples). As a reader, Evelyn was always already writing.

One possible explanation for Evelyn's lackadaisical treatment of Aubrey, especially when set against the painstaking care that Aubrey took to attribute and preserve Evelyn's notes, is that Aubrey valued their friendship much more than Evelyn did. Although Aubrey referred to Evelyn as his "worthy Friend," this designation may have contained a component of wishful thinking as well as posturing for posterity. Evelyn does not seem to have responded with the same warmth; there are no letters from Evelyn, for example, in Aubrey's carefully compiled letter books. The one letter I have found from Evelyn to Aubrey was printed in the posthumous 1723 edition of *The natural history and antiquities of the county of Surrey*. Evelyn wrote in February 1676 with his comments on Aubrey's collections for Surrey (then in manuscript). He approved of Aubrey's work and offered several pages of information drawn from his and his family's life at Wotton, their Surrey estate.[163] In correspondence with others, Evelyn lauded Aubrey's "Inquisitive Genius."[164] However, signs of a more personal esteem are difficult to find. The absence of letters from Evelyn to Aubrey in Aubrey's letter books, when Aubrey took great pains to preserve letters from both friends and eminent acquaintances, suggests that Evelyn did not view Aubrey as a particular friend.[165]

Regardless of whether it sprang from a disregard of Aubrey as a person, Evelyn's appropriation of Aubrey's words illustrates the danger that such reading, copying, and rewriting could pose to authors. By copying some of Aubrey's manuscripts without attribution to their author, Evelyn introduced the possibility that he would use Aubrey's words in his own writing without attribution. Whether this was a slip of the pen or a deliberate omission, the threat to Aubrey was the same. Once separated from his name and partially rewritten as the first stage in the process of composing new treatises, Aubrey's words were as good as Evelyn's.

Indeed, when writing for print, Evelyn followed similar citation practices. In *Sylva,* a popular treatise on the cultivation of trees, Evelyn tended not to give the names of those who provided him information through correspondence or conversation except when those names belonged to nobility.[166] Information seemingly from conversation or correspondence appeared frequently in the text, marked by phrases such as "I am told" or "I hear."[167] Often, but not always, Evelyn anonymized the sources of information so presented, identifying it as having come, variously, from a "curious friend," "a worthy person," or a "husband" (or other tradesman).[168] Although he usually named nobility, he occasionally rendered them anonymous as well, while preserving their high status in his descriptions of them. For example, he relayed that "a great person in Devon, planted Oaks as big as twelve Oxen could draw, to supply some defect in an Avenue to one of his houses."[169] Evelyn recorded that this anecdote was transmitted to him by the late Charles Berkeley, Earl of Falmouth, once "Treasurer of his Majesties {Charles II's} Household."[170] This practice was intended to elevate both the text and Evelyn in the eyes of the reader. Evelyn provided fuller references to printed texts. He mentioned as authorities, among others, Joshua Childrey's *Britannia Baconica,* Robert Plot's *Natural history of Oxford-shire,* an unspecified work by Francis Bacon, Pliny's *Natural History,* the Elizabethan naturalist Hugh Plat, Henry Wotton (the English diplomat and translator of Vitruvius), and the physician and astrologer Girolamo Cardano.[171]

The contrast between Aubrey's and Evelyn's citation practices suggests that the social and economic dynamics of print could widen the distance between writers and readers, encouraging authors to drop the names of collaborators and informants from their texts.[172] Scribal exchange encouraged authors and readers to think of reading as a collaborative act. Aubrey selected readers who would participate in the labor represented in their papers, and his readers scribbled their annotations with the understanding that they would be read by the author.[173] Furthermore, Aubrey hoped that after his death, future naturalists would continue his work, using his papers as raw material for their natural histories. To this end, accurately sourcing and dating claims and observations was vitally important. Without such sourcing, Aubrey's project was guaranteed to stop with Aubrey; with it, the possibility remained that someone—if that someone presented himself—could take it up where he left off. For example, in recounting the history of a failed plan to connect Bristol and London by canal and the disposition of the papers relating to the project, Aubrey stated that he had "been the more full in this Account, because if ever it shall happen that any publick spirited man shall arise to carry-on such a usefull Work; they may know in whose hands the Papers that were so well considered heretofore, are now lodged."[174]

Yet writing for print alone did not account for Evelyn's citation practices. If that were the case, then John Ray too would have eliminated references to his correspondents from his printed works. Much depended on whom a book was directed at and on the author's conception of his own social position. With a printed book that attracted a larger readership beyond a small cadre of specialists, reading was less likely to be collaborative, as authors were less likely personally to select all, or even most, of their readers, though they might send presentation copies to a few chosen individuals. Issued in four editions between 1664 and Evelyn's death in 1706 and earning close to five hundred pounds for John Martyn, its publisher, by its third edition *Sylva* was such a popular book.[175] Though his readership was still fairly elite (given the reality of seventeenth-century publishing), the generality of Evelyn's readers consisted of people who were unlikely to be actual or potential collaborators. For these readers, detailed citations and references to minor country gentry might serve only to clutter the discourse with unnecessary details. Evelyn's *Sylva*, like other natural histories, selectively mirrored the social world out of which it came. In providing names of highborn informants, or at least an indication of when an anonymous informant was highborn, as well as names of print authors, Evelyn presented a particular vision of the social and intellectual world of which he was a part. For Evelyn, printed books and noble persons were the only sources that counted.

Conclusion

This chapter explored the relationships that obtained between Aubrey's *Naturall Historie* as a material text, the topographical vision of Britain that it communicated, and the social organism, the correspondence, that was its milieu. I have argued that the "Britain" communicated in *The Naturall Historie* was porous and unstable, open to revision and addition. In this it was a reflection of the media in which Aubrey and his readers constructed it, which transformed over time as Aubrey accumulated notes on loose papers, "tumultuarily stitch't" them together in order to share and preserve them, and then invited readers to add their notes as well. The text's openness to revision and addition was no accident or a simple property of manuscript as material text. Rather, Aubrey built the capacity for revision and addition into the text. He left spaces in his papers—the blank versos of each folio, the blanks in sentences for missing names, places, and dates—for information to accumulate. He filled those over the years as well as he was able and invited his readers to do the same.

The title of the book may have been *The Naturall Historie of Wiltshire,* but, Aubrey used the work as a repository for topographical observations about England, Wales, Scotland, and even the farther reaches of the world with which Britons came into contact or exerted authority—northern Africa and Jamaica, for example.[176] He sourced these observations from friends and fellows whom he named, providing a vivid image of the collaborative nature of early modern natural history: as the historian of science James Delbourgo has written of Hans Sloane and his collections, "collecting things meant collecting people."[177]

Aubrey's readers-annotators extended what Aubrey had begun, adding comments that for the most part reflected their own locally rooted expertise. In doing so, their notes illustrate one of the themes first explored in Chapter

1 of this book, that topographical writers attempted to hold in tension the national and the local without losing sight of either one. Because each reader possessed a different, locally grounded store of natural knowledge, each reader had something valuable to contribute to the project.

Ray's comments, on the other hand, in presuming to critique Aubrey, highlight the fragility of the topographical balance. Ray's knowledge of nature, more systematic and national in scale, could serve as a basis for denying more locally rooted, particularized authority and expertise. If Ray could—based on his knowledge of British plants, without ever having lived in Wiltshire—tell Aubrey that he had not seen a plant he claimed to have seen, what then was the role of local authority and local expertise? This tension was present in eighteenth-century botany, as European naturalists fanned out around the world, seeking to develop systematic knowledge of plants and identify botanical riches that could serve as (among other things) medicines and industrial resources, such as dyes. They often relied on indigenous informants to guide them toward useful plants but rarely represented these people, or the systems of knowledge in which they placed these botanical resources, in the books and reports they compiled for their fellows in Europe.[178] We continue to wrestle with this particular problem into the twenty-first century.[179]

The ways in which Aubrey, Tanner, Gale, Ray, and Evelyn read, annotated, copied, and wrote about *The Naturall Historie* also suggest the limitations of attempting a strict separation between print and scribal "cultures." Each culture was compounded of a range of practices. Although some of these practices were more associated with manuscript texts and some with printed texts, no practice was linked exclusively to one kind of text. The fear (and sometimes the fact) of plagiarism bedeviled manuscript exchange, but it was also strongly felt in the print context, as evidenced by authors' and stationers' efforts to construct a legal and cultural framework to protect printed texts from piracy.[180] In addition some of the more speculative effects of print culture—the elevation of the individual author, for example—can be found in both manuscript and print texts, as shown by the way in which Evelyn commonplaced Aubrey's *Naturall Historie of Wiltshire*. This may be evidence that practices and attitudes fostered by writing for print publication influenced how authors and readers produced and appropriated scribal texts.[181]

Print practices could point to, or support, collaboration through correspondence. John Ray liberally cited correspondents by name when he included information from them in his *Miscellaneous discourses.* By naming names, Ray rewarded correspondents for their contributions, helping maintain the stream of information flowing his way. But there was a diversity of practices here too. Evelyn erased correspondents' names from his printed texts as well as his commonplace notebooks. He preferred instead to grant names only to noble correspondents and print authors, a sign that his readership's familiarity with a name was an important criterion for its inclusion in the text. It may also be a sign of Evelyn's relatively high social status: correspondents such as Aubrey would continue sending him information even if Evelyn did not reward them with a mention in print (Evelyn's willingness to name noble correspondents is the exception that proves the rule). Ray, son of a blacksmith, may have initially required the mechanism of credit in order to maintain good relations with his correspondents. By the 1690s, when his eminence as a naturalist was widely recognized, it may have been an ingrained habit (and one that, though perhaps not as necessary as it once was, still helped funnel information his way).

One might compare Charles Darwin in his later years as a similarly homebound, and prolific, correspondent who, like Ray, used his correspondence to assemble vast reams of information about the natural world. Janet Browne has observed that once he settled in at Down House, correspondence became "his primary research tool."[182] Darwin, like Ray, was careful to credit those from whom he drew information. In *The Variation of Animals and Plants Under Domestication*, for example, Darwin extensively discussed the history of the domesticated pigeon, which pigeon fanciers had developed into a wide range of breeds. Darwin's footnotes are thick with acknowledgments of the particular pigeon fanciers (identified by name) who provided the data upon which Darwin built his theories.[183] Print authors' choices in these matters depended on their priorities, their understanding of their readership's expectations, and their relative social status.[184]

There is yet a further way in which the material topographical text serves as a mirror. It reflects Aubrey's social and financial position, the roles he took on within the scientific correspondence, his ambitions, and the ways in which they were constrained by financial precarity and accomplished through scribal collaboration. Aubrey's career as a scribal author can be understood only in terms of his social and economic position, particularly the startling reversal that he underwent when his fortunes collapsed at mid-life. Early in his life, print seems not to have been a priority for him. As a gentleman scholar and a landowner, he seems to have used scientific investigation as a hobby. He enjoyed it, and some of his friendships were formed around shared interests in experimental philosophy, mathematics, and antiquities. His scientific investigations also brought him into contact with royalty and nobility, as when he was summoned to discuss the monuments at Avebury and Stonehenge with Charles II, which led to his offering Charles and his queen a guided tour of Avebury. Yet publishing in these areas seems not to have been a major preoccupation. After he had lost his estates and his money, recognition through publication became deeply important to Aubrey, but it was frustratingly inaccessible. Aubrey's social and economic marginality led him to test the limits of correspondence: partly because he had difficulty getting his works into print, he shared near-finished scribal copies of his works.

For most naturalists, including Aubrey and his readers, correspondence was not (or was not meant to be) the end point of their efforts; though some were content, at one time or another, to contribute to the works of others without publishing under their own names, those who composed longer works, the products of sustained scientific investigation, usually sought to get them into print. Aubrey desired to be known as the author of printed works rather than just as a contributor to the work of others. That he did not make it into print until the end of his life was a mark of a certain kind of marginality. This was not a social or an intellectual marginality, at least not in the context of his contemporaries, with whom he shared many close bonds and scientific interests. Rather he feared that the work he had done would be lost or credited to someone else and that absent from print, he would be invisible to history. This was a source of great anxiety for him.

Aubrey's marginality and the ways it affected his engagement with script and print are useful tools for understanding the moral economy of early modern science. As a collaborator, Aubrey was capable of undertaking research tasks for his friends—he checked inscriptions on monuments for his antiquarian friend Anthony à Wood, attempted to impose himself on Robert Plot as a collaborator, and worked for John Ogilby surveying Surrey. However, because he was not a print author, he was unable to offer other kinds of acknowledgment and support that made the scientific correspondence run smoothly, such as the recognition of his collaborators in print. Had he possessed the visibility that print accorded, he could have, if he wished, used it to reward and promote others in his correspondence.

Aubrey's case shows that by the late seventeenth century scribal exchange held a vital place in late seventeenth-century natural history and antiquarian studies as the material and social foundation of topographical visions of Britain. Aubrey's readers responded enthusiastically to his project, and though he (and they) might have preferred also to see the text printed, in manuscript the pages of *The Naturall Historie* came to embody at least a small piece of the vast collective aims of British naturalists. Ironically, as Aubrey surely knew, given that manuscript copy of text that had been printed was often tossed into the dustbin, his failure to print helped to ensure the survival of his *Naturall Historie,* with its key evidence of the collaborative construction of seventeenth-century topographical visions of Britain.

Yet Aubrey's story also illustrates that in late seventeenth-century natural philosophical circles, moving to print was assumed by many, though not all, to be the end goal of scribal exchange. But print required some measure of social and financial capital. How did naturalists get into print, especially from social and financial positions akin to Aubrey's? How did they bring their versions of local history and their visions of Britain into print? In the next chapter I turn to a closer exploration of how naturalists manipulated their correspondence in order to produce the financial and social capital they needed to get their works published. Correspondence mediated print; that is, naturalists printed through and for their correspondence.

Chapter 5

Publics of Letters: Printing for
(and Through) Correspondence

In seventeenth-century Britain naturalists were among the first to exploit subscription as a means for financing publication of their books. Just over half of the books published by subscription before 1700 were in "scientific" disciplines: natural philosophy, geography, mathematics, medicine, and natural history.[1] Booksellers and authors financed publication through subscription because scientific books were often expensive to publish and readerships were relatively small. Booksellers were reluctant to take on such projects without guaranteed funding. In many cases authors (or their friends and family members) served as publishers, collecting subscriptions, buying paper, contracting with printers, and distributing copies.

The publication of Francis Willughby and John Ray's heavily illustrated *Historia piscium* (1686), funded in part by a subscription raised from fellows of the Royal Society, is a well-known example. It illustrates both the potentially enormous expense of learned scientific publishing, the greatest part of which often lay in the production of engravings and woodcuts, and the way in which subscription could be used to cover those costs. Subscribing fellows kicked in varying amounts; their donations to the project were memorialized in the work's engraved plates, each of which recorded the name of a generous subscriber-patron. Samuel Pepys, then president of the Royal Society, donated over sixty guineas, and his name was inscribed on eighty of the plates.[2] Ideally, of course, subscription would meet all the costs, but this was not the case with the *Historia piscium*. The subscribers' investment in the book was massive—£163 was collected—but not massive enough. Ultimately the edition of five hundred copies cost £360 to produce; some of the excess may have been made up from Royal Society dues.[3] In 1687 Robert Hooke and Edmond Halley received their salaries as curator of experiments and clerk, respectively, in the form of copies of the book.[4] Almost one hundred years later the Royal Society had made back only £111 1s. 5d. selling copies of the *Historia piscium*, many of them at sharp discounts off the original subscription price.

As the example of the *Historia piscium* shows, the British "market" for learned print was extremely limited even into the eighteenth century.[5] This problem was neither new nor limited to Britain.[6] Neither were British naturalists the only ones to consider subscription as part of the solution to it. Wilhelm Gottfried Leibniz proposed that the state should fund scientific printing and that scientific societies, in particular the Berlin-based Sozietät der Wissenschaften, should censor worthless books and, as the Royal Society sometimes did, support the worthy by organizing subscription schemes.[7]

This chapter explores how subscription undertakers—particularly authors superintending their own subscriptions—sold their books, emphasizing in particular the "social marketing" strategies that they employed (to borrow a term of art from modern-day social media business practices). In a typical subscription publication, undertakers assembled a text (including engravings or woodcuts as well as manuscript copy); issued subscription proposals (two-sided broadsheets advertising the book and the subscription terms); collected subscribers' names, addresses, and money (usually half at the time of subscription, half upon receipt of a book); hired and paid printers, artists, and engravers; and oversaw the distribution of books.[8] Printed ephemera·produced in the course of subscription publication, including subscription proposals, advertisements, and lists of subscribers as well as authors' correspondence, offer a window into relations between scientific authors and their readers. This material shows authors-undertakers and booksellers pursuing a range of marketing strategies. Quite frequently they mobilized a rhetoric of public benefit against the supposed profit-mindedness of commercial booksellers, arguing that subscription made possible the production of books that redounded to the nation's good and its honor but would never be printed if profit were the only motive for publishing a book. They also mobilized relationships between individuals as well as the power of famous and prominent names, advertising the names of noble, gentle, and learned subscribers in order to induce others to subscribe. In addition booksellers and authors-undertakers promoted their books through their correspondence.

I focus in particular on this third strategy, arguing that authors-undertakers printed through and for their correspondence. Just as conversation was mediated through the correspondence, so was print. An examination of two subscription projects undertaken by Edward Lhuyd shows that successful authors-undertakers assembled readerships letter by letter and contact by contact. They personally managed subscription schemes by issuing advertisements, canvassing for subscribers, accounting for the income and expenditure of money, and hiring printers. Subscription thus enmeshed authors and correspondents in a web of promises, receipts, half-payments, proposals, and appeals to subscribe. If all went well—that is, if a printed book emerged at the end of this process—the readership was an expanded version of the undertaker's correspondence.

I further argue that within topographical studies, subscription was more than just an engine for financing book production: to borrow more analogies from modern social media, projects were "crowd-sourced" as well as "crowd-funded." Undertakers designed projects such that subscribers were also content producers, as seen through an analysis of Edward Lhuyd's use of subscription in his *Archaeologia Britannica* project, in which Lhuyd raised subscriptions to fund research travel as well as book publication. Lhuyd directly involved his subscribers in the process of producing books. He distributed to them printed research questionnaires and asked them to return detailed information relevant to the project on standardized forms—a kind of "printing for manuscript," to borrow a term coined by Peter Stallybrass.[9] Lhuyd encouraged subscribers to share observations and material artifacts relevant to the project via the post as well as face-to-face when he traveled to conduct research. Lhuyd was not alone in inviting readers to shape content. In some cases undertakers invited subscribers to superintend the production of images for their books. There were more subtle pressures too: authors selected content and areas of emphasis based at least in part on what they knew about their subscribers' interests.

Ultimately subscription ephemera and authors' correspondence reveal the construction of print natural history and antiquarian studies as a collaborative process, one in which texts and their readerships were assembled piece by piece and person by person. This mode of using subscription to facilitate collaborative research and writing as well as funding was particularly well suited to topographical studies because of its dependence on the contributions of informants distributed across the land. Effectively subscription undertakers such as Lhuyd used print to scale up the process of collaboration through the correspondence. The body of papers, correspondence, and returned questionnaires that Lhuyd's project resulted in was something like an expanded version of John Aubrey's *Naturall Historie of Wiltshire*. Whereas Aubrey had four readers who were also writers, Lhuyd brought together a body of contributors that numbered in the hundreds. In addition, as in Aubrey's case, the image of Britain that emerged from the project was developed in collaboration between "author" and "readers." Jointly they defined the boundaries of the nation.

Learned Print and the Public Good

In the seventeenth and eighteenth centuries printing was one of many enterprises funded by subscription. Joint-stock companies founded and promoted for both "public and private profit" were increasingly common features of the cultural and commercial landscape, as Daniel Defoe recognized in his *Essay upon projects* (1697).[10] The rhetoric of public benefit was used to promote a wide range of cultural and financial enterprises. There were subscription schemes for everything from theater construction, to educational lecture series, to life and fire insurance, to funds that were used to secure the release of soldiers and sailors taken into captivity while serving along the coast of North Africa.[11] In the late 1660s the Royal Society ran a subscription (failed, unfortunately) to fund a perpetual dream of theirs, the establishment of a philosophical college with laboratory and meeting rooms for fellows and lodging for the society's employees.[12] Some of these enterprises, such as the joint-stock East India Company, produced financial profits for subscribers and stockholders, while others, such as printing, tended to produce more intangible benefits, contributing to the common good as well as the intellectual and cultural enrichment of subscribers. In 1651, for example, the printer William Dugard asked readers to subscribe to the publication of Thomas Harding's *Historie of the Church* either in the interest of "the publick good, or to their own private contentment."[13]

Naturalists and booksellers promoted the printing of natural history and other scientific works as services undertaken for the public good. This way of thinking about natural history and husbandry, in particular, had gained steam during the civil war and commonwealth periods. It was embedded deeply in the thinking of the intelligencer Samuel Hartlib.[14] Progress in the sciences—particularly improvement in husbandry, natural history, and other disciplines that might contribute to the expansion of trade—was central to Hartlib's conception of public service (as discussed in Chapter 1). In particular, no branch of learning did more to support "the comforts and Publick Use of a Societie" than husbandry.[15] Husbandry, in turn, could not advance unless natural history was set upon a sturdy foundation.[16] Hartlib dedicated himself to disseminating and publicizing news of projects and developments in husbandry, natural history, and trade. He maintained an extensive correspondence through which he aggregated and shared scribal news and information.[17] Because making science public was a key part of his plan, he also published letters and treatises generated by his correspondents; unless correspondents laid their own restrictions on dissemination in advance, they and he assumed that many of the things sent to him were fair game for printing.[18] Books superintended by Hartlib included *The Reformed Librarie Keeper* (1650) by John Dury, Gerald Boate's *Irelands Naturall History* (1652), and *The Reformed Virginian Silk-Worm* (1655), a collection of essays by various authors on the husbandry of silkworms and bees. The rhetoric of public service was woven through this corpus.[19]

Through the seventeenth century, undertakers continued to use the rhetoric of public benefit when publishing learned scientific works. Moses Pitt's 1678 proposals for a new atlas included a declaration signed by (among others) Christopher Wren, John Pell, Thomas Gale, and Robert Hooke testifying that "this Work will be of great Use, and for the Honour of the Nation."[20] Brabazon Aylmer proposed an edition of the late Isaac Barrow's sermons, noting that he undertook the project for "the accommodation of all Persons, and making more publick the said Book."[21] Such terms could be used to justify broadening a subscription and making a book accessible to more buyers. According to the 1693 proposals for Edmund Gibson's revised edition of Camden's *Britannia*, the subscription was initially undertaken without the benefit of public advertisements, and many gentlemen had already signed on. But it was "thought fit for the general advantage" to canvass publicly for subscriptions by means of a printed advertisement.[22] We see here the rhetoric of public advantage and public benefit as a marketing tool: the proposals imply a select readership of gentlemen that could now be joined by those who learned of the subscription only through the printed proposals.

The rhetoric of public benefit was often directly opposed to a rhetoric that denigrated booksellers' concerns about profit. Even after the Royal Society agreed to pay for sixty copies of an algebra treatise by John Wallis at a rate of three half-pence per sheet, no bookseller was willing to take on the project. The Royal Society, collaborating with Oxford bookseller Richard Davies, offered up the edition more broadly to the reading public in the hopes that signing up more subscribers would tip the project into profitability, and "encourage the Bookseller to proceed."[23] In another example, proposals issued by Oxford University Press in 1680 called upon honored "Persons of eminent Quality and Learning" to organize the publication of scholarly books for the press. These books (represented by a list of sixty-seven printed on the back) included diverse works of theology, chronological and antiquarian studies, chorography, travel narratives, church history, and classical mathematics, philosophy, and literature, and many of them were to be prepared from manuscripts in the Bodleian Library. [24] Perhaps this was an attempt to generate work for the university press by drawing on the library's catalog of unpublished manuscripts. Groups of twenty-five persons were invited to organize subscriptions for any book on the list. As long as they purchased five hundred copies at a fair price, the press would print an edition of the book. The prospective undertakers would be given control over the layout, design, and quality of their edition. The press's proposal promoted this work as a "public service" that would contribute to the "honor and improvement of knowledge." In this advertisement, issued in the wake of the press's conflict with a group of London stationers over the rights to print and sell Bibles, psalters, and schoolbooks (a dependably profitable trade), "Persons of eminent Quality and Learning" were contrasted with "men of Trade, only intent upon their gain, [who] will not be at the expence and hazard of such impressions."[25] The press's advertisement drove home the point that public service—in this case the printing of learned books—ran counter to the pursuit of private gain.

Yet appeals to the public good and profit-mindedness could occupy the same space, as booksellers' subscription advertisements showed. No one could accuse, for example, the bookseller John Dunton of failing to attend to his own profits. Dunton was, among other things, the impresario behind the *Athenian Mercury*, a weekly paper that ran in the 1690s. The *Athenian Mercury* was the organ of the "Athenian Society," an invented learned society. In the *Mercury*'s pages the Athenians offered answers to readers' real and invented questions, satirizing the work of the Royal Society in the process. The paper also ran ads, including some for other books printed or projected by Dunton. In 1692 Dunton advertised a natural history of Britain that would include "all Artificial and Civil Things Remarkable in England and Wales, Scotland, Ireland, and all the Forreign Plantations depending on them." He invited readers to participate with him in a "Design so much for the Honour and Profit of the English Nation" and send in items to be included, promising that anything of "Service to the Publick, or to particular Persons" would be inserted.[26] Dunton used the rhetoric of public benefit and public service but by no means disclaimed profit for himself. If his proposed natural history would redound to the "Honour and Profit of the English Nation," so too was it meant to profit his bottom line.

Dunton's advertisement also speaks to the themes articulated in the first chapter of this book. Dunton's natural history of England, Wales, Scotland, Ireland, and their foreign plantations, or colonies, was meant to serve the "Honour and Profit of the English Nation." This "Britain," crafted by an English undertaker for a largely English audience, was one in which England was dominant.

Making the List: Social Strategies for Selling Books

In this section I turn to the social strategies that authors-undertakers and booksellers used to secure subscriptions and finance book production. "Social strategies" included a range of tactics, from offering free books to individuals who assembled a group of subscribers to publishing the subscription list. The boldfaced names on the subscription list, that is, those that belonged to members of the nobility and gentry or well-known scholars, were a marketing tool, as readers were eager to own books also owned by the gentry and nobility. The subscription readership was a social body. In selling books, undertakers drew on the relationships between readers, whether those really existed or were aspirational. Subscription lists, circulated on broadsheet advertisements and in books, with the well-born and high status represented in large type, were, much like topographical images of Britain, reflections of the nation to itself.

Undertakers offered subscription as an opportunity to become a literary patron. Their patronage was recognized through the mechanism of the subscription list. These lists were more or less extravagant. Those who subscribed to John Aubrey's *Monumenta Britannica* would have the honor of having their own names and titles as well as the names of their homes listed in the book, implying a readership of propertied gentry and nobility.[27] Similarly, Richard Blome's *Exact Book of Geography* included the "names, titles, seats and coats" of arms of members of the nobility and gentry who subscribed to

the book.[28] Edward Lhuyd was somewhat apologetic in offering to list in the
book those who funded his research trip through the Celtic regions of Britain
and France, as if this were too small a return for their support. In a letter to
Thomas Tonkin in March 1703, he wrote of his subscribers, "All the return I
can make them, will be copies of what I shall print, and the mentioning in
the title page, that 'twas done at their command and expences, &c. with a
catalogue of the subscribers, and the book dedicated to them in general."[29]
As we see in this letter, the subscription list took the place of a dedication to
a particular patron: patronage and its rewards were dispersed across hundreds
of readers.

The names of prominent subscribers were used to promote books: booksellers hoped to induce more readers to subscribe by publishing preliminary
subscription lists in their advertisements. In this context, the ultimate subscriber was the king, who, in addition to providing substantial financial
support, sometimes allowed his name and endorsement to be used in subscription advertisements and proposals. Charles II supported geographical
volumes in this way. Of course the king's promise of financial support was
not the same as cash in hand. In February 1682 Charles II agreed to give
Captain Greenville Collins two hundred pounds to finance the printing of
his new collection of coastal surveys. A year later Collins still waited on his
money from the king. In the meantime he had spent five hundred pounds
on his survey and was in danger of being arrested for outstanding debts. He
waited until April 1683 for the balance of the promised two hundred pounds
to arrive.[30]

Whether or not he made good on his financial promises, the king's support did function as a powerful advertising tool. In his 1669 recommendation
of Blome's *Exact Book of Geography*, the king called on the nobility as well as
the nation's societies for the advancement of learning and commerce (including, presumably, the Royal Society) to subscribe to the work. He advised
justices of the peace, sheriffs, and mayors to offer their assistance to Blome
so that his maps and descriptions of England, Scotland, and Ireland could be
made as accurate as possible.[31] A few years later Charles named John Ogilby
his royal cosmographer. In 1672 the king issued a declaration of support for
Ogilby's project to survey England and Wales. This was a collaborative project; Aubrey, for example, was deputized by Ogilby to survey Surrey. The
final result was Ogilby's *Britannia*, a road atlas (discussed in Chapter 1 of this
book). In supporting the project, Charles recommended Ogilby "to all lords,
archbishops, bishops, Lords Lieutenant, Deputy Lieutenants, Universities,

Heads of Colleges, Deans and Chapters, Sheriffs, Justices, etc., in England and Wales."[32] Advertising his own contribution of five hundred pounds to the undertaking, Charles directed his subjects to give generously. Additional noble names—those of the Earls of Bridgewater, Sandwich, Essex, and Anglesey and Lord Holles—further bolstered the project.[33]

Subscription lists were widely distributed prior to publication to encourage further subscribers to join up. The social marketing function of the lists was clear in their design.[34] An appeal for Moses Pitt's *English atlas*, proposed as an eleven-volume set of maps (of which four were eventually produced), listed a formidable array of royal subscribers: not only Charles II but also his queen, the Duke of York, Prince Rupert, and the prince elector of the Palatine. From there the list descended through luminaries such as Robert Boyle and Elias Ashmole, bishops, ambassadors, government officials (Samuel Pepys was one), fellows and principals of Oxford and Cambridge colleges as well as the colleges as corporate bodies, lawyers, physicians, apothecaries, merchants, students, and private gentlemen.[35] Even tradesmen showed up, such as William Nott, bookbinder to the queen.[36] Pitt's list identified subscribers by their titles, professional qualifications, and civic and ecclesiastical positions of authority, in addition to rank. Proposals for Nehemiah Grew's *Museum Regalis Societatis* (1681) listed nobility (including bishops) in capital letters while reducing others to conventionally capitalized italics.[37]

That such aspirational appeals—which promised readers that they could join a select social set simply by buying a book—were likely to move books can be seen in evidence that customers were willing to pay a premium for the privilege of owning copies of books also owned by royalty and nobility. In April 1667 Samuel Pepys purchased a "finely bound and truly coloured" copy of Paul Rycaut's *The present state of the Ottoman Empire*. The copy he purchased was one of six in which the illustrations were hand-colored; four of the remaining five copies, he proudly noted, were owned by Charles II, the Duke of York, the Duke of Monmouth, and Lord Arlington. Pepys paid fifty-five shillings for his copy, though he judged that the same book similarly colored had gone for twenty shillings before the Great Fire. While the price was partly driven up by the destruction of copies during the Great Fire, it was worth paying in part because of the company of "readers" Pepys joined when he bought the book.[38]

Not all subscription marketing was aspirational. Booksellers and author-undertakers also sold books by taking advantage of direct relationships between their readers. A common feature of many subscription proposals was the "buy six (or sometimes five), get one free" deal.[39] In proposals for printing a book of the mathematician Isaac Barrow's sermons, the undertaker Brabazon Aylmer offered a seven-for-six deal "for the encouragement of all Persons who shall subscribe, or procure Subscriptions for six Books, at the rate aforesaid."[40] Readers taking advantage of these deals may have assembled groups of subscribers through their correspondence or local acquaintance. One individual might take the free book, or groups of readers might distribute the discount across their group. In making these offers, undertakers assumed that the correspondence and face-to-face relationships between potential readers would do some of the work of selling books for them. Aylmer's offer suggests the possibility that a single individual might subscribe for six books; undertakers may also have used "buy six, get one free" deals as a volume discount for regional booksellers. Aylmer appointed multiple booksellers in Cambridge, Oxford, Norwich, Bristol, and Exeter, as well as individuals in smaller towns, including Barnstable and Grantham, to receive subscriptions and money from "Subscribers that live in the Country."[41] Such booksellers would be able to pool subscriptions from local readers and pick up the free copies to dispose of as they wished.

"Social strategies" for selling books shaped the content of the books: undertakers offered subscribers opportunities to display their social status in finished books. With topographical works this increased the degree to which, as mirrors of the nation, they selectively reflected the wealthy and highborn back at themselves. This was done with subscription lists, of course, but also through the sponsorship of engraved plates. Given their expense, individual plates were often paid for by subscribers who, at the very least, were rewarded with a dedication on the plate (as with Willughby and Ray's *Historia piscium*). Or one might dedicate a plate to a potential patron in hopes of a reward, as the naturalist and collector James Petiver did in his *Musei Petiveriani*. This was a risky strategy, though: because Petiver did not necessarily have established relationships with those to whom he dedicated plates, some observers (such as the German traveler Zacharias Conrad von Uffenbach) regarded such behavior as déclassé.[42]

In some cases undertakers crafted the visual contents of the plates around individual subscribers. The plates in Plot's *Natural History of Oxford-shire* (1677) largely depicted natural and antiquarian curiosities (oddly shaped fossils, for example, or fragments of Roman urns), many of which were discovered on the estates of those who paid for the plates.[43] In the successor volume, *The Natural History of Stafford-shire* (1686), Plot cut to the chase, offering views of subscribers' homes and building works.[44] Likewise the county maps included in both *Oxford-shire* and *Stafford-shire* put the social world and the natural world on display. Locations of gentle and noble estates were pinpointed, and the borders of the maps showed the coats of arms of county grandees. In the introduction to *Stafford-shire*, Plot touted the ways in which the *Stafford-shire* map was an improvement over the county map printed in *Oxford-shire*: the coats of arms were arranged alphabetically by family names around the map and were keyed to the locations of the families' houses in the map grid.[45] For Plot and his readers, representing the social geography of their counties was just as, if not more, important than displaying the areas' natural features.

The creation of the printed topographical book as a representation of the hierarchical British social world was a deeply collaborative process between authors and readers. Undertakers of antiquarian works invited readers to participate directly in choosing and commissioning engravings to be included in histories of their counties and cities. In 1683 Henry Keepe offered readers the opportunity to provide engravings for his four-volume history of Westminster Abbey. He invited in particular noble readers whose ancestors were buried or memorialized in the abbey to commission engravings of their forbears' monuments. But the invitation was extended to those not so dignified as well, who could contribute a minimum of three pounds toward an engraving of the memorial of one of the "many ancient graceful Tombs and Monuments (of Persons of great Eminence) . . . whose Families are totally extinct." Regardless of whether one sponsored one's own family's monument or that of an extinct family, each plate would be engraved with the sponsor's coat of arms. Keepe further invited subscribers to select artists of their choice to execute their engravings.[46] Sir Henry Chauncey, in proposals for *The history and antiquities of Hertfordshire*, did not go quite so far as Keepe did in directly inviting readers to submit their own engravings, but he did list subscribers who had already committed to sponsoring engravings of their local towns as well as their country seats, indicating that this was an option.[47]

In inviting readers to sponsor and choose monuments, seats, and prospects for engravings, undertakers used the subscription process to offer personalized books that directly illustrated individuals' sense of their own and their families' just place in history and in the ordered, hierarchical world of the shire. The pleasure that subscribers took in these representations of their place in that world could only have been enhanced by knowing, via the mechanism of the subscription list, precisely who else in their social set had purchased a copy of the book and thus would see the engravings of their homes and monuments (if they opened the book). This attachment to the local world, its history and its hierarchies, suggests that for all that authors and their collaborators may have been engaged in a broader project of constructing "Britain" as a topographical object, the parish and the county were the most significant spheres of concern for many readers (and, to be fair, for many authors as well). For some, the pleasures of county natural histories and antiquarian studies lay in the ways they lifted up local society and local landscapes, reflecting, embodying, and preserving them in print.

"Vendible, as Well as Useful": Lhuyd's *Lithophylacii Britannici ichnographia*

The social foundations of printing by subscription can be further delineated through an exploration of two subscription projects superintended by Edward Lhuyd, their author. The first is Lhuyd's *Lithophylacii Britannici ichnographia* (1699), a geological field guide with a particular focus on fossils. The title means, roughly, "Map of the British Stone Cabinet."[48] The second is Lhuyd's *Archaeologia Britannica* project, projected in the mid-1690s as a multivolume study of the languages, antiquities, customs, and natural history of Britain. Each project in its own way illustrates how authors-undertakers worked through and for their correspondence in order to bring their projects forward as printed books.

Before turning to Lhuyd's projects, briefly consider a failed subscription project: Aubrey's *Monumenta Britannica*. In its failure it highlights authors-undertakers' dependence on their correspondence in raising subscriptions. In 1693, nearing the end of his life, John Aubrey proposed to print his *Monumenta Britannica* by subscription. In opting to superintend a subscription scheme, Aubrey was not a new-media trailblazer; numerous learned authors— and sometimes their friends and family members, including widows— managed their own subscriptions.[49] Yet Aubrey's proposals fell flat: they were met with awkward silences and half-hearted promises of assistance. Edward Lhuyd, by then curator of the Ashmolean, attempted to assist Aubrey by distributing printed proposals among his acquaintances at Oxford. However, Lhuyd asked to be excused if his efforts were not successful. "As many as I have discours'd with," he wrote Aubrey, "have a good opinion of the Book; but my acquaintance is very small, & interest and Authority much lesse."[50]

When Lhuyd heard rumors that Aubrey was claiming that Lhuyd had communicated firmer support—an offer from Jonathan Edwards, one of the delegates of the press, to finance all publication costs—Lhuyd wrote swiftly to disabuse him of this notion.[51] John Ray, though he encouraged Aubrey to print this and other projects (as we saw in Chapter 4), was unable to offer much support in the way of canvassing for subscriptions. The intellectual poverty of his country acquaintance was his excuse: he was unable to distribute Aubrey's proposals to more than a few people because his Essex neighborhood was "barren of Wits; heer being but few either of the gentry or Clergy who mind anything that is ingenious."[52] Former vice chancellor Ralph Bathurst, away from Oxford during the summer break, committed to purchasing two copies but could, at best, promise payment in two months, and he discouraged Aubrey from printing his treatise at the university press, given how expensive new, accurate engravings would be.[53] Aubrey raised as many as 112 subscriptions, but that was not enough to secure publication.[54]

Aubrey's story highlights the author-undertaker's dependence on his correspondence. When he was unable to persuade friends and associates to support his project, it was likely to fail. For a project to be successful, friends had to be willing not only to buy books; they also had to be persuaded to hawk the book themselves. Although willing enough to purchase copies for their own use, none of Aubrey's friends really wanted to promote his design. Aubrey's correspondence was fairly broad, but his ability to mobilize it on behalf of his project was limited. It may have been that they knew Aubrey too well. By this point in his life, Aubrey had worked on many different natural historical and antiquarian projects but had never successfully brought one to completion. His friends may not have felt it was worth supporting a project that might never be finished. Timing too may have played a factor. As Michael Hunter has observed, Aubrey released his subscription advertisements just as Edmund Gibson's efforts to revise Camden's *Britannia* were gaining steam. This larger project may have crowded Aubrey's book off the stage, as many of his correspondents (including Lhuyd and Tanner) were preoccupied with work on the *Britannia*, and many of Aubrey's potential subscribers may have purchased Camden instead.[55] In any case, without his friends' help, the edition failed.

The possible failure of a subscription—usually due to an undertaker's failure to gather sufficient funds—loomed over every proposed project.[56] To counteract these fears, and reassure potential subscribers that their books would appear as promised, undertakers included in advertisements statements that so much of an edition had been written or printed already or plates had already been engraved. The booksellers William Battersby, Henry Rhodes, and John Taylor noted in their proposal for William Salmon's illustrated herbal that the book would be delivered speedily in part because the engravings had already been completed before proposals were issued.[57] On occasion John Dunton explicitly promised to refund customers' money in the event of a failed subscription, providing receipts for that purpose.[58] In his "Proposals For Printing of Holwell's Book of Dialling," John Holwell, whose primary business was private instruction in mathematics ("dialling" referred to constructing and using sundials), went to extreme lengths to reassure subscribers. Rather than collecting up their initial payments to pay the printer, he directed that the money would remain with his subscription agents (booksellers and instrument makers in England and Ireland) until delivery.[59]

That Edward Lhuyd's first subscription publication, *Lithophylacii Britannici ichnographia*, did not fail was a testament to the strength of his social connections, particularly among Royal Society fellows. Edward Lhuyd initially sought to publish this work through the university press at Oxford. These efforts failed when the delegates of the press, a committee of university faculty, rejected the book. In 1699, however, the book was published with the support of ten subscribers, all of whom were affiliated with the Royal Society. The *Lithophylacii Britannici ichnographia* was successfully published because it earned the support of the right people: once alerted to Lhuyd's trouble, Hans Sloane and Samuel Pepys took up his cause. Lhuyd's eventual success and the means by which he achieved it demonstrate the interconnectedness of authors, booksellers, and readers. They were known to each other as friends and acquaintances, participants in the common project of exploring, and publicizing, the natural world. In addition their roles were fluid: authors were readers of each other's books, and both readers and authors could take on the role of publishers (for example, the general subscription proposals issued by Oxford University Press, examined above, explicitly called on would-be book buyers to take on the functions of publishers). Lhuyd's success as an author depended on his abilities to negotiate these relationships.

Writing to Martin Lister in 1694, Lhuyd explained that he intended his first published work to be a catalog he was then calling his *Lithologia*, a small field guide, or "pocket book to be carried into stonepits."[60] Initially, Lhuyd estimated that it would take him just twelve months to ready the catalog for the press; he thought he might make up some of the plates from the plates of shells Lister used in the appendixes to his 1685 edition of Jan Goedaert's

De insectis.[61] But his official duties at the Ashmolean intervened, as did other research projects, and three years passed. In January 1697 Lhuyd decamped to Marcham, a village a little over eleven miles' distance southwest of Oxford, to finish a fair copy of the text.[62] Lhuyd sent the finished copy (minus a few of the drawings) to Lister via his London solicitor, Walter Thomas, at the end of March 1697 with a request for Lister's comments.[63]

Lhuyd explicitly designated Lister's copy for marking up, asking that when Lister had finished perusing it, he send it on to the physician Tancred Robinson and John Ray for their comments.[64] Robinson, in addition to his skills as an herbalist, was adept at shifting books through the press; he assisted Ray in the publication of *The Wisdom of God Manifested in the Works of the Creation* (1691).[65] One might compare Lhuyd's prepublication circulation of the fair copy to Aubrey's sharing of *The Naturall Historie*. Both men distributed scribal copies of their works in the hope of securing written feedback; however, Lhuyd did it as a step toward printing, which, as Aubrey's story illustrated, was the more conventional path for naturalists' books.

Lhuyd hoped to publish his book through the university press in a modest edition of three hundred copies, illustrated with the newly engraved plates that by this time he had decided were necessary.[66] To do so Lhuyd needed more than just Lister's feedback on the text. As an unknown author, his chances of publication at the university press were slim unless the work was supported by some person known and respected by the press.[67] The expensive engravings he planned for his book, not to mention the fact that the delegates of the press were, in Lhuyd's words, "utter strangers to these studies," further reduced Lhuyd's chances of being published.[68] Lister was a benefactor to the university; among other things, he regularly donated large quantities of books and objects to the Ashmolean Museum.[69] If he approached the delegates with Lister's imprimatur, Lhuyd was confident that the university would print his catalog despite the cost of the engravings, which, at eighteen shillings a table (the usual rate that the engraver charged the university), seemed "most unreasonably dear" even to Lhuyd.[70]

In a few weeks Lister duly returned his approval of the text. Lhuyd responded jubilantly in a letter of 6 April 1697: "Nothing can be greater encouragement to me, than the approbation of so competent a judge; but the character you are pleas'd to give that small piece and its author heaps more honour on them than they are able to support."[71] However, the testimonial of learned men proved insufficient.[72] Lhuyd's edition was blocked by the press's financial troubles. The university press depended on the Stationers'

Company of London to subsidize learned editions by buying up to five hundred copies of each edition. In exchange, the university leased to the stationers its rights to print Bibles, prayer books, and grammars and other textbooks, extremely profitable stock. But the stationers, claiming they lost money by being forced to buy learned books that did not sell, resisted maintaining their end of the bargain.[73] Stonewalled by the stationers, the delegates of the press held off making a decision on Lhuyd's book. According to Lhuyd, the delegates delayed because the stationers were reluctant to take their required copies, claiming they had "been losers by all the books the University have lately publish'd; and that they'll be their tenants no longer."[74]

In an early letter to Lister explaining the delay, Lhuyd struck an optimistic note, reporting that he expected the disagreement between the press and the stationers to be resolved within five or six weeks.[75] Over the ensuing months, though, Lhuyd gradually lost his faith in the university press. Writing to John Lloyd in May 1697, he expressed one final hope that "about a month hence things will be better setld: tho' I believe 'twill be Christmasse ere my Book is printed off."[76] But the matter was not settled in Lhuyd's favor. In a meeting that took place as Lhuyd was struggling to get his book published, the delegates resolved "that great care be taken by the Delegates for Printing, to recommend such Books to the Press as are Vendible, as well as Usefull."[77] Lhuyd's book was rejected on these grounds.

"Vendible, as well as Usefull": Lhuyd's *Lithophylacii Britannici ichnographia* met the second condition but, according to the delegates of the press, not the first. Even with the approval of such noted scholars, authors, and university patrons as Lister and Ray—and even though the press was specifically dedicated to "learned" works—the question of financing nixed Lhuyd's chances of printing at Oxford.

The conflict over Lhuyd's catalog cannot simply be chalked down to a question of inadequate finances. Clearly the university did not stop printing books altogether. The financial difficulties simply sharpened their choices, forcing them to set priorities regarding the kinds of books they published. Lhuyd pinned the blame on John Meare, vice chancellor and ex-officio delegate. Several of the delegates "seem'd very inclinable" to the project; however, the "present Vice-Chancellor will hear nothing of it; tho I told him to whom 'twas dedicated {Lister} & how great a benefactor he has been."[78] The press's lack of finances, while a real enough problem, provided a convenient excuse for Meare when he wanted to turn down a book. From Lhuyd's perspective, this seemed to have as much to do with disciplinary priorities as with vendibility: as Lhuyd had written to Lister when he was first beginning to strategize about the book's publication, "the Delegates are utter strangers to these studies."

If the fossil catalog was going to make it into print, Lhuyd would have to find another publisher and another means of financing it. Tancred Robinson's publishing expertise now came in handy. In the spring of 1698 Lhuyd decided to send the manuscript to Robinson, who had located a bookseller willing to "venture it."[79] However, financing was still a problem: who was to pay for the edition? Lhuyd was not the only one frustrated with the situation. In a letter to Arthur Charlett, the master of University College, Oxford, Hans Sloane decried the sorry state of learned publishing with particular reference to Lhuyd's sufferings, complaining that booksellers "would (& will if not speedily prevented) ruine most good books that are proposed to be printed."[80] With Samuel Pepys, Sloane called upon fellows of the Royal Society to finance the book. Though the level of personal attention that Lhuyd's book received from the fellows was somewhat unusual, overall fellows of the Royal Society were used to personally pledging their financial support for books. In these decades it was not uncommon for authors and publishers to canvass among Royal Society fellows, even presenting their works and the subscription terms at weekly meetings.[81] Ten fellows subscribed for an edition of 120 copies, with 10 copies each to the subscribers and the remaining 20 for the author. The business, according to Hans Sloane, was settled in a quarter of an hour.[82] The list of subscribers was short and select: it included Isaac Newton, Hans Sloane, Lister, Francis Aston, Tancred Robinson, and Claude Joseph Geoffroy, fellow of both the Paris Académie Royale des Sciences and the Royal Society.[83]

The rest of the subscription list was made up of boldfaced names, another example of the way in which subscription lists mirrored the hierarchical social world of early modern Britain. The book's publication was also supported by John Somers, William III's lord chancellor and then president of the Royal Society; Charles Sackville, the sixth Earl of Dorset, who was made a fellow of the Royal Society in 1699; and Charles Montague, chancellor of the treasury and former president of the Royal Society (1695–1698).[84] Although the book itself was dedicated to Lister, these men, all wealthy and well placed in the government of William and Mary, were listed first among the subscribers. The subscription list thus displayed the connections between the scientific and the political establishments in the 1690s as well as the weight accorded famous names in the context of subscription publications.

"Vendible, as well as Usefull": clearly Lhuyd's catalog was useful enough to leading fellows and officers of the Royal Society. However, for these subscribers, vendibility was no longer a concern. Though the subscribers spent on the order of forty-five pounds on the edition, they did not seek to recoup their costs through sales.[85] Their copies instead went out as gifts to their correspondents in Britain and abroad. Newton shared his copies with other Cambridge scholars, while Lister and Sloane sent some of theirs to Italy, Germany, and other corners of the Continent. Ten books went directly to Paris, presumably through Claude Joseph Geoffroy, fellow of the Royal Society and *eleve* of the Académie Royale des Sciences. Lhuyd distributed his copies as gifts to subscribers to his *Archaeologia Britannica* project, particularly those who were scholars themselves.[86]

Subscribers distributed the book as an example of the best scientific work being done in Britain about Britain: rather than being valuable for any revenue it might generate in sales, it was valuable for the way it could be used to bolster the British scientific reputation, a perennial concern. Historically authors gifted books to their patrons and fellow scholars in the Republic of Letters as a way of strengthening and reinforcing relationships. Tycho Brahe, who used his riches to fund his publications, distributed copies of his books to actual and potential patrons as well as other astronomers.[87] Lhuyd's near-contemporary John Ray gave books to correspondents who provided particularly useful information for his own projects (as noted in Chapter 4).[88] However, the gifting of the *Lithophylacii Britannici ichnographia* was about more than just strengthening relationships. Almost all the copies were given away, most of them by the subscribers rather than by the author. In 1706 Thomas Hearne, an Oxford antiquary, noted that Lhuyd's "Name became famous, particularly upon Publication of a small Book in 8o about Fossiles: which is writ in Latin, & has (together with other Things in the Philosophical Transactions) given occasion to Dr. Sloan often to say that he thinks Mr. Llhwyd the best Naturalist now in Europe."[89] Sloane and his fellow subscribers gave the book away to show their correspondents an example of the work being done by British naturalists.

The history of Lhuyd's *Lithophylacii Britannici ichnographia* demonstrates that the correspondence was a vital source of funding and support for learned publications. Scholars, whose printing needs were not always met by the London stationers or even by the university press at Oxford, acted as patrons and agents for each other's books. Sloane even went so far as to accuse booksellers of "ruining" good books. In this world a commercial failure and learned success could have very little to do with each other. No one, except perhaps the printer who received his fee from the subscribers, made any money from the publication of the *Lithophylacii Britannici ichnographia*. Yet it was distributed at home and abroad as a representation of and an emissary for British science and the British scientific community, as embodied by the names on the subscription list.

Printing for and Through the Correspondence: Lhuyd's *Archaeologia Britannica*

Lhuyd's second subscription project was run on a very different scale from that of *Lithophylacii Britannici ichnographia*. Although enormously successful in one sense—it earned Lhuyd a sturdy place among both British and European naturalists—with only ten subscribers, the publication of Lhuyd's fossil catalog was a relatively small project from an undertaker's standpoint. Lhuyd's *Archaeologia Britannica* was a different beast. The *Archaeologia* consumed the last fifteen years of Lhuyd's life; subscribers and contacts numbered in the hundreds and were distributed across Wales, Ireland, Scotland, Cornwall, and Brittany. He planned a multivolume treatise but in the end finished only the first volume—*Glossography* (1707), the linguistic component—before his death in 1709. Based on the strength of this treatise, Lhuyd has come to be regarded as the originator of the modern study of Celtic languages.[90]

Unlike the *Lithophylacium Britannicum*, which was published by subscription only as a last resort, *Archaeologia Britannica* was conceived from the beginning as a subscription project. Lhuyd himself acted as the undertaker, with some assistance from Walter Thomas, the London solicitor whom he hired to help manage the inflow and outflow of subscription monies.[91] Furthermore he used subscription not just to fund printing the finished books but also to pay for the years of research, travel, and writing that would go into producing those books. This was an innovative use of subscription; typically it was employed only as a way of covering printing costs. But Lhuyd, whose ambition far outstripped his financial resources, reached out to his correspondence to support his research. As a scheme for funding research travel, rather than just publication, Lhuyd's subscription venture, even more than most, echoed the joint-stock companies of his day, which originated largely as vehicles for funding international travel and commerce and distributing the profits to investors.[92] In the case of Lhuyd's scheme, investors' returns were the finished books (which, in the subscription lists, recognized the social position of those investors within Wales and the nation as buyers of a book such as Lhuyd's) and possibly a deeper knowledge of their local environment. Those who subscribed minimal amounts (on the order of ten shillings) did not get books but only their names in the list of benefactors, set alphabetically with those who gave much more.[93]

The history of *Archaeologia Britannica* shows how authors-undertakers such as Lhuyd could use subscription to scale up the work of the correspondence. In this project Lhuyd sought to reconstruct the historical relationships between the peoples of Ireland, Scotland, Wales, Cornwall, and Brittany (as discussed in Chapter 1). As one of the first such projects, his work fostered a sense of a common "Celtic" culture where one did not necessarily exist, as the peoples of the individual "Celtic" nations were more focused on themselves and their relationships with England than on each other. Along the way Lhuyd brought into being a "Britain" that did not include England. This work required extended research travel as well as the cultivation of local correspondents distributed across the land. Lhuyd relied on his subscribers as sources of financing and as sources of content, and he used printed subscription advertisements and other tools, such as printed research questionnaires, to develop a cohort of collaborators distributed across Celtic Britain.

There was some tension in Lhuyd's conception of "Britain" (as discussed in Chapter 1). At times his Britain seemed confined primarily to Wales; at other times he extended Britain to cover Scotland, Ireland, Cornwall, and Brittany, though never England. A close examination of the strategies he used to gin up subscription and maintain relations with his correspondents, as well as subscribers' and correspondents' responses to his project, reveals the social basis of these tensions. Though Lhuyd sought to establish the connections between the "Celtic" peoples of Britain, his subscribers and his correspondents were settled most thickly in Wales, and he designed his printed instruments, his subscription proposals and questionnaires, to cater to that audience. His readership, in turn, responded enthusiastically, taking pride in a serious study of their culture, language, and history. This was no small beans in a literary world dominated by the English and in which the Welsh—and their language especially—were routinely denigrated and mocked.

In 1695 Lhuyd issued a prospectus titled "A Design for a British Dictionary."[94] At the outset of the project, he proposed a comparative study of Welsh, Greek, Latin, Cornish, Irish, and Breton; a comparative study of Celtic customs; an account of all ancient Welsh monuments of both Celtic and Roman origin; and a thorough account of the Welsh soils, waters, fossils, plants, and animals. Lhuyd projected that his research could be completed over a series of four or five summer trips into Wales. It would be necessary to visit each of the other Celtic-speaking countries at least once for comparative purposes. Travel was an absolutely vital part of his plan, for "the want of such actual Surveying, hath been in all Ages the occasion of much Error and Ignorance in Writings of this Nature."[95] Lhuyd promised to produce the linguistic study within five years and the archaeological and antiquarian volumes after two years more. He made no guarantees with respect to the natural history, which he thought he might publish in Latin, "not being able to guess how tedious it may prove."[96]

None of this could be accomplished without substantial financial backing, as Lhuyd bluntly told his potential subscribers:

> It's well known, no kind of Writing requires more Expences and Fatigue, than that of Natural History and Antiquities: it being impossible to perform any thing accurately in those Studies, without much Travelling, and diligent Searching, as well the most desert Rocks and Mountains, as the more frequented Valleys and Plains. The Caves, Mines, and Quarries must be pry'd into, as well as the outward Surface of the Earth; nor must we have less regard to the Creatures of the Sea, Lakes, and Rivers, than those of the Air and Dry Land. But 'tis not the Expences of Travelling we are only to regard; the Charges of the Figures or Draughts of such new Discoveries as will occur, must needs be much more considerable: not to mention, that a Correspondence as extensive as we can settle it, must be maintain'd with the Curious in these Studies; and such new Books purchas'd, as are pertinent to our Design; and that Labourers (especially in Mines and Quarries) are to be rewarded for preserving such things, as they shall be directed to take Notice of.[97]

This passage nicely illustrates how a topographical representation of a nation was compounded out of travel, conversation, reading, and correspondence. The naturalist aspired to map and record everything on land and water, taking notice of what was above ground as well as below, in mines and quarries. There was also much reading and writing, particularly of correspondence, to be done: just as one traveled across the land, one also had to "settle" a correspondence across that land.

One ran through money just sitting at one's desk, what with expenses for drawing and engraving figures, buying books, and maintaining the required correspondence with other naturalists and antiquarians. The natural son of an impoverished Welsh gentleman, Lhuyd received no set salary for his work as keeper of the Ashmolean and lived as he could off the museum and library admissions fees—the keeper's was "but a mean Place," according to the antiquary Thomas Hearne.[98] To pay his research expenses, Lhuyd proposed a new kind of subscription scheme. Where previous undertakers had asked for money merely to finance printing, Lhuyd asked that the Welsh (as well as Cornish, Scottish, and Irish, though Lhuyd emphasized the Welsh) gentry, clergy, and nobility fund his research for a five-year term by pledging a certain amount to be paid once a year starting 1 March 1696. Asking only for as much as donors might be willing to contribute (rather than setting a price, as in book proposals), Lhuyd apologized in advance for what might be seen as the "profuse Liberality" of such a request. While acknowledging that "such an Encouragement is above my Merits," he promised to carry out the design to the very best of his abilities.[99] Over the next five years some two hundred people, most of them Welsh, donated a total of £360 5s.[100] Giving started out high at £110 10s. in 1696 but dropped over the years to just £11 by 1700.[101] Lhuyd began using the money right away, setting out on a six-month tour of Wales in April 1696.[102] In the spring of 1697 he set off once more. He would not return to Oxford until March 1701.[103]

Over the life of the project, Lhuyd employed a range of "social strategies" for encouraging subscriptions and subscriber participation. Building and working the right social connections were crucial. Lhuyd's "social strategies," which he enacted through correspondence and face-to-face interaction with subscribers and informants, included distributing proposals and information on the project through personal contacts, discreetly advertising the names of prominent subscribers and the amounts for which they subscribed, and inviting his subscribers to become intellectual as well as financial supporters of the work, primarily through the mechanism of the research questionnaire.

Lhuyd distributed subscription proposals primarily through friends and acquaintances among the Welsh gentry and clergy. As he was a Welshman, Welsh contacts were most readily available to him. He designed the promotional materials to take advantage of this. Even though *Archaeologia Britannica* was a comparative project, the printed materials emphasized that he would focus primarily on Welsh antiquities and natural history. Given the importance of regional and local affiliations in the social and political identities of the gentry and nobility, this was a canny move on Lhuyd's part: it could only encourage Welsh gentry, clergy, and nobility to participate.

In this Welsh context (as across the country as a whole), the right names were valuable tools of persuasion. In his effort to cultivate Welsh subscribers, Lhuyd did not put an equal amount of energy into pursuing every local squire who might have once picked up a fossil. Instead in each county he sought out one or two members of the gentry and nobility, well-off men who were known and respected by their peers. He used those names to promote the project and assemble a team of subscribers; six to ten per county would be enough.[104] One of his first goals, for example, was to sign John Vaughan, Earl of Carbery, Royalist politician, governor of Jamaica from 1674 to 1678, and president of the Royal Society from 1686 to 1689. Carbery was most useful not for his Royal Society connections, however, but for the respect and honor he commanded in the southern Welsh county of Carmarthenshire, his home. Conscious of the etiquette of patronage, Lhuyd pursued Carbery through intermediaries, including Martin Lister. If Carbery would recommend the proposals to a few gentlemen in Carmarthenshire, Lhuyd wrote to Lister, "I doubt not but 'twill be well recd in that countrey."[105] Carbery's prominence was such that his name carried weight outside of Carmarthenshire as well. Lhuyd particularly asked Lister to get Carbery's signature and return the paper to him so that he could show it to other Welsh scholars in Oxford.[106] Lhuyd planned to use the physical evidence of Carbery's subscription to persuade his Oxford colleagues to support the project and promote it among their acquaintances across Wales.

Lhuyd sometimes communicated not only subscribers' names but also the amounts for which they subscribed. If potential subscribers saw that their neighbors contributed generously, they might also be inclined to do so. In a letter to John Lloyd of Denbighshire in northern Wales, Lhuyd listed all the subscribers in Denbighshire and Flintshire, a neighboring county, along with the amounts they gave. He asked Lloyd, who gathered subscriptions as Lhuyd's agent, to tell potential subscribers the names and the amounts if they asked.[107] Tellingly, Lhuyd gave Lloyd the names and amounts only of contributors local to Denbighshire and Flintshire. When the gentry dug into their pockets to support Lhuyd's travels, they compared themselves not to some national, or London, standard of giving but to those immediately around them.

Although Lhuyd tried to raise competition among neighbors, he also took some care not to seem immodest in his requests for money. The balance he attempted to strike reflected a tension at the heart of subscription publication, particularly author-managed subscriptions: raising money from one's friends and acquaintances could be seen as taking advantage of them. In the early seventeenth century George Wither thought to use subscription to finance the publication of *Fidelia*, a volume of his poetry. However, in the end Wither felt uncomfortable taking his friends' money: "remembering how far it would be from his disposition to lay claim to proffered gratuities, he wholly repented himself of what indeed he never well approved of."[108] He returned the money he had collected, gave the books away for free, and granted the copyrights to the stationer George Norton.

Though he never suffered a change of mind or heart as George Wither did, Lhuyd claimed that he sought subscriptions only from those with both ample means and sincere interest in his project. In a letter to his Welsh friend Richard Mostyn, Lhuyd expressed a desire to limit the number of his subscribers to "those who have good estates, and are of their own free choice (& not purely from the example of their neighbours) disposed to favour the undertaking."[109] On the face of it, taking this line would seem to restrict the number of potential subscribers as well as revenue. However, disclaiming greed in this way could also be read as another strategy for encouraging subscriptions. Socially and financially Lhuyd's position was limited; he had no personal income of his own and no social standing beyond what he had earned as a scholar. Because he depended on the goodwill of the gentry, clergy, and nobility for the success of his project, if Lhuyd appeared greedy in his aims, he was likely to fail. This was only truer because he relied on his friends to do much of the work of distributing proposals and collecting subscriptions for him. His friends volunteered on his behalf for the sake of friendship, their enthusiasm for his projects, the pleasure of his company when he traveled (as we saw in Chapter 3), and any return favors he might be able to do for them in his "Station at Oxford," such as procuring for them books to which they were otherwise unable to get access.[110] If he overburdened them or appeared to be gaining personally from their labor, why should they help him? Later in the same letter to Mostyn, Lhuyd expressed delighted surprise that two of his earliest subscribers had given so much—five pounds and forty shillings, respectively; it was, he wrote, much more than he hoped for, but "these are persons of the greatest estates."[111] By communicating exact amounts with a pleasing modesty, Lhuyd combined two strategies in one neat stroke.

But if such strategies as advertising the names of prominent supporters and making known to potential subscribers how much their neighbors had given could be used to sell a project, they could also backfire on the under-taker. Although Carbery subscribed to the *Archaeologia Britannica*, he put himself down for a very small amount. By the winter of 1696 Lhuyd had to hush up Carbery's subscription for fear that his stinginess set the bar too low and would encourage others with less means to reduce their giving.[112] Car-bery, it turned out, was probably more trouble than he was worth; when it came time to pay for the first volume of the *Archaeologia Britannica* in 1707, he denied his signature in the subscription book and refused to pay for his copy, which had been custom printed for him on large-format paper.[113]

In this instance a peer's word won out over a written record. Carbery's refusal to pay for his copy of the book offers an interesting data point in the history of the relationship between speech and writing. Carbery's unmistak-able signature was there in the subscription book, and yet he chose to deny it, trusting that if it was his spoken word against his written word, his spoken word (seconded by his servant in this case) would carry the day. Historians have suggested that over the course of the early modern period, literacy grad-ually took precedence over orality, particularly in the realms of historical and legal evidence: whereas, for example, at the beginning of the period, oral testimony could be used to defend historical property claims in the courts, by the end of the period, written evidence was usually required.[114] Though this was not a court case, and so not the most high-stakes or high-visibility test of the value of spoken testimony versus written evidence, Carbery's suc-cessful denial of the signature illustrated the ways in which social status could enhance the force of the spoken—though perhaps not its truth value. Lhuyd clearly believed that Carbery was lying. In any event, Lhuyd probably should have known not to trust Carbery, a notorious libertine who was dogged by rumors that while he was governor of Jamaica he had sold Welsh servants in his household for slaves.[115] Given this reputation, even if Carbery had come through with his promised support for the project, it is possible that advertising him as a subscriber would not have been the most winning strategy.

Another obstacle Lhuyd encountered as he canvassed for subscriptions through his correspondence was the intermittent reliability of his friends. They might recommend Lhuyd's project to others, obtain their promise to subscribe, but forget to obtain a signature and a written guarantee of the amount right away (thus making it easier for those who were inclined to do so to lower their subscriptions after they heard how little Carbery had pledged).[116] Lhuyd hired the London solicitor Walter Thomas in part to combat this problem. As Lhuyd's solicitor, he was paid for diligent follow-up. The nature of the difficulties that Lhuyd encountered and his solution to them—employing a solicitor to manage the subscriptions—suggest the limits of the social approach to financing research and book production. One could not always trust—or compel—one's friends and acquaintances to act on one's behalf.

Taken together, Lhuyd's "social strategies" for gaining subscriptions show a scholar building support for his project point by point, person by person. Some of his strategies, such as advertising the name of Lord Carbery, were more intimate versions of those used by commercial publishers such as Moses Pitt and John Ogilby. Others, such as discreetly communicating to potential subscribers how much others had donated, were more tailored to his project, given that his project was unlike a regular book subscription in that there was no set subscription price. What the strategies shared was a sensitivity to the social mores of the correspondence and an emphasis on local connections and local contexts: Lord Carbery's name mattered because it was prominent within Welsh circles, particularly within Carmarthenshire. Lhuyd's potential subscribers cared what their neighbors gave but not what somebody distant from them might have given. Although Lhuyd may have seen a broader national vision animating his project, his supporters among the Welsh gentry and clergy were unlikely to make that their focus.

Parochial Queries: Subscribers as Content Producers

In addition to asking his subscribers for money, Lhuyd solicited their active participation in his research program: he treated his subscribers as content producers.[117] In December 1696, after returning from a six-month exploratory trip into Wales, he issued "Parochial Queries in Order to A Geographical Dictionary, A Natural History, &c of *Wales*." Thirty-one questions covered antiquities, the names and seats of local gentry, manuscripts ("Ancient or late Copies," which were useful for tracking linguistic history), local customs, inscriptions, livestock, lakes and rivers, caves, diseases, agricultural practices, seashells, and fossils. Respondents were encouraged to answer the queries in blanks after each question—Lhuyd's were the first queries to include such blanks—or write directly on a separate sheet and return their answers to one of Lhuyd's local contacts, who would remit them to Lhuyd's assistant at the Ashmolean or to Walter Thomas in London.[118] (See Figure 7.)

The role that the "Parochial Queries" played in Lhuyd's project illustrates well one of the key themes of this book: that constructions of Britain as a topographical object were anchored on the social foundations of the correspondence. The strength and layout of that foundation helped determine the appearance and size of the final building. Creating a body of knowledge about Britain depended on creating a body of social connections as well, people distributed across the land in which any particular investigator was interested. Lhuyd, clearly aware of these social foundations, expended much effort in cultivating the connections that would encourage individuals to respond to the queries and to engage with him as he traveled. It was through the questionnaires, in particular, that Lhuyd molded the subscription base into something like a scaled-up correspondence.

Some 4,000 copies of the four-page questionnaire were printed and disbursed through Lhuyd's correspondence to the gentry and clergy of Wales, Ireland, Scotland, and Cornwall.[119] In marketing the queries, Lhuyd played on potential contributors' hometown pride, asking those who distributed queries for him to emphasize to potential respondents "that it lies chiefly in their own powers, whether a compleat or imperfect account be given of their country."[120] Lhuyd received around 150 replies. At least 30 or so came in as query sheets partially or wholly completed, and additional responses were written as letters.[121]

Lhuyd used the questionnaires to prepare the ground for his research travels through Wales, Ireland, Scotland, Cornwall, and Brittany, which lasted four years, and to keep information moving after his travels were over. Querying locals helped him to discover what manuscripts, coins, monuments, and natural or archaeological sites might be worth investigating on the ground. It also helped him identify knowledgeable locals—both the gentle and the "vulgar," with whom Lhuyd, fluent in Welsh, could speak directly during his travels.[122] In some ways the "Vulgar" could better aid Lhuyd than the gentle could. They were more likely, for example, to know all the Welsh names of plants, animals, and places, which Lhuyd needed to know for his comparative analysis of Celtic languages, whereas the learned and literate would be more likely to speak and write primarily in English. In the case of local place names, Lhuyd judged "an illiterat shepheard" more reliable than bishops and other men of learning.[123] "Vulgar" informants might assist him by preserving fossils, plants, and odd stones that crossed their paths; he was

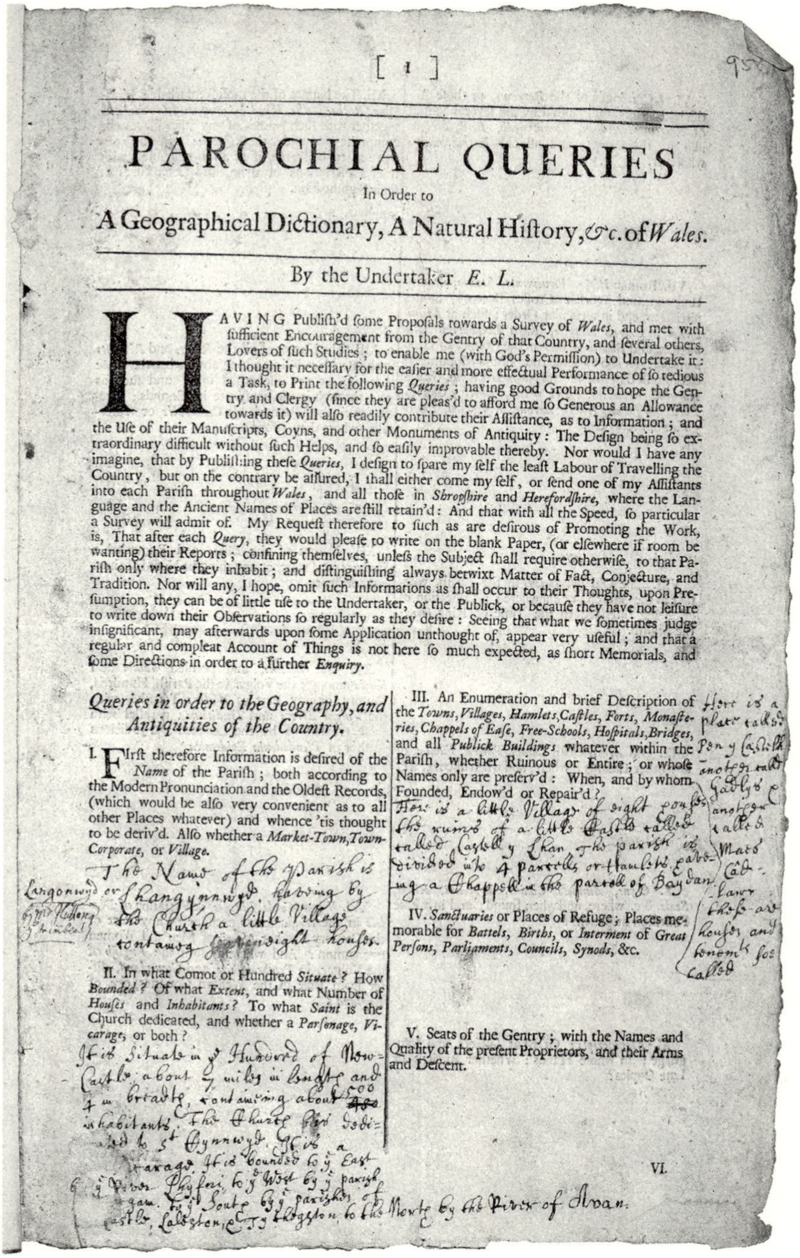

PAROCHIAL QUERIES

In Order to

A Geographical Dictionary, A Natural History, &c. of Wales.

By the Undertaker *E. L.*

HAVING Publish'd some Proposals towards a Survey of *Wales*, and met with sufficient Encouragement from the Gentry of that Country, and several others, Lovers of such Studies ; to enable me (with God's Permission) to Undertake it : I thought it necessary for the easier and more effectual Performance of so tedious a Task, to Print the following *Queries* ; having good Grounds to hope the Gentry and Clergy (since they are pleas'd to afford me so Generous an Allowance towards it) will also readily contribute their Assistance, as to Information ; and the Use of their Manuscripts, Coyns, and other Monuments of Antiquity : The Design being so extraordinary difficult without such Helps, and so easily improvable thereby. Nor would I have any imagine, that by Publishing these *Queries*, I design to spare my self the least Labour of Travelling the Country, but on the contrary be assured, I shall either come my self, or send one of my Assistants into each Parish throughout *Wales*, and all those in *Shropshire* and *Herefordshire*, where the Language and the Ancient Names of Places are still retain'd : And that with all the Speed, so particular a Survey will admit of. My Request therefore to such as are desirous of Promoting the Work, is, That after each *Query*, they would please to write on the blank Paper, (or elsewhere if room be wanting) their Reports ; confining themselves, unless the Subject shall require otherwise, to that Parish only where they inhabit ; and distinguishing always betwixt Matter of Fact, Conjecture, and Tradition. Nor will any, I hope, omit such Informations as shall occur to their Thoughts, upon Presumption, they can be of little use to the Undertaker, or the Publick, or because they have not leisure to write down their Observations so regularly as they desire : Seeing that what we sometimes judge insignificant, may afterwards upon some Application unthought of, appear very useful ; and that a regular and compleat Account of Things is not here so much expected, as short Memorials, and some Directions in order to a further *Enquiry*.

Queries in order to the Geography, and Antiquities of the Country.

I. First therefore Information is desired of the *Name* of the Parish ; both according to the Modern Pronunciation and the Oldest Records, (which would be also very convenient as to all other Places whatever) and whence 'tis thought to be deriv'd. Also whether a *Market-Town, Town-Corporate*, or *Village*.

[handwritten notes]

II. In what Comot or Hundred *Situate* ? How *Bounded* ? Of what *Extent*, and what Number of *Houses* and *Inhabitants* ? To what *Saint* is the Church dedicated, and whether a *Parsonage, Vicarage*, or both ?

[handwritten notes]

III. An Enumeration and brief Description of the *Towns, Villages, Hamlets, Castles, Forts, Monasteries, Chappels of Ease, Free-Schools, Hospitals, Bridges*, and all *Publick Buildings* whatever within the Parish, whether Ruinous or Entire ; or whose Names only are preserv'd : When, and by whom Founded, Endow'd or Repair'd ?

[handwritten notes]

IV. *Sanctuaries* or Places of Refuge ; Places memorable for *Battels, Births*, or *Interment* of Great *Persons, Parliaments, Councils, Synods*, &c.

V. Seats of the Gentry ; with the Names and Quality of the present Proprietors, and their Arms and Descent.

VI.

Figure 7. Edward Lhuyd, "Parochial Queries in Order to A Geographical Dictionary, A Natural History, &c. of *Wales*," Bod MS Ashmole 1820, 95r. Reproduced by permission of the Bodleian Library, Oxford. The first page of one of Lhuyd's "Parochial Queries," filled out for the parish of Lhangynnwyd (or Langonwyd) by a respondent identified in the margin as "Mr. Hutton, the Incumbent," or the parish priest. This is one of 44 responses preserved in Bod MS Ashmole 1820, out of a total of about 150 that Lhuyd received, many of which were submitted as letters rather than as filled-out questionnaires.

particularly interested in formed stones brought up from underground by miners. On the other hand, gentle and noble informants could help by allowing him access to their estates, where he could copy the manuscripts in their libraries, trace inscriptions on ancient monuments, and collect what he could of the fossils, rocks, and plants. Interestingly, Lhuyd traveled not just to observe nature and collect specimens firsthand but to collect the query sheets. Though Lhuyd's printed instruction encouraged respondents to return their answers to Lhuyd's local contacts or to mail them in, Lhuyd also collected them as he traveled.

In Lhuyd's hands, print was not just a tool for answering immediate research questions; it was also a tool for growing the correspondence in a somewhat more permanent fashion: this is what I mean by printing for correspondence. Lhuyd hoped that the correspondence he built with subscription proposals and questionnaires would continue on after the immediate purposes of those instruments had been fulfilled. After he returned from his four-year ramble, he asked subscribers to continue to send on information. To Richard Mostyn he wrote, "Being after a tedious ramble of four years at length return'd to the place from whence I set out . . .'tis my Duty to return most humble Thanks to my best Friends and greatest Patrons, who have enabled me to {have} performd such expensive Travails; and necessary I should entreat their farther assistance as to correspondence and Information, in case anything may occur remarkable, during the time I shall be culling out of the pertinent part of my collection and digesting it for the Presse."[124] Even after his travels were done, Lhuyd's "best Friends and greatest Patrons" could continue to help him by sending him useful observations as well as material artifacts as they came to their notice. Traveling also provided opportunities to foster longer-lasting connections: as he traveled, Lhuyd met with correspondents, providing them with personal attention that made them feel like valued participants in his project and encouraged them to keep information moving. When Lhuyd failed to pay these social calls, it resulted in breaches in his relationships with his informants, stopping up the flow of information (as discussed more extensively in Chapter 3).[125]

Lhuyd's correspondence hummed with the business of distributing the "Parochial Queries," allowing us to inspect, almost brick by brick, the social foundations of his topographical Britain. Most of them went to Wales, where, as a Welshman, he had the most contacts, with a few copies reserved for Cornwall, Ireland, and Scotland. He wrote to an associate in North Wales:

I sent by Mr K. Eaton a parcel of *Queries* to Mr Price of Wrexham, with a great many more to your worship directed to be left with your Br{other}, half a dozen to Chancellor Wyn {Robert Wynne, a fellow of Jesus College} (from his brother William) a dozen to Dick Jones, the like number betw. Ken. Eytyn and his Father; two to Mr Humphreys of Maerdy, four to your brother David; and about 50 to the parson of Dôl Gelheu. His Fellow Travailler Mr John Davies took with him a good parcel for Anglesey, and about a douzen to the Schoolmaster of Bangor. I shall dispose of them to other countreys as I have opportunities; but must trouble you to prevail with your Kinsman to disperse them in Flintshire where I have no acquaintance at all. I have printed four thousand of them; so that I can affoard three to a parish; or more or lesse as occasion requires; besides a sufficient number for Cornwall &c[126]

As this letter illustrates, in Wales, Lhuyd's contacts were thickly layered and defined by family relationships. Queries passed between brothers, fathers and sons, and kinsmen. Lhuyd relied on kin networks: in Flintshire, where he knew no one, he asked his correspondent to share the questionnaires with a "kinsman" who could distribute them broadly there. Queries were also transmitted through multiple layers of relationship, with Lhuyd transmitting queries to "Mr Price of Wrexham" via "Mr K. Eaton" and to Robert Wynne of Jesus College via his brother William. In addition he pinpointed the locally prominent, sending queries through schoolmasters and parsons, those who had no fame beyond their own locale but were well known within it and would know who else to target as recipients of the queries.

In contrast, Lhuyd's contacts were much thinner on the ground in the rest of "Britain," and it was harder to know how and to whom to distribute the questionnaires. Kin relationships could not serve him outside of Wales. Instead, Lhuyd worked through more distant contacts. Before he began traveling, he sent copies to Scotland via the naturalist Martin Lister. He particularly targeted the Highlands. Lhuyd's knowledge of the social landscape of antiquarian studies and natural history in the Scottish Highlands was relatively meager, but he did manage, through John Aubrey, to identify James Garden, the Aberdeen antiquary, as a possible point of contact. Garden was "a person of considerable interest in the Highlands, amongst the clergy" and so might be able to disseminate a number of questionnaires.[127] Neither Lhuyd nor Lister knew Garden personally; however, Lhuyd asked Lister to approach him, perhaps because given Lister's prominence within Royal Society circles, an unlooked-for letter from him might receive a better reception. Lhuyd also asked Lister to canvass his acquaintances who might have contacts in the Highlands; through a Dr. Grey and a Dr. Wallace, known to Lister, Lhuyd distributed more queries.[128] Whereas there were three questionnaires per parish in Wales, there were many fewer for all of Cornwall, the Scottish Highlands, and Ireland. Though exact numbers are hard to come by, in his letters to Lister, Lhuyd mentioned sending a "parcel" and a "quire" north to the Highlands.[129] (A quire would have been twenty-four or twenty-five questionnaires.)

Not only was Lhuyd's correspondence thickest in Wales. As a research instrument, the queries were crafted for the investigation not of *Celtic* languages, antiquities, and natural history but of *Welsh* languages, antiquities, and natural history. They were "Parochial Queries in Order to A Description of Wales," and several asked questions particular to Wales. A question on regional linguistic variation, for example, specifically asked respondents to give information on differences between English as spoken in southwestern Wales and as spoken in the western counties of England.[130] There was no similar question about differences between Scots Gaelic as spoken in the Scottish Highlands versus the Lowlands. Which is not to say that Lhuyd was uninterested in such questions; this was precisely the kind of question he explored once he was on the ground traveling. The printed questionnaire was something of a blunt instrument, crafted for the majority of potential respondents rather than tailored to each individual.

Though the queries were distributed across the "British" parts of Britain, they were neither designed nor distributed with all the "British" in mind. This approach was a deliberate one, reflecting not only the limitations of the printed questionnaire but also Lhuyd's own Welsh partisanship.[131] Martin Lister suggested altering the questionnaires for distribution in Scotland, but Lhuyd refused.[132] Yet this approach could also limit Lhuyd's ability to trace the historical connections between British peoples and languages, connections in which he was deeply interested. Ultimately, Lhuyd received most, if not all, of the replies to his printed queries from Wales and a few of the English counties along the border where some Welsh was still spoken and Welsh place names persisted.

The printed questionnaires were not the end of the story of Lhuyd's researches in Ireland, Scotland, Cornwall, and Brittany. Once he hit the ground a few years later, Lhuyd identified a few more "persons of considerable interest" in Ireland and Scotland, including the learned antiquary John Beaton in the Scottish Highlands.[133] Rather than using the printed queries, Lhuyd sent a specially tailored, handwritten list of queries to Colin Campbell, a minister in Ardchattan, about a hundred miles northwest of Glasgow.[134] In this list, which he wrote after a conversation with the minister, Lhuyd asked detailed and knowledgeable questions about antiquities, folk customs, and folklore in the Highlands. He hoped that this single contact would share the queries with a friend or three who might be able to provide additional perspectives. He also compiled a list of individuals in Scotland in possession of Gaelic manuscripts, counting six such collectors, including some on the remote isles of Skye and Uist (to Lhuyd, "Wyst an Island beyond Sky").[135]

Though Lhuyd's contacts in Scotland were fewer and farther between, one can picture him developing his sense of the relationships between the Scottish, Irish, and Welsh, the factors that united them as "British," as he traveled. Chief among these was an oppositional relationship to the English. He was intensely curious about "British" history, antiquities, languages, and customs outside of Wales, as evidenced by his conversation and correspondence with Colin Campbell and others in the Highlands. That Lhuyd made the effort to travel so far north was an index of his curiosity: as he noted in a letter to the Dubliner Thomas Molyneux (younger brother of William), many a southerner, as well as an Irishman, regarded the Highlanders as barbarous people on account of "the Roughness of their Countrey as Consisting very much of Barren Mountains and Loughs and their Retaining their Antient Habitts Custom and Language" (a "lough" is a loch).[136] Contrary to expectation, Lhuyd was happily surprised to find "a great Deal of Civility and kindness as well in the Highlands as the Lowlands."[137] Furthermore his experiences of the Highlanders caused him to question the common opinion that they were "Barbarous and inhospitable": after all, many Englishmen counted the Welsh "Barbarous" and the Irish "Wild" because (from an English perspective) they too lived in rough, unwelcoming country.[138]

The linguistic data that Lhuyd collected, both in response to the printed questionnaires and in more informal conversation and correspondence during and after his travels, suggest something of the complexity of Lhuyd's "Britain," as well as the enthusiasm with which local gentry and clergy communicated their small piece of it. In terms of the content they provided, Lhuyd's Welsh respondents tended to focus narrowly on providing information about their parish, as requested by the queries.[139] However, one sees hints of respondents' wider perspectives on relationships among the various peoples and languages of greater Britain, particularly in response to Lhuyd's question about linguistic variation, which did ask for comparisons between English as spoken by the Welsh and by the English, particularly in southwestern Wales and in the West Country in England.[140] One respondent in Carmarthenshire discriminated between "British" and "English" names and vocabulary, seeming to use "British" as a synonym for Welsh (consistent with the widely held belief that the Welsh were the remnant of the ancient British).[141] Another respondent observed that in the Gower peninsula (in southwestern Wales, not far from Cardiff) many "people both highe & lowe" who had been born in the time of Queen Elizabeth spoke an English in which "f's" and "s's" were pronounced as "v's" and "z's," as they did in the West Country.[142] Historically these pronunciations were shared across the northern and southern reaches of the Gower peninsula, but there were some differences as well: in the north they tended to season their English with more Welsh vocabulary.[143] However, times were changing: though past generations in the Gower peninsula had used many English words that were outdated in their time, the old words were disappearing, perhaps a sign that this part of Wales was becoming more closely connected with the rest of England.[144]

Lhuyd's study of Scots and Irish Gaelic revealed similarly highly localized variations in those languages. One of the key methods he followed in studying these languages was essentially natural historical: he collected words. He copied into notebooks the word lists from John Ray's *Dictionariolum trilingue* (1675), a student dictionary with common words in English, Latin, and Greek, broken down by category.[145] The category headings were not unlike the chapters in a county natural history. They began with natural categories, such as the heavens, "stones and metals," "plants," "four-footed beasts," before proceeding to the human and the divine, with sections devoted to words related to human bodies, diseases, food, God, "moral virtues and vices," and schools. Like a natural history, this dictionary attempted to be a systematic, ordered representation of a portion of the world, though this portion was defined linguistically rather than territorially. As Lhuyd traveled, he recorded in his notebooks the equivalents of Ray's words in Scots and Irish Gaelic (two dialects each) and Breton.[146] Words were captured from interviews with those he met as he traveled; he recorded words in a phonetic alphabet based on Welsh orthography, doing his best to record pronunciation in the various dialects he encountered.[147] Lhuyd also recorded the Scottish minister John Beaton's pronunciation of the first two chapters of the book of

Genesis.[148] As Beaton read it in Irish Gaelic, Lhuyd took dictation using his phonetic alphabet. Beaton, the scion of a scholarly family whose members had long served as physicians to the "Lords of the Isles," the rulers of the seacoasts and islands in northwestern Scotland, used classical Gaelic pronunciation in reading the Bible to Lhuyd.[149] His use of it was evidence of the long, and ongoing, history of contacts and interconnections between Ireland and northwestern Scotland, as this was the "literary" Gaelic used in Ireland.

In sum, Lhuyd's work in Ireland and Scotland recording vocabulary in four Gaelic dialects and a Scotsman's pronunciation of literary Irish Gaelic opened up a small window onto the complexity of the relationships between British languages and cultures, a complexity that archaeologists and linguists are still parsing. His correspondents' responses to the queries opened up similar complexity in Wales. Lhuyd's Welsh respondents differentiated between the English and the "British," but they also noted regional variation in how English was spoken within Wales and traced similarities between Welsh and English uses of the English language. These comments highlighted the linguistic links between Wales and England, suggesting that parts of southwestern Wales were linguistically integrated with the nearer parts of England as much as with the rest of Wales, while a bit farther north, linguistic identity shaded more Welsh. The terrain of Britain was complex and shifting. As Lhuyd's original question about linguistic variation and his research methods more broadly acknowledged, Celtic Britain was by no means linguistically pure. Neither were Ireland, Scotland, Wales, Cornwall, and Brittany linguistically unified; language varied with the terrain. This was why localized studies, sourced from an array of correspondents spread across the land, were so important in constructing Lhuyd's vision of Britain as a topographical and historical object.

Conclusion

Lhuyd's experiences with two different subscription projects illustrate how readerships were built from the ground up and how different those readerships could be, even with books written by the same author. Readerships formed one by one, as authors contacted their friends and potential patrons and they, if sufficiently interested, contacted their friends and acquaintances to see if they might be willing to buy the books. If an author failed to mobilize his social connections, a book could fail, as Aubrey's inability to bring forward the subscription for his *Monumenta Britannica* showed.

Sensitive to the ways in which a readership could dissolve, or never mate-
rialize, if not properly attended to, undertakers supervised the process carefully, trying to ensure that proposals got into the hands of the right people
at the right time and through the proper channels. When successfully assembling financing for research and publication for *Archaeologia Britannica,*
Lhuyd signed prominent subscribers and showed evidence of their subscription to others; he asked his agents to pass on (discreetly) how much others
had subscribed for; and he enlisted his Welsh contacts, rather than booksellers, to distribute proposals and collect subscriptions and payments for him.
What these tactics shared was an emphasis on building local contacts and
connections.

Authors-undertakers as well as commercial publishers such as John
Ogilby, Moses Pitt, and John Dunton leveraged (or attempted to leverage)
social relationships and the power of famous names in an effort to open
people's pockets. When individual subscribers' names were used as promotional tools, it depended on the project whether locally prominent or nationally famous names had more persuasive power. For Lhuyd, for example, the
Earl of Carbery's support mattered (for better or for worse) for the respect he
may (or may not have) commanded among his Welsh neighbors and compa-
triots. Although Lhuyd was well connected to the Royal Society through
Robert Plot, Hans Sloane, Martin Lister, and John Ray, and fellows of the
Royal Society supervised and funded the publication of his *Lithophylacii Britannici ichnographia,* the subscribers to the *Archaeologia Britannica* were
mainly Welsh gentry, clergy, lawyers, physicians, and scholars. Lhuyd's strategies for building a subscriber base were thus somewhat different from those
followed by undertakers pushing books whose appeal was less tied to geography, such as broader atlases, mathematical treatises, and herbals. In those
cases subscription undertakers canvassed nationally for subscriptions through
booksellers around the country, and they promoted their projects with the
names of nationally prominent subscribers. Across the board, subscription
lists became selective mirrors of the British social world, even, in their typog-
raphy and ordering, reproducing British social hierarchies.

Lhuyd invited subscribers to participate directly in providing content for
his research as well as in financing it. In some sense, because Lhuyd sought
to reconstruct histories of language and culture in Celtic Britain, his potential
readers and subscribers *were* his content. In transforming subscribers into
content providers, Lhuyd made use of long-established habits of soliciting
and trading natural historical and antiquarian information within the natural

historical and antiquarian correspondence. In effect he built his readership in the image of the correspondence, as a (hopefully) scaled-up version of it. Book and readership were created together, as the content that Lhuyd projected for the book determined where he sought readers and the interests of the readers and material they provided helped fill the pages of the books.

Lhuyd was not the only undertaker to pursue subscribers as content providers, though none, perhaps, did it on quite so grand a scale in the seventeenth century. Undertakers invited subscribers to pay to have their county seats depicted in studies of local antiquities and natural history, or they could contribute accounts of curiosities of art and nature; natural specimens; ancient monuments, coins, and manuscripts; and unusual occurrences, such as earthquakes and fierce storms, to be included in works that surveyed history, nature, and the providences that God bestowed upon his people.

These efforts suggest increasing ambitions for comprehensiveness on the part of learned antiquaries and naturalists as well as an awareness that financial support and personal, intellectual investment in books went hand in hand. Though sometimes honored more in the breach than in the observance, extensive correspondence and conversation with knowledgeable individuals along with personal observations and careful attention to manuscript and other historical records had formed the foundation of learned natural history and antiquarian studies since the late sixteenth century. In late seventeenth-century subscription projects, as this chapter has shown, what was new was the use of print instruments (subscription proposals and queries), distributed through booksellers and through existing correspondence, to reach and recruit greater numbers of potential informants.

Lhuyd's printed vision of Britain as an object of topographical and historical inquiry, represented by the linguistic volume of *Archaeologia Britannica,* was a product of a collaborative process between Lhuyd and his subscribers and correspondents. Lhuyd's work showed how the "correspondence," the social relationships between investigators, subscribers, and respondents working together at a distance, functioned as the foundation of any construction of Britain as a topographical object. Lhuyd defined Britain from the "margins"—the Celtic margins—arguing that the history of Britain was a history spread out across Wales, Scotland, Ireland, Cornwall, and even Brittany, places defined by related languages. Yet digging deeper into the project, especially into Lhuyd's use of the questionnaire as a tool for collecting data and managing and disciplining collective observation, we see more clearly the balance between the Welsh focus of the project and Lhuyd's

broader curiosity about, but limited access to, the rest of "Britain." Lhuyd
by no means broke free (or desired to break free) of his and his sponsors' and
primary respondents'—the gentry and clergy of Wales—dominant interest in
their own national history and topography. Lhuyd, a Welshman and inheritor
of a historical tradition that identified "British" as Welsh, pushed the Welsh
emphasis of his project.[150] Yet in his travels he conducted fine-grained linguistic work on Irish Gaelic, Scots Gaelic, Cornish, and Breton, the first such
work of its kind, and developed a deeper appreciation for the similarities that
bound the scattered peoples of his Britain. In Lhuyd's work we see how, on
social, material, and intellectual levels, a naturalist brought the local and the
national to bear on each other, compounding a "national" vision of Britain
out of local particulars gathered from individuals scattered across the Celtic
lands.

Chapter 6

"The Manuscripts Flew About
like Butterflies": Self-Archiving
and the Pressures of History

Despite their heavy reliance on papers and manuscripts—as documented throughout this book—seventeenth-century British naturalists and antiquaries lived in a world that did not much care for them. Writing a thought down and expecting it to be preserved, especially after one's death, was something of a desperate act: the possibility of loss or destruction was always present, and anything other than accidental preservation (the child of neglect) required vast resources of social, financial, and institutional capital. Sometimes the destruction of a manuscript was a deliberate response to its content, as was the case with religious-book burning. More commonly, however, manuscripts were destroyed through reuse or recycling, as John Aubrey recalled in some detail in *The Naturall Historie of Wiltshire*:

> Anno 1633. I entered into my Grammar at the Latin Schoole at
> Yatton-Keynel, in the Church: where the Curate Mr Hart taught
> the eldest Boyes, Virgil, Ovid, Cicero &c. The fashion then was to
> save the Forules of their Bookes with a false cover of Parchment
> sc{ilicet} old Manuscript. Which I was too young to understand;
> But I was pleased with the Elegancy of the Writing, and the coloured
> initiall Letters. I remember the Rector here [Mr: Wm. Stump.] great
> gr{and} Son of St{ump} the Cloathier of Malmesbury] had severall
> Manuscripts of the Abbey: He was a proper Man, and a good Fel-
> low, and when He brewed a barrel of speciall Ale, his use was to

stop the bung-hole (under the Clay) with a sheet of Manuscript: He sayd nothing did it so well. which me thought did grieve me then to see. Afterwards I went to Schoole to a Mr. Latimer at Leigh-Delamer (the next Parish) where was the like use of covering of Bookes. In my grandfathers dayes, the Manuscripts flew about like Butterflies: All Musick bookes, Account bookes, Copie bookes &c. were covered with old Manuscripts, as wee cover them now with blew Paper, or Marbled Paper. And the Glovers at Malmesbury made great Havock of them, and Gloves were wrapt up no doubt in many good pieces of Antiquity. Before the late warres a World of rare Manuscripts perished here about: for within half a dozen Miles of this place, were the Abbey of Malmesbury, where it may be pre-sumed the Library was as well furnished with choice Copies, as most Libraries of England: and perhaps in this Library we might have found a correct Plinys Naturall History, which Canutus a Monk here did abridge for King Henry the second. Within the afore said compass was Broadstock Priory, Stanley Abbey, Farleigh Abbey, Bath Abbey 8 miles: and Cyrencester Abbey 12 miles. Anno 1638. I was transplanted to Blandford-Schoole in Dorset to Mr William Sutton. Here also was the use of covering of Bookes with old Parch-ments, sc{ilicet} Leases &c. but I never saw any thing of a Manu-script there. Here about were no Abbeys or Convents for Men. One may also perceive by the binding of old Bookes, how the old Manu-scripts went to wrack in those dayes. About 1647. I went to Parson Stump out of curiosity to see his Manuscripts, whereof I had seen some in my Childhood; but by that time they were lost, and dis-perst: His sonns were Gunners, & Soldiers, and scoured their Gun-nes with them, but he shewed me severall old Deedes granted by the Ld Abbotts, with their seales annexed: which (I suppose) his Sonn [Capt. Thomas Stumpe of Malmesbury] hath still."[1]

In this passage (see Figure 8) Aubrey mentions four of the many uses of old manuscripts, none of which involved reading: covering books, wrapping gloves, cleaning guns, and stopping up the bungholes of kegs of beer. With the exception of legal records having to do with land tenure (Aubrey's refer-ence to leases notwithstanding), the matter of parchment and paper was often much more useful to most people than any text that might be written on them.[2] Aubrey linked this destruction to the dissolution of the monasteries and the consequent emptying of their libraries under Henry VIII. Manuscripts were everywhere, and yet they were being cut up, torn to pieces, and worn out by use until soon they could be found nowhere. Who could tell what had been lost in the process? Aubrey mourned the loss of a correct copy of Pliny the Elder's *Natural History*, only one of the untold thousands of texts dispersed and destroyed in the dissolution of the monasteries.

In this chapter I argue that early modern British naturalists and antiquaries searched out and attempted to preserve not only manuscripts but also the increasingly large volume of handwritten papers they produced in the course of their work. They established archives as institutions where papers could be deposited and made publicly accessible down through history. Antiquaries concerned themselves with the survival of papers and manuscripts because their research depended on parchments and papers dating back centuries, deep into the "middle age," as early moderns had begun to refer to the time between the fall of Rome and the Reformation.[3] Their preservationist instincts were sharpened by the historical memory of the dissolution of the monasteries, and the dispersal of their libraries, under Henry VIII.[4] As Aubrey's reflections, which he labeled "a Digression," showed, the dispersal of the monastic libraries haunted antiquaries well into the seventeenth century, encouraging them to redouble their efforts to save what time and chance had left them. Because naturalists shared interests, methods, and concerns with antiquaries and topographers, they also tended to share an interest in preserving manuscripts. County natural histories, such as those compiled by Robert Plot and Aubrey, as well as linguistic studies, such as Lhuyd's were built in part out of the diligent study of manuscript records scattered in private homes, cathedral and church buildings, and the public libraries of Oxford and Cambridge.[5]

However, the determination to preserve papers and manuscripts came not only from the antiquarian branch of the intellectual family. Naturalists were also concerned with preserving papers because they generated a wealth of them in the course of their work. Naturalists, inspired by the writings of Francis Bacon, viewed their papers not as the by-products of producing printed knowledge but as the fundamental stuff of knowledge, repositories of facts and observations for future generations of naturalists. As naturalists grew these collections and used them daily as the foundation for correspondence with each other and printed treatises that might be shared with larger readerships, their value became increasingly apparent. For a growing number of naturalists, preserving papers thus became an imperative.

A Digression.

Anno 1633 J entred into my Grammar at the Latin-Schoole
at Yatton-Keynel, in the Church: where the Curate Mr Hart taught the
eldest Boyes; Virgil, Ovid, Cicero &c. The fashion then was to save the
Forules of their Bookes with a false cover of Parchment fc. old Manuscript. Which J was too young to understand; But J was pleased with
the Elegancy of the writing, and the coloured initiall Letters. J remember
the Rector here [Mr Wm Stump] great gr: Son of St. the Clothier of
Malmesbury] had severall Manuscripts of the Abby: He was a proper
Man, and a good Fellow, and when He brewed a barrell of speciall Ale,
his use was to stop the bung-hole (under the Clay) with a sheet of Manuscript:
He sayd nothing did it so well. which me thought did grieve me then to See.
Afterwardes J went to Schoole to Mr Latimer at Leigh-Delamer (the next
Parish) where was the like use of covering of Bookes. Jn my grandfathers
dayes, the Manuscripts flew about like Butter-flies. All Musik bookes,
Account-bookes, Copie bookes &c. were covered with old Manuscripts, as wee
cover them now with blew Paper, or Marbled Paper. And the Glovers at
Malmesbury made great Havock of them, and Gloves were wrapt up no
doubt in many good pieces of Antiquity. Before the late warres a World
of rare Manuscripts perished here about: for within half a dozen Miles
of this place, were the Abbey of Malmesbury, where it may be presumed
the Library was as well furnished with choice Copies, as most Libraries
of England: and perhaps in this Library we might have found a correct Plinys
Naturall History, which (annuius a Monk here did abridge for King
Henry the second. Within the afore said compass was Broad-stock Priory,
Stanley-Abbey, Farleigh Abbey, Bath Abbey 8 Miles: and Cyrencester Abbey
12. miles.   Anno 1638 J was transplanted to Blandford-Schoole in

Jn Mr Wm Gardi
ners time it
was the most emi
nent Schoole for
the Education of
Gentlemen in
the West of Eng-
land.

Dorset to Mr Wm Sutton. Here also was the use of covering of
Bookes with old Parchments, fc. Leases &c. but J never saw any thing of a
Manuscript there. Here about were no Abbeys or Convents for Men. One
may also perceive by the binding of old Bookes, how the old Manuscripts went
to wrack in those dayes. About 1647. J went to Parson Stump out
of curiosity to see his Manuscripts, whereof J had seen some in my Childhood, but by that time they were lost, and disperst: His Sonns were Gunners
& Soldiers, and scoured their Gunnes with them, but he shewed me severall

Archives were instruments of the new science.[6] Seventeenth-century naturalists and antiquaries created new institutions—most prominently the libraries of the Ashmolean Museum and the Royal Society—to protect and preserve their books and papers. Their efforts to invent the archive revealed the connection between the development of a historical consciousness in Stuart Britain and the material culture of scientific communication. They also suggested that naturalists possessed a growing sense of confidence that the scientific project had become self-sustaining, that their work would be continued by others after their deaths, if only they could establish public institutions that would securely preserve, protect, and promote science in an ongoing way. That is, they became more oriented toward the future. The twin developments of a historical consciousness and future orientation were deeply related to each other.

If archives were instruments of the new science, they were by no means neutral instruments.[7] Rather, the values and tensions of the correspondence were baked into archives at their founding. This chapter presents the archival strategies and archival histories of three different figures: Samuel Hartlib, John Evelyn, and John Aubrey. Hartlib, Evelyn, and Aubrey approached the preservation and use of papers and manuscripts in ways that were distinctive of their places in the scientific correspondence. Their starting points within the correspondence helped shape the subsequent histories of their papers after their deaths. As with one's ability to participate in natural history and antiquarian studies in print, a naturalist's social class and level of financial resources played particularly important roles here. For example, Aubrey's fraught position in the correspondence can be read in the history of the donation of his papers to the Ashmolean, which stretched out over a decade. He sent material to the archive in part because, having failed to extend himself in print, he feared that once he died, his work and name would be lost to history unless he managed to lodge his manuscripts "in some publick Repository."[8] Yet even as he sent his material, hoping that others would read and make use of it, he continued to fear its misappropriation.

The archival story is also a national story intertwined with the development of England, Scotland, Wales, and Ireland as well as Britain (whether it was more or less than the sum of its parts) as nations and the development of understandings of history, language, culture, and the land as foundations of national identity. The antiquarian hunt for manuscripts released from the dissolved monasteries was keyed to the project of establishing England's national and religious identity independent from Rome. Through the seventeenth century, naturalists' and antiquaries' sense of the fragility of their materials, and their efforts to preserve them, was linked to the religious and civil disturbances that, among other things, further shaped British national identities, as well as relations between England, Scotland, Wales, and Ireland. Aubrey's archival drive was rooted as much in his fears that national instability endangered his manuscripts as it was in the fear that his own lack of personal resources would prevent their survival.

Papers or Manuscripts?

The very names by which naturalists, antiquaries, and topographers called the written documents they dealt with can tell us a lot about their understanding of their historical status and their ongoing role in the creation of knowledge. Most historians would surely include papers in the archives of seventeenth-century naturalists within the compass of our understanding of "manuscript" (indeed library classifications preface call numbers for such documents with "MS"). But what would seventeenth-century naturalists and antiquaries have made of our definition? They tended to draw a line between "papers"—daily work products—and "manuscripts"—the illuminated parchments of an earlier age. But this line itself was mobile, shifting with time and the concerns of the individual demarcating it. The ways in which scholars negotiated between these terms reveal both the place of manuscripts within their own lives and work and the changing relationship between science and history over the second half of the seventeenth century.

Handwritten texts became manuscripts only in contrast to printed books and papers. "Manuscript" was thus a late coinage in the history of the book, arising in the second half of the sixteenth century. According to the *Oxford English Dictionary*, although any handwritten text could be a manuscript, many of the early uses of the word suggest that it frequently (though not exclusively) referred to a subset of handwritten texts: those written on parchment or vellum before the advent of printing. Seventeenth-century naturalists and antiquaries concurred: they usually referred to the products of their pens as "papers" rather than "manuscripts." Papers typically included loose sheets, notes from experiments and observations, commonplace books, correspondence, and drafts of treatises. Naturalists also used the word "archives" to refer to these collections.[9] Loose papers belonged in the gentlemanly or scholarly library but were housed separately from bound printed books. They could be classed or stored with pamphlets, unbound books, and other loose printed material.

"Papers" could also refer to bound, handwritten books. In his diary Robert Hooke often used "books" and "papers" to refer to Royal Society account books, letter books, and loose letters and treatises, as when he was surveying and sorting the books and papers left in Royal Society secretary Henry Oldenburg's lodgings after his death.[10] In his instructions to his grandson and heir concerning the disposition of his library, John Evelyn listed together his "Writings & papers, as Copys of Letters Common-place-Books, and several unpolished draughts, collected at severall times, & confusdly packd up or bound without any order, altogether Imperfect & most of them Impertinent."[11] These various kinds of handwritten materials were united primarily by their disorder and by the fact that they were written by Evelyn (or Richard Hoare, his scribe and secretary) in the course of his work. Interestingly some of Evelyn's "Writings & papers" were bound and yet still disordered; one might contrast Aubrey's sense that binding up his loose papers was part of a process of ordering them (discussed in Chapter 4). Binding did not necessarily mean pressing papers into an ideal order.

In contrast, the term "manuscript" was usually applied to older, bound, handwritten books. Hooke, though he referred to Royal Society records as "papers" and "books," used "manuscripts" in referring to the "Arundell library manuscripts," the body of classical and medieval texts that formed part of the library donated to the society by Henry Howard, Duke of Norfolk, in 1667.[12] Edward Lhuyd, in his *Parochial Queries in Order to a Geographical Dictionary, a Natural History &c. of Wales*, included the question "Manuscripts: Of what Subject and Language; In whose Hands; Whether Ancient or Late Copies?"[13] In the course of his research into Celtic natural history, antiquities, and languages Lhuyd consulted, transcribed, and (whenever possible) obtained the originals of Welsh, Cornish, Irish and Scottish Gaelic, and Breton manuscripts in private and public libraries scattered across Britain and France. Evelyn wrote an entire treatise on the history of manuscripts, largely for the education of those interested in collecting them. In this work he used "manuscripts" exclusively to refer to ancient and medieval texts, whether of papyrus, parchment, or paper.[14] Evelyn instructed his readers not only in the material history of the manufacture, ornamentation, and storage of manuscripts but also where to search for them and how to read the unfamiliar scripts and languages in which they were written.[15] Several times Evelyn abbreviated manuscripts "MSS." The very use of this abbreviation among naturalists and antiquaries was a mark of the frequency with which they dealt in and discussed manuscripts.

In his evocative description of the various ways of recycling parchment, Aubrey clearly marked the differences between "papers" and "paper books" and the manuscripts of the middle age. "Musick bookes, Account bookes, Copie bookes," all seventeenth-century scribal books, were not manuscripts. First and foremost, then, manuscripts were old, but not just old: in this passage, "manuscript" refers specifically to sheets with elegant writing and "coloured initiall Letters," those exquisite products of an earlier monastic scribal culture. Manuscripts were different from "old parchments, sc{ilicet} Leases," which were much plainer utilitarian legal and economic documents. In Dorset schoolboys, lacking a richly stocked monastic library, covered their books with drab uncolored parchment sheets. In Wiltshire, where the Abbey of Malmesbury was but one of many local sources of manuscript, they covered them in pages bright with "coloured initiall Letters."[16]

Manuscripts were produced by monks before the English Reformation and were objects worthy of preservation and study. "Musick bookes, Account bookes, Copie bookes," though handwritten, were not manuscripts but paper books. Their pages were filled with music for divine service as well as recreation (both were often copied by hand in the sixteenth and seventeenth centuries), household and business accounts, and schoolchildren's copy texts.[17] These sorts of books were ordinary objects, tools for daily work and worship. Manuscripts, on the other hand, were products of the past, meant to be admired, studied, and used in the construction of historical accounts. Only by some kind of horrid mistake were manuscripts part of everyday life, ripped apart to make the coverings and bindings of scribal and printed "paper books."

Although the rough distinction between papers and manuscripts held through much of the seventeenth century, naturalists sometimes referred to their papers as manuscripts. The shift between the terms may have indicated a change in a scholar's understanding of his documents. Aubrey began calling his papers manuscripts as he reached the end of his life, when he became occupied with efforts to secure their preservation, primarily through donating them to the Ashmolean Museum. He considered willing them to Wood but worried that Wood was "not very young, & a mortall man" and that after Wood's death his nephew would stop guns with them (that is, use them for wadding when loading his gun) or they would be "putt under Pies."[18] For Aubrey, "papers" were rougher notes not yet possessed of historical status, while "manuscripts"—finished papers—were ready to take up their permanent home in the Ashmolean and bear the scrutiny of future generations. This is clear in the way Aubrey differentiated between museum-ready "manuscripts" and unfinished "papers." Writing to Wood in 1690, Aubrey noted that he had planned to send to Oxford "4 volumes of MSS of my owne" but had held them back because the Royal Society first desired transcriptions of them. In the same letter Aubrey wrote, "I long to be at Oxford to finish my papers there."[19] Aubrey referred there to the process of transforming papers into manuscripts, cleaning them up and reordering them, retranscribing sections that were difficult to read, and binding them into books arranged by genre or topic.[20] Edward Lhuyd, who as keeper of the Ashmolean received Aubrey's donation, assisted in this process. He asked Aubrey for a list of "tracts . . . as well the printed as M.SS." to assist him in cataloging the collection and offered to have Aubrey's letters bound, a task that Aubrey ultimately took care of himself.[21] The two naturalists agreed: copied, bound, and transferred to the archive, Aubrey's papers were no longer the loosely filed, disorganized products of daily work but rather useful collections out of which future generations of naturalists might draw new knowledge.[22] Conscious of their historical status as a body of documents in a library, Aubrey called his papers "manuscripts."[23]

The astrologer, antiquary, and museum founder Elias Ashmole blurred the distinctions between books, papers, and manuscripts in ways that may have reflected how he stored materials in his library. In the course of collecting and transcribing the writings of the Elizabethan mathematician and natural philosopher John Dee, Ashmole used a variety of terms to refer to the materials he handled. In August 1672 he received "a parcell of Doctor Dee's Manuscripts, all written with his owne hand." This parcel contained texts corresponding to five separate books; Ashmole had them bound into two volumes.[24] Elsewhere, Ashmole referred to this same collection as "Doctor Dees originall Bookes & Papers," "divers Bookes in Manuscript, & Papers," and "severall things in MS."[25] Other collections of Dee's writings were labeled simply "Manuscripts" and "papers."[26]

Ashmole's separation of this trove of Dee's writings into "Manuscripts" or "Bookes in Manuscript" and loose "Papers" mapped onto the ways in which they were physically separated in his library. In the well-ordered gentleman's library, the rough working division between manuscripts (medieval, monkish, illuminated) and papers (contemporary handwritten materials, bound or loose) did not quite hold. The division instead fell between bound books and loose sheets, as these required somewhat different kinds of storage. In his *Instructions concerning erecting of a library*, Gabriel Naudé advised shelving bound manuscript books as one would printed books—books in each format intermingled on shelves and in catalogs—and gathering loose papers up into "bundles and parcels according to their subjects."[27] Both kinds of materials were precious and thus worth protecting. Manuscripts "of great consequence" were to be placed away from prying eyes, on the highest shelves and "without any exteriour Title."[28] Loose manuscript sheets too were not to be left out on the library table. These especially were "daily obnoxious" to being stolen, borrowed, and copied; as with valuable manuscripts, they were to be placed on an even higher shelf, "upmost of all," with only the librarian knowing where to find them.[29] Echoing these divisions, in his will Ashmole divided the written material that he wished to bequeath to his museum—which included illuminated medieval manuscripts as well as the more recent papers of John Dee and the astrologers Simon Forman, Richard Napier, and William Lilly—into "Manuscript bookes" and "other Manuscript papers not yet sorted nor bound up."[30] In Ashmole's library books and papers were organized by format rather than time period. Ashmole's specification of "Manuscript papers not yet sorted nor bound up" echoes the link that Aubrey perceived between sorting and binding. Specifying that these were "Manuscript papers" also hints at another sense of "papers" as loose *printed* material.

In his extensive correspondence with both naturalists and religious reformers, the intelligencer Samuel Hartlib referred to the papers of both the living and the dead as "manuscripts."[31] Perhaps Hartlib's more general use of the word may be explained by the fact that, as a Prussian immigrant with little interest in antiquarian studies, he was not immersed in the cultural memory of the dissolution or involved in the latter-day search for monastic manuscripts. That cultural memory, and the material signs that the dissolution had left in the landscape, could play a key role in directing, or creating, an interest in antiquities. Monastic ruins and stories of England before the Reformation inspired a love of antiquities in the young Aubrey. In his *Brief Lives* he noted that he had "a strong and early impulse to antiquitie" and was "alwayes enquiring of my grandfather of the old time, the rood-loft, etc., ceremonies, of the priory, etc."[32] Compared to Aubrey, Hartlib had much less reason to distinguish between illuminated parchments and inky papers.

Yet despite the variation in terminology, differences between Hartlib's pursuit of the manuscripts of a living scholar versus his quest for those of a dead scholar indicate that, like Aubrey, he made a connection between the end of a naturalist's life and the understanding of his papers as a finished body of work. Only after a naturalist's death did Hartlib become interested in locating and collecting the entire corpus of his unprinted work, including notes toward future treatises, commonplace books, letters, and other fragments.[33] While a naturalist was alive, his papers were his working materials, his to share as he wished—though Hartlib, always a persistent correspondent, would press him to share as much as possible. After a naturalist passed away, his papers were a finished (by fiat of death, if nothing else) corpus of manuscripts from which other, living naturalists might glean insights that they could develop in their own work. The naturalist's death transformed scattered papers into a manuscript collection, the pieces of which had to be identified, tracked down, and gathered together.[34] Hartlib and his successors did not approach the papers of the dead with the sensibility of a modern professional historian (a point to which I will return below). Nonetheless then, as now, the death of the author constituted the manuscript collection as a historical object.

Religious Violence and the Destruction of Manuscripts

Naturalists' and antiquaries' interests in manuscripts, as well as the distinctions they drew between papers and manuscripts, were rooted in the history of the dispersal of medieval libraries that accompanied the dissolution of the English monasteries. The greatest damage was done between 1536, when Parliament passed the first act for the suppression of the monasteries, and 1558, when Elizabeth I came to the throne. The monastic libraries were emptied. The destruction visited the college and university libraries of Cambridge and Oxford as well, though not as consistently. The books were recycled, sent abroad, and taken into private libraries. Meanwhile a few antiquaries, such as John Leland and John Bale, selectively salvaged monastic manuscripts as they traveled around the country on commission from Henry, who sought books for the royal library, especially books that could be used to help make the case for his supremacy over an independent Church of England.[35] These books were not safe either, though; some of them were dispersed again after

Henry's death because the Crown had neither the space nor the financial resources to hold on to them.[36]

In the decades after the dissolution, monastic manuscripts were used and collected as instruments of the Reformation, pry bars for widening the fissures between Protestant and Catholic Britain. As Jennifer Summit has argued, the libraries formed out of these books were neither politically nor theologically neutral institutions. In the decades following Henry VIII's declaration of independence from the church, collectors, institutions, authorities, and individual readers recollected medieval manuscripts and organized new libraries to demonstrate, and inculcate, particular kinds of literacy; for many Protestant collectors, this meant an antimonastic literacy controlled by royal authority. The destruction of one kind of library was necessarily yoked to the formation of other kinds.[37] For example, in the early 1550s, when Bale was exiled from Ireland, he was forced to abandon the manuscript books he had collected in England during the dissolution. In a letter to Matthew Parker, he made it clear that he believed that the "obstynate papystes" in Ireland immediately busied themselves with suppressing these manuscripts for the good of the Roman Catholic Church.[38]

Flushed out of the monastic libraries, manuscript books were ubiquitous. Available everywhere in seemingly endless supply, their very ubiquity doomed them to destruction through casual use. Despite efforts at preservation, much was lost in the 1530s and 1540s. In the same letter to Parker, written in 1560, Bale vividly described the places to which manuscripts had been dispersed. He had found manuscript books where one might expect to find them, such as "stacyoners and boke bynders store howses." But they also lay hidden in "grosers, sopesellars, taylers, and other occupyers shoppes, some in shyppes ready to be carryed over sea into Flaunders to be solde—for in those uncircumspect and carelesse dayes, there was no quyckar merchaundyce than library bookes."[39] Elsewhere, Bale described the use of manuscripts in bookbinding, candlestick scouring, and boot cleaning.[40] Tradesmen hoarded and sold vellum and parchment because these could be put to many uses. Ironically parchment was a key ingredient in paper manufacture. After forming and drying the sheets, the papermakers dipped them in "size," water boiled with shavings of parchment or vellum, and dried them again. This sealed the paper, making it more durable. In the late medieval period, paper used for writing and printing was sized; by the late seventeenth century, size was still applied to writing paper but not necessarily to paper used for printing.[41]

During Elizabeth's reign churchmen, scholars, and the queen's leading ministers continued to work on rebuilding library collections, still with largely, though not entirely, sectarian ends in mind. Archbishop of Canterbury Matthew Parker, who built a library that included more than five hundred manuscripts, was, like his predecessors, inspired to collect at least in part by the need to establish a historical record that would legitimize the Church of England's separation from Rome.[42] Elizabeth's minister William Cecil, Baron Burghley, sought manuscript records to provide historical evidence to bolster a specifically English national identity and Elizabeth's claims to the throne.[43] John Dee proposed during the reign of Queen Mary that dispersed manuscripts be sought out and collected for the Royal Library; Tudor naturalists were as interested in medieval manuscripts as their seventeenth-century counterparts would be.[44]

Though much was preserved, over the next hundred years the rubbishing of manuscripts continued and the dispersal of the monastic libraries haunted antiquaries and naturalists through the British civil war. Dugdale, writing during Oliver Cromwell's reign as lord protector, lamented the dissolution of the monasteries and "the destruction and spoil of many rare Manuscripts."[45] In the early 1680s one draft of Elias Ashmole's terms for establishing the Ashmolean Museum included a special provision in case of "civil wars or like calamities": if they should come, Oxford was to invest his gift in land, rather than spending it on the museum and a professor to lead it.[46] In his reflections on the use and abuse of manuscripts, Aubrey mixed his centuries, referring in one breath to the destruction wrought by the violence of both the civil war during the 1640s and the Reformation of his grandfather's day, when "the Manuscripts flew about like Butterflies." These were wars and tumults of religion, but because the destruction was motivated by economic necessity and ignorance as well as ideology, manuscripts on natural philosophy, mathematics, and natural history were destroyed along with theological ones. Aubrey suspected that, at the very least, a more perfect copy of Pliny's *Natural History* had been lost in the destruction of Malmesbury Abbey.[47]

Seventeenth-century naturalists and antiquaries, steeped in histories of the dissolution, transferred their deeply rooted sense of the fragility of Britain's cultural patrimony to their own papers and manuscripts. As in Bale's day, papers continued to be recycled through ordinary everyday use. The learned seemed to have been particularly fixated on the notion that papers would be used to "line pies." This practice was attested to in contemporary cookery books: in *The accomplish'd lady's delight in preserving, physic, beautifying and cookery* (1675), Hannah Woolley recommended assembling (and possibly baking) a venison pasty on top of sheets of "Cap-paper," the kind of paper in which grocers and mercers wrapped goods, well-sprinkled with flour.[48] Printed sheets were also recycled in this fashion as well as in other, unsavory ways, judging by the lines of John Dryden's poem "Mac Flecknoe," written in 1676: "From dusty shops neglected authors come, / Martyrs of pies, and relics of the bum."[49] The waste of manuscript (both "papers" and medieval parchment) to stop and scour guns and line pies haunted Aubrey: recall his complaints that Parson Stump's sons had cleaned their guns with manuscript.[50] After Bishop Seth Ward's death, Aubrey rescued from his study a paper that was "destined with many other good papers and letters, to be put under pies."[51] According to Ashmole, John Dee's papers were being used to line pies before they came into his hands. After a London confectioner and his wife discovered them in a secret compartment in a chest they had purchased secondhand in the early 1640s, "they made no great matter of these Bookes &c: because they understood them not; which occasioned their Servant Maide to wast about one halfe of them under Pyes & other like uses, which when discovered, they kept the rest more safe." Fortunately the papers, though not the chest, were saved from the Great Fire in 1666, and the lady's second husband, a warder in the Tower of London, knew of Ashmole and his interests and thought he might like to see them.[52]

Although many manuscripts were lost through recycling or accident rather than burnt by clergymen, confessional conflict was also, of course, directly responsible for their destruction, with many prayer books, service books, and theological works burnt by royal and parliamentary fiat during the reigns of Henry VIII and his son Edward.[53] During the English Reformation and in the first generation or two following it, some saw theologically motivated book burning, in the right context and for the right reasons, as a positive good. Matthew Parker wrote that Pope Gregory the Great had selectively burned a Roman library holding only pagan works so that "the Scriptures of God should be more read and studied."[54] Similarly, Parker saw the despoliation of the monastic libraries, on the whole, as a positive good. The dissolution was like a purging fire: the books that had been lost were full of pernicious Popish error, while those that survived carried in them the true, pure religion, having been shepherded through by God's providence.[55] Parker lent providence a helping hand, allowing his binders to use leaves and fragments from thirteen-and fourteenth-century liturgical books to bind and repair manuscripts that he wished to save, such as those that provided evidence for the early history of the church in England.[56]

As the rupture with Rome receded into the past, though, the learned came to see religious book burning more and more as an act born of ignorance rather than a true desire to promote Christianity. There was a generational shift in the attitudes of collectors who assembled libraries from the ruins of the monasteries: while those in Parker's generation were fierce partisans to the cause of the English church, later collectors, such as Robert Cotton and Thomas Bodley, were more "ecumenical" in their tastes (though still steeped in and motivated by religious controversy).[57] As Alexandra Walsham has argued, by the late seventeenth and eighteenth centuries, attitudes shifted even more, and many antiquaries beheld monastic ruins with an impartial eye, as part of British history, rather than as sites that provoked active religious controversy. Some even gave voice to a romantic longing for the world that was lost when the monasteries were destroyed.[58] It also became possible to see Protestant book burning as acts of ignorance and misplaced zeal rather than of faith. One of the respondents to Edward Lhuyd's "Parochial Queries" noted that during the civil war, Cromwellian agitators destroyed "a large British Manuscript History" once held in his parish. But "the Round-Heads of Pembrokeshire," in great ignorance, pronounced "All Books and papers, which themselves understood not, to be Popery" and cast them into a great bonfire.[59] Although this story—repeated to Lhuyd some fifty years after the fact may have been more of a local legend than an accurate historical account, its telling suggests a perceived link between Protestant religious violence (and ignorance) and the destruction of historical records.

Lhuyd, working in the late seventeenth and early eighteenth centuries, cooperated with Protestant and Catholic antiquaries alike; apparently the intensely partisan religious feelings and beliefs that had motivated sixteenth-century antiquarian scholarship were alien to him.[60] For Lhuyd, the destruction of manuscripts—which he drily termed "the mismanagement of posterity"—was to be deplored regardless of who carried it out, Catholic or Protestant.[61] In the early eighteenth century Lhuyd corresponded with William Baxter about the ancient (possibly Celtic, or British, as Lhuyd called them) inhabitants of Spain. Some manuscripts that might have provided useful evidence, Lhuyd believed, had been destroyed by zealous religious reformers. He wrote to Baxter that "it is not to be questioned but several of the Primitive Christians had mistaken zeal as well as our reformers; and twas but 50 years ago that the Jesuit, Julian Manoir, being a missionair in Basbretaign {Lower Brittany}, obtained an order from his superiors to burn what British manuscripts & other books he should meet with, excepting such as tended to devotion and were approv'd of."[62] Although Manoir's book burning was inspired by theological zeal, it indiscriminately destroyed religious and secular books alike. Lhuyd further aligned it with similar activities undertaken both by "primitive Christians" and "our reformers."

Pursuing, Disseminating, and Cataloging Scientific Manuscripts

Whether papers and manuscripts were burned in a cleansing fire or used up lining pies, scouring guns, or wrapping gloves, the result was the same: a world impoverished of its own historical and scientific records. In response to this impoverishment, seventeenth-century naturalists and antiquaries sought to collect, preserve, and in some cases disseminate both the old and the new. In *The Advancement of Learning*, Francis Bacon defended antiquarian records as "spars from a shipwreck" that could be used to recover knowledge about the past that would otherwise be lost to "the deluge of time."[63] Naturalists and antiquaries were also motivated by their sense of the usefulness and fragility of their own records. Sixteenth- and seventeenth-century papers as well as medieval manuscripts lay scattered across the country, squirreled away in private libraries and in the studies of the recently deceased. Naturalists searched for papers just as they hunted down curious or obscure species of plants and animals, odd stones, or descriptions of extreme weather and faraway places, and they sought to preserve papers and manuscripts and make them accessible by collecting them in public repositories and by printing them. In the seventeenth century the Ashmolean Museum and the library of the Royal Society were formed in part as public repositories for scientific, technical, and antiquarian papers. In what follows, I focus primarily on the Ashmolean Museum as an exemplar of a "public repository."

Naturalists and antiquaries wrote much more than they could ever hope to print. Yet these papers, often (though not always) the products of activity directed toward producing print publications, were not wastepaper (to them, anyway). Whether in the form of letters, fragmentary notes, drawings, diagrams, tables, commonplace books noting observations taken from travel, conversation, reading, experiment, or complete finished treatises, papers could be mined for insights and observations that contributed to the advancement of natural, technical, and historical knowledge. Scholars had ample evidence of the usefulness of papers in their working lives: they regularly consulted their notes and papers while writing correspondence and also relied on papers left behind by previous investigators. John Leland's were among those widely consulted (as observed in Chapter 4).

Convinced that papers, even fragmentary and partial ones, harbored important insights, Samuel Hartlib pursued both religious and scientific manuscripts as a key part of his work as an intelligencer from the 1630s until his death in 1662.[64] Working through his correspondence among the learned of England and Europe, he hunted for manuscripts and papers. In his *Ephemerides*, or diary, he recorded who had seen or heard of caches of letters, unprinted treatises, or even notes and fragments. He sought the papers of recently deceased contemporaries as well as those of naturalists of previous generations, including George Starkey, Francis Bacon, John Dee, Robert Fludd, Joachim Jungius, the mathematician Peter Cruger, and members of the Northumberland circle, especially Thomas Harriot and Walter Warner. Hartlib's work encouraged others. In 1650 Robert Childe wrote from New England to tell Hartlib that one of the primary missions of the chemical club he was forming would be collecting and publishing chemical manuscripts.[65]

Hartlib closely linked preservation and dissemination, maintaining central stocks of papers from which he extracted and copied material to send to others. In Hartlib's proposed Parliament-funded "Office of Address," the intelligencer installed therein was to "have and keep . . . all manner of Registers, Inventories, Catalogues and Lists containing the Peculiar Objects whereof he should furnish Information" to all who repaired to him.[66] Hartlib maintained a catalog of the scribal treatises in his possession; this facilitated the preservation and circulation of those treatises as well as his personal access to them.[67] When he obtained papers, even those of the deceased, Hartlib copied and redistributed them to those whom he thought would best use them to generate new knowledge for the public good. Hartlib believed that a naturalist's death fully transferred responsibility for circulating a collection: with the naturalist no longer able to do so, Hartlib felt it his duty, for the good of the scientific correspondence and the renovation of natural knowledge, to find those papers and keep them moving. If he obtained, for example, the fragmentary remains of Francis Bacon's papers, he planned to copy and disseminate them among his correspondence as a way of encouraging others to produce and share their papers; "the only and best use of such fragments," he wrote, "is to improve them by way of correspondency as a bate to obtaine the like from others."[68]

The early fellows of the Royal Society enthusiastically searched out manuscripts. Soon after the society was founded, the mathematician John Pell, who had worked with Hartlib to locate papers produced by the Northumberland circle, led the effort to collect and print Harriot's writings. This undertaking foundered upon the fellows' inability to procure any of his manuscripts (though some turned up in the eighteenth century).[69] The papers of the astronomer Lawrence Rooke and the physician William Harvey were similarly sought after.[70] The society also proposed to use its powers as licensers of the press to print treatises by Roger Bacon and the stellar catalog of the fifteenth-century Persian astronomer Ulugh Beg, both of which could be found in the Bodleian Library. At the very least, they meant to encourage the university press at Oxford to print these works at their own expense.[71] Aubrey wrote to Wood, on behalf of the society, to request a list of Bacon's manuscripts: "The R. Societie have a wonderfull Esteeme of Friar Roger Bacon, and desire you to send me [for them] the names of all the Treatises he wrote. They wish the University would print them."[72] In the society's ambitious plan, Hooke would be deputized to review the manuscripts before they were printed.[73] There are resonances here with the Oxford press's advertisement (discussed in Chapter 5) seeking individuals to superintend subscriptions to support printing manuscripts in the Bodleian.

For the most part, as Adrian Johns has observed, these plans failed once fellows realized how expensive and onerous collecting and printing manuscripts were.[74] But their interest and a sense of the usefulness of manuscripts and papers to natural history and antiquarian projects persisted. Edward Lhuyd's 1696 linguistic and geographical questionnaire specifically asked respondents to identify any manuscripts extant in their neighborhoods by their authors, transcribers, subjects, languages, and dates.[75] Lhuyd also welcomed originals or copies of "any Letters, Papers, or Manuscripts" that respondents thought might be relevant to his investigation.[76] The Royal Society asked Henry Howard, Duke of Norfolk, who, in addition to donating his family's library to the society, served as Charles II's ambassador to the emperor of Morocco, to keep an eye out for "any Antient Manuscripts that may possibly have been translated out of the Antient Greeks, either in Geometry, Astronomy, Physick, or Chymistry" in Moroccan libraries.[77]

In 1673, before he composed his career-making natural histories and became keeper of the Ashmolean Museum, Robert Plot proposed traveling through England and Wales "for the Promotion of Learning and Trade."[78] Plot outlined his plan in a letter to John Fell, the dean of Christ Church. Modeling himself on John Leland and William Camden, Plot made gathering up dispersed predissolution manuscripts central to his plan, for many monastic manuscripts were still "lost to the World, lying secretly in Corners and in private Hands, no Man knowing either what MSS. there be, or where to find them."[79] If Oxford University and the Crown would provide the funding, he proposed to purchase as many manuscripts as private owners would relinquish and copy the rest. If owners proved immune to his money and his charms, he would at the very least produce a thorough catalog of manuscripts in private hands.[80] A wealth of secret knowledge rested with private owners who often had no idea of the value of what they held.

Plot's letter to Fell offers an instance of the casual, Anglo-centric ambiguity that characterized English naturalists' and antiquaries' writing on the relationships between topography, history, and nation. In his letter Plot connected the hunt for monastic manuscripts to the project of writing human and natural histories of the nation. Plot spoke of his project as well as Leland's and Camden's in terms of the contributions they made to the "Honour" and "Reputation" of the "Nation," and he described Leland's efforts as the "Foundation" upon which Camden built the "Superstructure" of his *Britannia*.[81] But which nation did he mean? His own proposed efforts Plot described as "a fair new Building erected (altogether as much to the Honour of the Nation) out of Materials they {Leland and Camden} made little or no use of."[82] Following in their footsteps, Plot sought to make a journey "at least through England and Wales" collecting manuscripts.[83] Later in the letter he collapsed Wales into England, referring to "my search of all the MSS in England."[84] Yet Plot surely knew that Camden's *Britannia* encompassed Scotland and Ireland as well as Wales and England. Indeed he implicitly recognized the mismatch between his plans and the template laid out by Camden in writing that he would make a journey "*at least* through England and Wales" (emphasis mine). He also sought to uncover the layered ethnic history of the island by recording "British, Roman, and Saxon" place names to add to available lists of English names, such as Henry Spelman's *Villare Anglicum* (1656).[85] Yet Plot's plan remained solidly Anglo-centric: he intended to deliver the collected manuscripts into English hands and implied that English scholars would be the primary users of them.[86]

Though Plot did not, in the end, carry out his ambitious scheme, later in the century the Oxford scholar Edward Bernard published something similar to what Plot had projected: his *Catalogi manuscriptorum Angliae et Hiberniae* (1697).[87] Bernard's *Catalogue of the manuscripts of England and Ireland* included a good deal of "scientific" materials, including books and papers on natural history, chemistry, antiquarian studies, mathematics, and medicine. Whereas Plot would have traveled to meet with manuscript owners and assess their collections, Bernard worked through the press, another example of a scholar using printed instruments to expand the reach of his correspondence. He advertised his project, inviting correspondents to assist him, in the London newspapers. In August 1694 he posted an advertisement in John Houghton's *Collection for Improvement of Husbandry and Trade* requesting "all lovers of Learning and Antiquity . . . to communicate a List of such Manuscripts as they are possessed of, in order to be inserted in the said general Catalogue."[88] This notice was repeated through summer and fall 1694.[89] Such advertisements in the "London Mercuries" were part of a concerted strategy to pull in manuscripts from private as well as public libraries.[90] The project was also publicized via a Latin broadside printed in Oxford, also in August 1694. This advertisement listed the libraries to be surveyed for the catalog (including the university and college libraries of Oxford and Cambridge, cathedral libraries, and notable private libraries such as those of Plot, Samuel Pepys, and Hans Sloane) and repeated the call for patrons of literature to assist in the program.[91]

Bernard's and Plot's methods for assembling their catalogs—Plot proposed extensive travel, while Bernard engaged correspondents as collaborators through the press (and, most likely, via correspondence)—aligned with those of learned topographers. Union catalogs such as those proposed by Plot and accomplished by Bernard were essentially topographical projects, in that they mapped the distribution of resources across the land. In their case the resource was written documents. Considered topographically, Bernard's project, like Plot's, was more English than British. The catalog covered primarily manuscripts in libraries in England, with a few libraries in Anglo-Ireland surveyed as well. Bernard drew in Irish manuscripts from several Dublin-based libraries.[92] Neither Scotland nor Ireland beyond Dublin was surveyed at all. The *Philosophical Transactions* review lauded Bernard's catalog for advertising to foreign scholars, to the "Honour and Credit of England" that a wealth of manuscripts could be found in English libraries, and more particularly at Oxford.[93]

However ostensibly "English" the manuscript catalog was, though, it also hinted at the permeability of the boundaries between English and Welsh, at least at elite levels. Bernard's preliminary advertisements suggested that at least one private Welsh library would be surveyed, that of Roger Mostyn, politician and subscriber to Lhuyd's *Archaeologia Britannica*.[94] In the event Mostyn's library was not included in the final catalog.[95] Even if it had been, the choice would not have been unequivocally "Welsh." To put it another way, there was no pure Welsh national identity, at least at elite levels. Though Mostyn's library was located in north Wales, and Lhuyd accounted it one of the richest sources of "Welsh authors" in Wales, Mostyn was thoroughly integrated into English political life.[96] His mother and his wife were English; among his sons were an MP for Yorkshire, a vice admiral in the navy, and an Anglican canon at Windsor; and he himself represented in Parliament boroughs in both Wales and England.[97] Mostyn's biography suggests that the English habit of identifying Wales as part of England (which the title of Bernard's catalog also participated in) was not just an artifact of English thoughtlessness or a projection of English authority; rather it reflected some measure of the reality of life for Welsh elites in seventeenth-century Britain. Perhaps "English" really could mean "British."

"All Is Lost That Is Not Deposited in Some Publick Repository"

John Aubrey was a consummate manuscript hunter. He consulted, collected, copied, organized, and attempted to preserve others' writings as well as his own. His writings abundantly illustrate how seventeenth-century naturalists used the manuscript materials they so hotly pursued. He copied some materials into his own notebooks. In his *Idea of Education of Young Gentlemen*, he justified his proposed method of teaching law with a quote from a quarto manuscript written by the early seventeenth-century lawyer John Selden: "Reports alone, teach not a man Lawe."[98] Aubrey noted that the manuscript was in the library of the Earl of Abingdon, in whose Wiltshire home he sometimes stayed (he was receiving mail there, for example, in October 1693).[99] He also assembled a collection of tracts on educational reform and related subjects, a kind of supplement to the *Idea of Education of Young Gentlemen*. In this "Collection of Grammaticall learning," written sheets were mixed with printed tables and pamphlets, some of which had been annotated. For example, the first item in the book consisted of a set of Latin grammar lists and tables attributed to the Popish Plot informant Israel Tonge. Two of these are hand-drawn, and three are printed; these sheets were collected together under a manuscript title page.[100]

In the search for these scraps of writing, Aubrey haunted dead men's studies. On a table summarizing various aspects of English law, tipped into his *Idea of Education of Young Gentlemen*, he wrote that he had taken it from Seth Ward's study after he died: "Seth Ward the Bishop of Salisbury studied the Common-Lawe—and I found this paper. [which is his owne hand-writing] amongst his scatter'd papers."[101] After Israel Tonge died in 1680, Aubrey wrote to Wood, "I suppose you heare that Dr Tong is dead, he hath left 2 Vol: MSS in Alkymy (which was his Talent) I shall retrieve a Catal{og} of all his Writings."[102]

If John Aubrey was keen to collect, use, and preserve the unprinted works of others, so much the more was he determined to save his own. For Aubrey, his own writings were extensions of self, prostheses that would carry his memory into the future if only they survived. In November 1692 Aubrey wrote to Anthony à Wood asking him to find his "Verses of the Robin-red-breast, to insert & pin it in my *Villa*. I should be very sorry to have it lost: and I see one is sure of nothing that is not in one's owne custodie: and when one is dead, all is lost that is not deposited in some publick Repository."[103] Aubrey's request to Wood was at once a lament and an expression of hope and faith—making it all the more ironical that his *Villa*, a description of Easton-Piers, his childhood home, and the verses pinned to it were among the few manuscripts of his that have not survived.[104] Aubrey was convinced of the potential value of every sheet of his papers, even seemingly inconse-quential slips and scraps, and was loath to see his materials slip away. Who knew what might contribute to the study of nature and antiquities in coming centuries? Beyond that, as his lament hinted, papers preserved in an archive also testified to one's existence, establishing one's place in history even if one had never published a word in print. Yet the wider world was hostile to the survival of these slips and scraps. If texts could be copied or printed, they might be secured that way. However, much material persisted in single drafts and was unprintable or uneconomical to print. Aubrey believed—desperately—that this material, so threatened by the wider world, would be secure in a "publick Repository."

Aubrey was not alone in placing his faith in a "publick Repository." In their travels and researches, naturalists and antiquaries particularly emphasized making manuscripts public and accessible. Efforts to collect and catalog manu-scripts in private hands, such as those projected by Plot and accomplished by

Bernard, were grounded in the belief that private manuscripts should serve the public good. Lhuyd reserved dark words for private collectors who refused to share what they owned or permit copying. Regarding some religious charters he wished to borrow, he complained to a Welsh correspondent, "I suppose no Gentlman that's any thing a scholar would scruple to lend them; but for those that are in other hands we are not to expect them."[105] According to naturalists, manuscripts were meant to be in public hands, or at least in hands willing to grant access to scholars.

For naturalists, gathering papers and manuscripts into public hands meant concentrating them in sites where they would always be accessible to them and future scholars. Their interest and efforts in this direction signaled a new and rising faith in public institutions. Not that long ago, the mid-sixteenth century, libraries had been emptied of their books. At Oxford's Bodleian library even the bookcases had been sold off.[106] Yet by the end of the seventeenth century naturalists came to view libraries and archives as important sites for preserving in perpetuity the manuscripts, papers, and books that were the foundations of their work. Even if libraries and archives could not be secured against the worst kinds of violence (as the histories of the monastic libraries showed), at one's death it was infinitely better to leave one's papers in an archive than behind in one's lodgings or in the hands of private collectors who might (or might not) allow them to be read and copied.

In founding the Ashmolean Museum to house his collection of books, papers, pamphlets, and natural and artificial curiosities, Elias Ashmole emerged as a key representative of the nascent faith in public institutions.[107] Ashmole donated to Oxford his collection of books, manuscripts, and natural and artificial rarities, much of which had descended to him from the Trades-cant family, who had long served as royal gardeners. Ashmole's library, with included a large proportion of manuscripts, was a key part of his donation; it formed a nucleus around which antiquarian and scientific manuscripts and books began to collect almost as soon as the museum opened.[108]

Seeking to guarantee the survival of his collection, Ashmole made his donation conditional on the erection of a purpose-built museum building and the adoption of a set of statutes governing the maintenance and use of the collection. The fragility of his materials must have been brought home to Ashmole in 1679 when, even as he and the university negotiated terms and construction commenced on the building, he lost a significant portion of his collections, including papers, books, medals, heraldic seals, prints, and over nine thousand coins, when a fire swept through the Middle Temple, where he kept chambers. A purpose-built museum was not total proof against accidents such as fire and flood, which visited the lucky and the unlucky alike (though a well-built stone building such as Ashmole's museum was better than a timber dwelling). On the other hand, if well designed in terms of its physical structure and the rules that governed it, well funded, and attentively tended to by its curators, a public museum might offer some measure of protection against other ills that constantly threatened manuscripts and other collections in private hands, such as neglect, pilfering, and dispersal.

Ashmole's faith in the museum as a public institution was not naive: he negotiated terms with the university that protected his collections with a set of rules and practices to guide the treatment of the material housed by the museum. Thus he required as a condition of his bequest not only that the university build a special museum to house the collections but also that they hire a keeper to curate them.[109] He donated not only his books and papers but also the locked chests in which to store them.[110] Ashmole further approved strict statutes, in place in 1688, requiring manuscripts to be kept in a separate closet within the library. Although anyone paying the admissions fee could enter the museum, "the Curious, & such others as are desirous" were allowed to read or transcribe the library's manuscripts only with the approval of the keeper.[111]

These conditions had much to do with the survival of the Ashmolean, and the materials it housed, over time. A building enacted a permanent commitment to preserve Ashmole's collections—and permanently celebrate Ashmole's name. The building also isolated Ashmole's collections from others in the university. Furthermore, without a keeper dedicated to maintaining and cataloging the material, it could have disappeared into private hands (those of greedy fellows and grubby undergraduates alike) without anyone so much as noticing. Ashmole's unusual (at the time) determination that the museum would be open to the public with a small admissions fee further secured the existence of the collection, as the fees paid the keeper's salary and lined the pockets of the board of visitors.[112]

Though now standard features of museums, the permanent curator, single-purpose building, and admission to a fee-paying public were relatively uncommon at the time.[113] None of these features guaranteed the survival of Ashmole's collection; for example, a dishonest, untrustworthy, or inattentive keeper could do great harm. During the eighteenth century there was more than one such keeper, beginning with Lhuyd's successor, David Parry, an intelligent and able man who also happened to be a drunk. He flagged in his care of the collections, particularly in his cataloging duties.[114] In addition the decay of at least some specimens, especially animal bodies, was inevitable, as Ashmole recognized and for which he prepared by requiring in his statutes that items "apt to putrefie & decay" be painted in a vellum book.[115] Without a building, a source of funding, and a keeper (provided the bad keepers did not do too much harm), the collections would most likely have been dispersed through the university and intermingled with other libraries and collections even faster than they did. The Royal Society's repository, for example, lacking in its first fifty years a secure and stable home, repeatedly fell into neglect and disarray as generations of fellows turned their attention toward and then away from their collections.[116] Even with the building and a keeper, items from the original Ashmolean were moved around the university over time as academic disciplines and institutional priorities shifted.[117] In the late nineteenth century, in particular, the keeper A. J. Evans refocused the Ashmolean's collections around arts and antiquities.[118] Materials that were initially housed at the Ashmolean were transferred to Oxford's Museum of Natural History, the Pitt Rivers Museum, and the Bodleian.[119] Edward Lhuyd's collection of fossils was repurposed by the geology department for teaching and research.[120]

Ashmole's attention to the institutional governance of his museum suggests a commitment to actively forming public institutions as secure repositories. At a time when collective memories of the ransacking of libraries and the destruction of manuscripts played constantly in the background, Ashmole purposefully fashioned his museum as a secure repository of scientific and antiquarian objects and texts.[121] The museum's openness to a paying public, in particular, suggests the cultural basis on which the virtuosi staked their faith in public institutions as the solution to the problem of preserving manuscripts. Where once these texts had been preserved in private hands, unknown to the world, or (before the Reformation) immured in ecclesiastical libraries whose privileges were resented by many, now they would be housed in institutions open to, and supported by, the public.

This openness to the public posed its own challenges. As second keeper, Lhuyd was frustrated by what he saw as paying visitors' lack of respect for the objects in the collection. He wrote of "the Liberty that some take in displaceing them, & occasioning the loss of some, and endammageing of several more; besides the general contempt, which the tumbling of things about, as if they were of no value, must expose them to."[122] From the keeper's perspective, early visitors did not know how to behave in a museum, another sign that the cultural form of the museum, as we know it, was under construction. Yet Lhuyd held out hope for the future if proper measures were taken. Lhuyd believed that the public could be taught how to comport themselves in a museum. He suggested posting the museum's statutes near the front door for all to read, so "that such as are unacquainted with collections of this kind, and the use that may be made of them, might in some measure be informed how to demean themselves amongst things that are acquired <& preserved> with so much Difficulty."[123] Perhaps a properly trained public's support would guarantee the museum's survival.

With the Ashmolean open to the paying public, there were tensions between access and preservation, especially when it came to the library of printed books and manuscripts, reinforcing the notion that in seeking to place manuscripts in "public" hands, scholars intended to make them accessible to a "public" that consisted primarily of themselves. Ashmole's statutes reflected this: visitors could view the rarities, but the use of papers and books was reserved for scholars. In this respect the museum was not so different from the "public" university libraries, which were generally open only to the learned, rather than the merely curious. Access to the Ashmolean library became even more restricted when the statutes were tightened during Lhuyd's tenure as keeper. Among other things, Lhuyd gained the right to, at his discretion, reject requests to read any given manuscripts. He could be countermanded only if a reader presented an order signed by four members of the museum's board of visitors.[124] Scholars relied on public support to fund the preservation of their papers after their deaths; and yet they sought to restrict access to the papers to imagined future colleagues, much as they did during life by exchanging material within their correspondence. They constructed the archive as a kind of correspondence in perpetuity.

Archival Strategies

John Aubrey began transferring his papers to the Ashmolean soon after the museum's founding. Aubrey's archival strategies—the ways in which he drew out the process of depositing his papers, the documents he chose to preserve, how he cataloged and organized them, whom he involved in their transfer—reveal scientific archives as sites of social negotiation. Kathryn Burns, speaking of colonial Peruvian archives, has written that "archives are less like mirrors than like chessboards."[125] Each document in an archive represents a move in the game of chess, an attempt to channel the truth along one direction or another, with the stakes being anything from property rights to historical esteem. In the case of Aubrey's self-archiving, we see that the collaborative habits of the correspondence, as well as its inequalities and tensions, continued into the archive. Aubrey's story also highlights the continuing entwinement of archive and nation, illustrating the extent to which civil and religious unrest continued to be felt as threats to the material continuity of history. A sense of security and safety at the national level could help one to believe that one's papers might survive. At the end of a tumultuous century, neither this security nor this belief was fully in place for Aubrey.

Nonetheless, Aubrey was something of a pioneer. Movement into public archives was slow at first. Only some had the ability, or desire, to take steps to secure their papers in this way. Some failed to organize their papers or make concrete arrangements for their preservation after their deaths; Robert Hooke was one such, and his papers were dispersed among various individuals and institutions, including the Royal Society.[126] Landed families had no need for public archives, maintaining papers and records in the libraries and muniment rooms of their estates unless the dead had previously ordered their destruction, and even in such cases heirs' lack of follow-through could ensure the papers' survival. John Evelyn expected that any papers he wished preserved would be maintained at his family estate. Conscious of his legacy, he issued instructions to his grandson and heir to "burn or otherways dispose of" loose notes, including copies of letters, reading notes, and rough drafts; thankfully the grandson was one of those heirs who failed to respect the wishes of the dead.[127]

Aubrey was particularly dogged in his pursuit of a public resting place for his archive. Though he found it by no means easy to protect his papers, he managed to do so with a combination of persistence and the right social connections. During the last eight or so years of his life, much of his time was consumed with first rearranging, ordering, and making fair copies of his papers and then superintending their transfer to Oxford, where they were deposited in the Ashmolean. Though he also took advantage of opportunities that arose to place copies of his papers in other repositories—depositing a copy of his *Naturall Historie of Wiltshire* in the Royal Society library at the society's request, for example—he saw the Ashmolean as the primary repository of his papers and the guarantor of his legacy.

Aubrey's strenuous efforts to secure the survival of his manuscripts stemmed in part from his failure to print the books he had spent his life writing; these included *An Idea of Education of Young Gentlemen* and *Monumenta Britannica*, to name just two. Though he published his *Miscellanies* in 1696, he had no books in print when he began transferring papers to the Ashmolean in the late 1680s. No manuscript of the *Miscellanies* survives, suggesting that in some cases print preservation and archival preservation were interchangeable.[128] Yet Aubrey's interest in the archives was not solely determined by his failure to print. As Kate Bennett has shown, Aubrey did not view the print and archival forms of preservation as interchangeable in all cases.[129] Some things had to go in the archive; they could not be represented fully in print even if one wished to print them. The biographical compendium *Brief Lives*, for example, included personal details that Aubrey felt were not printable while the subjects and those who knew them were still living.[130] Yet Aubrey wanted them to be available to future writers and historians. As another example, it might have been difficult to print *An Idea of Education* with its supporting materials, the "Collection of Grammatical Learning" that Aubrey had pieced together from various books and authors. In the early 1690s he maintained this material, which included printed books and pamphlets as well as manuscript texts, in a chest in Robert Hooke's rooms in Gresham College.[131] Fully conceived, *An Idea of Education* was not simply a one-volume treatise but a minilibrary supporting Aubrey's case for educational reform. The best way to preserve the full content of a project such as this, embodied in an assemblage of print and manuscript texts, was not to print the papers but to archive the books and papers.

Aubrey's choice of the Ashmolean as his papers' final resting place was his opening move on the archival chessboard and was conditioned by both social realities and his intellectual proclivities. Aubrey deposited his papers in the library of the Ashmolean Museum rather than the Bodleian Library— then and now the more conventional repository for manuscripts—for two reasons. The first was that he feared that John Wallis, the Savilian Professor of Geometry and keeper of the archives, might selectively suppress or destroy papers under his control in the Bodleian. Aubrey, having written in his *Brief Lives* that the mathematician was a plagiarist, did not wish to entrust to his care either that manuscript or any other.[132] His second reason was that the Ashmolean had been founded as a collection of natural and artificial objects, manuscripts, and experimental apparatus for the study of nature and antiquities, making it the perfect repository for a collection of papers that Aubrey thought of as raw materials, or "instruments," of Baconian science.[133] In a sense, as Kate Bennett has argued, Aubrey "published" his papers by depositing them in the Ashmolean.[134]

Transferring the papers to Oxford, either by private carrier, with a friend, or by transporting them himself (Aubrey used all three methods), was an inherently risky business. Once out of his direct control, his papers could easily fall into unfriendly hands. Someone might attempt to print his works—or, more likely, extract materials from them for incorporating into texts of his own—destroy or deny the originals, or take credit for his labors. More prosaically, papers could be lost in transit. Poorly secured in the carrier's cart, they could easily fall onto the road.[135] Alternatively, if a carrier did not recognize the address of the recipient, he might hold on to the package. Unless the sender wrote a letter under separate cover to the recipient notifying him of the delivery, the recipient would never know to claim it.[136]

If Aubrey died without securing the survival of his papers, he and the work to which he had dedicated his life were equally damned to historical obscurity. He began transcribing and ordering his papers and wrote to his friend Anthony à Wood in 1689,

> As soon as they are donne I will send them to you: for fear of Death's preventing me. For Life is uncertain: and this morning I was anguishi{d} and if I die, before I send them <to you> all will be lost: there is no trust (hardly) to any body: and I know you are so much a Gentleman, that you will not doe me wrong by putting out anothers Labours under your own name. A thing too common in this World . . . Had not you &c: goaded me on to putt my papers in order, I am satisfied they would have perished. I thanke you for it.[137]

Though this letter suggested that delivering the papers was a discrete event, this was but one of many letters Aubrey sent to Oxford negotiating their transfer. As can be surmised from this letter, Aubrey believed that his papers were unlikely to survive after his death if left behind in his temporary London lodgings or the rooms he sometimes shared with Robert Hooke in Gresham College—there were too many cases of papers so abandoned being pillaged or put under pies. In the end Aubrey feared the loss of his legacy more than he feared the plagiarism, theft, or loss of his papers while they were on the road or in others' hands. Aubrey started sending boxes of his writings to

Wood, who at the time was one of the few men Aubrey felt he could trust, for him to peruse and then deposit in the Ashmolean. Yet even when writing to Wood, whom he ostensibly trusted, Aubrey sounded a cautionary note: "I know you are so much a Gentleman, that you will not doe me wrong by putting out anothers Labours under your own name."

Aubrey's fear of plagiarism was an ever-present refrain in his life, even when writing to one of his most trusted friends. In this case his fears were not misplaced. Aubrey and Wood's relationship dissolved just a few years later when, after years of drawing on Aubrey's papers to develop his biographical compendium *Athenae Oxonienses* (1691), Wood published it without crediting Aubrey at all.[138] When the book was negatively received—many objected to Wood's publication of rumors and gossip, jottings that Aubrey had shared with him privately—Wood even pointed to Aubrey as a scapegoat, though Aubrey, characteristically, had recommended discretion in printing anything that might be scandalous.[139] Even close collaborations and friendships could be torn apart by misunderstandings over the use of scribally communicated texts.

Even if friends could be trusted, external events could still endanger papers, much as in centuries past. Aubrey's faith in Wood's ability to preserve his papers fluctuated with the rise and fall of political and religious unrest. In the fall of 1688, as the Roman Catholic James II struggled to maintain his grip on the throne, only to flee England and cede it to the Dutch Protestant William of Orange in December, even suspicions of Catholic sympathies were enough to draw the inquisitive eye of officials and the popular anger of the mob. These were nervous, combustible months.[140]

Wood was a potential target of any anti-Catholic action. Though he always denied having converted, he had Catholic friends and patrons.[141] Friendly relations with known Catholics were enough to arouse the suspicions of one's Protestant neighbors. Since the Reformation, Protestants and Catholics, including Protestant and Catholic antiquaries, had gone their separate ways as their families were increasingly less likely to intermarry and move in the same social circles.[142] Hence the ties of friendship with which men voluntarily bound themselves looked all the more suspicious.

In the face of civil and religious disturbance, even Aubrey abandoned his commitment to preserving all papers. He once thought himself at risk of censure or injury for having expressed "friendship" with the Church of Rome in a letter to Wood in the mid-1670s. In 1676 he wrote to his friend, "If you die; or, one knows not some time or other as the World runs madding, wheth your papers may be sifted & examined. Therefore ex abundanti cautelâ, I would entreat you to burne (or exp blott out) a passage in a letter of mine, about 1674, or 5, wherein I expressed my friendship to the Ch: of R. {Church of Rome} God blesse us, from another Rebellion."[143] ("Ex abundanti cautela" is a Latin legal tag meaning "out of an abundance of caution.") Aubrey wrote this note on a separate piece of paper and sent it enclosed in another letter; even this slip was intended to be destroyed. Even here Aubrey could not resist adding historical detail and context, noting that he had expressed some amiable feelings to the Catholic Church when he "was invited to take a Benefice"—earlier in the decade, on the run from his creditors, he had considered taking up holy orders, perhaps Jesuit, perhaps Anglican.[144] Regardless, that Wood did not burn this scrap suggests that Aubrey's anxieties about sharing his sympathies with Rome in writing, even with a "trusted" friend, were not misplaced.

Indeed just a few years later, as fears of a Catholic takeover of the government were stoked by Israel Tonge's revelations about the Popish Plot (which was eventually discovered to be a hoax), the vice chancellor of Oxford rifled through Wood's papers in his rooms opposite Merton College for evidence that Wood had converted to Catholicism.[145] Nine years later, as the country turned against James II and the "World ran madding" once again, these suspicions were enough to fuel not only Aubrey's fears for his papers' safety but also Ashmole's.[146] On 23 October 1688 Aubrey wrote angrily to Wood, transmitting their patron's message that certain sensitive papers he had shared with him should immediately be moved to the museum for safekeeping:

> Mr Ashmole is much vex't at my managem{en}t of this business . . . I told Mr Ashmole in May, before I came to Oxon, that you should have the perusal of all, in the first place: I expected (you know) the receipt of the Things when I was there: and now he tells me the reason: Scilicet because You are lookt upon as a P———{Papist} and in these tumultuous Turns your papers will be searcht, which is like enough, for people grow mad by changes of————{religion?} and so of leaving of any thing in your hands, it would be a means to have them lost; wherefore (in passion) he desires that those papers that I conceive fitt to be kept secret, should be all sealed-up (after you have donne with them) and <then> putt in the Museum; not to be opened till after my death: and I thinke his advise is very solid and sedate.[147]

Wood filled out Aubrey's blank "P———" as "Papist." Given the sensitivities of the time, one wonders why. Perhaps the meaning of "P———" was so obvious that nothing was saved by leaving it blank. In any case, in a way, in annotating the letter, Wood showed himself once again to be more committed even than Aubrey to the preservation of sensitive papers.

Aubrey repeated his concerns again in a letter to Wood dated 22 December 1688. By then Aubrey was furious (as was Ashmole) that Wood had still not transferred the boxes of papers to the Ashmolean. He described a thrilling sick-bed scene, witnessed by him and an unnamed Oxford scholar, a kinsman of Ashmole's:

> Mr Wood! Last Tuesday I went to see Mr Ashmole (whom I found ill) He lately received a letter from Dr Plott about the things that I sent to Oxford <and sayes that> He desired you to send to the Musaeum, but you denied it: and would not let him—See the Catalogue, that I sent. Mr Ashmole desired to speake with me about it: and is most outrageously angry: and charged me to write to you, as soon as I could, and to order you to put the Box in the Musaeum: for he looks upon you as a P. and sayeth, so does the whole University, and there was present at this angry fitt of his, an Oxford scholar (I thinke his kinsman) who owned what, Mr Ashmole sayd. Mr Ashmole saies that now there is such care and good method taken, that the Bookes in the Musaeum, are more safe, than those in the Libraries, or Archives: and he says, he expects to heare of your being plundered, and papers burnt, as at the Sp{anish} ambassadors at Wild-house, where were burnt MSS and Antiquities invaluable: such as are not left in the world and he further bids me tell you, that if you shall refuse to deliver the things sent downe by me, to Oxford, that he will never looke on you as a Friend: and will never give a farthing more to the University of Oxford.[148]

Anti-Catholic tensions ran high, and Aubrey feared more than the ordinary sorts of loss and destruction—papers lining pies and wrapping gloves. The anti-Papist "mobile," or mob, was abroad.[149] Aubrey urged Wood to act swiftly because he feared that his manuscripts would be "rifled by the Mobile."[150] He worried that Wood's own writings were in danger too of "being confounded by the Mobile."[151] They had burnt down the Spanish ambassador's house in London; might not similar mobs coalesce in Oxford around rumors of a scholar's Catholic sympathies? It had happened before: there were stories of both Catholics and radical Protestants alike burning books and manuscripts thought to be heretical, and of books getting caught up in general waves of destruction. In these troubled times, Aubrey wanted his papers in Ashmole's museum. Ashmole had made stringent efforts to establish his museum as a secure public archive. "Such care and good method" guaranteed that Aubrey's papers were much safer there, in a public museum, than in a private dwelling, Wood's attic rooms in Merton Street.

Aubrey's efforts to transfer his papers continued through the 1690s. The process reflected Aubrey's uneasy place in the correspondence and his habit of sharing material with a number of correspondents while constantly worrying that they were making improper use of it. The unrest of the revolution of 1688–1689 and the threat of religious violence that endangered them gradually receded (though that unrest continued elsewhere, with James's and William's armies clashing in Ireland), but the transfer of the papers did not settle into an easy rhythm. In these years Aubrey communicated more with Lhuyd, as curator of the Ashmolean, about the gift of his papers. Yet by no means did he commence sending the papers directly to the museum.

In the 1690s Aubrey shifted gears from sharing material with Wood, and asking that it be sent to the Ashmolean in times of danger, to transferring material to the museum for archiving. As in the letter to Wood above, which mentioned at least four people (Ashmole, Aubrey, Plot, and Wood) with stakes in the movement of his writings into the Ashmolean, Aubrey continued to involve large numbers of people in the process of depositing his papers in the archives. Aubrey involved many friends with similar interests in antiquities and natural history by sending them papers with instructions to send them on to the Ashmolean after perusing them. He asked Lhuyd, who as curator was in charge of receiving donations, to allow certain named persons to remove the manuscripts from the museum for their own perusal. This led to much confusion about where Aubrey's works belonged, whether in the museum or in the hands of one of Aubrey's associates. Lhuyd was often left to wonder whether Aubrey meant to give a manuscript to the museum or was just using the Ashmolean as a centrally located pick-up and drop-off point for his Oxford readers.

The peregrinations of Aubrey's *Monumenta Britannica*, his treatise on British antiquities, provide one example of the circuitous paths Aubrey's manuscripts traced to the museum. *Monumenta Britannica* wandered especially widely because Aubrey was hoping to see it printed and because its contents were of particular interest to those then at work, such as Lhuyd, on the revised edition of Camden. In the winter of 1693–1694, Aubrey sent the *Monumenta Britannica* manuscript to Oxford.[152] On 4 March 1694 Lhuyd wrote to Aubrey that he had received another delivery of Aubrey's books and requested Aubrey to "in your next {be} pleased to acquaint me whether you give them now to the Museum or onely deposit them for the present in my custody. Mr. Tanner brought me the key of your Box: and I have deliverd him your Monumenta Brit{annica}. But no other papers for he desired no more."[153] Lhuyd was unsure whether the present delivery was intended for the museum or not. He also gave *Monumenta Britannica,* then in his custody at the Ashmolean, to Thomas Tanner, annotator of *The Naturall Historie of Wiltshire.* While in Lhuyd's keeping, *Monumenta Britannica* circulated to other readers as well, without, it seems, Aubrey's permission. In a letter dated 29 May 1694, Lhuyd wrote to Aubrey that "Dr. Edwards I know is very sensible of the true worth of your labours, as he was pleased to declare upon perusal of your <u>Monumenta Brittanica</u>."[154] Lhuyd had "presumed" to show *Monumenta* to Edwards—the same Jonathan Edwards whom Aubrey had hoped might be able to fund the book's print publication—before giving it to Tanner.[155] Though Lhuyd acted without express authority in showing the manuscript to Edwards, the gesture was well-meant, as it was the sort of thing that could have helped Aubrey gain more subscriptions to pay for printing.

Once the manuscript was in Tanner's possession, he sent it back to Aubrey, who still hoped to have it printed.[156] Before his death Aubrey sold the copy to the London bookseller Awnsham Churchill, one of the undertakers of the 1695 revised Camden.[157] Churchill did not bring forth an edition, but his heirs held on to the manuscript until 1836—a long century during which a number of antiquaries took and shared notes from the original manuscript, as well as a copy made by Thomas Gale—before the Bodleian purchased it for fifty pounds (Aubrey's other manuscripts would not join it there until they were relocated to the Bodleian in 1860).[158] *Monumenta Britannica* traced a circuitous path. Stops along the way included Aubrey, Lhuyd, Edwards, Tanner, Aubrey again, a bookseller and his family, and numerous eighteenth-century antiquaries until finally, and posthumously, the book came to rest in a public repository. Along the way copies and notes drawn from it proliferated. Indeed "at rest" is a strange way to describe its current position in the Bodleian, given that the book continues to be copied, extracted, and printed.[159]

Aubrey dispersed his papers widely, seemingly encouraging these complicated exchanges. Yet he did not always look favorably on requests to use or peruse his papers, as he was concerned that even as they entered the archive he would be robbed of all credit for having written them. When Plot was curator, Aubrey hesitated to deposit his manuscripts in the Ashmolean, for fear that Plot "will and must have the benefit: and (no doubt) would have the Credit too."[160] Lhuyd, at work on his contribution to the forthcoming revised edition of Camden's *Britannia* being superintended by Edmund Gibson, once requested to check *Monumenta Britannica* for information on Welsh antiquities, including Caerphilly castle near Cardiff. In October 1693 he wrote to Aubrey in polite terms asking permission to study the relevant papers, some of which were then in the Ashmolean, while others were in Gibson's possession: "Pray let me hear from you at your leasure; & let me know whether you permit me to open your box for my own private use. What Mr. Gibson has of your's I would also beg the perusal of, when he has done."[161] Although Lhuyd promised Aubrey that he would "be carefull to doe you right, and <not> rob you of any part of that honour and thanks that is due to you from the curious and ingenious," Aubrey responded rather touchily, denying him access: "my Monumenta Britannica, I doe not thinke fit to be shewn, till the Britannia (now in hand) is published: for then I should loose the Credit of it, and the Creame would be skimmed to imbelish that Designe and then who would buy or print my Collections?"[162] In November, Lhuyd wrote apologetically to Aubrey that he could not "in the least blame your Caution in communicateing your Monumenta Britannica" and reduced his request to a transcription of material relating to Welsh antiquities, Caerphilly castle in particular, saying that he "did not expect or desire a perusal of your MSS."[163]

In this exchange between Aubrey and Lhuyd, we see in action the persona of the curator as disinterested caretaker of the museum and its contents. Lhuyd was by no means a perfect steward of the Ashmolean; for one thing, his research drew him away from his post for years at a time.[164] Nevertheless, Lhuyd's letters displayed a dedication to his role as curator that was an important part of the "care and good method" that ensured the relative safety of the materials housed in the Ashmolean. This persona had its roots in an older, patronage-based system of institutional management: especially while Ashmole was still alive, Lhuyd paid close attention to maintaining the collection in good order because his patron demanded it and thus his job depended on it.[165] Yet, Lhuyd's attention to care and good method also seemed to reflect a more abstract (and perhaps more modern) sense of fidelity to one's duty as a public servant. In requesting to peruse *Monumenta Britannica* and other papers as he prepared his contributions to the revised *Britannia,* he drew a distinction between "public" and "private" uses of Aubrey's papers. In reviewing the papers and extracting notes, Lhuyd said that he would be making "private use" of them. That Lhuyd made this distinction suggests that he believed that his public duties as keeper were separate from his private responsibilities and interests as a scholar. As much as he may have wanted to study Aubrey's *Monumenta Britannica,* he felt bound to treat it primarily as a donation to the museum, rather than as a resource available for his own use. At the same time, Lhuyd was probably aware that such attention to protocol was strategically good sense, as it encouraged Aubrey to share his materials (as he eventually did), trusting that his goodwill would not be abused. Similarly, when Lhuyd communicated in print material drawn from Aubrey's manuscripts, he carefully and respectfully cited Aubrey.[166]

Lhuyd's curatorial persona was also on display in the work he did processing Aubrey's donation. Working in the face of Aubrey's tetchy indecision, Lhuyd built the information architecture that would make Aubrey's materials findable, and thus accessible to future readers. He organized and cataloged Aubrey's papers as well as the pamphlets and books he donated. He grouped some materials by format or genre: he had bound loose pamphlets that Aubrey had donated and offered to have the correspondence bound as well.[167] To aid him in preparing a catalog, Lhuyd requested from Aubrey a list specifying which of his writings he was donating. Lhuyd entered Aubrey's donations into the museum's library catalogs, separating printed books from manuscripts.[168] In order that there might not be any errors in the catalog, he repeatedly queried Aubrey to pin down precisely which books and papers he meant to donate and which he was only storing temporarily at the museum.[169]

The pains that Lhuyd took to ensure that the collection was accessioned to the Ashmolean with "care and good method" suggest that he was thinking about the needs of present and future users of the materials, as well as curators: to be accessible, materials would have to be kept in good order. Lhuyd's efforts to subdue Aubrey's unruly donation were part of broader attempts on his part to keep the library's collection of printed books and manuscripts in order. These had begun when he was Plot's assistant and given primary responsibility for keeping the museum catalog up to date.[170] But Lhuyd's attention to maintaining the catalogs did not fail after he became keeper and

Ashmole had died. In the early 1690s, for example, he sorted, sent out for binding, paginated, and cataloged the hundreds of loose pamphlets and papers (printed and manuscript) that arrived at the museum after Ashmole's death.[171] As he became more engaged in topographical work and more experienced as keeper, Lhuyd delegated some of these responsibilities to a sub-keeper, whose work he checked, at least occasionally.[172] From the mid-1690s Lhuyd and his assistant Robert Thomas began cataloging donations in Anthony à Wood's copy of Thomas Hyde's 1674 Bodleian Library catalog, which they had interleaved with sheets for new entries after Wood donated it to the museum with the rest of his library. (This kind of use of a copy of Hyde's catalog, one of the easiest to use and fullest bibliographies of books in print then available, was common both in Britain and abroad.[173]) Lhuyd complained mightily about cataloging work and the time it took from his researches in geology, antiquities, natural history, and languages, but he took care to do it or delegate it responsibly—yet another sign of the distinction he drew between private interests and public duties.[174]

Seventeenth-Century Papers in Eighteenth-Century Archives

After the deaths of their originators, the papers of seventeenth-century naturalists went on to varied lives of use, destruction, and neglect, generating histories that ultimately vindicated Aubrey's pursuit of an archive for his manuscripts. Hartlib was unable to provide for the survival of his papers after his death. As he neared the end of his life, some of his materials were destroyed by a house fire. The remainder were further depleted by untrustworthy friends who took what they would from the ill and aging Hartlib. After his death in 1662, William Brereton, a friend and natural philosopher, purchased the remnant of Hartlib's collection. At Brereton's Cheshire country house, the cleric John Worthington cataloged and ordered the papers, all the while allowing others, including the mathematician Seth Ward and possibly John Milton, to remove or burn items in the collection, some of which cast their "involvement in the affairs of the Commonwealth and Protectorate in not quite the uncommitted light that they hoped to put abroad *post facto*," as Mark Greengrass has put it.[175] The collection was broken up, and some of the papers emerged later in the British Library and Yale University Library. In 1933 George Osborn, professor of education at Sheffield University, rediscovered and obtained for his university a large portion of the original archive;

this material has since been made available electronically through the Hartlib Papers Project.[176] Robert Boyle's archives too were reorganized and trimmed after his death, though the primary concern of those doing the trimming seems to have been his reputation rather than their own. In the 1740s Thomas Birch and Henry Miles discarded many letters that they thought reflected inappropriately on Boyle, including "family letters, begging letters, letters from alchemists and other 'enthusiasts.'"[177] William Wotton, an eighteenth-century biographer, absconded with some papers while researching his life of Boyle, though these were eventually returned to the main archive.[178]

Aubrey deposited his papers in the Ashmolean precisely in order to avoid the posthumous mutilation that Hartlib's and Boyle's collections suffered. The papers that Aubrey and Ashmole gave to the museum have largely survived intact to the present day, with some exceptions: the second book of Aubrey's *Wiltshire Antiquities* was lost, for example, when his brother permanently borrowed it from the library in 1703.[179] We see here the shaky emergence of the orientation toward the future that continues to be embodied by the modern archive. However, as Hartlib's activities, widespread attitudes toward manuscripts, and even Aubrey's hesitations over depositing his papers show, this attitude was by no means stabilized or universally shared, nor would it be for many years. Into the eighteenth century the personal papers of figures regarded as having some historical importance were hardly treated as sacrosanct: witness Miles, Burch, William Wotton, and Aubrey's brother "borrowing" or removing materials from archives, even institutional ones.

In contrast to both Hartlib and Aubrey, neither of whom possessed estates at which their libraries and archives could be maintained by their heirs, John Evelyn was able to preserve his papers by keeping them in the family. Evelyn's security in this respect highlights the way that financial and social stability conditioned the decisions that naturalists made regarding the circulation, publication, and preservation of their papers and manuscripts, and the way in which their manuscripts were treated after their deaths. Aubrey fixed his hopes on the "public repository" because he thought it was reasonably secure and because the ideals according to which it was established reflected his own beliefs about the development of natural and historical knowledge. Yet it was true that if his papers and manuscripts had been left in private hands, they would have been particularly insecure, particularly likely to be disseminated and destroyed after his death because they would not be passed down and preserved in a home handed down to his heirs.

It would be equally wrong to suggest that papers maintained in family homes were necessarily preserved exquisitely down to the present. This was far from the case. Houses were sold; heirs were careless. They could have as little regard for the papers' potential to contribute to historical or natural knowledge as any gunner, baker, or fishmonger using paper or parchment to scour guns, line pies, or wrap fish. The history of Evelyn's papers offers a case in point. Evelyn's now-famous *Kalendarium* (his diary) lay dormant in an "old ebony cabinet of neglected papers" at the Evelyn home in Surrey until William Bray, a lawyer and antiquary, along with the "autograph collector" and librarian William Upcott rediscovered it in the 1810s while cataloging the Evelyn family's library.[180] Just in time too: "the ladies of the house . . . had already begun to use 'scraps' from the archive as pattern papers. The kitchen drawers and sewing baskets were filled with them."[181] (The fact that these papers were still hardy enough to serve for sewing patterns is, perhaps, a testimony to the quality of seventeenth-century paper.) Bray, recognizing its value to historical study, brought out an edition of the diary in 1818.[182] The larger body of documents continued to be maintained by the Evelyn family until 1949, when it was removed to the library of Christ Church College, Oxford, before being sold to the British Library in 1995.[183]

"The ladies of the house" should not be too harshly regarded for treating Evelyn's archive as scrap paper: this would hardly be fair, given that these were papers that no one had much looked at since Evelyn's death and that Evelyn himself had commanded at least some of these scraps to be burnt. The treatment that Evelyn's papers received, however, does suggest that no repository, public or private, could guarantee the survival of one's papers. When writings were packed up in closets and cupboards in a family estate, benign neglect until someone came along to recognize their "value" was perhaps the best preservative. Of course neither could the rediscovery of one's papers guarantee their survival, especially when one of the discoverers was a professional autograph hunter.

If the goal was to preserve one's papers in order to raise one's visibility among naturalists and antiquaries and to make them available for future study, as it was for Aubrey, the public repository may have been better than the private estate. In the early eighteenth century a group of printers under-took to publish *The natural history and antiquities of the county of Surrey* derived (they claimed) from two of Aubrey's original manuscripts, one in private hands and one in the Ashmolean; this was, in fact, the sort of thing

Aubrey had hoped would happen.[184] In the 1740s and 1750s readers annotated both the Royal Society copy and the Ashmolean copy of Aubrey's *Naturall Historie of Wiltshire* with comments that indicated a fundamental sympathy with Aubrey's project of documenting local natural history, agricultural practices, arts, and antiquities. These readers, like Aubrey's contemporary readers, participated in the text by adding topically related factual information from counties that were not Wiltshire. In the fair copy, one reader responded to Aubrey's observation on an extraordinarily long-lived goose: "a Goose is now living (anno 1757) at Hagley Hall in Worcestershire full Fifty years old."[185] (See Figure 9.) Perusal of one of Aubrey's manuscripts, in which he saw a drawing showing the historical development of window architecture through the Gothic period, led the antiquary Charles Lyttleton to the study of medieval architecture.[186] Evelyn's papers tucked away in Surrey were comparatively little used and little consulted until their rediscovery.

Conclusion

In the seventeenth century naturalists and antiquaries, understanding both older and contemporary writings as foundational to their scholarship, worked to collect, copy, and preserve manuscripts and papers. Yet they did not view these materials as "historical" documents, that is, as "primary sources" that would be studied and interpreted by historians whose aims and understanding were not fundamentally continuous with their own. Nor did they necessarily share modern historical and archival assumptions (as varied and vexed as these are) about what the responsibilities of a *public* repository are. Aubrey, Plot, and Ashmole sought to preserve their papers for the use of other naturalists and antiquaries—people they assumed would share the same basic outlook, preconceptions, and methodology. Modern historians, on the other hand, are generally engaged not in continuing the seventeenth-century scientific project but in understanding it and its implications for the present, though there is a fuzzy area of overlap between continuing and understanding.

The disjunctions between past and present approaches to history, as well as emerging points of conjunction, are perhaps best represented by the ways seventeenth-century scholars did and twenty-first-century historians do treat archival documents. Early moderns did not necessarily regard the physical medium, the paper itself, as having an intrinsic historical value—recall the

164

The Partridges [Perdix Tridgis] and Black-birds in Northwilts, are bigger than those of South Wilts: and the Black-birds doe sing lowder and a shriller noise.

Wilton parish Steuerton &c. Deuxpooles at master Amphteus and Lord Colerus. G. I find one at Longleat at S.L. Weymouth's?

At my Lord Stourton's house at Stourton, is the Aire of a White Wood-cock: [Gallinago-Sachona] Killed in the Parke there: but that is not so very uncommon

a Goose is now living (Anno 1757) at Hagley Hall in Worcestershire full Fifty yeares old.

Ganders [Anser Xω̄] are vivacious Animals, e.g. that that defended the Capitol, lived . . . . . yeares. But in my Neighbourhood Farmer Ady of Segary had a Gander that was fifty yeares old: which the Soldiers Killed: He and his Gander were both of the same age.

Sea-mewes [Fulica, Gavia] plentie of them at Clem-donne: else where in Wiltshire I doe not remember any. There are Presages of Wea-ther made by them

Virgil: Georg: liber.

*Jam sibi tum curvis male temperat unda carinis,
Cum medio celeres revolant ex aequore Mergi,
Clamoremq; ferunt ad littora cumq; marinae
In sicco ludunt Fulicae: notaeq; paludes
Deserit, atq; altam supra volat Ardea nubem.*
            Englished thus by Mr T. May.

See Mr Willoughbys of Birds.

*Then Seas are ill to saylers evermore
When Cormorants fly crying to the Shore,
From the mid-sea, when Sea-fowle pastime make
Upon dry land: when Herns the Ponds forsake
And mounted on their wings doe fly Aloft.——*

For the Prick of a Thorne.
R. a piece of the Slough of an Adder, and tye it to the wrong side of the finger, or &c. that is prickt with a Thorne: it will open the Orifice, that you may pluck it forth. from Mrs Markey S. Jo: Hoskyn's aunt.

Figure 9. John Aubrey, *Memoires of Naturall Remarques in the County of Wilts*, RS MS 92, p. 164. Reproduced by permission of the Royal Society. This page was annotated by an eighteenth-century reader. In response to Aubrey's observation of a long-lived goose, the reader wrote, "A Goose is now living (Anno 1757) at Hagley Hall in Worcestershire full Fifty years old." Though this reader would not have been exposed to the comments left by Aubrey's contemporary readers (which were in Aubrey's working draft, then in the Ashmolean), his response to the text resembled theirs. He treated the text as one in which he was permitted (even encouraged) to intervene and added an observation topically related to what Aubrey had written, but from a county that was not Wiltshire, expanding the geographical remit of the book.

practice of destroying (or failing to preserve) scientists' correspondence once an edition had been printed. Value inhered in the information, not in the paper or the handwriting in which it was stored. Papers were rarely retained if the information they contained was available in other forms. Likewise from the sixteenth through eighteenth centuries, antiquaries happily annotated and otherwise added to, rebound, and mixed together manuscripts and papers of both recent and medieval vintage. Few twenty-first-century historians would write their own thoughts in the margins of an early modern manuscript or printed book. Even if they wished to, the owl eyes of the librarians patrolling the reading rooms where the books are available for consultation—not to mention the security cameras positioned above—are usually an effective deterrent.

Yet in Aubrey we see a dedication to the slips and scraps, to the idea that documents need to be maintained in public repositories because they may well be unique in representing knowledge and information that would not otherwise be preserved. This might be by accident: things had chanced such that certain papers had not been printed. Or it might be the result of a deliberate choice to stick to scribal preservation: certain materials could not be printed by either the legal and moral standards or the etiquette of the time, but that did not mean the information they contained should be lost. Or they represent a person: Aubrey's slips and scraps were extensions of himself, and entombed in the archive, they offered him the opportunity to survive death. These attitudes are somewhat more in keeping with modern archival and historical values. Archival institutions seek to preserve the unprinted, the messy rough drafts, the correspondence, the notebooks and index cards. They maintain secret and sensitive records until the day that these can be legally unsealed. We trust them to carry forward some record of our societies and culture, if not us as individuals.

But if Aubrey's story displays a prophetic enthusiasm for the "public repository," it reveals a certain ambivalence as well. Reluctant to exchange disseminating his work in the present for its secure preservation after his death, he sent material to Lhuyd only to ask for it back or allow friends to take it out of the archive. In addition, despite Lhuyd's best efforts, Aubrey struggled to believe that his papers would be safe in the Ashmolean. Although one of the earliest and most enthusiastic donors of material to the Ashmolean, he recoiled when Lhuyd touched on his old sensitivities to other people using (and misusing) his work in print without crediting him. Though the archive had been built—its physical structure was in place—the concomitant mental and cultural structure, an understanding that an archive was a secure location whose personnel could be trusted as custodians of one's papers, had not put down deep roots.

Lhuyd managed the tension between the desire to share one's work freely and the fear that it would be misused by striving to separate public duties from private interests, by adopting something of a curatorial persona through which he embodied the idea of the archive as neutral repository. But Aubrey could not abandon at the door of the museum the anxieties that had long been a part of his correspondence-driven life. He could not guarantee that future naturalists using his work would properly attribute credit to him (a constant worry throughout his life) or that future generations would remember him in a way he would recognize. Indeed perhaps Aubrey's worst fears have been realized in the common image of him as a gullible gossip, promoted by unsympathetic readings of *The Miscellanies*, his one printed work, and the editor Andrew Clark's sour presentation of Aubrey in his 1898 edition of *Brief Lives*.[187] Sealing his remains in the archive entailed both a preservation of self and a giving up of that same self. Yet placing his faith in the future, he deposited as full a record as possible, preserving, insofar as it was possible, every page, every scrap, every note.

Of course today the understanding of the archive as a neutral site and the archivist as its objective custodian is by no means universal.[188] In any case, even where it is broadly accepted, this understanding is a form of archival ideology that some (though not all) archives as institutions and archivists as individuals strive to embody in their day-to-day workings. It has been a powerful ideology, legitimizing the powers of empires and conditioning the formation of history as an academic discipline.[189] As an ideology, it contributes to hiding from us the inner workings of the archive: the negotiations over where and how documents are stored; the disputes over who is allowed to use them and when; and the transformations and losses that occurred as collections of papers passed into the archive and became manuscripts.

In seeking to ensure the survival of their papers at a time when, whether public or private, libraries, museums, and other repositories were anything but secure, early modern British naturalists and antiquaries proved instrumental in creating this archival ideology. In the process they participated in the creation of ideologies of the nation as well. Antiquaries' and naturalists' individual efforts to search out, collect, and preserve manuscripts and papers (their own and previous generations') as well as the establishment of "public repositories" to house them were responses to civil and ecclesiastical unrest.

Naturalists such as Aubrey and Elias Ashmole hoped that public repositories might serve to overmaster the forces that imperiled papers. As warehouses of antiquarian and natural historical papers, they were also wells from which narratives that reinforced historical and land-based conceptions of "British" identity could be drawn. Manuscript catalogs such as Edward Bernard's served a similar purpose, working on a scale that was at once larger and more modest. A union manuscript catalog cost less than a museum, both in its construction and in its perpetuation, but it made visible and more accessible a wide array of papers and manuscripts distributed across the land, held in both private and public hands. It was a necessary, but not sufficient, step toward making manuscripts available for topographical research, for creating histories of the land and images of the nation.

Yet the legacy of these projects for the development of conceptions of Britain as a nation was mixed. More often than not, public repositories and catalogs were held up as national icons of England, Scotland, Wales, or Ireland, individually rather than of "Britain" as a whole. Furthermore, in the centuries since they were laid in the archive, rather than being a foundation for visions of "Britain," seventeenth-century topographical papers and manuscripts have been used in ways that have bolstered individual national identities and exposed the tensions and differences between England, Scotland, Wales, and Ireland.

Conclusion

Paper *Britannias*

The printed Britannia*s of* the seventeenth century bear witness to a shared discourse of the nation in seventeenth-century Britain, one constructed in the context of long-distance collaborations and transmitted more broadly and preserved for the future in print. In these books educated Britons, many of them city-dwellers and most of them Protestants, parsed the relationship between the local and the national in the overlapping realms of culture, language, economic life, human descent, husbandry, and nature. They offered visions of Britain in which local particulars (and particularities) contributed to the overall strengthening of the nation. They transmitted visions of the "imagined community" rooted in the land and in a correspondence that spanned England, Wales, Scotland, and Ireland, helping to provide the ideological basis for greater British union in the eighteenth century.[1] Though not yet an invention that anyone was ready to die for (to paraphrase Benedict Anderson), their nation was an imagined community in that it existed not as political fact but as a projection, rich with affect and social meanings, into the spaces between correspondents, readers, and authors.[2]

Yet the unified vision promised by the words "Britannia" or "Britain" in the titles of natural historical and antiquarian books often dissolved on closer inspection. Each book, each printed *Britannia*, was a different edition of the nation. Neither were these books always internally consistent, or unambiguous, in how they denominated Britain and identified its constituent parts. Some of these differences had to do with the variety of approaches that topographers followed—whether they focused on trade, husbandry, linguistic difference, antiquities, roads, or the "politique divisions of Princes," in John Ogilby's phrase.[3] The internal and external differences were not surprising in a century with often bitter conflict between and among the

English, Irish, Welsh, and Scottish. The differences in various writers' views of Britain, as well as the hierarchies and inconsistencies internal to each work, spoke especially to English presumptions of intellectual and political dominance and to Irish, Welsh, and Scottish push-back against those presumptions. In the eyes of many English writers, "Britain" was already an empire, with Scotland, Ireland, and Wales playing the part of colonies. Yet Scottish, Irish, and Welsh naturalists, accompanied by some of the English, some of the time, elaborated visions of "Britain" as a realm of national equals.

However diverse these *Britannia*s were, naturalists and antiquaries worked out, constructed, and composed them in a common context, their correspondence. Through correspondence many individual investigators, both the undertakers of large treatises as well as the gentry and clergy who took an interest in neighborhood antiquities and natural history, were directly known to each other or separated by only one or two degrees of acquaintance. Correspondence was the foundation upon which the superstructure of the printed *Britannia*s rested. It provided a social forum, a disciplinary community, in which naturalists and antiquaries shared information, observation, objects, drawings, and books and manuscripts. It was a setting in which local knowledge and local perspectives could be compiled and viewed within a national context and a national perspective. It was a medium that materially structured naturalists' and antiquaries' intellectual projects, which depended on the seemingly endless accumulation of information represented in books, manuscripts, notebooks, papers, and other objects.

To a certain extent differences between and within the *Britannia*s became visible in print because individuals collaborated across political, cultural, and geographical divides in their correspondence. Though the majority of the contributors to the revised 1695 edition of Camden's *Britannia* were English, there were Welsh, Scottish, and Irish scholars participating as well, creating a text that offered a range of ways for understanding Britain as a nation amalgamated from local and regional particulars. One could also look to the different works on "Britain" produced by Edward Lhuyd. His work on the 1695 *Britannia* revision inspired him to begin his *Archaeologia Britannica*, a project that began to establish, through rigorous comparative study, the commonalities between the languages and antiquities of Scotland, Ireland, Wales, Cornwall, and Brittany. This was a Britain minus England. In the context of his field guide to fossils, Lhuyd worked within a Britain that was largely, if not entirely, English (initially he had planned an intensely local study, limiting himself to figured stones picked up in and around Oxford), despite the fact that the book's title, *Lithophylacii Britannici ichnographia*, pronounced it a guide to *British* fossils.[4] Even this latter (apparent) conflict is not inexplicable: the field guide was written in Latin and intended for European as well as British audiences. Perhaps keeping in mind that "external" audience, before whom it was desirable to make a good show as a demonstration of national scientific acumen, those who undertook to print the volume gave it a title that linked it to the whole island of Britain rather than just the English portion of it. The printed *Britannias* were shaped not only by internal forces; British naturalists also acted on how they saw their nation relative to others.

The collaborative processes—and polyvocal results—characteristic of topographical writing were on display in John Aubrey's manuscript *Naturall Historie of Wiltshire*. In its "tumultuarily stitch't up" state, with its annotations in multiple hands, the manuscript showed naturalists generating topographical knowledge by accreting local particulars through the correspondence.[5] Though Aubrey initially crafted *The Naturall Historie of Wiltshire* as a local history, with its boundaries defined by the county lines first drawn under the medieval Saxons, he and his annotators constantly pushed it beyond those boundaries, bringing in references to other counties as well as Wales, Scotland, Europe, and the Americas. This escape from locality was driven by Aubrey and his fellows' devotion to a Baconian topographical methodology, which encouraged contributors to add annotations derived from their own experiences of particular places at particular times (as well as, on occasion, their reading). The content of the eventual product depended very much on perspectives that individuals brought to the table.

If the material remains of *The Naturall Historie of Wiltshire* were a "mirror, not a telescope" (to borrow Joshua Childrey's phrase), they reflected not only the British landscape but also the community of writers and readers that assembled that knowledge.[6] Aubrey collected the annotations of John Evelyn, John Ray, Thomas Tanner, and Thomas Gale not only for the information they provided but also for the sake of his relationships with them. He used the manuscript as a vehicle for materially representing the community of his friends and collaborators. Their attention to the manuscript was a way, for Aubrey, of confirming his contribution to natural history and antiquarian studies. This function of the annotations was particularly important to Aubrey because at the point in his life when he solicited them, none of his writings had yet appeared in print.

Aubrey's predicament as someone who deeply desired to see at least some of his works in print and yet for the most part failed to get them there made him something of an edge case by the late seventeenth century, when naturalists often (though not always) assumed that substantial treatises were destined for print publication. Aubrey found himself in this situation in part because of the financial collapse he suffered at mid-life. Prior to that collapse he had been less interested in print publication, but afterward getting something into print—though by no means everything—became a more important goal for him. It is this transition and his subsequent "marginality" that make his career such a valuable window onto the interconnected moral and financial economies of the late seventeenth-century learned correspondence. If Aubrey knew better than anyone the benefits of collaborative work, he also felt more sharply the anxieties it provoked, most prominently the fear that friends with whom he shared materials would steal credit from him by publishing them under their own names. His letters were rife with such worries. Yet given the nature of the intellectual project in which he was engaged and Aubrey's social position within the correspondence, refusing to share information was not an option available to him.

Conversation was mediated through the correspondence. The transmission and preservation of conversational details in letters and other forms of writing were key to sustaining an "imagined community" on a national scale. Though it never fully captured conversation, correspondence allowed investigators to engage in conversation-at-a-distance. Through their exchanges, naturalists created for themselves a kind of virtual presence in conversations for which they could not be physically present. They asked correspondents to remember them in talking to mutual acquaintances and in some cases even gave correspondents instructions on what to say in conversations with third parties. The interplay of correspondence and conversation was particularly crucial in the topographical fields, where investigators' and informants' distribution across the land was a precondition for the production of new knowledge, and investigators sought to maintain over time acquaintances they had first begun in conversation.

In creating systems for archiving and sharing conversations, naturalists allayed their anxieties that their exchanges were just so much empty talk. These anxieties had deep spiritual and philosophical roots, evident in the fact that naturalists and intelligencers (such as Henry Oldenburg) felt the need to situate natural philosophical conversation as a morally and spiritually improving practice. In the scientific societies, clubs, and scribal news bureaus of the seventeenth century, the virtuosi lashed conversation to various forms of writing, including correspondence and meeting minutes, as a way of making it productive, of ensuring that insights that appeared in the course of conversations would be given permanence and shared with those who were not present.

Printed *Britannia*s and regional histories were constructed for and through the correspondence. In the everyday exchange of letters, naturalists and antiquaries shared information that made its way into their printed works. They circulated scribal drafts of their books to gauge reception, build support, and get others' suggestions and corrections. They amplified the relationship between correspondence and print using printed instruments such as query sheets and subscription proposals. These papers, printed as broadsheets or bifolios (if particularly extensive), were the ephemera of collaborative knowledge-making, circulated in bookshops, coffeehouses, and in letters. They advertised proposed projects and invited potential readers to contribute money to finance research and printing as well as information that would be included in the books. Authors-undertakers multiplied the reach of their proposals and queries by enlisting allies among their correspondents to do the work of signing subscribers and connecting them to new informants. If successful, the subscription process resulted not only in a printed book but also in an expanded correspondence. As with Aubrey's *Naturall Historie* but on a much larger scale, individual subscribers helped to determine a book's content—and thus the image of the nation it conveyed—as well as bring it into existence by financing its printing.

Naturalists and antiquaries may have been driven to subscription publication by financial realities (their books were expensive and had limited readerships), and yet subscription was also a publication strategy that played to the strengths of learned correspondence as a medium. Subscription publication's emphasis on "social marketing" made it a good fit for topographical works insofar as they were developed within interconnected communities of gentry, nobility, clergy, and scholars. Understanding and relaying social geography were already intimate parts of documenting natural and human history regardless of whether a book was published by subscription, but they became even more visible in subscription lists and related ephemera. Topographical readerships were microcosms of the nation's elite readers, "Publics of Letters." Subscribers' names appeared in the books with titles, places of residence, and academic degrees attached. Typographical hierarchy, with the famous names of powerful people listed first in the largest types, reflected British social hierarchies.

As the seventeenth century drew to a close, the correspondence came to rest in the archives. Across the sixteenth and seventeenth centuries, waves of ecclesiastical and civil disorder washed books, manuscripts, and papers out of libraries and into general circulation, where they were repurposed and often destroyed. In response, naturalists created new "public" spaces for housing their books, papers, and collected naturalia and artificialia. The Ashmolean Museum represented once such space. In depositing their materials in these repositories, naturalists such as John Aubrey hoped to protect them against the general destruction that usually visited collections of papers (especially when they were not maintained at a private estate) and make them available to future generations of naturalists. These institutions were not independent from the correspondence; they were infused with its values and anxieties, as illustrated by the complicated set of maneuvers by which Aubrey staged the arrival of his papers at the Ashmolean. Furthermore efforts such as those undertaken (or projected) by Robert Plot, Edward Bernard, Aubrey, and Lhuyd to collect, catalog, and preserve not only the medieval manuscripts that had survived the dissolution of the monasteries but also the papers of the late seventeenth-century learned were self-consciously national projects, intended to bolster the image of Britain and/or England as realms of learning. Here, as elsewhere, naturalists differed on which "nation" was being bolstered, but at least some of the time they seemed to imply a broader concept of "Britain" not entirely dominated by the English.

What happened to the correspondence and to these visions of nation and nature as the Stuart era, with its convulsions and obsessions, passed into history? A look at the uses and fates of the materials that naturalists left behind, in and outside of the archive, hints at the answers. Strikingly the histories of these materials show topography in the eighteenth century not as a ground for national union but as a realm in which the component parts of Great Britain and Ireland became more isolated from each other rather than less.

First vignette, of three. By the time of his death in 1709, Edward Lhuyd had developed a substantial collection of manuscripts and papers in Irish Gaelic, Welsh, Scots Gaelic, Cornish, and Breton. These included both medieval originals and transcriptions as well as his own notes, all testifying to the history of the Celtic languages and the relationships between them. They had enormous value for the study of the Celtic languages, and there was a fair amount of interest in them. In the years immediately after his death, Lhuyd's former colleagues perused and raided them, taking away items that they felt might be good additions to their own collections of working papers.[7] The papers were ill attended by the new keeper, Lhuyd's former assistant, David Parry, who by all accounts was more often at the pub than at his post.[8]

However, the university could not be persuaded to hold on to them. Lhuyd had died owing about eighty pounds in total, some of it to the university and its printer, primarily for the printing of his *Archaeologia Britannica,* whose costs had not been fully covered by the subscription.[9] As a way of covering the debts owed it and others, the university took into its own possession most of his printed books and sold off his manuscripts.[10] In the mid-1710s, after an extended competition between various collectors, Lhuyd's Celtic manuscripts were purchased by Sir Thomas Sebright, an Englishman; Humfrey Wanley, librarian to the first and second Earls of Oxford, whose manuscripts eventually formed one of the cornerstones of the British Museum's library, had attempted to get them, but to no avail.[11] Additionally, a Cornish vocabulary fetched up at the library of the Earls of Macclesfield via Moses Williams, one of Lhuyd's assistants at the Ashmolean, whose library was purchased by William Jones, a mathematician who served as a tutor to the astronomer George Parker, second earl of Macclesfield.[12]

The Sebright family held on to most of the papers through the eighteenth century. During that time Welsh scholars complained mightily that they were secreted away in an English library, unavailable to those who would use them to advance scholarship on Celtic antiquities, natural history, and languages (particularly Welsh).[13] Yet their complaints belied the reality that the manuscripts were widely consulted by interested scholars and that copies and originals circulated among Welsh and English antiquaries and linguists.[14] By the early nineteenth century, though, the collection had been further broken up. The Sebrights donated the Irish materials to Trinity College Dublin in the 1780s and 1790s, a benefaction brokered by Edmund Burke.[15] Material related to Scots Gaelic and antiquities was mixed in with this lot, as Lhuyd did not separate his notes on Scots and Irish Gaelic into different notebooks.[16] The seventh baronet gave some of the Welsh manuscripts (roughly 180 volumes) to a Welsh cousin of his in the 1790s; the rest were purchased at auction in 1807 by a number of people, including a future president of the Cymmrodorion Society, a learned society (still in existence) devoted to the study and promotion of Welsh culture.[17] Most of the surviving Welsh collections, severely depleted by three separate house fires, have since found their way to the National Library of Wales and the Cardiff Public Library.[18] Some papers eventually ended up at the British Library and the Bodleian.[19]

Second vignette. From 1721 to 1730 a consortium of printers active in the London newspaper trade, including the printer Elizabeth Nutt and her son Richard, published *Magna Britannia et Hibernia, Antiqua & Nova*, a topographical history of England.[20] They began by issuing the work serially, as a supplement to a five-volume world atlas published by Elizabeth Nutt and her husband John from 1711 to 1717.[21] Each "number" surveyed the history, antiquities, religious foundations, gentry families, and grand estates of one or more counties; these were collected together for the 1721–1730 publication of *Magna Britannia*. The text was based largely on Camden's *Britannia*; the undertakers claimed to be making extensive use of Gibson's 1695 revised edition.[22] Camden lived a long life through the eighteenth century, serving as a source for many of the topographical and antiquarian views of Britain aimed at wider audiences, including Daniel Defoe's *Tour Through the Whole Island of Great Britain*.[23] The undertakers of *Magna Britannia* eschewed Camden's method of touring the country by following its major rivers, preferring to proceed alphabetically from county to county.[24] They beefed up the coverage of local notables and charitable Protestant religious foundations in each county; the latter was done to give the lie to Catholic slanders that Protestants were no match for Catholics in the charity department.[25] The description of each county also includes a table showing all the clerical livings in the county, their current holders, the patrons in whose gifts they lay, and their annual value. The dedication went to George I—not an uncommon strategy for works on British antiquities and geography in the period. With a German king on the throne and the Catholic Stuarts always on the horizon, English antiquaries and geographers tended to emphasize the Saxon strain in Britain's history, which they linked to its present-day Hanoverian rulership.[26]

Despite the title, in *Magna Britannia et Hibernia* the undertakers eschewed any coverage of Ireland, Scotland, and Wales. In the preface they disclaimed any responsibility for the rest of Britain: no person or society of persons existed who could write a topographical study of the entire country, because anyone undertaking such a thing "must be a Soldier, statesman, Philosopher, Divine, Lawyer, Orator, and Poet; yea more than all these, abounding with Wit, of an unbounded Spirit, and biased with no Interest or Passion."[27] The undertakers classed such a person with other impossible inventions, including "the perpetual Motion, or the Philosopher's Stone."[28] They thus proposed to contribute what they could to the general history of the nation, for it was only by collaborative effort, each man doing his part, that the "greatest Cities" grew from a few simple dwellings.[29] In addition to jettisoning Ireland, Wales, and Scotland, the undertakers of *Magna Britannia et Hibernia* eschewed running up and down the country for manuscript sources on which to base their history, as was the custom of learned antiquaries; they had "neither Interest nor Leisure enough" for that.[30] Instead they compiled their account from printed sources, throwing in the occasional, anonymous letter for good measure.[31] This was a book aimed at an audience broader and much less specialized than the learned topographical correspondence.

Taken together, these two vignettes suggest that one response to greater British union in the eighteenth century was to retreat into closer identification with regional cultures and traditions. Scotland and England became "Great Britain" in 1707, the very year Lhuyd's *Archaeologia Britannia* was published. In 1800 the British Parliament officially incorporated Ireland into Great Britain by an Act of Union, creating the United Kingdom of Great Britain and Ireland, thereby attempting (ultimately unsuccessfully) to resolve Ireland's troubled status vis-à-vis Britain and more particularly England.[32] Historians (Linda Colley most prominently) have argued that in this expanding empire there was room for English, Welsh, Scots, and at least some of the Irish to develop a sense of "British" identity that, while it did not erase more local loyalties, could be drawn upon as an ideological basis for national unity: this, perhaps, was an invention men were willing to die for.[33] This "Britishness" was of a print public, consumed in newspapers and in public spectacles, such as the coronations and funerals of the Hanoverian monarchs, beginning especially with George III.[34] It was anti-Catholic; it was anti-French; and it depended on an oceanic perspective: "Britannia" ruled the waves, not England, Scotland, Wales, or Ireland.[35] It was a Britishness expressed abroad, as the English, Scots, and Welsh left their island to create and become denizens of an expanded empire.[36] Hans Sloane, as an Irish Protestant who rose to great heights by combining colonial service in Jamaica with a thriving medical practice in London, exemplified these trends.[37]

Yet at home this Britishness remained profoundly contested, ambiguous, and even ignored.[38] For example, Lhuyd's unified "British" collection of manuscripts was first purchased by an English collector and then divided between Ireland and Wales, and Welsh scholars in particular felt frustrated when the materials were in English hands. Into the twenty-first century scholarship on Lhuyd and his contributions to the fields of linguistics, geology, and antiquarian studies has been concentrated in academic journals devoted to Welsh history, literature, and culture.[39] *Magna Britannia* was aimed at the broader newspaper-buying public rather than a somewhat narrow learned correspondence. Serialization, in making topographical writing affordable, brought it to larger readerships.[40] Yet although the title page of *Magna Britannia* proclaimed it to be a history of Great Britain and Ireland, the text shunned Scotland, Ireland, and Wales (Cornwall made it in). *Magna Britannia* was a *Britannia* for an English print public. It abandoned even the pretense of constructing a topographical history based on extended travel, collaboration, and correspondence. The public at which it was aimed was perhaps best represented in the tables that accompanied the description of each county, which named not only the clergy who held the living in the parishes but also their patrons. These tables were the ghost of the seventeenth-century learned correspondence—many of whose members had been clergy and their gentle and noble patrons—haunting the text. But these tables represented a "public" at once enlarged and constricted, from the seventeenth-century point of view. It was a social body expanded beyond the point where individual members could all know each other, and yet it included only clergy with livings in England.

In the eighteenth century, antiquarian views of Britain saw the landscape with English eyes. As topographical writing became more popular with non-specialists in the middling classes, moving beyond the narrow, elite sphere of the correspondence, the conflict and ambiguity in its representations of a land-based Britain slid into a new register. Specialist studies continued, and specialists shared information in common forums, such as the refounded Society of Antiquaries; however, in books designed for broader print readerships, defining Britain was no longer a joint project in quite the same way as it had been. Over the eighteenth century, especially with the lapse of the Licensing Act in 1695, the print trade expanded not only in London but also in Ireland and Scotland, with thriving trades taking root in the cities of Dublin, Glasgow, and Edinburgh.[41] Yet the English market for printed topographical studies remained the largest and thus had a genre-defining power. In this market antiquities became separate from scientific study, with agricultural improvement and natural history becoming their own distinct genres. Nonspecialist views of the antiquities of Britain emphasized the picturesque, leaning solidly on the "aesthetic of the ruin," in Rosemary Sweet's phrase.[42] They also concentrated particularly on English antiquities, especially those that dated to the medieval era. When Welsh and Scottish antiquities were included, it was with the English book market in mind as well, as Welsh and Scottish sites—but not comparable ones in Ireland—attracted English tourists, who planned and remembered their trips through such books.[43]

A last vignette. In 1847 the self-taught antiquary John Britton published *The Natural History of Wiltshire*, an edition of Aubrey's *Naturall Historie* transcribed and redacted from the manuscript in the library of the Royal Society. Britton was no slouch; he and his partner Edward Wedlake Brayley made their names as leaders of a consortium of authors who worked on the twenty-seven-volume *The Beauties of England and Wales* (1801–1816). In researching just the first five volumes, the two crisscrossed the counties, largely by foot, covering some thirty-five hundred miles.[44] Wiltshire-born Britton felt a sense of kinship with Aubrey and sought to restore his reputation, even then somewhat dim because of the "superstitious" character of his *Miscellanies* (1696), a commonplace collection of omens, apparitions, witchcraft, and sorcery.[45] In addition to *The Natural History of Wiltshire*, Britton published a memoir of Aubrey's life. He rejected the notion that Aubrey was "an especial votary of superstition," arguing that he was a product of the "gloom and illiteracy" of the dark age—the seventeenth century—in which he lived.[46] Even the eminent men of those years, "Harvey, Wren, Flamsteed, and Newton . . . were slaves and victims to the superstition and fanaticism of their age."[47]

Britton also set Aubrey's *Naturall Historie of Wiltshire* firmly in a local context. The edition was published by the Wiltshire Topographical Society; most of Britton's editorial notes point to further reading in the history, topography, and antiquities of Wiltshire. Britton redacted and summarized the text first and foremost with an eye toward distilling the manuscript down to only those portions that shed light on life in Wiltshire.[48] Whereas Aubrey's *Naturall Historie* reached out toward Britain, broadly defined, setting local particulars in national context, Britton's *Natural History* was firmly reined in, no longer extending beyond its county boundaries. Topography had turned inward. Yet some things endured, for example a fascination with the grand estates of the nobility: Britton dubbed Aubrey's description of Wilton House, the home of the Earls of Pembroke, "exceedingly interesting" and expanded it with extensive explanatory notes.[49] From Britton's perspective, the science of Aubrey's *Naturall Historie* was hopelessly out of date, if not backward to begin with. What survived, however, was the value of the *Naturall Historie* as a mirror of the social world of Britain, as it was instantiated on the land.

Notes

INTRODUCTION

1. Scribal exchange practices in the sciences shared some features with "scribal publication," as that phenomenon has been discussed by Harold Love and others, and this book builds on work that has been done on postprint scribal cultures by literary scholars and historians of the book. Their studies have focused primarily on scribal practices within literary, religious, and legal circles. My book differs from these studies in certain key respects, showing that not all scribal cultures functioned in the same way: the development of practices for creating, exchanging, circulating, and preserving texts depended on a host of factors, including the intellectual priorities of writers and readers, governmental regimes and cultural norms restricting (or encouraging) the use of print, and the properties of the available technologies. On early modern literary, religious, and legal scribal cultures, see McKenzie, "Speech-Manuscript-Print" (1990); Marotti, *Manuscript, Print, and the English Renaissance Lyric* (1995); Love, *The Culture and Commerce of Texts* (1998); Beal, *In Praise of Scribes* (1998); Woudhuysen, *Sir Phillip Sydney and the Circulation of Manuscripts, 1558–1640* (1996); Ezell, *Social Authorship and the Advent of Print* (1999); Howard-Hill, "Nor Stage, Nor Stationers Stall Can Showe" (1999); Marotti and Bristol, eds., *Print, Manuscript, Performance* (2000); Scott-Warren, "Reconstructing Manuscript Networks" (2000); Marotti, "Folger MSS V.a.89 and V.a.345: Reading Lyric Poetry in Manuscript" (2001); McKitterick, *Print, Manuscript and the Search for Order, 1450–1830* (2003); and Brayman Hackel, *Reading Material in Early Modern England* (2005), 25–34. On scribal cultures and practices beyond Britain's shores, see Moureau, ed., *De bonne main* (1993); Hall, *Ways of Writing* (2008); and Richardson, *Manuscript Culture in Renaissance Italy* (2009).

2. Lambarde, *A perambulation of Kent* (1576), 387: "And, as touching the description of the rest of the Realme, knowing by the dealing in this one, that it wilbe harde for any one man (and much more for my self) to accomplishe all, I can but wishe in like sorte, that some one in each Shyre, would make the enterprise for his owne Countrie, to the end that by ioyning our pennes and conferring our labours (as it were) *Ex symbolo*, wee may at the last by the union of many parts and papers, compact a whole and perfect bodie and Booke of our English antiquities."

3. Sweet, *Antiquaries* (2004), 310–311.

4. On the long, gradual, conflicted history of Great Britain as a political and cultural entity, the creation of a "British" identity, and relations between England, Wales, Scotland, and Ireland, see Hechter, *Internal Colonialism* (1975); Jenkins, *The Making of a Ruling Class* (1983); Hill, "The Protestant Nation," in *The Collected Essays of Christopher Hill*, vol. 2 (1986),

21–36; Kearney, *The British Isles* (1989); Elton, *The English* (1992); Wormald, "The Creation of Britain" (1992); Helgerson, *Forms of Nationhood* (1994); Samuel, "British Dimensions" (1995); Ellis and Barber, eds., *Conquest and Union* (1995); Bradshaw and Roberts, eds., *British Consciousness and Identity* (1998); Williamson, "Patterns of British Identity," in *The New British History*, ed. Burgess (1999), 138–173; Sweet, *Antiquaries*; Claydon, *Europe and the Making of England, 1660–1760* (2007); Colley, *Britons* (1992); and Walsham, *The Reformation of the Landscape* (2011). These citations are necessarily representative, not comprehensive.

5. See also Mendyk, *"Speculum Britanniae"* (1989); Cormack, "Good Fences Make Good Neighbors" (1991); Parry, *The Trophies of Time* (1995); Olwig, *Landscape, Nature, and the Body Politic* (2002); Withers, *Geography, Science, and National Identity* (2001); and Broadway, *"No Historie so Meete"* (2006).

6. Childrey, *Britannia Baconica, or, The natural rarities of England, Scotland, and Wales* (1660), "The Preface to the Reader."

7. Walsham, *The Reformation of the Landscape.*

8. Cormack, "Good Fences Make Good Neighbors," 656.

9. On the development of this tradition, see Ogilvie, "The Many Books of Nature" (2003); and Ogilvie, *The Science of Describing* (2006).

10. See Kusukawa, "The *Historia Piscium* (1686)" (2000); and Ogilvie, "Attending to Insects" (2012).

11. Though they may not have always followed Bacon to the letter, the vision was, broadly (and rhetorically), Baconian. See Lynch, *Solomon's Child* (2002). On Baconism and Baconian method in seventeenth-century natural history, see Shapiro, *A Culture of Fact* (2000), esp. 63–85, 105–138; Daston, "Marvelous Facts and Miraculous Evidence in Early Modern Europe" (1991); Cormack, "Good Fences Make Good Neighbors"; Clucas, "In Search of 'The True Logick,'" in *Samuel Hartlib and Universal Reformation,* ed. Greengrass, Leslie, and Raylor (1994), 51–74; and Daston and Park, *Wonders and the Order of Nature, 1150–1750* (2001), esp. "Strange Facts," 215–253.

12. Bacon, *The Great Instauration,* in Bacon, *New Atlantis and The Great Instauration,* ed. Weinberger (1980), 16–17.

13. Ray to Willughby, 25 February 1659, quoted in Raven, *John Ray, Naturalist* (2nd ed., 1950), 111.

14. The acknowledgments are spread across two prefaces (one of which also appeared in the first edition). See Ray, *Synopsis methodica stirpium Britannicum* (2nd ed., 1696), "Preface" and "Preface to the Second Edition," sig. (a2v)–(a4r) and sig. (b4 + 2r–v).

15. Harkness, *The Jewel House* (2007), 214–216, 241–253.

16. In his 1610 preface to the reader, Camden wrote only that in preparing his *Britannia,* he had "conferred with most skillful observers in each country" (Camden, *Britain, Or a chorographicall description of the most flourishing kingdomes, England, Scotland, and Ireland, and the ilands adioyning,* trans. Holland [1610], 4). See also Mendyk, *"Speculum Britanniae,"* 54. On Camden's emphasis on gathering facts and observations from personal experience, see Cormack, "Good Fences Make Good Neighbors," 658–660.

17. See Mosley, *Bearing the Heavens* (2007).

18. Pumfrey, "Ideas Above His Station" (1991); Iliffe, "In the Warehouse" (1992); Hunter, "Hooke the Natural Philosopher," in *London's Leonardo,* ed. Bennett (2003), 155–157; Westfall, *Never at Rest* (1983), 241–247, 272–274, 382–390, 446–452. See also the essays in Hunter and Schaffer, eds., *Robert Hooke* (1989).

19. Stewart, *The Rise of Public Science* (1992); Richard Westfall, "Sir Isaac Newton (1650–1715)," *ODNB*.

20. Blair, "Note Taking as an Art of Transmission" (2004), 105.

21. On "information overload" in early modern natural history, see Ogilvie, "The Many Books of Nature"; more generally, see Blair, *Too Much to Know* (2010).

22. John Ray to Martin Lister, 15 July 1676, in Ray, *Philosophical letters between the bate learned Mr. Ray and several of his ingenious correspondents, natives and foreigners* (1718), 141–142. For another, similar example, see Lister to Ray, n.d., in Ray, *Philosophical Letters*, 60.

23. Samuel Dale to Edward Lhuyd, February 1703, RS item EL/D1/39.

24. On these dynamics, see Eisenstein, *Divine Art, Infernal Machine* (2012).

25. Evelyn, "Of Manuscripts," in *Memoirs*, vol. 2, pt. 1, ed. Bray (1818), 340.

26. Margócsy, "Refer to Folio and Number" (2010); Bleichmar, "The Geography of Observation," in *Histories of Scientific Observation*, ed. Daston and Lunbeck (2011), 373–395.

27. John Ray to John Aubrey, 27 October 1691, in Aubrey, *The Naturall Historie of Wiltshire*, Bod MS Aubrey 1, 13r.

28. For similar sentiments, see Lhuyd to Aubrey, 2 March 1693, Bod MS Aubrey 12, 241r.

29. See Eisenstein, *The Printing Revolution in Early Modern Europe* (1979); Johns, *The Nature of the Book* (1998); and their exchange in the pages of the *American Historical Review*: Eisenstein, "An Unacknowledged Revolution Revisited" (2002); and Johns, "How to Acknowledge a Revolution" (2002). On the common assumptions shared by Johns and Eisenstein, see also Dane, *The Myth of Print Culture* (2003), 15–16; and Gitelman, *Paper Knowledge* (2014), 8–9.

30. On ways in which the legal and economic structures of the early modern book market could encourage the production of revised editions of popular books, see Hoffman, "The Montaigne Monopoly" (1993); Mann, "A Mongrel of Early Modern Copyright," in *Privilege and Property,* ed. Deazley, Kretschmer, and Bently (2010), 58.

31. John Evelyn, annotated copy of *Sylva* (3rd ed., 1679) (BL Add. MS 78348).

32. For example, in the section on chestnut trees, he added a reference to the sixteenth-century German humanist Janus Cornarius's description of the different varieties (Evelyn, BL Add. MS 78348, 44). In some cases he added citations for facts already included in the text, further shoring up the quality of the evidence (Evelyn, BL Add. MS 78348, 55). In other cases he referenced personal experience, as in an addition describing an improved method for extracting sap from birch trees (Evelyn, BL Add. MS 78348, 74).

33. On early modern readers' marks in their books, see Grafton and Jardine, "Studied for Action" (1990); Andersen and Sauer, eds., *Books and Readers in Early Modern England* (2001); Brayman Hackel, *Reading Material in Early Modern England*; and Sherman, *Used Books* (2008).

34. Turner, *A compleat history of the most remarkable providences, both of judgment and mercy, which have hapned in this present age* (1697), "Letter to the Reader," sig. bv.

35. See Moss, *Printed Commonplace-Books and the Structuring of Renaissance Thought* (1996); Yeo, "Notebooks as Memory Aids" (2008); Blair, *Too Much to Know,* chap. 5, "The Impact of Early Printed Reference Books"; and Yeo, *Notebooks, English Virtuosi, and Early Modern Science* (2014).

36. Francis Willughby and John Ray, *De historia piscium* (1686), copy in the library of the Royal Society.

37. See Armitage, "Greater Britain" (1999).

38. Houghton, *A Collection for Improvement of Husbandry and Trade* (1692–1703).

39. On the bequest of papers across the generations of scholarly families, as well as between scholarly colleagues, see Blair, *Too Much to Know*, 115–116.

40. Walker, MacGregor, and Hunter, eds., *From Books to Bezoars* (2012).

CHAPTER I

1. Rowena Mason, "David Cameron Says Queen 'Purred Down Line' After Scotland No Vote," *Guardian*, 23 September 2014, http://www.theguardian.com/politics/2014/sep/23/david -cameron-queen-purred-down-line-scotland-no-vote (accessed 17 April 2015).

2. Ogilby, *Britannia, volume the first or, an illustration of the Kingdom of England and dominion of Wales* (1675), sig. B1r. See also Hindle, *Roads and Tracks for Historians* (2001), 52.

3. See Speed, *The theatre of the empire of Great Britaine* (1611), 162–166; and Carew, *The survey of Cornwall* (1602), f. 2r.

4. Kidd, *British Identities Before Nationalism* (1999), 86–90. See also Roberts, "Tudor Wales, National Identity and the British Inheritance," in *British Consciousness and Identity,* ed. Bradshaw and Roberts (1998), 8–42.

5. See Wrightson, *Earthly Necessities* (2000).

6. Colley, "Britishness and Otherness" (1992); Armitage, *The Ideological Origins of the British Empire* (2000).

7. Camden, *Britain* (1610), 4.

8. Camden, *Camden's* Britannia, newly translated into English (1695), "The Preface to the Reader."

9. Camden, *Camden's Britannia, newly translated into English* (1695), "To the Right Honourable Sir John Sommers, Knight," sig. A1r.

10. Pocock, "British History" (1975).

11. In addition to multiple reprints of Camden's *Britannia*, see also Speed, *The theatre of the empire of Great Britaine*; Camden, *The abridgement of Camden's Britannia with the maps of the several shires of England and* Wales (1626); Speed, *England, Wales, Scotland and Ireland described and abridged* (1627); Childrey, *Britannia Baconica, or, The natural rarities of England, Scotland, and Wales* (1660); Enderbie, *Cambria triumphans, or, Brittain in its perfect lustre shewing the origen and antiquity of that illustrious nation* (1661); Blome, *Britannia, or, A geographical description of the kingdoms of England, Scotland, and Ireland* (1673); Ogilby, *Britannia*; Sammes, *Britannia antiqua illustrata* (1676); Anon., *Britannia reflorescens* (1684). For an overview of this century of English antiquarian scholarship, see Parry, *The Trophies of Time* (1995).

12. For example, the text of Speed, *The theatre of the empire of Great Britaine*, was primarily sourced from Camden. Speed's book was then further replicated through the century in various editions and abridgements, as can be seen in a search of the *English Short Title Catalogue* (estc.bl.uk; accessed 2 May 2015).

13. On this tendency and the ways in which it came into conflict with historical reality in early modern Britain, see Wormald, "The Creation of Britain: Multiple Kingdoms or Core and Colonies?" (1992). Wormald's answer is "neither."

14. Wormald, "The Creation of Britain," 187.

15. See, for example, Cormack, *Charting an Empire* (1997). Cormack's study deals in the connections between geography (in which she includes descriptive geography, mathematical geography, with its close associations to cartography, and chorography) and the "ideology of imperialism in early modern England" (Cormack, *Charting an Empire*, 1). I see this ideology

as one facet of the greater problem of defining Britain, rather than just England. Similarly, Parry's excellent study of early modern antiquaries, *The Trophies of Time*, focuses largely on English perspectives. Scottish and Welsh antiquaries, such as Robert Sibbald and Edward Lhuyd, receive mentions but are assimilated into an English tradition. Similarly, Parry largely excludes Ireland, and Irish antiquaries, from consideration.

16. Childrey, *Britannia Baconica*, "The Preface to the Reader," sig. (A4 + 4v).

17. Childrey, *Britannia Baconica*, "The Preface to the Reader," sig. B1v.

18. Childrey, *Britannia Baconica*, "The Preface to the Reader," sig. B1r. Childrey antici-pated the eighteenth-century boom in domestic travel and tourism. See Henry, "The Making of Elite Culture," in *A Companion to Eighteenth-Century Britain,* ed. Dickinson (2002), 324, 326–327; and Ousby, *The Englishman's England* (1990).

19. Childrey, *Britannia Baconica*, "The Preface to the Reader," sig. (A4 + 4v)–B1r.

20. Childrey, *Britannia Baconica*, 61. See also 161–162, where he mentions stones in Cuba and Provence that may be similar to distinctive stones found in Yorkshire.

21. Childrey, *Britannia Baconica*, 55.

22. Childrey, *Britannia Baconica*, 103–104, 158–159, quotes on 103, 158.

23. Childrey, *Britannia Baconica*, 175–181.

24. Childrey, *Britannia Baconica*, 101.

25. Childrey, *Britannia Baconica*, 173.

26. Childrey, *Britannia Baconica*, 59.

27. Childrey, *Britannia Baconica*, 61.

28. Robert Sibbald, *Advertisement* (1682). On Sibbald, see Withers, "Geography, Science, and National Identity in Early Modern Britain" (1996).

29. Hartlib, "To His Excellency Oliver Cromwel," in Boate, *Irelands Naturall History* (1652), sig. A3r–v.

30. See Wennerlind, *Casualties of Credit* (2011), esp. 44–82.

31. On the broader links between agriculture, the improvement of trade, and empire, see Drayton, *Nature's Government* (2000), esp. 50–82.

32. Aubrey, Bod MS 1, 5r.

33. Ogilby, *Britannia,* sig. A1r.

34. See Clark, " 'Now Through You Made Public for Everyone,' " in *Making Space Public in Early Modern Europe,* ed. Vanhaelen and Ward (2013), esp. 136–139. In his *Britannia*, Ogilby crafted a "narrational representation of the nation founded on history, quotidian activity and hopes for the nation's future" (136).

35. Ogilby, *Britannia,* sig. A1r.

36. Childrey, *Britannia Baconica*, 73, 100, 101, 103–104, 109.

37. Lhuyd to Richardson, 18 April 1699, *ESIO*, 14:415.

38. Lhuyd to Richardson, 18 April 1699, *ESIO*, 14:415.

39. Lhuyd to Richardson, 18 April 1699, *ESIO*, 14:415.

40. Carew, *The survey of Cornwall,* 56r.

41. Carew, *The survey of Cornwall,* 56r.

42. Lhuyd, *Archaeologia Britannica* (1707), sig. b2r.

43. Ray, *A collection of English words, not generally used* (1674), "To the Reader," sig. (A4 + 1r).

44. On Ray's interest in language, particularly in the universal character as a means of classifying and assigning proper names to things, see Kusukawa, "The 'Historia Piscium' (1686)" (2000), 183–185.

45. On the connections between natural history and the study of languages, see Cooper, "Latin Words, Vernacular Worlds" (2007).

46. John Ray, *Dictionariolum trilingue* (1675); Campbell and Thomson, *Edward Lhuyd in the Scottish Highlands 1699–1700* (1963), 91–100.

47. Pittock observes the extension of this phenomenon into the nineteenth and twentieth centuries in *Celtic Identity and the British Image* (1999).

48. Aubrey, *Villare Anglicanum,* Bod MS Aubrey 5, 10r.

49. For a recap of modern scholarly debates on the identities and interrelationships between early British peoples as well as these early peoples' relations to modern-day inhabitants of Great Britain and Ireland, see Snyder, *The Britons* (2003).

50. On the development of such a "national past" for England, see Woolf, *The Social Circulation of the Past* (2003), 12–13.

51. See Sweet, *Antiquaries* (2004), esp. 119–153. On English denigration of "Celtic" identity, see Pittock, *Celtic Identity and the British Image.*

52. Jones, *The most notable antiquity of Great Britain vulgarly called Stone-Heng* (1655), 3–4.

53. Aubrey, *Monumenta Britannica,* ed. Fowles (1980–1982), 1:25.

54. Aubrey, *Monumenta Britannica,* ed. Fowles, 1:23.

55. On eighteenth-century approaches to "British" (i.e., Welsh) antiquities, see Sweet, *Antiquaries,* 120–121, 139–142.

56. Kidd, *British Identities Before Nationalism,* 87–88; Parry, *The Trophies of Time,* 3–4.

57. Kidd, *British Identities Before Nationalism,* 83–90.

58. Kidd, *British Identities Before Nationalism,* 86.

59. Edward Lhuyd, "A Design of a British Dictionary, Historical and Geographical" (1695).

60. Ellis, "Some Incidents in the Life of Edward Lhuyd," *ESIO,* 14:51. See also Anne O'Sullivan and William O'Sullivan, "Introduction," in Lhuyd, *Archaeologia Britannica* (1971); and Cram, "Edward Lhuyd's *Archaeologia Britannica*" (2010), 75–96.

61. Lhuyd, "A Design of a British Dictionary, Historical and Geographical."

62. Lhuyd, "A Design of a British Dictionary, Historical and Geographical."

63. Lhuyd, *Archaeologia Britannica* (1707), t.p.

64. Lhuyd, *A compleat translation of the Welsh preface to Mr. Lhuyd's Glossography, or Archeologia Britannica* (1710?), 10–11.

65. Lhuyd to Henry Rowlands, 12 March 1699/1700, *ESIO,* 14:428.

66. Campbell and Thomson, *Edward Lhuyd in the Scottish Highlands 1699–1700,* 91–92.

67. Cram, "Edward Lhuyd's *Archaeologia Britannica,*" 84.

68. Cram, "Edward Lhuyd's *Archaeologia Britannica,*" 84.

69. See Roberts, "Tudor Wales, National Identity and the British Inheritance," 21–22, 35–36.

70. Jenkins, "Seventeenth-Century Wales," in *British Consciousness and Identity,*" ed. Bradshaw and Roberts (1998), 213–235.

71. Robertson, "Union, State and Empire," in *An Imperial State at War,* ed. Stone (1994), 237–250.

72. Colley, *Britons,* 13–17.

73. Jenkins, "Seventeenth-Century Wales," 218–220.

74. Lhuyd, *Archaeologia Britannica* (1707), sig. b2r.

75. Speed, *The theatre of the empire of Great Britaine,* 166.

76. Lhuyd, *Archaeologia Britannica* (1707), "Dedication," sig. bᵢᵥ.

77. Canny, "Irish Resistance to Empire? 1641, 1690, and 1798," in *An Imperial State at War,* ed. Stone (1994), 290–302.

78. Lhuyd, "Additions to Penbrokshire," in Camden, *Camden's Britannia newly translated into English,* 637; Parry, *The Trophies of Time,* 351.

79. See, for example, Arnold Boate's description of his brother Gerard's plan for a four-volume history of Ireland: the fourth volume was to concern "the Natives of Ireland, and their old Fashions, Lawes, and Customes; as likewise the great paines taken by the English, ever since the Conquest, for to civilize them, and to improve the Countrie" (Arnold Boate, "To the Reader," in Gerard Boate, *Irelands Naturall History,* sig. (A4 + 2v)).

80. McCormick, *William Petty and the Ambitions of Political Arithmetic* (2010), 207.

81. Canny, "Irish Resistance to Empire? 1641, 1690, and 1798," 292.

82. Canny, "Irish Resistance to Empire? 1641, 1690, and 1798," 300.

83. McCormick, "Alchemy in the Political Arithmetic of Sir William Petty (1623–1687)" (2006).

84. Roberts, "Tudor Wales, National Identity and the British Inheritance," 30.

85. Parry, *The Trophies of Time,* 353.

86. Lhuyd, *Archaeologia Britannica* (1707), 267–268.

87. Lhuyd, *Archaeologia Britannica* (1707), sig. c2r.

88. William Baxter, "A Letter from Mr William Baxter to Dr Hans Sloane," *Phil. Trans.* 311 (1707): 2444. Baxter's endorsement was also printed separately at Oxford and distributed with the title page of *Archaeologia Britannica.*

89. Lhuyd to John Lloyd, 1 September 1708, National Library of Wales MS Peniarth 427, 80, trans. Helen Watt and Brynley Roberts, EMLO.

90. Roderic O'Flaherty to Lhuyd, 22 November 1707, Bod MS Ashmole 1817a, 52r, EMLO. See also O'Flaherty to Lhuyd, April 1708, Bod MS 1817a, 57r, EMLO. Both letters transcribed by Helen Watt and Brynley Roberts.

91. William Lewes to Lhuyd, 1 March 1708, Bod MS 1816, 53–54, trans. Helen Watt and Brynley Roberts, EMLO.

92. Edward Lloyd to Lhuyd (spelled Lluyd by the correspondent), 11 August 1708, Bod MS Ashmole 1816, 207r, trans. Helen Watt and Brynley Roberts, EMLO.

93. This is not to say that there were not Irish Catholic antiquaries, but that they were generally not well represented in works written from the English perspective. See Sweet, *Antiquaries,* 142–146, 228.

94. Mendyk, *"Speculum Britanniae,"* 51; Cormack, "Good Fences Make Good Neighbors" (1991), 660; Sweet, *Antiquaries,* 120–121, 160, 310–311; Broadway, *"No Historie so Meete,"* 32–33.

95. Camden, *Britain* (1610), t.p.

96. Camden, "Scotland," in Camden, *Britain* (1610), 3.

97. Camden, "Scotland," in Camden, *Britain* (1610), 3.

98. Camden, *Camden's* Britannia newly translated into English, t.p.

99. William Nicolson to William Dugdale, 23 November 1685, in Camden, *Camden's Britannia newly translated into English,* 841.

100. Camden, *Camden's Britannia newly translated into English,* "The Preface to the Reader."

101. Walters and Emery, "Edward Lhuyd, Edmund Gibson, and the Printing of Camden's *Britannia,* 1695" (1977), 109.

102. Walters and Emery, "Edward Lhuyd, Edmund Gibson, and the Printing of Camden's *Britannia*, 1695," 109.

103. Walters and Emery, "Edward Lhuyd, Edmund Gibson, and the Printing of Camden's *Britannia*, 1695," 112.

104. Walters and Emery, "Edward Lhuyd, Edmund Gibson, and the Printing of Camden's *Britannia*, 1695," 111.

105. Camden, *Camden's Britannia newly translated into English*, "The Preface to the Reader," sig. air.

106. "Warrant of Appointment as Geographer Royal," in Withers, "Geography, Science, and National Identity in Early Modern Britain," 65–66.

107. Withers, "Geography, Science, and National Identity in Early Modern Britain," 62.

108. Fox, "Printed Questionnaires, Research Networks, and the Discovery of the British Isles, 1650–1800" (2010), 619; Charles W. J. Withers, "Sibbald, Sir Robert (1641–1722)," *ODNB*.

109. Camden, *Camden's Britannia newly translated into English*, 901.

110. Camden, *Britain* (1610), 26–27.

111. Camden, *Camden's Britannia newly translated into English*, xxix–xxx.

112. Sibbald, "The Thule of the Ancients," in Camden, *Camden's Britannia newly translated into English*, 1100.

113. Sammes, *Britannia antiqua illustrata*; "An Account of Some Books . . . Britannia Antiqua Illustrata, or, The Antiquities of Ancient Britain, Derived from the Phoenicians," *Phil. Trans.* 11 (1676): 596–598; Graham Parry, "Aylett Sammes (c. 1636–c. 1679)," *ODNB*; Parry, *The Trophies of Time*, 308–330.

114. Interestingly, though no etymology has been decisively reconstructed for Britain, Bochart's suggestion that it comes from the ancient Phoenician word for tin continues to circulate, judging by entries on "Britain" in the *OED* and on Wikipedia (though the *OED* prefers an etymology that links "Britain" to the Old Welsh "Priten"). See also Snyder, *The Britons*, 12, which notes that though "Britain," "Britannia," and "British" are first seen in writing in ancient Greek and Roman sources, they bear a striking resemblance to the ancient British and Welsh words for the Picts and for Britain, respectively.

115. Colley, "Britishness and Otherness," 314.

116. Camden, *Britain* (1610), "Ireland," 72–73, 63.

117. Camden, *Britain* (1610), "Ireland," 68.

118. Speed, *The theatre of the empire of Great Britaine*, 167.

119. Camden, *Britain* (1610), "Ireland," 119–139.

120. Camden, *Britain* (1610), 139.

121. Camden, *Britain* (1610), 139.

122. Boate, *Irelands Naturall History*, t.p.

123. Samuel Hartlib, "To His Excellency Oliver Cromwel," in Boate, *Irelands Naturall History*, sig. (A4 + 1v).

124. Canny, "Irish Resistance to Empire? 1641, 1690 and 1798," 300.

125. Fox, "Sir William Petty, Ireland, and the Making of a Political Economist, 1653–87" (2009), 400. On the depths of English anti-Catholicism, see Colley, "Britishness and Otherness," 316–321.

126. See Buck, "Seventeenth-Century Political Arithmetic" (1977).

127. Slack, "Government and Information in Seventeenth-Century England" (2004), 34–36; McCormick, *William Petty and the Ambitions of Political Arithmetic*, 168–208, 259–284.

128. See Bod MS Ashmole 1813.

129. Andrews, "Science and Cartography in the Ireland of William and Samuel Molyneux" (1980), 236–243.

130. Michael Harris, "Moses Pitt and Insolvency in the Booktrade in the Late 17th Century," in *Economics of the British Booktrade 1605–1939,* ed. Myers and Harris (1985), 181; Harris, "Moses Pitt (*bap.* 1639, *d.* 1697)," *ODNB.*

131. Moses Pitt, "Proposals for Printing a New Atlas" (1678); Johns, *The Nature of the Book,* 452; Peter van der Krogt, "Gerhard Mercator and His Cosmography," 122.

132. Fox, "Printed Questionnaires, Research Networks, and the Discovery of the British Isles, 1650–1800," 615, 619; Andrews, "Science and Cartography in the Ireland of William and Samuel Molyneux," 238.

133. Nollaig Ó Muraíle, "Roderic O'Flaherty," *ODNB;* Sharpe, ed., *Roderick O'Flaherty's Letters, 1696–1709* (2013).

134. William Molyneux, "Whereas there is an accurate account and description of Ireland designed to be made publick in the English Atlas undertaken by Moses Pitt of London" (1682); Johns, *The Nature of the Book,* 452.

135. Robertson, "Union, State and Empire," 240–241; James G. O'Hara, "William Molyneux (1656–1698)," *ODNB.*

136. Molyneux, *The case of Ireland's being bound by acts of parliament in England, stated* (1698); O'Hara, "William Molyneux (1656–1698)," *ODNB.*

137. Molyneux, "Preface to the Reader," in *The case of Ireland's being bound by acts of parliament in England, stated,* sig. (A4 + 3v). See also Molyneux, *The case of Ireland's being bound by acts of parliament in England, stated,* 106, where he refers to the "Insolencies and Barbarities of the Irish Papists."

138. Molyneux, *The case of Ireland's being bound by acts of parliament in England, stated,* 20.

139. Molyneux, *The case of Ireland's being bound by acts of parliament in England, stated,* 18–21. See Hill, "Ireland Without Union," in *A Union for Empire,* ed. Robertson (1995), 271–298, esp. 280–281.

140. Molyneux, *The case of Ireland's being bound by acts of parliament in England, stated,* 97–98.

141. Hill, "Ireland Without Union," 287–288.

142. Compare Colley, "Britishness and Otherness," 309–329. See also Hechter, *Internal Colonialism* (1975). Though overly schematic in his treatment of the early modern period (and too willing to see the "Celtic Fringe" as a region with a common set of political and cultural concerns), Hechter develops a model of colonialism that captures some of the complexities of the loyalties and identities developed by non-English Britons.

143. Cañizares-Esguerra, *How to Write the History of the New World* (2001).

CHAPTER 2

1. John Aubrey to Anthony à Wood, 28 July 1692, Bod MS Ballard 14, 98.

2. Fiennes, *The Journeys of Celia Fiennes,* ed. Morris (1947); Guldi, *Roads to Power* (2012).

3. Daston, "The Ideal and Reality of the Republic of Letters in the Enlightenment" (1991); Jardine, *Erasmus, Man of Letters* (1993); Bots, *Commercium Litterarium, 1600–1750* (1994); Greengrass, Leslie, and Raylor, eds., *Samuel Hartlib and Universal Reformation* (1994); Iliffe,

"Material Doubts" (1995); Goldgar, *Impolite Learning* (1995); Lux and Cook, "Closed Circles or Open Networks" (1998); Miller, *Peiresc's Europe* (2000); Biagioli, *Galileo's Instruments of Credit* (2006), esp. chap. 1, "Financing the Aura: Distance and the Construction of Scientific Authority"; Harkness, *The Jewel House* (2007). For a more material perspective on correspondence, see the work of Steven J. Harris, including "Networks of Travel, Correspondence, and Exchange," in *Cambridge History of Early Modern Science*, vol. 3, ed. Park and Daston (2008), 341–362; and Harris, "Confession-Building, Long-Distance Networks, and the Organization of Jesuit Science" (1996).

4. "Diffusion" is one of the effects attributed to the printing press by Elizabeth Eisenstein. As book historians have recognized, however, diffusion could not have taken place without material transportation networks. See the essays in Myers and Harris, eds., *Spreading the Word* (1990).

5. O'Neill, "Dealing with Newsmongers" (2013).

6. Hartlib, *A faithfull and seasonable advice* (1643). In a three-page description of the "correspondencie," Hartlib uses the word five times (sig. A3r–A4r).

7. Edward Lhuyd to Martin Lister {1696 or 1697}, *ESIO*, 14:321.

8. Lhuyd to Lister {December 1696}, *ESIO*, 14:320.

9. Lhuyd to Lister, 23 April 1696, *ESIO*, 14:305. John Woodward was the author of *An essay toward a natural history of the Earth . . . with an account of the universal deluge* (1695). The book and the man were much disliked by Lhuyd.

10. Roos, "The Art of Science" (2012), 23–24.

11. Johns, "Miscellaneous Methods" (2000), 167–168.

12. HO, 2:646–647; quoted in Johns, "Miscellaneous Methods," 168.

13. Lux and Cook, "Closed Circles or Open Networks," 179–211.

14. George Garden to Henry Oldenburg, 17 February 1677, HO, 13:215–216.

15. Robert Plot to John Aubrey, 15 {?} 1676, Bod MS Aubrey 13, 139r.

16. John Ray to Lhuyd, 18 January 1691/92, Bod MS Ashmole 1817, 216r.

17. Edward Tyson to Dr. Plot, 26 February 1680/81, *ESIO*, 12:2; Tyson to Plot, 24 March 1680/81, *ESIO*, 12:3.

18. Ray to Lhuyd, 7 November 1692, Bod MS Ashmole 1817, 219r.

19. Lhuyd to Lister, 5 December 1695, *ESIO*, 14:297.

20. Daybell, *The Material Letter in Early Modern England* (2012), 109–147. See also Robinson, *Britain's Post Office* (1953), 1–37.

21. Daybell, *The Material Letter in Early Modern England*, 7–8.

22. Daybell, *The Material Letter in Early Modern England*, 120–121.

23. Daybell, *The Material Letter in Early Modern England*, 126–127.

24. Harkness, *The Jewel House*, 18, 24–25.

25. Daybell, *The Material Letter in Early Modern England*, 110.

26. Daybell, *The Material Letter in Early Modern England*, 126.

27. Daybell, *The Material Letter in Early Modern England*, 126.

28. Robinson, *Britain's Post Office*, 25.

29. Abel Swall, *Proposals for printing by subscription, Cambden's Britannia, English* (1693?).

30. Cowan, *The Social Life of Coffee* (2005), 175–177.

31. John Aubrey (his cousin) to John Aubrey (the naturalist), 12 April {1681?}, Bod MS Aubrey 12, 10v; William Ball to Aubrey, 22 August 1688, Bod MS Aubrey 12, 19r–20v; William Brown to Aubrey, 9 September 1645, Bod MS Aubrey 12, letter 19, 35–36.

32. See James Garden to Aubrey, 25 March 1694/95, Bod MS Aubrey 12, 134r–135v.

33. Lhuyd to Lister, 15 December 1699, *ESIO*, 14:418.

34. Lhuyd to Tancred Robinson, 15 December 1699, *ESIO*, 14:421.

35. See Vickery, *Scientific Communication in History* (2000), 69–72.

36. See Oldenburg to Lady Ranelagh, 22 August 1657, HO, 1:130; Oldenburg to Samuel Hartlib, 20 March 1657/58, HO, 1:157.

37. Marie Boas Hall, *Henry Oldenburg* (2002), 179; Rob Iliffe, "'In the Warehouse'" (1992).

38. Aubrey to Wood, January 1673, Bod MS Wood F.39, 253v; Hunter, *John Aubrey and the Realm of Learning* (1975), 64.

39. See Albert, *The Turnpike Road System in England, 1663–1840* (1972); Gerhold, ed., *Road Transport in the Horse-Drawn Era* (1996), 139–164; and Hey, *Packmen, Carriers and Pack-horse Roads* (1980).

40. Aubrey, Bod MS Aubrey 2, f. 89r.

41. Gerhold, *Road Transport in the Horse-Drawn Era*, 139–164.

42. Albert, *The Turnpike Road System in England, 1663–1840*, 169; Hey, *Packmen, Carriers and Packhorse Roads*, 218.

43. Hey, *Packmen, Carriers and Packhorse Roads*, 218.

44. Hey, *Packmen, Carriers and Packhorse Roads*, 210–211.

45. Taylor, *The carriers cosmographie* (1637). See Watt, "Publisher, Pedlar, Pot-Poet," in *Spreading the Word,* ed. Myers and Harris (1990), 71.

46. See, for example, the listings in Houghton's *Collection for Improvement of Husbandry and Trade*, 5, no. 97 (8 June 1694) (Bod Hope Folio 22).

47. Houghton, *Collection*, 5, no. 105 (3 August 1694) (Bod Hope Folio 22).

48. Robert Peirce in Bath to William Musgrave, 11 April 1685, Bod MS Ashmole 1813, 295r–v.

49. Peirce to Musgrave, 11 April 1685, Bod MS Ashmole 1813, 295v.

50. Ray to Aubrey, 18 November 1691, Bod MS Aubrey 13, 175r.

51. Aubrey to Wood, 3 August 1691, Bod MS Wood F.39, 429r.

52. Aubrey to Wood, St John Evangelist's Day {27 December}, 1679, Bod MS Wood F.39, 327.

53. Lhuyd to Aubrey, 12 February 1687, Bod MS Aubrey 12, 240r.

54. Plot to Aubrey, {9} February 1675/76, Bod MS Aubrey 13, 137v.

55. Plot to Aubrey, {9} February 1675/76, Bod MS Aubrey 13, 137r; Mendyk, *"Speculum Britanniae"* (1989), 176–177.

56. Francis Aston to Plot, 31 January 1682, Bod MS Ashmole 1813, 7v.

57. William Molyneux to William Musgrave, 4 April 1685, Bod MS Ashmole 1813, 283r.

58. Michael Hunter, *The Royal Society and Its Fellows, 1660–1700*, 196–199, 210–211.

59. For Petty's scheme, see Aston to Plot, 27 March 1683, Bod MS Ashmole 1813, 16r–17v. Aston exchanged with Plot and Musgrave multiple letters on the contents of *Philosophical Transactions*. See Aston in London to Plot, 5 April 1683, Bod MS Ashmole 1813, 18r–19v; and Aston to Musgrave, 15 January 1684, Bod MS Ashmole 1813, 182r–183v.

60. In addition to the letters from Aston already cited, see Aston to Musgrave, 1 May 1684, 146r–147v; Aston to Musgrave, 3 July 1684, 160r–161v; and Aston to Musgrave, 15 January 1684, 182r–183v—all in Bod MS Ashmole 1813.

61. Aubrey to Musgrave, 27 February 1684/85, *ESIO*, 12:268, original letter in Bod MS Ashmole 1813, f. 234r–235v. See also Bennett, "John Aubrey's Collections and the Early Modern Museum" (2001).

62. Alick Cameron, "Musgrave, William (1655–1721)," *ODNB*.

63. Elias Ashmole, "Statutes, Orders, & Rules for the Ashmolean Museum," dated 24 June 1686 (Bod MS Ashmole 1820, 296r).

64. See Findlen, *Possessing Nature* (1994); Daston and Park, *Wonder and the Orders of Nature, 1150–1750* (1998); and Cook, *Matters of Exchange* (2007).

65. See Kusukawa, "The 'Historia Piscium' (1686)" (2000), 179–197; Ogilvie, "Attending to Insects" (2012), esp. 361–362.

66. Lhuyd, *Lithophylacii Britannici ichnographia* (1699).

67. Lhuyd, "Instructions for Collecting Plants on Cader Idris," Bod MS Ashmole 1820, 182r. See also *ESIO,* 14:70.

68. Lhuyd, "Parochial Queries," Bod MS Ashmole 1820, 74r–178r, 239r–v.

69. Lhuyd to Lister, 15 December 1699, *ESIO*, 14:419.

70. Ray to Lhuyd, 28 March 1690, Bod MS Ashmole 1817, 213r.

71. Lhuyd, "Instructions for Collecting Plants on Cader Idris," Bod MS Ashmole 1820, 182r.

72. Lhuyd to John Lloyd, 16 July 1695, *ESIO*, 14:279.

73. Lhuyd, "Instructions for Collecting Plants on Cader Idris," Bod MS Ashmole 1820, 182r–v. Unless otherwise noted, all citations in this paragraph are to this document.

74. Lhuyd, Bod MS Ashmole 1820, 182v.

75. Lhuyd, Bod MS Ashmole 1820, 182v; *ESIO*, 14:73.

76. Lhuyd, Bod MS Ashmole 1820, 182v.

77. Bod MS Lister 36, ff. 72–73; in Roos, "The Art of Science," 23.

78. Ray to Lhuyd, 25 November 1691, Bod MS Ashmole 1817, 215r.

79. Ray to Lhuyd, 18 January 1691/92, Bod MS Ashmole 1817, 216r; Ray to Lhuyd, 5 April 1692, Bod MS Ashmole 1817, 217r.

80. Ray to Lhuyd, 7 November 1692, Bod MS Ashmole 1817, 219r.

81. Ray to Lhuyd, 28 December 1692, Bod MS Ashmole 1817, 220r.

82. Edward Lhuyd, *A Design of a British Dictionary, Historical and Geographical* (1695), 2.

83. See, for example, John Earle's description of the antiquary: "Hee will goe you forty miles to see a Saint's Well, or a ruin'd Abbey; and if there be but a Crosse or stone footstoole in the way, hee'l be considering it so long, till he forget his journey" (Earle, *Micro-Cosmographie* [7th ed., 1660], 33–34; quoted in Sweet, *Antiquaries* [2004], xiii).

84. Plot to John Fell {c. 1673}, *ESIO*, 12:336–337.

85. Plot to Fell {c. 1673}, *ESIO*, 12:344.

86. Bod MS Ashmole 1820, 197r.

87. Plot to Fell {c. 1673}, *ESIO*, 12:344–345.

88. Lhuyd to Lister, 26 June 1699, *ESIO*, 14:418.

89. Lhuyd to Tonkin, 29 November 1700, *ESIO*, 14:435–437.

90. Lhuyd to Tonkin, 29 November 1700, *ESIO*, 14:436.

91. Lhuyd to Henry Rowlands, 10 March 1701, *ESIO*, 14:439.

92. Lhuyd to Rowlands, 10 March 1701, *ESIO*, 14:439–440.

93. Lhuyd to Rowlands, 10 March 1701, *ESIO*, 14:440.

94. See also Lhuyd to Richard Mostyn, 26 April 1701, *ESIO*, 14:443–445.

95. Stroup, *A Company of Scientists* (1990); Biagioli, *Galileo, Courtier* (1993); Moran, *Alchemical World of the German Court* (1991); the essays in Moran, ed., *Patronage and Institutions* (1991), esp. Eamon, "Court, Academy, and Printing House," 25–50.

96. Moran, *Alchemical World of the German Court.* See also Ashworth, "The Habsburg Circle," in *Patronage and Institutions*, ed. Moran, 137–167, on the ways in which mathematicians seeking Hapsburg patronage in the seventeenth century shaped their research around that end.

97. Eamon, "Court, Academy, and Printing House," 25–50.

98. James Long to Aubrey, 16 July 1676, Bod MS Aubrey 12, 267v. For similar expressions of regard, see also Long to Aubrey, n.d., Bod MS Aubrey 12, 288r.

99. Plot to Aubrey, 9 {February?} 1675/76, Bod MS Aubrey 13, 137r. The ellipsis marks an illegible word.

100. See James Garden to Aubrey, 15 June 1692, Bod MS Aubrey 12, 123r–124v. Garden also provided Aubrey with instances of the second sight and action, or movement, at a distance, which Aubrey compiled with other instances of occult phenomena for publication in his *Miscellanies* (1696). See James Garden to Aubrey, 20 January 1693/94, Bod MS Aubrey 12, 129r–130v; James Garden to Aubrey, 4 May 1694, Bod MS Aubrey 12, 132r–33v; and James Garden to Aubrey, 25 March 1694/95, Bod MS Aubrey 12, 134r–135v.

101. See James Garden to Aubrey, 15 June 1692, Bod MS Aubrey 12, 124r.

102. Koerner, "Daedalus Hyperboreus," in *The Sciences in Enlightened Europe,* ed. Clark, Golinski, and Schaffer (1999), 389–422.

103. Koerner, "Daedalus Hyperboreus," 390.

104. Both Aubrey and Garden profited by this exchange, as Aubrey related to Anthony à Wood. See Aubrey to Wood, 20 August 1692, MS Bod F. 51, 4r.

105. Lhuyd to Lister, 6 January 1697/98, *ESIO*, 14:321.

106. Phillip Mathew to Lhuyd, 3 November 1685, Bod MS Aubrey 12, 321r.

107. Lhuyd to Lister, {1696 or 1697} *ESIO*, 14:321; Ray to Lhuyd, 5 April 1692, Bod MS Ashmole 1817, 217r; Ray to Lhuyd, 7 November 1692, Bod MS Ashmole 1817, 219r.

108. Compare Findlen, "Economy of Scientific Exchange in Early Modern Italy," in *Patronage and Institutions*, ed. Moran (1991), 5–24. Findlen argues that patronage gifts were primarily symbolic offerings marking hoped-for or existing social relationships, rather than practical assistances rendered to advance scientific research projects.

109. For examples in the early modern British and Spanish Empires, see Schiebinger, *Plants and Empire* (2004), 29; and Barrera-Osorio, "Local Herbs, Global Medicines" in *Merchants and Marvels,* ed. Smith and Findlen (2002), 167.

CHAPTER 3

1. John Evelyn to Robert Boyle, 3 September 1659, in John Evelyn, *Diary and Correspondence*, ed. Bray (1854), 3:116–120, quote on 116.

2. Evelyn to Boyle, 3 September 1659, in Evelyn, *Diary and Correspondence*, ed. Bray, 3:118. An "olitory garden" is a kitchen garden, planted with cooking herbs and everyday vegetables.

3. Evelyn to Boyle, 3 September 1659, in Evelyn, *Diary and Correspondence*, ed. Bray, 3:119.

4. Evelyn to Boyle, 3 September 1659, in Evelyn, *Diary and Correspondence*, ed. Bray, 3:120.

5. Evelyn to Boyle, 3 September 1659, in Evelyn, *Diary and Correspondence*, ed. Bray, 3:116.

6. Francis Bacon, *Sylva Sylvarum* (1627).

7. Hartlib, *Considerations Tending to the Happy Accomplishment of Englands Reformation in Church and State* (1647), 37–58; DiMeo, "Openness vs. Secrecy in the Hartlib Circle," in *Secrets and Knowledge in Medicine and Science, 1500–1800*, ed. Leong and Rankin (2011), 119–121.

8. Lynch, *Solomon's Child* (2002), 13–19; Rupert Hall and Marie Boas Hall, "The Intellectual Origins of the Royal Society" (1968); Frank, "John Aubrey, F.R.S., John Lydall, and Science at Commonwealth Oxford" (1973).

9. See Wellman, *Making Science Social* (2003); *A general collection of discourses of the virtuosi of France*, trans. Havers (1664); *Another collection of philosophical conferences of the French virtuosi*, trans. Havers and Davies (1665). Additionally, though not the focus of this chapter, shops were also important sites of scientific conversations across Europe—see, for example, Valentina Pugliano on pharmacy shops as sites of conversation among sixteenth-century Italian naturalists (Pugliano, *Botanical Artisans* (2012), 318–325.

10. Darley, *John Evelyn* (2006), 156–157; Cope, "Evelyn, Boyle, and Dr. Wilkinson's 'Mathematico-Chymico-Mechanical School'" (1959), 30–32.

11. Camden, *Britain* (1610), 4.

12. Compare McKenzie, "Speech-Manuscript-Print" (1990).

13. Sprat, *The history of the Royal Society, for the improving of natural knowledge* (1667); Shapin, *A Social History of Truth* (1994), esp. 114–125.

14. Biagioli, *Galileo's Instruments of Credit* (2006), 44–75.

15. James Long to Aubrey, January 30 1686/87, BOD MS Aubrey 12, 283r.

16. Oldenburg, "Admonitions and Directions of a good parent to his Child, especially a Son," Henry Oldenburg, n.d., BL Add. MS 4458, f. 115v.

17. Oldenburg, BL Add. MS 4458, f. 109r.

18. Oldenburg, BL Add. MS 4458, f. 115r.

19. Greengrass, "Samuel Hartlib and Scribal Publication" (1997), 60; Hartlib, *Considerations tending to the happy accomplishment of England's reformation in church and state*.

20. Lister, "Preface" to his *Historiae animalium Angliae tres tractatus* (1678), 3, in Roos, "The Art of Science" (2012), 26.

21. See Daston and Galison, *Objectivity* (2007), on this kind of scientific oversight of artists and engravers, which they term "four-eyed sight."

22. Margócsy, "Refer to Folio and Number" (2010), 63–89.

23. Shapin, "Pump and Circumstance" (1984); Shapin and Schaffer, *Leviathan and the Air Pump* (1985).

24. John Ray to John Aubrey, 20 December 1692, Bod MS Aubrey 13, v. 177r; Aubrey to Ray, 15 December 1692, in Ray, *The Correspondence of John Ray* (1848), 269.

25. See Carey, "Compiling Nature's History" (1997).

26. On queries as a way of directing or controlling travel, see Carey, "Compiling Nature's History," 271–275.

27. Edward Lhuyd, "Parochial Queries" (1697), 4.

28. Robert Plot, *Quaer's to be propounded to the most ingenious of each county in my travels through England.* (1674).

29. Lhuyd, "Parochial Queries," 4.

30. Evelyn, BL Add. MS 78329, 14r. See also Francis Bacon's advice in his essay "Of Travaile," in Francis Bacon, *The essayes or counsels, civill and morall* (1625), 100–104.

31. Lhuyd, *Archaeologia Britannica* (1707), sig. br.

32. Lhuyd to Richard Richardson, 21 January 1699, BL Sloane MS 4062, ff. 297–298, trans. Helen Watt and Brynley Roberts, EMLO.

33. Heal, "The Idea of Hospitality in Early Modern England" (1984), 70.

34. Heal, "The Idea of Hospitality in Early Modern England," 69–70.

35. Heal, "The Idea of Hospitality in Early Modern England," 72, 74–75. See Matt. 25:35–36, Rom. 12:13, and Heb. 12:2 for exhortations to hospitality in the Christian New Testament.

36. See, for example, Harkness, "Managing an Experimental Household" (1997). Unfortunately, for want of space, this chapter does not consider the crucial role of women in brokering conversations and relationships within the home. I plan to consider women's roles in such conversations (and more broadly, the gender dynamics that shaped them) in a future essay on domestic mathematical, chemical, and natural philosophical conversation in the Pepys and Evelyn households. See also Woolf, "Speaking of History," in *The Spoken Word*, ed. Fox and Woolf (2002), which considers how men and women talked about history in polite domestic settings in the seventeenth and eighteenth centuries.

37. Bod Ashmole 1820, f. 197r. Plot's letter was signed by Bathurst (chancellor), Barrow (pro-vice-chancellor), John Wallis, James Hyde, and William Levinz (president of St. John's College).

38. Plot, *The natural history of Oxford-shire* (1677), 171. Other examples include a conversation with the bishop of Oxford about barley growing that occurred at his estate Gaunt-House (153). Plot thanks (among others) a "Mr. *Wildgose, Physitian* at *Denton*, and an ingenious *Chymist*" (89–90); "ingenious Mr. *Munday*, Physitian" in Henly upon Thames (101); and "the Reverend and Ingenious Mr. *Clark*, Rector of *Dreyton* near *Banbury*" (103) for providing him with or showing him particular geological specimens.

39. James Long to Aubrey, 3 June 1682, Bod MS Aubrey 12, 275r; Long to Aubrey, n.d., Bod MS Aubrey 12, 288r.

40. Long to Aubrey, 3 June 1682, Bod MS Aubrey 12, 275r; Long to Aubrey, n.d., Bod MS Aubrey 12, 288r.

41. See Lhuyd to Martin Lister, 23 April 1696, *ESIO*, 14:306; and Lhuyd to John Lloyd, 13 August 1701, *ESIO*, 14:462.

42. Lhuyd to Lloyd, 25 October 1696, *ESIO*, 14:311.

43. Lhuyd, *Archaeologia Britannica* (1707), sig. c1v.

44. Lhuyd to Lloyd, 13 August 1701, *ESIO*, 14:461–462.

45. Ray to Aubrey, 24 August 1692, Bod MS Aubrey 13, 176r.

46. Sprat, *The history of the Royal Society*, 41. More broadly, complaints about the dullness of country life from the early modern to the present are legion.

47. John Williams to Lhuyd, 4 November 1693, Bod MS Ashmole 1817b, f. 297r.

48. Isaac Hamon to Lhuyd, 26 April 1698, Bod MS Ashmole 1815, f. 166, in Emery, "Edward Lhuyd and Some of His Glamorgan Correspondents," 109.

49. John Williams to Lhuyd, 31 March 1696, MS Ashmole 1817b311, in Emery, "Edward Lhuyd and Some of His Glamorgan Correspondents," 70.

50. Williams to Lhuyd, 31 March 1696, MS Ashmole 1817b311, in Emery, "Edward Lhuyd and Some of His Glamorgan Correspondents," 70.

51. Sprat, *The history of the Royal Society*, 111–115, quote on 112.

52. Aubrey to Wood, 22 October 1681, Bod MS Tanner 456a, 27; quoted in Hunter, *John Aubrey and the Realm of Learning* (1975), 34.

53. Aubrey to Wood, 7 August 1669, Bod MS Wood F.39, 123.

54. Edmond Gibson to Aubrey, 12 February 1692/93, BOD MS Aubrey 12, f. 138c–r.

55. Pepys, *Diary*, 3 June 1663, 4:172. See also the entry for 21 July 1663, 4:236.

56. Pepys, *Diary*, 27 June 1663, 4:201.

57. Pepys, *Diary*, 5 July 1663, 4:218; 14 October 1663, 4:334. In the latter entry, Pepys wrote, "Up and to my office, where all the morning—and part of Sir J. Mennes spent as he doth everything else, like a fool, reading the Anatomy of the body to me, but so sillily as to the making of me understand anything that I was weary of him."

58. See Pincus, "Coffee Politicians Does Create" (1995), 811. On the history of early modern London coffeehouses, especially as sites for natural philosophical conversation, see Cowan, *The Social Life of Coffee* (2005); and Johns, "Coffeehouses and Print Shops," in *The Cambridge History of Early Modern Science*, ed. Daston and Park (2008), 3:320–340.

59. Pincus, "Coffee Politicians Does Create," 812.

60. Pepys, *Diary*, 3 November 1663, 4:361–362, quote on 362.

61. Pepys, *Diary*, 8 August 1666, 7:239.

62. Pepys, *Diary*, 8 August 1666, 7:239.

63. *OED*.

64. Johns, "Coffeehouses and Print Shops," 336–337.

65. Johns, *The Nature of the Book* (1998), 554–558.

66. Phillip Skippon to Ray, {between 13 December 1667 and 24 January 1667,} in Ray, *Philosophical Letters* (1718), 27–28.

67. Simon Schaffer, "Regeneration" (1998), 103.

68. See Johns, "Coffeehouses and Print Shops," 336; Shadwell, *The virtuoso* (1676), 28–31.

69. Shadwell, *The virtuoso*, 30.

70. Shadwell, *The virtuoso*, 72–75.

71. Selwood, *Diversity and Difference in Early Modern London* (2010), 36.

72. Harris, *London Crowds in the Reign of Charles II* (1987), 191–203.

73. Shadwell, *The virtuoso*, 72.

74. Shadwell, *The virtuoso*, 74.

75. Shadwell, *The virtuoso*, 74–75.

76. Shadwell, *The virtuoso*, 75.

77. Selwood, *Diversity and Difference in Early Modern London,* 36; Pfister, "Craft Guilds and Technological Change," in *Guilds, Innovation and the European Economy, 1400–1800*, ed. Epstein and Prak (2008), 186–187.

78. Aubrey, Bod MS 2, f. 66r–67r, quote on 67r.

79. Harris, *London Crowds in the Reign of Charles II*, 192.

80. Hooke, *Diary*, 235. See also Chico, "Gimcrack's Legacy" (2008), 31; and Hunter, *Science and Society in Restoration England* (1981), 70.

81. Hunter, *Science and Society in Restoration England*, 177.

82. Wotton, *Reflections upon Ancient and Modern Learning* (1697), 419.

83. Pepys, *Diary*, 5 July 1663, 4:218.

84. Sprat, *The History of the Royal Society*, 103.

85. Sprat, *The History of the Royal Society*, 103.

86. Sprat, *The History of the Royal Society*, 104.

87. Sprat, *The History of the Royal Society*, 67–71, 92, 111–115.

88. Sprat, *The History of the Royal Society*, 114–115, quote on 114.

89. Dear, "Totius in Verba" (1985); Shapin and Schaffer, *Leviathan and the Air Pump*; Shapin, "Who Was Robert Hooke," in *Robert Hooke*, ed. Hunter and Schaffer (1989), 253–286; Shapin, *A Social History of Truth*; Iliffe, "Material Doubts" (1995).

90. Compare Livingstone, "Science, Site and Speech" (2007) and *Dealing with Darwin* (2014), in which Livingstone explores how the interpretation and appropriation of Darwinian evolution varied across localities. Livingstone discusses here the concept of "speech spaces": even if one keeps the focus mostly on Scots Calvinists and their diaspora (as Livingstone does), Darwinian evolution is interpreted differently in different places because conversational protocols and cultural and intellectual concerns are locally particularized. Though Livingstone directs his focus to the role of face-to-face encounters, including conversations and public lectures, in the appropriation of Darwinian ideas, in practice the "speech space" is a bit like a localized public sphere, in that Livingstone considers not only what individuals said to each other face-to-face, but also what they wrote in publications with locally defined readerships.

91. Carey, "Compiling Nature's History," 269–292.

92. See Henry, "The Origins of Modern Science" (1998), 103–110.

93. Marie Boas Hall, *Henry Oldenburg* (2002), 58. See RS MS/557–574, the secretaries' minutes covering 1662–1761, and MS/575–579, a series of "rough minutes" covering 1685–1711.

94. Henry Oldenburg to Lister, 10 June 1676, HO, 12:332–334.

95. RS Journal Book Copy (JBC)/4/49–50; Oldenburg to Lister, 11 May 1672, HO, 9:64–65.

96. RS JBC/4/49–50.

97. Johns, "Miscellaneous Methods" (2000), 171–172.

98. See Dolan, *True Relations* (2013), 111–153; and Burns, *Into the Archive* (2010), 20–41.

99. Oldenburg to Lister, 12 December 1672, 356; Lister to Oldenburg, 17 December 1672, 364–366; Oldenburg to Lister, 28 December 1672, 373; Lister to Oldenburg, 1 January 1672/73, 377–378; and Lister to Oldenburg, 8 January 1672/73, 397–401: all letters in HO, vol. 9. See also RS JBC/4/73–74; and Roos, *Web of Nature* (2011), 153–166.

100. Lister to Oldenburg, 8 January 1672/73, HO, 9:397–401.

101. See Biagioli, "From Book Censorship to Academic Peer Review" (2002), 11–45.

102. Luke Hodgson to Oldenburg, 15 May 1676, HO, 12:288–289.

103. See Feingold, "Of Records and Grandeur," in *The Archives of the Scientific Revolution*, ed. Hunter (1998), 171–184.

104. See Marie Boas Hall, *Henry Oldenburg*, 295–298, quote on 295; HO, 13:intro, xxvi–xxvii.

105. Birch, *The history of the Royal Society of London* (1756–1757), 3:343, in Feingold, "Of Records and Grandeur," 175.

106. Richard Waller to Hans Sloane, 23 January 1699, BL Sloane MS 4043, f. 189–190, in Hunt, "Sloane as a Collector of Manuscripts," in *From Books to Bezoars*, ed. Walker, MacGregor, and Hunter (2012), 291 n60. See Feingold, "Of Records and Grandeur," 175–176, for other, similar instances.

107. The Hooke Folio, RS MS/847; transcript and page images available at http://livesand letters.ac.uk/cell/Hooke/Hooke.html, accessed 23 April 2015. See also Hunt, "Sloane as a Collector of Manuscripts," 203.

108. BL Sloane MS 3342.

109. Johns, "Miscellaneous Methods," 173.

110. Ghobrial, *The Whispers of Cities* (2013), 44, 55, 64.

111. Ghobrial, *The Whispers of Cities*, 44.

112. Ghobrial, *The Whispers of Cities*, 42–64.

113. See Johns, "Miscellaneous Methods," 173, 182–183.

114. Johns, "Miscellaneous Methods," 162–164.

115. Johns, "Miscellaneous Methods," 182.

116. HO, 9:377–378.

117. Secord, *Victorian Sensation* (2000), 155–170, 187–190; Secord, "How Scientific Conversation Became Shop Talk," in *Science in the Marketplace,* ed. Fyfe and Lightman (2007), chap. 2.

CHAPTER 4

1. These volumes are now in the Bodleian Library (Bod MS Aubrey 1, 2). There are two extant copies of *The Naturall Historie of Wiltshire*, the working draft in the Bodleian and a fair copy in the Royal Society library. The fair copy was made over 1690 and 1691 at the request of the Royal Society (Royal Society MS 92; hereafter RS MS 92). In this chapter, unless the Royal Society copy is specifically being discussed, citations are to the Bodleian copy, as that was the copy Aubrey shared with his readers. On the history of Aubrey's papers, see Hunter, *John Aubrey and the Realm of Learning* (1975), 233–242.

2. John Aubrey to Anthony à Wood, 17 August 1685, Bod MS Wood F.39, 375r.

3. John Ray to Aubrey, 18 November 1691, Bod MS Aubrey 13, 175r.

4. See Aubrey to Wood, 5 and 10 July 1690, Bod MS Wood F.39, 405r–v.

5. Methodologically, compare the essays in *Critical Inquiry* 31 (2004), a special issue devoted to the "arts of transmission," which considers "material culture, a history of practices and skills, and a history of forms of thought" as interconnected (Chandler, Davidson, and Johns, "Arts of Transmission" [2004], 3).

6. Aubrey, Bod MS Aubrey 1, 2v.

7. On early modern readers and reading, see Grafton, "Kepler as a Reader" (1992); Grafton and Jardine, "Studied for Action" (1990); Sherman, *John Dee* (1995); Cavallo and Chartier, eds., *A History of Reading in the West* (1997); Johns, *The Nature of the Book* (1998); Jagodzinski, *Privacy and Print* (1999); Richardson, *Printing, Writers, and Readers in Renaissance Italy* (1999); Sharpe, *Reading Revolutions* (2000); Blair, "Annotating and Indexing Natural Philosophy," in *Books and the Sciences in History,* ed. Frasca-Spada and Jardine (2000); Baron, Walsh, and Scola, eds., *The Reader Revealed* (2001); Jackson, *Marginalia* (2001); Andersen and Sauer, *Books and Readers in Early Modern England* (2001); Blair, "Scientific Readers" (2004); Hackel, *Reading Material in Early Modern England* (2005); and Blair, "Errata Lists and the Reader as Corrector," in *Agent of Change*, ed. Baron, Lindquist, and Shevlin (2007), 21–41.

8. Note that "scribal" here refers to handwritten texts, whether written or copied by their authors or professional scribes hired for taking dictation or making copies. On professional scribes and the manuscripts they made, see Beal, *In Praise of Scribes* (1998).

9. On Aubrey's biography, scientific interests, and scholarly methods, see Powell, *John Aubrey and His Friends* (1963); Hunter, *John Aubrey and the Realm of Learning*; Bennett, "Materials Towards a Critical Edition of John Aubrey's *Brief Lives*" (1993); and Bennett, "Editing Aubrey," in *Ma(r)king the Text*, ed. Bray, Handley, and Henry (2000), 271–290.

10. Aubrey, Bod MS Aubrey 1, 25v.

11. See, for example, Plot, *The natural history of Oxford-shire* (1677); and Plot, *The natural history of Stafford-shire* (1686). There were also county histories that focused more on social history and antiquities. See Blount, *The 1675 Thomas Blount Manuscript History of Herefordshire,* trans. and ed. Reeves, trans. and research Botzum and Botzum (1997).

12. Plot, "To the Reader," in Plot, *The natural history of Oxford-shire*, sig. b2iv.

13. Hunter, *John Aubrey and the Realm of Learning,* 69.

14. Although I would by no means argue that county natural histories eliminated strange marvels, their emphasis on usefulness over wonder differentiates county natural histories from the seventeenth-century natural historical tradition described by Daston and Park in *Wonders and the Order of Nature, 1150–1750* (1998), 215–301.

15. Thirsk, "Making a Fresh Start," in *Culture and Cultivation in Early Modern England,* ed. Leslie and Raylor (1992), 15–34.

16. Mendyk, *"Speculum Britanniae"* (1989), 40–43; Cormack, "Good Fences Make Good Neighbors" (1991), 655–661; Aubrey, Bod MS Aubrey 1, 8v–11v and 14r–23v.

17. Wear, "Making Sense of Health and the Environment in Early Modern England," in Wear, *Health and Healing in Early Modern England* (1998), 119–147; Siraisi, *Medieval and Early Renaissance Medicine* (1990).

18. Kupperman, "Fear of Hot Climates in the Anglo-American Colonia Experience" (1984).

19. On the preference for local remedies and controversy over the use of exotic medicines, see Wear, *Knowledge and Practice in English Medicine, 1550–1680* (2000), 72–78.

20. Aubrey, Bod MS 1, 104r.

21. Aubrey, Bod MS Aubrey 1, 5r.

22. Aubrey, Bod MS Aubrey 1, 6r–7r.

23. Aubrey, Bod MS Aubrey 1, 3r,

24. Aubrey, Bod MS Aubrey 1, 6r.

25. Wormald, "The Creation of Britain" (1992), 180.

26. Aubrey, Bod MS Aubrey 1, 5r, 6r.

27. Aubrey to Wood, 24 October 1674, Bod MS Wood F. 39, 282r.

28. On Plot, see *ESIO,* vols. 4 and 12; Mendyk, "Robert Plot" (1985); Mendyk, *"Speculum Britanniae,"* 193–205; Welch, "The Foundation of the Ashmolean Museum," in *Tradescant's Rarities,* ed. MacGregor (1983), 40–58.

29. Aubrey to Wood, 24 October 1674, Bod MS Wood F. 39, 282r. See also Bennett, "John Aubrey's Oxfordshire Collections" (2000). For contacts between Aubrey and Plot via Wood, see also Aubrey to Wood, 12 January 1674/75, Bod MS Wood F.39, 288r; Aubrey to Wood, 25 February 1674/75, Bod MS Wood F. 39, 292r; Aubrey to Wood, 27 November 1675, Bod MS Tanner 456A, 19r; Aubrey to Wood, Twelfth-day {6 January} 1675 {probably 1675/76}, Bod MS Ballard 14, 72.

30. See Aubrey to Wood, 27 November 1675, Bod MS Tanner 456A, 19r; and Aubrey to Wood, Twelfth-day {6 January} 1675 {probably 1675/76}, Bod MS Ballard 14, 72.

31. Aubrey to Wood, Twelfth-day {6 January} 1675 {probably 1675/76}, Ballard 14, 72.

32. Aubrey, *The natural history and antiquities of the county of Surrey* (1723), vol. 1, first flyleaf, verso. See also Hunter, *John Aubrey and the Realm of Learning,* 71–72.

33. Aubrey to Wood, 27 November 1675, Bod MS Tanner 456A, 19r.

34. Aubrey to Wood, 25 February 1674, Bod MS Wood F.39, 292r.

35. Aubrey to Wood, 25 February 1674, Bod MS Wood F.39, 292r.

36. Aubrey to Wood, 3 August 1691, Bod MS Wood F.39, 429v; Aubrey, Bod MS Aubrey 1, 6r.

37. In addition to Aubrey's letters to Wood, see Edward Tyson to Robert Plot, 26 February 1680–1681; Tyson to Plot, 24 March 1681 and 10 November 1683, *ESIO,* 12:2, 3, 45.

38. Aubrey, Bod MS Aubrey 1, 6r–7r. Plot did begin one more project, a natural history of London and Westminster, though it was cut short by his death. See Plot, *Enquiries to be*

propounded to the most sincere and intelligent in the cities of London and Westminster, in order to their history of nature, arts, and antiquities (1693?), Bod Don.a.3, 6–7.

39. Powell, *John Aubrey and His Friends*, 130–131, 133.

40. "Some Account of this Work, and Its Author," in Aubrey, *The natural history and antiquities of the county of Surrey*, 1:iv.

41. Wood, *Life and Times of Anthony Wood*, ed. Clark (1891–1900), 2:474–475.

42. Adam Fox, "John Aubrey (1626–1697)," *ODNB*.

43. Aubrey to Wood, Easter Tuesday 1670, Bod MS Tanner 456A, 9r. See also Powell, *John Aubrey and His Friends*, 115–126.

44. Hooke, *Diary*, 70; Fox, "John Aubrey (1626–1697)," *ODNB*.

45. Powell, *John Aubrey and His Friends*, 140, 143, 145–146. The number of addresses was derived from those recorded in Aubrey's correspondence, Bod MS Aubrey 12, 13.

46. Thomas Tufton to Aubrey, 19 April 1675, Bod MS Aubrey 13, 213.

47. "Some Account of this Work, and Its Author," in Aubrey, *The natural history and antiquities of the county of Surrey*, 1:xii.

48. On self-fashioning, see Daston and Sibum, eds., *Science in Context* 16 (2003): 1–269, a special issue on scientific personae; Hsia, "Mathematical Martyrs, Mandarin Missionaries, and Apostolic Academicians," in *Institutional Culture in Early Modern Society*, ed. Goldgar and Frost (2004), 12–15; and Biagioli, *Galileo, Courtier* (1993), esp. 11–101.

49. Aubrey, Bod MS Aubrey 1, 7r.

50. *OED;* Evelyn to Aubrey, 8 February 1675/76, in Aubrey, *The natural history and antiquities of the county of Surrey*, 1:sig. A4 + 3r.

51. Aubrey, *The natural history and antiquities of the county of Surrey*, 1:sig. A4 + 4v.

52. Camden, *Britain* (1610), 4–5; Dugdale, *The antiquities of Warwickshire illustrated* (1656), A3r–v; Edward Lhuyd to Martin Lister, 4 August 1702, *ESIO*, 14:468–469; Lhuyd to Richard Mostyn, 2 November 1707, *ESIO*, 14:534–535; Lhuyd to John Lloyd, 23 November 1707, *ESIO*, 14:536–537. Plot recorded the use of manuscript sources in the footnotes in his natural histories of Oxfordshire and Staffordshire.

53. For numerous examples, see Broadway, *"No Historie so Meete"* (2006).

54. Mendyk, *"Speculum Britanniae,"* 44–46; Phillip, *The Bodleian Library in the Seventeenth and Eighteenth Centuries* (1983), 41; Leland, *The Itinerary of John Leland the Antiquary*, ed. Hearne, 9 vols. (1710–1712).

55. Mendyk, *"Speculum Britanniae,"* 47, 60–73, 261n44; Woolf, *The Social Circulation of the Past* (2003), 169.

56. See Aubrey to Wood, 7 March 1679/80, Bod MS Tanner 456A, 23r; and John Aubrey, fragment of the title page to *An Essay Toward the Description of the Co{unty} of Surrey*, n.d., Bod MS Wood F. 49, 39r.

57. Aubrey, Bod MS 1, 7r.

58. Bod MS Aubrey 10, 2r.

59. Hornblower and Spawforth, eds., *Oxford Classical Dictionary* (1996).

60. Aubrey identified Tanner as his "Aristarchus" in the dedicatory letter to the Earl of Abingdon in his *Miscellanies* (1696). He noted there that he hoped Tanner would take over his *Description of the North Division of Wilts*, also deposited in the library of the Ashmolean Museum (Aubrey, *Miscellanies* [1696], "The Dedication," sig. A3 + 1r).

61. Aubrey to Wood, 3 August 1689, Bod MS Wood F.40, 372.

62. Johns, *The Nature of the Book*, 488–489; Harkness, *The Jewel House* (2007), 55–56, 95–96.

63. Johns, *The Nature of the Book,* 489.

64. Johns, *The Nature of the Book,* 488–489.

65. See Aubrey, Bod MS Aubrey 1, 18r, 51r, for two examples.

66. Aubrey, Bod MS Aubrey 1, 3r.

67. Aubrey, Bod MS Aubrey 1, 3r. Aubrey also noted that the artist David Loggan had drawn his picture "to be engraven for this Book" and that "Mr. Ed. Lloyd <of the Musaeum> tells me, there are petrified shells, both in South, & North Wales."

68. Aubrey, Bod MS Aubrey 1. 3v. The observations for Surrey and Flintshire were separated from *The Naturall Historie* before it was deposited at the Bodleian (or were never included; see Hunter, *John Aubrey and the Realm of Learning,* 100). Aubrey prepared his observations on Surrey as a separate manuscript titled *A Perambulation of Surrey* (Bod MS Aubrey 4), later edited by Richard Rawlinson and published by the bookseller Edmund Curll as *The natural history and antiquities of the county of Surrey* in 1718. This text was reissued in 1723 with a new title page identifying W. Mears and J. Hooke as the publishers. Though some of the front matter was reordered in at least some copies of the reissue, the 1718 and 1723 texts are from the same printing. In this chapter I cite the 1723 *Surrey,* as I consulted Houghton Library's physical copy of that text. Aubrey did not collect his observations on Flintshire into a separate volume.

69. Aubrey, Bod MS Aubrey 1, 12r.

70. Aubrey, Bod MS Aubrey 1, 2r, 2v, 4r–8r, 8v–11v.

71. Ray to Aubrey, 27 October 1691, Bod MS Aubrey 1, 13r.

72. Aubrey, Bod MS Aubrey 1, 14r–23r.

73. Aubrey, Bod MS Aubrey 1, 26r–27r.

74. Aubrey, Bod MS Aubrey 1, 28–30.

75. Pressing botanical samples between the pages of books was a common way to store them; naturalists laid up entire books of plants. Compare John Evelyn's *Hortus Hyemalis* (BL Add. MS 78334). See also Zytaruk, "'Occasional *Specimens,* Not Complete *Systemes*'" (2001), 189–191.

76. Aubrey, Bod MS Aubrey 1, 35v.

77. Aubrey, Bod MS Aubrey 1, 124r.

78. Andrew Paschall was the first to read *The Naturall Historie* in book form. Aubrey sent it to him in 1685, shortly after he organized his papers and completed the preface (dated 6 June 1685). Aubrey probably sent him the history of Wiltshire as a model—Paschall, a Cambridge-educated clergyman who corresponded with Aubrey and others on the "universal character," was then considering writing a natural history of Somersetshire, where he had his living. Paschall did not annotate the text (Aubrey to Wood, 17 August 1685, Bod MS Wood F.39, 375r).

79. Aubrey to Wood, {11 March 1690?}, Bod MS Wood F.39, 400r. Although Aubrey used these words to describe Wood, they also reflect back on their author.

80. Aubrey to Wood, 5 and 10 July 1690, Bod MS Wood F.39, 405r–v. Aubrey worked with B. G. Cramer, clerk to the Royal Society, to produce the fair copy. See Hunter, *John Aubrey and the Realm of Learning,* 89n1.

81. Aubrey to Wood, 3 August 1691, Bod MS Wood F.39, 429r–v.

82. Aubrey to Wood, 10 July 1690, Bod MS Wood F. 39, 405v.

83. Britton, "Introduction," Aubrey, *The Natural History of Wiltshire,* ed. Britton (1847), vii.

84. He certainly read it before Evelyn; he may also have come before Ray. Evidence for the time line comes from Evelyn's commonplacing of *The Naturall Historie*. He copied into his notes some of Gale's annotations, though without crediting Gale. See Evelyn, *Adversaria*, BL Add. MS 78333, 1v; Aubrey, Bod MS Aubrey 1, 25r.

85. In the "Introduction" to Aubrey's *Natural History of Wiltshire*, John Britton notes that Evelyn likely read Aubrey's *Idea of Education* in May 1692 (Aubrey, *The Natural History of Wiltshire*, ed. Britton [1847], vii). Evelyn also read Aubrey's *A Perambulation of Surrey* (Bod MS Aubrey 4) later that summer. See Aubrey to Wood, 28 July 1692, Bod MS Ballard 14, 98. Evelyn also read some of Aubrey's collections for Surrey in 1675/76. See Evelyn to Aubrey, 8 February 1675/76, in Aubrey, *The natural history and antiquities of the county of Surrey*, 1:sig. A3r–(A4 + 3r).

86. Tanner read the manuscript after Aubrey sent it to the Ashmolean, probably in the spring of 1694. In a letter dated 4 March 1693/94, Lhuyd wrote to Aubrey that he planned to retrieve "your history of Wiltshire" from Tanner the next day (Bod MS Aubrey 12, 252v–253r).

87. Aubrey, Bod MS Aubrey 2, 155r.

88. Aubrey, Bod MS Aubrey 2, 159r.

89. Over a scholar's lifetime, the leaves of the *album amicorum* could grow into a lasting memorial to friendship, correspondence, and connections in the humanist republic of letters. See Harkness, *The Jewel House*, 44–47; Swan, "On the Same Page " (2014).

90. Aubrey, Bod MS Aubrey 1, 3v. In Aubrey's rendering of Evelyn's initials, the "J" and the "E" are intertwined. This mark closely resembles the monogram Evelyn used in his own papers and stamped on the bindings of his books, an "I" over an "E." Evelyn, however, usually wrote his cipher in block print, while Aubrey joined the letters. Aubrey similarly marked John Evelyn's comments in his *Perambulation of Surrey*. On the title page of that work, he noted "that the Annotations marked JE are <of> John Evelyn, Esq, R.S.S." (Bod MS Wood F.49, 39v).

91. Evelyn, *Memoires for my Grandson*, BL Add. MS 78515, 33v.

92. Aubrey, Bod MS Aubrey 1, 22r.

93. Compare Bennett, *Materials Toward a Critical Edition of John Aubrey's Brief Lives* (1993), 25. Bennett argues that Aubrey adopted an informal style in the *Brief Lives* in accordance with his belief that his manuscripts were not finished products but historical resources for future generations of biographers.

94. See Thirsk, *Food in Early Modern England* (2007), esp. 229–328.

95. Gale, Bod MS Aubrey 2, f. 85v.

96. Ray to Aubrey, 18 November 1691, Bod MS Aubrey 13, 175r.

97. Ray and Aubrey, Bod MS Aubrey 1, 108v–109r; Ray and Aubrey, Bod MS Aubrey 1, 107r.

98. See Kusukawa, "The 'Historia Piscium' (1686)" (2000), 179–197; and Chambers, *The Reinvention of the World* (1996), 64–65. The profusion of local names for plants was a practical problem across early modern Europe. See Rankin, "Becoming an Expert Practitioner (2007), 41.

99. Aubrey, Bod MS Aubrey 1, 14v; Aubrey and Ray, Bod MS Aubrey 1, 15r.

100. Ray and Aubrey, Bod MS Aubrey 1, 108v. See also Ray and Aubrey, Bod MS Aubrey 1, 107r and 110v–111r.

101. Ray, Bod MS Aubrey 1, 107r.

102. Ray and Aubrey, Bod MS Aubrey 1, 11v.

103. Ray to Aubrey, 27 October 1691, Bod MS Aubrey 1, 13r.

104. Aubrey, Bod MS Aubrey 1, 132v. Aubrey credited this observation to the cleric and classicist Christopher Wase.

105. Evelyn, in Aubrey, Bod MS Aubrey 1, 132v. See also 132r, where Evelyn challenged Long on which county had the best-tasting rabbit.

106. Evelyn and Aubrey, Bod MS Aubrey 1, 76–77.

107. See Bod MS Aubrey 1, 32v; Bod MS Aubrey 1, 155ar; Aubrey, *The natural history and antiquities of the county of Surrey*, 1:sig. A4r. On the Evelyn family's long history in Surrey, see Sullivan, "Their 'Own Sweet Country," in *John Evelyn and His Milieu*, ed. Harris and Hunter (2003), 281–292.

108. Plot, *The natural history of Oxford-shire*, tables 1–16. A typical dedication reads, "To the right Worsp. the learned and curious Artist Sr. Thomas Penyston Baron. This 8th Table of formed Stones whereof the 4th 5th and 7th were found in his own grounds is humbly presented by RP. LLD" (table 8).

109. Evelyn, Bod MS Aubrey 1, 27r. Evelyn also mentioned books by Varro, Eusebius Nieuzebrigensis, Burnet, and Samuel Hartlib as well as his own *Sylva* and "herbals" by Ray and Morrison.

110. Evelyn, Bod MS Aubrey 1, 32v.

111. Evelyn, Bod MS Aubrey 1, 86v.

112. The attributions are in a different shade of ink from the comments, suggesting they were written in at a different time and by a different person.

113. Gale and Aubrey, Bod MS Aubrey 1, 10r, 9v.

114. Gale, Bod MS Aubrey 1, 25r.

115. Gale, Bod MS Aubrey 1, 24r.

116. Gale, Bod MS Aubrey 2, 85v.

117. Tanner, Bod MS Aubrey 1, 110r.

118. Tanner, Bod MS Aubrey 1, 48r.

119. In another instance Tanner wrote that he had "heard it credibly reported that Coale has been found in Urafont parish about 50 or 60 years since"; Tanner reported that the coal had not been dug up because the deposit was too deep in the ground and the workmen were too few (Bod MS Aubrey 1, 75v).

120. Tanner, Bod MS Aubrey 1, 122r. See also his extension of Aubrey's entries on birch, beech, and chestnut trees (Bod MS Aubrey 1, 120r–121r).

121. Tanner, Bod MS Aubrey 1, 122r.

122. For two examples, Aubrey and Ray, Bod MS Aubrey 1, 108v–109v.

123. Aubrey and Ray, Bod MS Aubrey 1, 110r.

124. Aubrey, Ray, and Evelyn, Bod MS Aubrey 1, 66r. On "Morison's herbal," see Feola and Mandelbrote, "The Learned Press," in *History of Oxford University Press, vol. 1: Beginnings to 1780*, ed. Gadd (2013), 330–337.

125. Contrast Plot's representation of Oxfordshire in *The natural history of Oxford-shire* (1677), as analyzed by Campbell in *Wonder and Science* (1999), 101–109, as an "island." Plot's *Oxfordshire* was more strictly carried out as one chapter in the "body and book" of British topography.

126. Aubrey to Wood, 3 August 1689, Bod MS Wood F.40, 372.

127. Hunter, *John Aubrey and the Realm of Learning*, 35; Vivienne Larminie, "Fell, John (1625–1686)," *ODNB*.

128. Aubrey to Wood, 27 December 1679, Bod MS Wood F. 39, 327.

129. Aubrey, Bod MS Aubrey 1, 87r–102r.

130. Aubrey, Bod MS Aubrey 1, 88r–89r.

131. Aubrey to Wood, 13 February 1692, Bod MS Wood F.39, 438; quoted in Powell, *John Aubrey and His Friends*, 219.

132. Ray cited and reproduced letters from Edward Lhuyd, Tancred Robinson, Richard Waller, William Cole, and others (Ray, *Miscellaneous discourses* [1692], 92–94, 108–109, 122–125, passim).

133. See also Hunter, *John Aubrey and the Realm of Learning*, 84.

134. Ray, *Miscellaneous discourses*, 124.

135. Westfall, *Never at Rest* (1983), 446–453.

136. Westfall, *Never at Rest*, 452; Hunter, *John Aubrey and the Realm of Learning*, 84.

137. Ray to Aubrey, 24 August 1692, Bod MS Aubrey 13, 176r.

138. Thanks to Ann Blair for this suggestion.

139. This is a signal theme in the history of the reading of printed matter, first introduced to the field by Roger Chartier. See, for example, Chartier, *The Order of Books*, trans. Cochrane (1994), 1–23; Grafton and Jardine, "Studied for Action"; Watt, *Cheap Print and Popular Piety 1550–1640* (1991); Sherman, *John Dee*, esp. 53–114; Grafton, *Commerce with the Classics* (1997); Johns, *The Nature of the Book*, 384–386; and Sharpe, *Reading Revolutions*. Brayman Hackel is particularly strong on the material aspects of appropriation in her book *Reading Material in Early Modern England* (2005).

140. Love, *The Culture and Commerce of Texts* (1998), 79–89.

141. Browne, *A true and full coppy of that which was most imperfectly and surreptitiously printed before under the name of Religio medici* (1643), sig. A1r–v. Andrew Crooke published the authorized *Religio medici* as well as the surreptitious and imperfect editions, two of which were printed in 1642. Concurrently with Browne's authorized copy, Kenelm Digby printed his observations on *Religio medici* based on his reading of the unapproved copy. See Digby, *Observations upon Religio medici* (1643).

142. Evelyn, *Adversaria: Historical, Physical, Mathematical, Mechanicall &c promiscuously set downe as they Occur in Reading, or Casual Discourse*, BL Add. MS 78333, 1r–7r. *Adversaria* were a particular kind of reading notes; they differed from commonplace notes in that they were "generally presented in the order of the text from which they were produced," while commonplace notes were "copied and sorted under a thematic or topical heading to facilitate retrieval" (Blair, "Note Taking as an Art of Transmission" [2004], 87). However, these categories have not been applied universally, either in the early modern period or at present (Blair, "Note Taking as an Art of Transmission," 87, 99). Though Evelyn's notes follow the order of *The Naturall Historie*, he made them more like commonplace notes by attaching marginal subject headings to each note. In the present day, "commonplace" is more familiar as a term for these kinds of notes. For both reasons I refer to them throughout the text as commonplace notes, rather than *adversaria*.

143. Evelyn also edited for brevity, paraphrased, and editorialized (Yale, "Manuscript Technologies" (2008), 139–141). These kinds of changes were not unusual; see Blair, "Note Taking as an Art of Transmission," 86–87, 100.

144. Evelyn, BL Add. MS 78333, 4r.

145. Aubrey and Evelyn, in Aubrey, Bod MS Aubrey 1, 147v.

146. Jackson, *Marginalia*, 62. The antiquary Francis Douce also assisted John Brand in the revision and expansion of his *Observations on Popular Antiquities* (1777) by marking up a copy of the first edition interleaved with blank pages (Jackson, *Marginalia*, 62).

147. Blair, "Note Taking as an Art of Transmission," 104–106; Gingerich, "An Early Tradition of an Extended Errata List for Copernicus's 'De Revolutionibus'" (1981), 47; Jackson, *Marginalia,* 64–65.

148. Aubrey, Bod MS Aubrey 1, 15v.

149. Evelyn, BL Add. MS 78333, 1r.

150. Aubrey, Bod MS Aubrey 1, 5r. On the relationship between Aubrey and Harvey, see Williams, "Training the Virtuoso" (2012), 166.

151. Evelyn, BL Add. MS 78333, 1r.

152. Aubrey, Bod MS Aubrey 2, 111r.

153. Evelyn, BL Add. MS 78333, 6v.

154. Aubrey to Evelyn, 10 May 1692, Bod MS Aubrey 10, 1ar.

155. Evelyn, BL Add. MS 78351, 111r, 113r; Evelyn BL Add. MS 78515, 33r.

156. Evelyn, BL Add. MS 78351, 111r. F. 110r is also marked with the word "Aubry" and the overlapping triangles symbol.

157. Evelyn, BL Add. MS 78351, 112v.

158. Aubrey, Bod MS 10, 120r.

159. Aubrey, Bod MS 10, 121r; Evelyn, BL Add. MS 78351, 112r.

160. Evelyn, BL Add. MS 78351, 112r.

161. Evelyn, BL Add. MS 78351, 112r.

162. Aubrey, Bod MS 10, 78v.

163. Evelyn to Aubrey, 8 February 1675/76, in Aubrey, *The natural history and antiquities of the county of Surrey,* 1:sig. A3r–A4r + 3r.

164. Evelyn to Awnsham Churchill, 23 August 1693, Christ Church Evelyn Collection MS 39, no. 685 (now BL Add. MS 78298–78299); quoted in Hunter, *John Aubrey and the Realm of Learning,* 212.

165. Bod MS Aubrey 12, 13.

166. See Evelyn, *Sylva* (3rd ed., 1679). A note on the edition used here: I cite the third edition of *Sylva* because it was revised by Evelyn relatively close in time to when he would have been reading Aubrey's manuscripts.

167. Evelyn, *Sylva,* 41, 45, 48, and passim.

168. Evelyn, *Sylva,* 20, 45, 50.

169. Evelyn, *Sylva,* 21.

170. Evelyn, *Sylva,* 21.

171. Evelyn, *Sylva,* 15–16, 17, 26, 34, 259. Further examples include references to "Mr. Blith" and "Mr. Cook" (27, 43), who were probably Walter Blith and Moses Cook, authors of seventeenth-century treatises on husbandry and forest trees.

172. Compare Harkness, *The Jewel House,* 220, 236, 240–241, on the Elizabeth naturalist Hugh Plat's citation practices. He retained references to individuals who gave him information but removed them from his printed works—this was a way of elevating his "brand" as a print author.

173. Note that this was not always the case; readers might be chosen for other reasons as well. When Aubrey circulated *An Idea of Education of Young Gentlemen,* he selected some readers not only as collaborators but also as potential patrons of the educational reform scheme described in the book. See Aubrey, Bod MS Aubrey 10, 2r.

174. Aubrey, Bod MS Aubrey 1, 51r.

175. Nummedal and Findlen, "Words of Nature," in *Thornton and Tully's Scientific Books, Libraries and Collectors,* ed. Hunter (2000), 190.

176. Bod MS Aubrey 1, 142v, 18v.

177. Delbourgo, "Collecting Hans Sloane," in *From Books to Bezoars,* ed. Walker, Mac-Gregor, and Hunter (2012), 9–23, quote on 17.

178. Schiebinger, *Plants and Empire* (2004).

179. See, for example, Osseo-Asare, *Bitter Roots* (2014).

180. See Johns, *The Nature of the Book.*

181. Compare Marotti, *Manuscript, Print, and the English Renaissance Lyric* (1995), 329–330. Marotti notes that English poetry manuscripts became more "print-like" over the course of the seventeenth century: compilers came to include tables of contents, indices, running heads, "typographical" shifts between different parts of the text, and titles for individual poems. Poems were also increasingly assigned authors, especially well-known ones such as John Donne and Robert Herrick. This focus on "name" authors suggests that literary authorship, much like scientific authorship, could function as a kind of brand, as Harkness argues in *The Jewel House.*

182. See Browne, *Charles Darwin* (2002), 10–13, quote on 11; and Secord, "Nature's Fancy" (1981).

183. Darwin, *The Variation of Animals and Plants Under Domestication* (1868), 1:131–224. On Darwin and pigeons, see Secord, "Nature's Fancy." On acknowledgment practices in nineteenth-century natural history, see Secord, "Corresponding Interests" (1994), 398.

184. Though not prominently featured here, the preferences of the booksellers who published natural history also played a role. See Johns, "Natural History as Print Culture," in *Cultures of Natural History,* ed. Jardine, Secord, and Spary (1996), 106–124; and Hoffman, "The Montaigne Monopoly" (1993), 308–319.

CHAPTER 5

1. Of forty-nine books printed by subscription before 1700, twenty-five were in natural history, natural philosophy, medicine, geography, or mathematics. Learned books, in which category I include theology, biblical criticism, history, and philology in addition to disciplines associated with the study of nature and mathematics, accounted for forty-two of the forty-nine books. Of the remaining seven books, five were poetic or literary (including two editions of Milton's poems, a translation of *Don Quixote,* and Dryden's translation of the poems of Virgil) and two were unknown. See Robinson and Wallis, *Book Subscription Lists* (1975); and Wallis and Wallis, *Book Subscription Lists* (1996). Compare Woolf, *Reading History in Early Modern England* (2000), 285, which shows (using data from Robinson and Wallis) "history," a category in which Woolf includes antiquarian studies and chorography, as 32 percent of all books published by subscription up to 1730. On subscription publishing in the sciences, see also Johns, *The Nature of the Book* (1998), 450–453.

2. Kusukawa, "The 'Historia Piscium' (1686)" (2000), 187.

3. Kusukawa, "The 'Historia Piscium' (1686)," 191.

4. Kusukawa, "The 'Historia Piscium' (1686)," 192.

5. See also Johns, "Miscellaneous Methods" (2000), 166.

6. On earlier British and continental cases, see Nummedal and Findlen, "Words of Nature," in *Thornton and Tully's Scientific Books, Libraries and Collectors,* ed. Hunter (2000), 171, 202–205; and Kusukawa, *Picturing the Book of Nature* (2012), 55–61.

7. Nummedal and Findlen, "Words of Nature," 202–205.

8. For insight into the financial arrangements that authors-undertakers made with presses (regardless of whether they published by subscription or self-financed) as well as an overview of subscription financing practices, see Carter, *A History of the Oxford University Press* (1975), 250–253.

9. Stallybrass, "Printing for Manuscript" (2006).

10. Clapp, "The Beginnings of Subscription Publication in the Seventeenth Century" (1931), 199.

11. Clapp, "The Beginnings of Subscription Publication in the Seventeenth Century," 200–203; Colley, *Captives* (2004).

12. Hunter, *Science and Society in Restoration England* (1981), 39.

13. *There is a very large Historie of the Church* (1651), Bod MS Wood 658, item 799.

14. See, inter alia, Hartlib and Plattes, *A description of the famous kingdome of Macaria* (1641); Hartlib, *Considerations tending to the happy accomplishment of Englands reformation in church and state* (1647); and Hartlib, *A further discoverie of the office of publick addresse for accomodations* (1648).

15. Hartlib, Preface to Boate, *Irelands Naturall History* (1652), sig. A3r.

16. Hartlib, Preface to Boate, *Irelands Naturall History*, sig. A3r–A3v.

17. Clucas, "Samuel Hartlib's 'Ephemerides,' 1635–1659, and the Pursuit of Scientific and Philosophical Manuscripts" (1991).

18. Greengrass, "Samuel Hartlib and Scribal Publication" (1997), 59; DiMeo, "Openness vs. Secrecy in the Hartlib Circle," in *Secrets and Knowledge in Medicine and Science, 1500–1800*, ed. Leong and Rankin (2011), 109; Pal, "Information Factory" (2013).

19. The rhetoric I discuss here intersects somewhat with historiography on the concept of the "public sphere" in seventeenth- and eighteenth-century British literary and political history. This concept is a controversial one, especially when applied to the seventeenth century. However, in this chapter I am not seeking to identify a "public" in the seventeenth century or dispute the existence of one. Rather, I am examining how seventeenth-century naturalists, booksellers, and their readers used and responded to concepts such as "public benefit" and "public service" to sell books by subscription and how these concepts intersected with the ways naturalists sold books through their correspondence. See Habermas, *The Structural Transformation of the Public Sphere,* trans. Burger (1991). On historians' use of the "public sphere" as an analytical category, see Rupp, "The New Science and the Public Sphere in the Premodern Era" (1995); Mah, "Phantasies of the Public Sphere" (2000); Baldwin, "The 'Public' as a Rhetorical Community in Early Modern England," in *Communities in Early Modern England,* ed. Shepard and Withington (2000), 199–215; Knights, *Representation and Misrepresentation in Later Stuart Britain* (2006), 48–53; Cowan, "What Was Masculine About the Public Sphere?" (2001); and Cowan, *The Social Life of Coffee* (2005), 149–151, 255–256, 261–262.

20. Moses Pitt, *Proposals for printing a new atlas* (1678).

21. Brabazon Aylmer, *Proposals for the first volume of the works of the eminently learned Dr. Isaac Barrow* (1682).

22. Abel Swall, *Proposals for printing by subscription, Cambden's Britannia, English* (1693).

23. *A Proposal about printing a Treatise of algebra, historical and practical* (1683).

24. University of Oxford, . *An advertisement, concerning the printing and publishing of ancient and other usefull books* (1680), in Bod MS Wood 658, item 775, dated "Sept 1680" in pencil.

25. Larminie, "The Fell Era 1658–1686," in *The History of the Oxford University Press,* ed. Gadd, 99–100; University of Oxford, *An advertisement, concerning the printing and publishing of ancient and other usefull books.*

26. John Dunton, preface to "The Supplement to the Fifth Volume of the Athenian Gazette" (London: John Dunton, 1691/92), collected in Bod Hope Folio 3.

27. *Proposals for printing Monumenta Britannica, written by Mr. John Aubrey* (1693), in Bod MS Wood 658, item 780, dated by hand "Apr. 10 1693."

28. *Calendar of State Papers (Domestic Series)* (hereafter *CSPD*), Reign of Charles II, SP29/441, n. 65, in McKenzie and Bell, *A Chronology and Calendar of Documents Relating to the London Book Trade, 1641–1700* (2005), 1:622.

29. Edward Lhuyd to Thomas Tonkin, 16 March 1702–1703, *ESIO*, 14:486.

30. *CSPD*, Reign of Charles II, SP29/423, n. 44, in McKenzie and Bell, eds., *A Chronology and Calendar of Documents Relating to the London Book Trade, 1641–1700*, 2:360.

31. *CSPD*, Reign of Charles II, SP29/262, n. 158, in McKenzie and Bell, eds., *A Chronology and Calendar of Documents Relating to the London Book Trade, 1641–1700*, 1:616.

32. *CSPD*, Reign of Charles II, Entry Book 36, p. 93 (11 July 1672), in McKenzie and Bell, eds., *A Chronology and Calendar of Documents Relating to the London Book Trade, 1641–1700*, 2:39. On Ogilby and Blome's various subscription-based endeavors, see Clapp, "The Subscription Enterprises of John Ogilby and Richard Blome" (1933). On the lottery and subscription that Ogilby set up to fund his *Britannia*, see Clark, "Now Through You Made Public for Everyone" (2013), 127.

33. *CSPD*, Reign of Charles II, Entry Book 36, p. 93 (11 July 1672), in McKenzie and Bell, eds., *A Chronology and Calendar of Documents Relating to the London Book Trade, 1641–1700*, 2:39.

34. Compare similar "social advertising" strategies—as K. A. James has termed them—used by the apothecary James Petiver and the Scottish physician Patrick Blair, who promoted Petiver's work. See James, "Humbly Dedicated" (2004), 318, 323–324; Swann, *Curiosities and Texts* (2001), 90–96; and Delbourgo, "Listing People" (2012), 739–742.

35. *A Catalogue of the Subscribers Names to the* English Atlas, *now Printing at the* Theater *in* Oxford (1680?), Bod MS Wood 658, item 791; Johns, *The Nature of the Book*, 451–453.

36. *A Catalogue of the Subscribers Names to the* English Atlas, *now Printing at the* Theater *in* Oxford, Bod MS Wood 658, item 791.

37. Nehemiah Grew, *Whereas a book entituled, Musaeum Regalis Societatis* (1680), Bod MS Wood 658, item 794. This use of the subscription list—as a space for articulating social hierarchies—continued into the eighteenth century, even as (at least for some subscription books) edition size expanded. See Yeo, *Encyclopaedic Visions* (2001), 47–49.

38. Pepys, *Diary*, 8 April 1667, 8:156. Pepys noted his judgments about the prices and the actual price paid in both his diary and on the back side of the title page of the book (Pepys, *Diary*, 8:156 n2).

39. See, for example, *Proposals for printing of Holwell's book of dialing* (1684), Bod MS Wood 658, item 789; *For Printing the* Manuscripts *of Dr.* WILLIAM HOWELL, *late Chancellour of* Lincoln, *being the following Parts of his* Institution of General History (1685), Bod MS Wood 658, item 786*; *The translation of* Homers Works *into English verse being undertaken by* John Ogilby (1660), Bod MS Wood 658, item 790; and Grew, *Whereas a book entituled, Musaeum Regalis Societatis* (1680), Bod MS Wood 658, item 794.

40. Aylmer, *Proposals for the First Volume of the Works of the Eminently Learned Isaac Barrow* (1682). See also *Proposals for the Printing of a Book of William Leybourn's* (1693).

41. Aylmer, *Proposals for the first volume of the works of the eminently learned Dr. Isaac Barrow* (1682).

42. Delbourgo, "Listing People," 740–741. Petiver's use of subscription points toward the commercial aspects of scientific exchange in the early modern Republic of Letters. See Dániel Margócsy, *Commercial Visions* (2014), esp. 39–40 on Petiver and the commercial exchange of natural history specimens.

43. See, for example, Plot, *The natural history of Oxford-shire* (1677), table 2 (at p. 92).

44. For an example, see Plot, *The natural history of Stafford-shire* (1686), table 29 (at p. 359).

45. Plot, *The natural history of Stafford-shire* (1686), sig. a1r–a1v.

46. Henry Keepe, *By HENRY KEEPE, formerly of New-Inn-Hall in the University of Oxford, Gentleman-Commoner, and now of the Inner-Temple London, Esq;. Having in The Year 1681. published a small Treatise, by way of* Essay to a more compleat History of *Westminster-Abbey* (1683), Bod MS Wood 658, item 800.

47. *Proposals for printing a book entituled, The history and antiquities of Hertfordshire* (1700), Bod MS Wood 658, item 812.

48. Hellyer, "The Pocket Museum" (1996), 43–60, quote on 47.

49. In addition to *Proposals for printing Monumenta Britannica, written by Mr. John Aubrey* (1693), Bod MS Wood 658, item 780; see Aylett Sammes, *Proposals concerning the printing of a* Chronological History *of England* (1677), Bod MS Wood 658, item 801; Grew, *Whereas a book entituled, Musaeum Regalis Societatis,* Bod MS Wood 658, item 794; Keepe, *By HENRY KEEPE, formerly of New-Inn-Hall in the University of Oxford, gentleman-commoner, and now of the Inner-Temple London, Esq;. Having in the year 1681. published a small treatise, by way of* Essay to a more compleat history of *Westminster-Abbey,* Bod MS Wood 658, item 800; *Proposals for printing of Holwell's book of dialing,* Bod MS Wood 658, item 789; Abel Wantner, *To the nobility, clergy, and gentry of the City an County of Gloucester* (1685?); *For Printing the* Manuscripts *of Dr.* WILLIAM HOWELL, *late Chancellour of* Lincoln, *being the following Parts of his* Institution of General History, Bod MS Wood 658, item 786*; Thomas Guidott, *Propositions touching printing a book entituled, De thermis Britannicis* (1686); and Lhuyd, *A Design of a British Dictionary, Historical and Geographical* (1695). The subscription for Howell's *Institution of General History* was superintended by his widow.

50. Lhuyd to John Aubrey, 29 April 1693, Bod MS Aubrey 12, 245r.

51. Lhuyd to John Ray, 29 May 1694, Bod MS Aubrey 12, 257r; Kilburn, "The Fell Legacy, 1686–1755," in *History of Oxford University Press, vol. 1: Beginnings to 1780,* ed. Gadd (2013), 113.

52. Ray to Aubrey, 4 July 1693, Bod MS Aubrey 13, 178r. For another example, see Ray to Aubrey, 7 May 1695, Bod MS Aubrey 13, 179r.

53. Ralph Bathurst to Aubrey, 25 August 1693, Bod MS Aubrey 12, 23r–v.

54. Hunter, *John Aubrey and the Realm of Learning* (1975), 89–90n8.

55. Hunter, *John Aubrey and the Realm of Learning,* 89–90n8.

56. For examples of overly ambitious—and at least partially failed—subscriptions, see Feola and Mandelbrote, "The Learned Press," in *History of Oxford University Press , vol. 1: Beginnings to 1780,* ed. Gadd (2013), 330–342.

57. William Salmon, *Proposals, for printing a compleat English herbal* (1710?), Bod MS Ashmole 1819, Item 13.

58. "*PROPOSALS* for Printing a Book Entituled *The Young Students Library,*" *Athenian Mercury,* intro. to vol. 3, 18 August to 17 October 1691 (Bod Hope Folio 3); "Proposals for the Printing of a Book of William Leybourn's," *Athenian Mercury* 9, no. 26, 11 March 1693 (Bod Hope Folio 4). These proposals also circulated freely as broadsides.

59. *Proposals for printing of Holwell's book of dialing* (1684), Bod MS Wood 658, item 789.

60. Lhuyd to Martin Lister, {1694}, *ESIO*, 14:236; Lhuyd to Lister, {c. 1695}, *ESIO*, 14:282.

61. Lhuyd to Lister, {1694}, *ESIO*, 14:236; Lhuyd to Lister, {c. 1695}, *ESIO*, 14:282; Jan Goedaert, *Johannes Goedartius de insectis, in methodum redactus: cum notularum additione. Operâ M. Lister* (1685).

62. Lhuyd to Lister, 30 January 1697, *ESIO*, 14:322.

63. Lhuyd to Lister, 28 March 1697, *ESIO*, 14:324.

64. Lhuyd to Lister, 16 March 1697, *ESIO*, 14:324.

65. G. S. Boulger, "Robinson, Sir Tancred (1657/58–1748)," rev. Kaye Bagshaw, *ODNB*.

66. Lhuyd to Lister, 30 January 1697, *ESIO*, 14:322; Lhuyd to Lister, 28 March 1697, *ESIO*, 14:324.

67. Lhuyd to Lister, 30 January 1697, *ESIO*, 14:322.

68. Lhuyd to Lister, 6 April 1697, *ESIO*, 14:326.

69. Lhuyd to Lister, 26 October 1696, *ESIO*, 14:312; Lhuyd to Thomas Tanner, 20 May 1698, *ESIO*, 14:371; Roos, *Web of Nature* (2011), 273.

70. Lhuyd to Lister, 28 March 1697, *ESIO*, 14:324–325. For Lhuyd's expectation that Lister's approval would guarantee publication, see also Lhuyd to Lister, 30 January 1697, *ESIO*, 14:322; and Lhuyd to Lister, 22 April 1697, *ESIO*, 14:327.

71. Lhuyd to Lister, 6 April 1697, *ESIO*, 14:326.

72. Lhuyd to Lister, 22 April 1697, *ESIO*, 14:327.

73. Carter, *A History of the Oxford University Press*, 105–106, 162–163, 180–181. This was a long-running conflict. See also Larminie, "The Fell Era, 1658–1686"; and Kilburn, "The Fell Legacy, 1686–1755," both in *History of Oxford University Press, vol. 1: Beginnings to 1780*, ed. Gadd.

74. Lhuyd to Lister, 22 April 1697, *ESIO*, 14:327.

75. Lhuyd to Lister, 22 April 1697, *ESIO*, 14:327.

76. Lhuyd to John Lloyd, {May 1697}, *ESIO*, 14:328.

77. Oxford Univ. Arch. W.P./R/8c/9, quoted in Carter, *A History of the Oxford University Press*, 162. The specific date of this meeting is unknown, but according to Carter, it occurred in 1697 or 1698 (Carter, *A History of the Oxford University Press*, 162).

78. Lhuyd to Tanner, 20 May 1698, *ESIO*, 14:371.

79. Lhuyd to Tanner, 20 May 1698, *ESIO*, 14:371.

80. Hans Sloane to Arthur Charlett, 4 July 1698, Bod MS Ballard 24, 66, EMLO.

81. See, for example, minutes from meetings of 24 March 1697, RS Journal Book Original (hereafter RS JBO)/10/20; 31 March 1697, RS JBO/10/20; 28 July 1703, RS JBO/11/29; 24 July 1712, RS JBO/11/304–305. In these instances subscriptions were taken for the posthumous second volume of Robert Morison's *Plantarum historiae universalis Oxoniensis* (1699), Lhuyd's *Archaeologia Britannica*, and John Ray's *Synopsis methodica avium et piscium* (1713).

82. Sloane to Charlett, 4 July 1698; Bod MS Ballard 24, 66, EMLO.

83. *Lithophylacii Britannici ichnographia*, subscription list. The list gives only nine subscribers. Sloane told Arthur Charlett, master of University College Oxford, that he and Samuel Pepys had come up with the plan to divide the edition among ten subscribers. Perhaps Pepys, though not included in the final list, was the tenth? See Sloane to Charlett, 4 July 1698, Bod MS Ballard 24, 66, EMLO; and Ellis, "Some Incidents in the Life of Edward Lhuyd," *ESIO*, 14:23.

84. Lhuyd, *Lithophylacii Britannici ichnographia*, subscription list.

85. This figure was reached by a bit of comparative calculation. Michael Burghers, the engraver of most of the plates, charged a standard price of 18s. per plate, and there were twenty-three engraved tables, so the engravings cost £20 14s., not counting the cost of the original drawings from which the engravings were made, at least some of which Lhuyd either drew or paid for himself (Lhuyd to Lister, 28 March 1697, *ESIO*, 14:324). For printing, including paper, the printer probably charged something on the order of three half-pence per printed sheet of text and three half-pence per engraved table. These were the rates that the Oxford bookseller Richard Davies charged the Royal Society for printing John Wallis's *Treatise of Algebra, Historical and Practical*, a quarto volume (*A Proposal about printing a Treatise of algebra, historical and practical* [1683]). With these rates, ten octavo sheets per book, and an edition size of 120, the cost of Lhuyd's book would have been around £45, or £4 10s. per subscriber (the book appears to have been printed as an octavo with half-sheet imposition to save on the cost of printing the letterpress; see Gaskell, *A New Introduction to Bibliography* (1995), 83 and fig. 52). These figures were on the high side of average book costs in the period (see Gaskell, *A New Introduction to Bibliography*, 178–179). Lhuyd's book was also a bit dear compared to other similar books printed by subscription in the 1680s and 1690s, but this may be due to the small edition size and the high number of engravings. The physician Thomas Guidott, for example, charged subscribers 5s. for his own *De thermis Britannicis* (London, 1691), a quarto volume on the medicinal and physical properties of the waters at Bath, sixty sheets with "several large Copper Cuts" (Guidott, *Propositions touching printing a book entituled, De thermis Britannicis*). On the other hand, Ray and Willughby's *Historia piscium* (in folio format with 187 plates) had total costs of 15s. per copy; see Kusukawa, "The 'Historia Piscium' (1686)," 191.

86. Ellis, "Some Incidents in the Life of Edward Lhuyd," *ESIO*, 14:24.

87. See Mosley, "Astronomical Books and Courtly Communication," in *Books and the Sciences in History*, ed. Frasca-Spada and Jardine (2000), 114–131.

88. See, for example, Ray to Aubrey, 20 December 1692, Bod MS Aubrey 13, 177r.

89. Hearne, *Remarks and Collections of Thomas Hearne*, ed. Doble (1885), 244.

90. Ellis, "Some Incidents in the Life of Edward Lhuyd," *ESIO*, 14:51. See also Anne O'Sullivan and William O'Sullivan, "Introduction," in Lhuyd, *Archaeologia Britannica* (1971).

91. Lhuyd to Lister, 9 February 1696, *ESIO*, 14:298.

92. Clapp, "The Beginnings of Subscription Publication in the Seventeenth Century," 200.

93. Lhuyd to Lloyd, St Steven's day (26 December) 1696, *ESIO*, 14:317.

94. Lhuyd, *A Design of a British Dictionary, Historical and Geographical*.

95. Lhuyd, *A Design of a British Dictionary, Historical and Geographical*, 2.

96. Lhuyd, *A Design of a British Dictionary, Historical and Geographical*, 2.

97. Lhuyd, *A Design of a British Dictionary, Historical and Geographical*.

98. See Hearne, *Remarks and Collections of Thomas Hearne*, 14 May 1706, 244.

99. Lhuyd, *A Design of a British Dictionary, Historical and Geographical*, 2.

100. R.T. Gunther, "Preparations for Travel," *ESIO*, 14:264. One hundred and ninety-eight subscribers were listed in the first (and only) volume of *Archaeologia Britannica*, published in 1707. Most of them were Welsh or had Welsh ancestry. They included the Earls of Clarendon, Pembroke, Denbigh, and Carbery; Martin Lister and Tancred Robinson; and local Welsh clergy and small landholders. There were fifteen lords or earls; six bishops; twenty-six baronets and knights; ninety-three esquires; thirteen M.A.'s; seven physicians; six bachelors or doctors of divinity; two doctors or bachelors of law; twenty listed simply as "of X"; and nine with no title or place of residence specified. Five were listed as royal officials.

101. Gunther, "Preparations for Travel," *ESIO*, 14:264.

102. Lhuyd to Lister, 23 April 1696, *ESIO*, 14:306; Lhuyd to Lloyd, 25 October 1696, *ESIO*, 14:311.

103. Lhuyd to Lloyd, 29 March 1697, *ESIO*, 14:325; Lhuyd to Richard Mostyn, 26 April 1701, *ESIO*, 14:443.

104. Lhuyd to Lister, 14 November {1695}, *ESIO*, 14:291.

105. Lhuyd to Lister, 14 November {1695}, *ESIO*, 14:290–291. See also Lhuyd to Lister, 5 December 1695, *ESIO*, 14:296.

106. Lhuyd to Lister, 14 November {1695}, *ESIO*, 14:291.

107. Lhuyd to Lloyd, St Steven's day (26 December) 1696, *ESIO*, 14:317.

108. George Wither, *The Poetry of George Wither,* ed. F. Sidgwick (London: A. H. Bullen, 1902), 91; quoted in Clapp, "The Beginnings of Subscription Publication in the Seventeenth Century," 208.

109. Lhuyd to Mostyn, 26 November 1695, *ESIO*, 14:293.

110. Lhuyd to Colin Campbell, 20 December 1699, in Campbell and Thomson, eds., *Edward Lhuyd in the Scottish Highlands 1699–1700* (1963), 4.

111. Lhuyd to Mostyn, 26 November 1695, *ESIO*, 14:293–294.

112. Lhuyd to Lister, 9 February 1696, *ESIO*, 14:298.

113. Lhuyd to Mostyn, 2 November 1707, *ESIO*, 14:535; Lhuyd to Mostyn, 6 December 1707, *ESIO*, 14:538.

114. Woolf, "The 'Common Voice'" (1988); Fox, "Custom, Memory and the Authority of Writing," in *The Experience of Authority in Early Modern England,* ed. Griffiths, Fox, and Hindle (1996); Woolf, *The Social Circulation of the Past* (2003), 13, 15–16.

115. K. Grudzien Baston, "Vaughan, John, third early of Carbery (bap. 1639, d. 1713)," *ODNB.*

116. Lhuyd to Lister, 9 February 1696, *ESIO*, 14:298.

117. Further examples of this dynamic can be seen in the production of William Turner, *A compleat history of the most remarkable providences, both of judgment and mercy, which have hapned in this present age* (1697), published by John Dunton and advertised in his newspaper, the *Athenian Mercury.* See "Proposals for Printing by Subscription An History of all the Remarkable Providences Which have hapned in this Present Age," *Athenian Mercury,* 17, no. 15, Tuesday, 22 May 1695 (Bod Hope Folio 5). See also 17, no. 16, 25 May 1695; and 18, no. 2, 20 July 1695, for instances of providences being sent in to be included in the book (all Bod Hope Folio 5). See also the careers of James Petiver and John Ogilby in James, "Humbly Dedicated," 323; and Clark, "Now Through You Made Public for Everyone," 139–141.

118. Lhuyd, "Parochial Queries," Bod MS Ashmole 1820, 77v. On the history of questionnaires as data-gathering tools in the early modern world, see Hunter, "Robert Boyle and the Early Royal Society" (2007): 1–23; Cooper, *Inventing the Indigenous* (2007), 119–120, 131–139; Barrera-Osorio, *Experiencing Nature* (2006), 81–100; Fox, "Printed Questionnaires, Research Networks and the Discovery of the British Isles, 1650–1800" (2010); Mendelsohn, "The World on a Page," in *Histories of Scientific Observation,* ed. Daston and Lunbeck (2011); and Yale, "Making Lists," in *Ways of Making and Knowing,* ed. Smith, Meyers, and Cook (2014).

119. See, for example, Lhuyd to Lloyd, St Steven's day, 1696 {26 December 1696}, *ESIO*, 14:316–318; and Lhuyd to Lister, 6 January 1697, *ESIO*, 14:321.

120. Lhuyd to Lloyd, St Steven's day, 1696 {26 December 1696}, *ESIO*, 14:317.

121. Bod MS Ashmole 1820, 76r–178v, 239r–v. It is possible that more query sheets were returned and simply not preserved, especially given the various destructions that visited Lhuyd's papers after his death. See also Morris, ed., *Parochialia*, 3 vols. (1909–1911); Emery, "A Map of Edward Lhuyd's *Parochial Queries in Order to a Geographical Dictionary, &c. of Wales* (1696)" (1958); Emery, "A New Reply to Lhuyd's *Parochial Queries* (1696)" (1958); Emery, "Edward Lhuyd and Some of His Glamorgan Correspondents" (1965); and Fox, "Printed Questionnaires, Research Networks, and the Discovery of the British Isles, 1650–1800," 603, 616.

122. Lhuyd, "Parochial Queries," Bod MS Ashmole 1820, 77r.

123. Lhuyd to Lloyd, 16 July 1695, *ESIO*, 14: 279.

124. Lhuyd to Mostyn, 26 April 1701, *ESIO*, 14:443.

125. Emery, "Edward Lhuyd and Some of His Glamorgan Correspondents," 69–71.

126. Lhuyd to Lloyd, St Steven's day, 1696 {26 December 1696}, *ESIO*, 14:316.

127. Lhuyd to Lister, 6 January 1697, *ESIO*, 14:321.

128. Lhuyd to Lister, 30 January 1697, *ESIO*, 14:322.

129. Lhuyd to Lister, 6 January 1697, *ESIO*, 14:321; Lhuyd to Lister [February 1696–1697], *ESIO*, 14:323.

130. Lhuyd, "Parochial Queries," Bod MS Ashmole 1820, 2.

131. See Jenkins, "Seventeenth-Century Wales," in *British Consciousness and Identity*, ed. Bradshaw and Roberts (1998), 219–220.

132. Lhuyd to Lister, Sunday morning {February 1697}, *ESIO*, 14:323.

133. "Edward Lhuyd and the Rev. John Beaton," in Campbell and Thomson, eds., *Edward Lhuyd in the Scottish Highlands 1699–1700*, 12–22.

134. Lhuyd to Colin Campbell, 20 December 1699, in Campbell and Thomson, eds., *Edward Lhuyd in the Scottish Highlands 1699–1700*, 4–5. Lhuyd also communicated queries for the Highlands to Robert Wodrow and James Fraser, an Inverness-shire minister (Campbell and Thomson, eds., *Edward Lhuyd in the Scottish Highlands 1699–1700*, 3).

135. "Lhuyd's Notes on Owners of Gaelic Manuscripts in Scotland in 1699," in Campbell and Thomson, eds., *Edward Lhuyd in the Scottish Highlands 1699–1700*, 9–11, quote on 9.

136. Lhuyd to {Thomas Molyneux}, 29 January 1700, in Campbell and Thomson, eds., *Edward Lhuyd in the Scottish Highlands 1699–1700*, 6.

137. Lhuyd to {Thomas Molyneux}, 29 January 1700, in Campbell and Thomson, eds., *Edward Lhuyd in the Scottish Highlands 1699–1700*, 6.

138. Lhuyd to {Thomas Molyneux}, 29 January 1700, in Campbell and Thomson, eds., *Edward Lhuyd in the Scottish Highlands 1699–1700*, 6.

139. See, for example, the responses collected in Emery, "Edward Lhuyd and Some of His Glamorgan Correspondents."

140. Lhuyd, "Parochial Queries," Bod MS Ashmole 1820, 2.

141. Bod MS Ashmole 1820, 143v.

142. Emery, "Edward Lhuyd and Some of His Glamorgan Correspondents," 106–108, quote on 108.

143. Emery, "Edward Lhuyd and Some of His Glamorgan Correspondents," 107.

144. Emery, "Edward Lhuyd and Some of His Glamorgan Correspondents," 106–108.

145. For an introduction to this aspect of Lhuyd's work and a transcription of his Scots and Irish Gaelic vocabulary notebooks, see Campbell and Thomson, eds., *Edward Lhuyd in the Scottish Highlands 1699–1700*, 91–218.

146. Campbell and Thomson, eds., *Edward Lhuyd in the Scottish Highlands 1699–1700*, 91.

147. Campbell and Thomson, eds., *Edward Lhuyd in the Scottish Highlands 1699–1700*, 91, 98; Cram, "Edward Lhuyd's *Archaeologica Britannica*" (2010), 78–82.

148. Campbell and Thomson, eds., *Edward Lhuyd in the Scottish Highlands 1699–1700*, 77–87.

149. Campbell and Thomson, eds., *Edward Lhuyd in the Scottish Highlands 1699–1700*, 12–22, 77.

150. See Jenkins, "Seventeenth-Century Wales," in *British Consciousness and Identity*, ed. Bradshaw and Roberts, 219–220.

CHAPTER 6

1. Aubrey, *Memoires of Naturall Remarques in the County of Wilts*, RS MS 92, 221–222. A marginal note at the line beginning "Dorset" reads, "In Mr. Wm. Gardners time, it was the most eminent Schoole for the Education of Gentle Men in the West of England." The "Forules of their Bookes" are probably the fore-edges of the books' covers.

2. Compare Gerhardt, "No quyckar merchaundyce than library bokes" (2007), 421–422. See also Fox, "Custom, Memory and the Authority of Writing," in *The Experience of Authority in Early Modern England*, ed. Griffiths, Fox, and Hindle (1996), 103; and Broadway, *"No Historie So Meete"* (2006), 121–126.

3. See Gadd and Gillespie, eds., *John Stow (1525–1605) and the Making of the English Past* (2004), in particular Gillespie, "Stow's 'Owlde' Manuscripts of London Chronicles," 57–67; Wright, "The Dispersal of the Libraries in the Sixteenth Century," in *The English Library Before 1700*, ed. Wormald and Wright (1958), 156–157, 170; Wright, ed., *Sir Robert Cotton as Collector* (1997); and Summit, *Memory's Library* (2008).

4. See Aston, "English Ruins and English History" (1973).

5. On the connection between John Aubrey's studies of natural history and antiquities, see Hunter, *John Aubrey and the Realm of Learning* (1975), 191–202.

6. In the last twenty years, the history of archives has generated a wealth of studies on archives as historical subjects, rather than simply as sources of history. This literature has focused primarily on archives as instruments of state and imperial governance. See Burton, ed., *Archive Stories* (2006); Stoler, *Along the Archival Grain* (2009); Burns, *Into the Archive* (2010); "Archival Knowledge Cultures in Europe, 1400–1900," a special issue of *Archival Science* 10 (2010); Soll, *The Information Master* (2009); Head, "Documents, Archives, and Proof Around 1700" (2013); and Weld, *Paper Cadavers* (2014). Hunter, ed., *Archives of the Scientific Revolution* (1998), stands out as a volume devoted to the archives of science.

7. The shift from viewing archives as neutral repositories to seeing them as sites thickly laden with ideology and politics is distinctive of scholarship on the history of archives. See *Archival Science* 2 (2002), a special double issue on "Archives, Records, and Power," especially the introduction, Schwartz and Cook, "Archives, Records, and Power," 1–19, 171–185; and Yale, "The History of Archives" (2015), for discussions of this conception of archives.

8. John Aubrey to Anthony à Wood, 8 November 1692, Bod MS Wood F. 39, 437.

9. See Hunter, "Introduction," in *Archives of the Scientific Revolution*, ed. Hunter, 11.

10. Hooke, *Diary*, entries of 21 September 1677, 314; 6 November 1677, 326; 19 November 1677, 329; 26 December 1677, 336; 28 December 1677, 337; 31 December 1677, 337–338; 1 January 1677/78, 338; 4 January1677/78, 338; 12 January 1677/78, 340.

11. Evelyn, *Memoires for my Grandson*, BL Add. MS 78515, 32r.

12. Hooke, *Diary*, 1 November 1677, 325; Henry Howard, Duke of Norfolk, *Bibliotheca Norfolciana* (1681), 126–153; Peck, "Uncovering the Arundel Library at the Royal Society" (1998), 4, 10. Note that *Bibliotheca Norfolciana*, a catalog of the library Henry Howard donated to the Royal Society, was primarily the work of William Petty. It is Howard, however, as the donor, whose name is listed on the title page. He is given as author in the *English Short Title Catalog*. See Hunter, *The Royal Society and its Fellows, 1660–1700* (1994), 21–22.

13. Lhuyd, *Parochial Queries in Order to a Geographical Dictionary, a Natural History &c. of Wales* (1697), 2.

14. Evelyn, "Of Manuscripts," 333–348. The manuscript copy of the treatise is no longer extant.

15. Evelyn, "Of Manuscripts," 339–348.

16. Aubrey, RS MS 92, 221.

17. Love, *The Culture and Commerce of Texts* (1998), 23–31; Monson, "Through a Glass Darkly" (1981), 64.

18. See Aubrey to Wood, 31 March 1690, Bod MS Wood F.39, 400r. See also Aubrey to Wood, 24 April 1690, Bod MS Wood F.39, 402–403; Aubrey to Wood, 5 and 10 July 1690, Bod MS Wood F.39, 405–406.

19. Aubrey to Wood, 10 July 1690, Bod MS Wood F.39, 405v.

20. See, e.g., Aubrey to Wood, 24 April 1690, Bod MS Wood F.39, 402r–v.

21. Edward Lhuyd to Aubrey, 3 April {1693}, Bod MS Aubrey 12, 243r; Lhuyd to Aubrey, 2 March 1693, Bod MS Aubrey 12, 241r; Aubrey to Wood, 24 April 1690, Bod MS Wood F.39, 402v; Aubrey to Wood, 10 July 1690, Bod MS Wood F.39, 405v.

22. Lhuyd generally used "MSS" to refer to Aubrey's materials. See Lhuyd to Aubrey, 16 November 1693, Bod MS Aubrey 12, 250r; Lhuyd to Aubrey, 9 January 1693/94, Bod MS Aubrey 12, 251r; and Lhuyd to Aubrey, 29 May 1694, Bod MS Aubrey 12, 257r. In a letter of 4 March 1693/94 as well as one letter for which no year is available but which was likely written about the same time, Lhuyd referred to Aubrey's "papers." "MSS" was otherwise standard in this series of letters (Lhuyd to Aubrey, 4 March 1694, Bod MS Aubrey 12, 253r; and Lhuyd to Aubrey, 27 February {1694}, Bod MS Aubrey 12, 260r).

23. Compare excerpts from Aubrey's letters quoted in Hunter, *John Aubrey and the Realm of Learning*, 75–92, where Hunter discusses Aubrey's efforts to methodize his writings. As quoted by Hunter, Aubrey used various words for his and others' written materials, including "papers" and "manuscripts" or "MSS." Instances of "papers" date to 1679–1685, before Aubrey transferred his collections to the Ashmolean (Hunter, *John Aubrey and the Realm of Learning*, 79, 80, 82). In quotations from 1692 to 1694, Aubrey exclusively used "manuscripts" or "MSS" (Hunter, *John Aubrey and the Realm of Learning*, 85, 87 can be securely dated; a third use of "MSS" on 83, taken from *Monumenta Britannica*, dates from the 1680s or 1690s).

24. Elias Ashmole, 20 August 1672, BL Sloane MS 3188, 2r–2v, and Ashmole, 10 September 1672, BL Sloane MS 3188, 2v–3r, in Josten, ed., *Elias Ashmole, 1617–1692: His Autobiographical and Historical Notes, His Correspondence, and Other Contemporary Sources Relating to His Life and Work* (1966), 3:1264–1265, 1270–1271 (hereafter *Autobiographical and Historical Notes*).

25. Ashmole, 20 August 1672, Bod MS Ashmole 1136, 47v; Ashmole, 10 September 1672, BL Sloane MS 3188, 2v–3; Elias Ashmole to Wood, 20 December 1672, Bod MS Wood F. 39, 59, in Josten, ed., *Autobiographical and Historical Notes*, 3:1264, 1271, 1288–89.

26. Ashmole, 29 January 1672, Bod MS Ashmole 1788, 158, in Josten, ed., *Autobiographical and Historical Notes*, 3:1242–1243.

27. Naudé, *Instructions concerning erecting of a library*, trans. Evelyn (1661), 80–82, quote on 81; McKitterick, *Print, Manuscript and the Search for Order, 1450–1830* (2003), 12–15.

28. Naudé, *Instructions concerning erecting of a library*, 81.

29. Naudé, *Instructions concerning erecting of a library*, 81–82, quote on 81.

30. "Ashmole's will," in Josten, ed., *Autobiographical and Historical Notes*, 4:1828–1832, quote on 1829.

31. Clucas, "Samuel Hartlib's 'Ephemerides,' 1635–1659, and the Pursuit of Scientific and Philosophical Manuscripts" (1991), 33–55.

32. Aubrey, *Brief Lives, Chiefly of Contemporaries, Set Down by John Aubrey*, ed. Clark (1898), 36–37.

33. See, for example, his interest in the papers of Peter Cruger, who died in 1639. See Clucas, "Samuel Hartlib's 'Ephemerides,' 1635–1659, and the Pursuit of Scientific and Philosophical Manuscripts," 43–44, 46–47, 50–51.

34. See Hartlib's catalog of Francis Bacon's extant manuscripts, compiled in 1639 (transcribed in Clucas, "Samuel Hartlib's 'Ephemerides,' 1635–1659, and the Pursuit of Scientific and Philosophical Manuscripts," 50–51).

35. See Gerhardt, "No quyckar merchaundyce than library bokes," 413. On the literary politics (and competing literacies, monastic and humanist) at play in the dissolution, see Summit, *Memory's Library*, 78–100.

36. Gerhardt, "No quyckar merchaundyce than library bokes," 413.

37. Summit, *Memory's Library*, esp. 1–15.

38. John Bale to Matthew Parker, 30 July 1560, in Graham and Watson, eds., *The Recovery of the Past in Early Elizabethan England* (1998), 17–18; quoted in Gerhardt, "No quyckar merchaundyce than library bokes," 408–409.

39. Bale to Parker, 30 July 1560, in Graham and Watson, eds., *The Recovery of the Past in Early Elizabethan England*, 17; quoted in Gerhardt, "No quyckar merchaundyce than library bokes," 409.

40. Bale and Leland, *The laboryouse journey and serche of Iohan Leylande* (1549), Giiir; quoted in Gerhardt, "'No Quyckar Merchaundyce than Library Bokes," 421.

41. See Houghton, *A Collection for Improvement of Husbandry and Trade* (1692–1703), 13:356–360 (19 May–16 June 1699) (Bod Hope Folio 23) for a description of paper manufacture. Issue 359 (9 June 1699) includes the method for boiling parchment and vellum to make "size," or gelatin, to seal the paper. On gelatin content in early modern paper, see Timothy Barrett, "Paper Through Time: Non-Destructive Analysis of 14th Through 19th Century Papers," http://paper.lib.uiowa.edu (accessed 20 May 2014).

42. Graham, "Matthew Parker's Manuscripts," in *The Cambridge History of Libraries in Britain and Ireland*, ed. Leedham-Green and Webber (2006), 322.

43. Wright, "The Dispersal of the Libraries in the Sixteenth Century," in *The English Library Before 1700*, ed. Wormald and Wright, 170. See also Summit, *Memory's Library*, 101–135; and Popper, "From Abbey to Archive" (2010), 249–266.

44. Wright, "The Dispersal of the Libraries in the Sixteenth Century," in *The English Library Before 1700*, ed. Wormald and Wright, 175.

45. Dugdale, *The Antiquities of Warwickshire Illustrated* (1656), sig. b3v.

46. Ashmole, "Propositions sent to my Lord Bishop of Oxford," Bod MS Rawlinson D. 912, 670r–71v, in Josten, ed., *Autobiographical and Historical Notes*, 4:1710.

47. Aubrey, RS MS 92, 221.

48. Woolley, *The accomplish'd lady's delight in preserving, physic, beautifying and cookery* (1675), 260–261.

49. Dryden, "Mac Flecknoe," in *The Poems of John Dryden, 1649–1681*, ed. Hammond (2014), 1:306, 323, quote on 323.

50. Aubrey, RS MS 92, 221.

51. Aubrey, Bod MS Aubrey 10, 65r.

52. Ashmole, BL Sloane MS 3188, 2v–3r, in Josten, ed., *Autobiographical and Historical Notes*, 1:184–186, 3:1270–1271, quote on 1271.

53. Summit, *Memory's Library*, 101–102.

54. Parker, "A Preface into the Byble," in *The Holie Bible* (1568), sig. iir, quoted in Summit, *Memory's Library*, 101.

55. Summit, *Memory's Library*, 103–104.

56. Graham, "Matthew Parker's Manuscripts," in *The Cambridge History of Libraries in Britain and Ireland*, ed. Leedham-Green and Webber, 330.

57. Summit, *Memory's Library*, 106–121, 138–142, 215–221, quote on 217.

58. Walsham, *The Reformation of the Landscape* (2011), 233–326.

59. Respondent to Lhuyd, *Parochial Queries in Order to a Geographical Dictionary, a Natural History &c. of Wales*, Bod MS Ashmole 1820, 143v.

60. Most notably with the Irish antiquary Roderic O'Flaherty. See Sharpe, ed., *Roderick O'Flaherty's Letters, 1696–1709* (2013).

61. Lhuyd to William Baxter, 7 September 1708, *ESIO*, 14:545.

62. Lhuyd to Baxter, 7 September 1708, *ESIO*, 14:545.

63. See Bacon, *Works*, ed. Spedding (1864), 8:423–424, quotes on 423.

64. Clucas, "Samuel Hartlib's 'Ephemerides,' 1635–1659, and the Pursuit of Scientific and Philosophical Manuscripts," 33–55.

65. Clucas, "Samuel Hartlib's 'Ephemerides,' 1635–1659, and the Pursuit of Scientific and Philosophical Manuscripts," 40.

66. Hartlib, *Considerations Tending to the Happy Accomplishment of Englands Reformation in Church and State* (1647), 46.

67. See Greengrass, "Samuel Hartlib and Scribal Publication" (1997), 56.

68. Hartlib, *Ephemerides*, 1639, Hartlib Papers, 30/4/27B; quoted in Clucas, "Samuel Hartlib's 'Ephemerides,' 1635–1659, and the Pursuit of Scientific and Philosophical Manuscripts," 42.

69. Clucas, "Samuel Hartlib's 'Ephemerides,' 1635–1659, and the Pursuit of Scientific and Philosophical Manuscripts," 44–45; Feingold, "Of Records and Grandeur," in *The Archives of the Scientific Revolution*, ed. Hunter (1998), 177.

70. Johns, *The Nature of the Book* (1998), 495; Feingold, "Of Records and Grandeur," in *The Archives of the Scientific Revolution*, ed. Hunter, 177.

71. See Johns, *The Nature of the Book*, 495–497.

72. Aubrey to Wood, n.d, MS Wood F.39, 318r.

73. Johns, *The Nature of the Book*, 495.

74. Johns, *The Nature of the Book*, 495–496.

75. Lhuyd, *Parochial Queries in Order to a Geographical Dictionary, a Natural History &c. of Wales*, 2.

76. Lhuyd, *Parochial Queries in Order to a Geographical Dictionary, a Natural History &c. of Wales*, 4.

77. "Inquires for Barbary Recommended by the R. Society to the Favour and Care of His Excellency the Lord Henry Howard, his Majesties Ambassadour Extraordinary to the Emperour of Marocco," RS Register Book Original 4 (1668–1675), 53.

78. Robert Plot to John Fell, c. 1673, *ESIO*, 12:336.

79. Plot to Fell, c. 1673, *ESIO*, 12:337.

80. Plot to Fell, c. 1673, *ESIO*, 12:337.

81. Plot to Fell, c. 1673, *ESIO*, 12:335–336.

82. Plot to Fell, c. 1673, *ESIO*, 12:336.

83. Plot to Fell, c. 1673, *ESIO*, 12:336

84. Plot to Fell, c. 1673, *ESIO*, 12:343.

85. Plot to Fell, c. 1673, *ESIO*, 12:343–344.

86. Plot to Fell, c. 1673, *ESIO*, 12:337, 343.

87. Bernard, *Catalogi manuscriptorum Angliae et Hiberniae* (1697). See also "A Letter Wherein is Given an Account of the Catalogues of Manuscripts Lately Printed at Oxford," *Phil. Trans.* 20 (1698): 442–460.

88. Houghton, *A Collection for Improvement of Husbandry and Trade,* 5:105, 3 August 1694.

89. Houghton, *A Collection for Improvement of Husbandry and Trade,* 5:107, 17 August 1694; 5:108, 24 August 1694; 5:112, 21 September 1694; 5:114, 5 October 1694.

90. Bernard, "De ratione & utilitate hujus catalogi epistola," in Bernard, *Catalogi manuscriptorum Angliae et Hiberniae,* vol. 1.

91. Edward Bernard, *Librorum manuscriptorum academiarum* Oxoniensis & Cantabrigiensis *& celebrium per* Angliam Hiberniamque *bibliothecarum catalogus cum indice alphabetico* (1694).

92. "A Letter Wherein is Given an Account of the Catalogues of Manuscripts Lately Printed at Oxford," *Phil. Trans.* 20 (1698): 453–454.

93. "A Letter Wherein is Given an Account of the Catalogues of Manuscripts Lately Printed at Oxford," *Phil. Trans.* 20 (1698): 459.

94. Edward Bernard, *Librorum manuscriptorum academiarum* Oxoniensis & Cantabrigiensis *& celebrium per* Angliam Hiberniamque *bibliothecarum catalogus cum indice alphabetico* (1694).

95. Edward Bernard, "In hisce Voluminibus continentur," in Bernard, *Catalogi manuscriptorum Angliae et Hiberniae,* vol. 1.

96. Lhuyd to Thomas Tanner {Spring 1698}, *ESIO*, 14:369.

97. G. Le G. Norgate, "Mostyn, Sir Roger, third baronet (1673–1739)," rev. M. E. Clayton, *ODNB*.

98. Aubrey, Bod MS 10, 68r.

99. Lhuyd to Aubrey, 13 October 1693, Bod MS Aubrey 12, 248v.

100. Aubrey, Bod MS Aubrey 22, item 1.

101. Aubrey, Bod MS Aubrey 10, 64–65. Brackets are original.

102. Aubrey to Wood, 13 {January?} 1681, Bod MS Wood F.39, 351v. Tonge's alchemical papers have not survived. For more on Aubrey's enthusiasms for others' papers, see Hunter, *John Aubrey and the Realm of Learning,* 64–65; and Bennett, "John Aubrey and the Printed Book" (2013), 399–400.

103. Aubrey to Wood, 8 November 1692, Bod MS Wood F. 39, 437.

104. Hunter, *John Aubrey and the Realm of Learning,* 239.

105. Lhuyd to John Lloyd, 23 November 1707, *ESIO*, 14:536. See also Lhuyd to Thomas Tanner, 12 April 1698, *ESIO*, 14:370; and Lhuyd to Thomas Tonkin, 16 March 1703, *ESIO*, 14:485. To Tanner, Lhuyd complained that a gentleman who had promised him access to his study in order to view and transcribe ancient Welsh manuscripts "was pleasd neverthelesse afterwards to refuse when I sent a purpose messenger twice to him." Writing to Tonkin, Lhuyd described how he "was refused access to the two Studies" where a number of manuscript "British Elegies" were "preserved in Parchment MSS."

106. Phillip, *The Bodleian Library in the Seventeenth and Eighteenth Centuries* (1983), 6.

107. Welch, "The Foundation of the Ashmolean Museum," in *Tradescant's Rarities*, ed. MacGregor (1983), 40–58.

108. Ashmole's library of manuscripts, donated to the museum after his death, numbered 620 volumes, out of a total of 1,758 books (C. H. Josten, "Biographical Introduction," in Josten, ed., *Autobiographical and Historical Notes*, 4:189n1).

109. See Welch, "The Foundation of the Ashmolean Museum," in *Tradescant's Rarities*, ed. MacGregor, 40–58. See also Elias Ashmole, "Statutes, Orders, & Rules for the Ashmolean Museum in the University of Oxon," Bod MS Ashmole 1820, 296r–297v (repr. in Josten, ed., *Autobiographical and Historical Notes*, 4:1821–1825). These were dated 24 June 1686 and signed by Ashmole.

110. Ashmole willed that his printed books, books of engravings (some hand-colored), and his "Manuscript books and other Manuscript papers not yet sorted nor bound up . . . be preserved in the Musaeum Ashmoleanum in Presses with locks and keys to bee provided for them" ("Copy of Elias Ashmole's Will," Bod MS Ashmole 1834, 62r–v; repr. in Josten, ed., *Autobiographical and Historical Notes*, 4:1828–1832, quote on 1829).

111. Ashmole, "Statutes, Orders, & Rules for the Ashmolean Museum in the University of Oxon," 24 June 1686, Bod MS Ashmole 1820, 296r. See also the copy of the statues in Josten, ed., *Autobiographical and Historical Notes*, 4:1823.

112. Ashmole, "Statutes, Orders, & Rules for the Ashmolean Museum in the University of Oxon," 21 June 1686, in Josten, ed., *Autobiographical and Historical Notes*, 4:1824–1825.

113. Swann, *Curiosities and Texts* (2001), 50–54; The Ashmolean Museum of Art and Architecture, "History of the Ashmolean," http://www.ashmolean.org/about/historyandfuture/ (accessed 8 September 2008).

114. MacGregor, "Edward Lhuyd, Museum Keeper" (2010), 69–72.

115. Ashmole, "Statutes, Orders, & Rules for the Ashmolean Museum in the University of Oxon," 21 June 1686, in Josten, ed., *Autobiographical and Historical Notes*, 4:1823.

116. Michael Hunter, *Establishing the New Science* (1989), 139–40, 153–55; Swann, *Curiosities and Texts*, 197–198.

117. Compare the breakup, over time, of Hans Sloane's collections. What remains of his original donation to the British nation is now divided between the British Museum, the British Library, and the Natural History Museum. See Walker, MacGregor, and Hunter, eds., *From Books to Bezoars* (2012).

118. "Ashmolean Museum," Finding Aid, Oxford University Archives, http://www .oua.ox.ac.uk/holdings/Ashmolean%20Museum%20AM.pdf (accessed 17 February 2014).

119. "Ashmolean Museum," Finding Aid, Oxford University Archives, http://www .oua.ox.ac.uk/holdings/Ashmolean%20Museum%20AM.pdf (accessed 17 February 2014).

120. MacGregor, "Edward Lhuyd, Museum Keeper," 73.

121. On the formation of early modern museums as social and intellectual spaces, see Impey and MacGregor, eds., *The Origins of Museums* (1983); Findlen, "Economy of Scientific

Exchange in Early Modern Italy," in *Patronage and Institutions*, ed. Moran (1991), 5–24; Outram, "New Spaces in Natural History," in *Cultures of Natural History*, ed. Jardine et al., 249–265; Findlen, *Possessing Nature* (1994); Swann, *Curiosities and Texts;* and Findlen, "Scientific Spectacle in Baroque Rome," in *Jesuit Science and the Republic of Letters*, ed. Feingold (2003).

122. Bod MS Ashmole 1820, 53r.

123. Bod MS Ashmole 1820, 53r.

124. "A Summary of the Statutes . . . of the Ashmolean Museum" (1696), Bod MS Ashmole 1820, 217v.

125. Burns, *Into the Archive*, 124.

126. Henderson, "Robert Hooke's Archive" (2009).

127. Evelyn, *Memoires for my Grandson*, BL Add. MS 78515 32r. On Evelyn's fear of humiliation or embarrassment, which may have inclined him toward wanting his rough drafts and notes destroyed, see Harris, *Transformations of Love* (2003), 42.

128. Hunter, *John Aubrey and the Realm of Learning*, 233.

129. Bennett, "Materials Towards a Critical Edition of John Aubrey's *Brief Lives*" (1993), 23, 25.

130. Bennett, "John Aubrey and the Printed Book," 405.

131. On the flyleaf of this volume, Aubrey wrote, "This Collection of Grammaticall learning, and another in 8o. is in relation to my Idea of the Education of the Noblesse" (Bod MS Aubrey 22, 1). See also Aubrey to John Evelyn, 10 May 1692, Bod MS Aubrey 10, 1ar.

132. Bennett, "John Aubrey's Collections and the Early Modern Museum" (2001), 216–217.

133. Bennett, "John Aubrey's Collections and the Early Modern Museum," 218.

134. See Bennett, "John Aubrey's Collections and the Early Modern Museum," 217. Bennett's argument as to the deliberateness of Aubrey's choices is further supported by the choices he made to disperse his books and papers among different repositories. For instance, he donated a number of printed books to the Royal Society (in addition to the fair copy of his *Naturall Historie of Wiltshire*), while at least a portion of his mathematical library went to Gloucester Hall at Oxford. See Buchanan-Brown, "The Books Presented to the Royal Society by John Aubrey, FRS" (1974), 167–193, esp. 173–183.

135. As discussed in Chapter 4, Aubrey feared that this had happened after his manuscript *Naturall Historie of Wiltshire*, mailed to the botanist John Ray for comments, did not return on schedule (Ray to Aubrey, 18 November 1691, Bod MS Aubrey 13, 175r).

136. See Lhuyd to Aubrey, 12 February 1687, Bod MS Aubrey 12, 240r (quoted in Chapter 2), for an example.

137. Aubrey to Wood, 3 August 1689, MS Wood F. 40, 372.

138. Graham Parry, "Anthony à Wood (1632–1695)," *ODNB*.

139. Bennett, "John Aubrey and the Printed Book," 410–411; Graham Parry, "Anthony à Wood (1632–1695)," *ODNB*.

140. See Pincus, *1688* (2009).

141. Graham Parry, "Anthony à Wood (1632–1695)," *ODNB*.

142. Broadway, *"No Historie so Meete,"* 95–100.

143. Aubrey to Wood, 11 September 1676, Bod MS Wood F.39, 302r.

144. Aubrey to Wood, 11 September 1676, Bod MS Wood F.39, 302r; Hunter, *John Aubrey and the Realm of Learning*, 32–34.

145. Graham Parry, "Anthony à Wood (1632–1695)," *ODNB*.

146. Aubrey to Wood, 11 September 1676, Bod MS Wood F.39, 302r.

147. Aubrey to Wood, 23 October 1688, Bod MS Tanner 456a, 34r. Wood left the second blank, in the phrase "changes of ———" as is, but it may likely be filled by "religion" or perhaps "government." See also the extract of this letter in Josten, ed., *Autobiographical and Historical Notes*, 4:1859–1861.

148. Aubrey to Wood, 22 December 1688, Bod MS Aubrey 12, 2r. As in the previous letter, "P" is short for "Papist." See also the extract of this letter in Josten, ed., *Autobiographical and Historical Notes*, 4:1861–1862.

149. Aubrey to Wood, 22 December 1688, Bod MS Aubrey 12, 2r–v.

150. Aubrey to Wood, 22 December 1688, Bod MS Aubrey 12, 2r.

151. Aubrey to Wood, 22 December 1688, Bod MS Aubrey 12, 2v.

152. Lhuyd to Aubrey, 4 March 1694, Bod MS Aubrey 12, 253r.

153. Lhuyd to Aubrey, 4 March 1694, Bod MS Aubrey 12, 253r.

154. Lhuyd to Aubrey, 29 May 1694, Bod MS Aubrey 12, 257r.

155. Lhuyd to Aubrey, 29 May 1694, Bod MS Aubrey 12, 257r.

156. Lhuyd to Aubrey, 29 May 1694, Bod MS Aubrey 12, 257r; Hunter, *John Aubrey and the Realm of Learning*, 89–90n8.

157. Hunter, *John Aubrey and the Realm of Learning*, 91.

158. Hunter, *John Aubrey and the Realm of Learning*, 91, 206; "Aubrey Manuscripts," http://www.bodley.ox.ac.uk/dept/scwmss/wmss/online/1500-1900/aubrey/aubrey.html (accessed 6 June 2012); "John Aubrey's Monumenta Britannica," http://www.bodley.ox.ac.uk/dept/scwmss/wmss/online/1500-1900/aubrey/aubrey2.ht ml (accessed 13 January 2015).

159. See, e.g., Aubrey, *Monumenta Britannica* (1980–1982).

160. Aubrey to Wood, 31 March 1690, Bod MS Wood F.39, 400r.

161. Lhuyd to Aubrey, 13 October 1693, Bod MS Aubrey 12, 248r.

162. Lhuyd to Aubrey, 13 October 1693, Bod MS Aubrey 12, 248r; Aubrey to Lhuyd, 19 October 1693, Bod MS Ashmole 1814, 100, trans. Helen Watt and Brynley Roberts, EMLO.

163. Lhuyd to Aubrey, 16 November 1693, Bod MS Aubrey 12, 250r. See also Hunter, *John Aubrey and the Realm of Learning*, 84–85.

164. MacGregor, "Edward Lhuyd, Museum Keeper," 64–65.

165. Lister to Lhuyd, 7 October 1690 and 31 October 1690; Lhuyd to Lister, 2 November 1690— all in Josten, ed., *Autobiographical and Historical Notes*, 4:1876–1877.

166. See, e.g., Edward Lhuyd, "Additions to Glamorganshire," in Camden, *Camden's Britannia newly translated into English* (1695), 618, where Lhuyd cites correspondence between Aubrey and the Scottish antiquary James Garden in the course of a comparative analysis of ancient monuments in Wales and Scotland. See also Hunter, *John Aubrey and the Realm of Learning*, 85.

167. Lhuyd to Aubrey, 2 March 1693, Bod MS Aubrey 12, 241r.

168. Lhuyd to Aubrey, 3 April {1693?}, Bod MS Aubrey 12, 243r; Lhuyd to Aubrey, "Sunday morning," Bod MS Aubrey 12, 262r.

169. Lhuyd to Aubrey, 4 March 1694, Bod MS Aubrey 12, 253r; Lhuyd to Aubrey, 27 February {year?}, Bod MS Aubrey 12, 260r; Lhuyd to Aubrey, "Sunday morning," Bod MS Aubrey 12, 262r.

170. Lhuyd to Lister, 28 August 1690, in Josten, ed., *Autobiographical and Historical Notes*, 4:1875.

171. Bod MS Ashmole 1820, f. 53r; Josten, ed., *Autobiographical and Historical Notes*, 4:1893–1895; MacGregor, "Edward Lhuyd, Museum Keeper," 59–60.

172. Lhuyd to Lister, 5 December 1695, *ESIO,* 14:296; Lhuyd to Lister, 26 October 1696, *ESIO* 14:312; MacGregor, "Edward Lhuyd, Museum Keeper," 60.

173. Wood's copy came preloaded with Wood's own notes. Wood had amended errors and marked entries with Bodleian shelf marks and factual additions, indicating the catalog was an important reference book for him. See Ovenden, "Catalogue of the Bodleian Library and Other Collections," in *History of the Oxford University Press,* ed. Gadd (2013), 287–289.

174. See Lhuyd to Lister, 5 December 1695, *ESIO,* 14:295–296.

175. On the posthumous history of Hartlib's papers, see Greengrass, "Archive Refractions," in *Archives of the Scientific Revolution,* ed. Hunter, 40–43, quote on 42.

176. Greengrass, "Archive Refractions," in *Archives of the Scientific Revolution,* ed. Hunter, 42–43; the electronic archive is available at "The Hartlib Papers," http://www.hrionline.ac.uk/hartlib/ (accessed 29 April 2015).

177. Hunter, ed., *Archives of the Scientific Revolution,* 8.

178. Hunter, ed., *Archives of the Scientific Revolution,* 6.

179. Hunter, *John Aubrey and the Realm of Learning,* 91, 241–242.

180. See Hofmann, Winterkorn, Harris, and Kelliher, "John Evelyn's Archive at the British Library" (1995), 148; Hunter and Harris, "Introduction," in Harris and Hunter, eds., *John Evelyn and His Milieu* (2003), 2; and Janet Ing Freeman, "Upcott, William (1779–1845)," *ODNB.*

181. Hofmann, Winterkorn, Harris, and Kelliher, "John Evelyn's Archive at the British Library," 148.

182. Julian Pooley, "William Bray, 1735/36–1832," *ODNB.*

183. Hofmann, Winterkorn, Harris, and Kelliher, "John Evelyn's Archive at the British Library," 149; John Young, "British Library Buys Record of 17th-Century Life and Times," *Times* (London), 9 March 1995, 9.

184. "Some Account of this Work, and Its Author," in Aubrey, *The Natural History and Antiquities of the County of Surrey* (1723), 1:i–ii.

185. Aubrey, RS MS 92, 164. Another reader annotated Aubrey's working draft, then housed in the Ashmolean, in the chapter on the "Falling of Rents." In this chapter Aubrey noted that it could be difficult to hire servants in the country because London employers drove up wages. He proposed a survey of servants' wages to quantify the problem. A reader felt moved to contribute to the project: "40S p an {shillings per annum} to a Servant maid is now in 1743 good wages to a servant maid in Warwickshire" (Bod MS Aubrey 2, 123r).

186. Sweet, *Antiquaries* (2004), 249.

187. This attitude also appears in Tylden-Wright, *John Aubrey* (1991).

188. See, e.g., Weld, *Paper Cadavers,* 13, on archival politics and "thinking archivally" in the context of political disputes.

189. Derrida, *Archive Fever,* trans. Prenowitz (1998); Steedman, *Dust* (2002); Stoler, *Along the Archival Grain.*

CONCLUSION

1. Anderson, *Imagined Communities* (1991).

2. Anderson, *Imagined Communities,* 141.

3. Ogilby, "Preface," *Britannia* (1675), sig. Bir.

4. Hellyer, "The Pocket Museum" (1996), 47.

5. John Aubrey, Bod MS 1, 7r.

6. Childrey, *Britannia Baconica* (1660), sig. A4 + 4v.

7. Rees and Walters, "The Dispersion of the Manuscripts of Edward Lhuyd" (1974), 150–151.

8. Rees and Walters, "The Dispersion of the Manuscripts of Edward Lhuyd," 150.

9. Ellis, "Some Incidents in the Life of Edward Lhuyd," in *Early Science in Oxford*, vol. 14, ed. Gunther (1945), 45–46.

10. Rees and Walters, "The Dispersion of the Manuscripts of Edward Lhuyd," 150.

11. Rees and Walters, "The Dispersion of the Manuscripts of Edward Lhuyd," 150–152.

12. Rees and Walters, "The Dispersion of the Manuscripts of Edward Lhuyd," 153.

13. Rees and Walters, "The Dispersion of the Manuscripts of Edward Lhuyd," 149, 158.

14. Rees and Walters, "The Dispersion of the Manuscripts of Edward Lhuyd," 159–165.

15. Rees and Walters, "The Dispersion of the Manuscripts of Edward Lhuyd," 154.

16. Campbell and Thomson, *Edward Lhuyd in the Scottish Highlands 1699–1700* (1963), xxvii–xxxii.

17. Rees and Walters, "The Dispersion of the Manuscripts of Edward Lhuyd," 155–156, 171.

18. Rees and Walters, "The Dispersion of the Manuscripts of Edward Lhuyd," 148, 157–158, 172.

19. See Rees and Walters's checklist of Lhuyd's manuscripts, which is useful in tracing the papers' ownership history ("The Dispersion of the Manuscripts of Edward Lhuyd," 175–178).

20. *Magna Britannia et Hibernia, antiqua & nova*, 6 vols. (1720–1731). On Elizabeth Nutt and the Nutt family of printers, see Horden, "'In the Savoy' John Nutt and His Family" (1988), esp. 14; Margaret R. Hunt, "Nutt, Elizabeth (b. in or before 1666, d. 1746)," *ODNB*; and McDowell, *The Women of Grub Street* (1998), passim. Authorship is usually attributed to the Essex antiquary Thomas Cox, but that may only be due to his sharing a name with the Thomas Cox who sold volumes 3–6. See Richard Riddell, "Cox, Thomas (1655/6–1734)," *ODNB*. Anthony Hall, fellow of Queen's College, Oxford, may be the author, in the sense that he collected and organized the text for the book (though it is unclear how much new writing he did). His authorship is suggested by an advertisement for the work printed in vol. 4 of *Atlas geographus* (1714). The advertisement, dated 30 November 1713, appears just after the title page.

21. Sweet, *Antiquaries* (2004), 310–311; Richard Riddell, "Cox, Thomas (1655/6–1734)," *ODNB*; "Advertisement," in *Atlas geographus*, vol. 4 (1714). An advertisement for *Magna Britannia* appears in each volume of *Atlas geographus*.

22. *Magna Britannia et Hibernia, antiqua & nova*, 1:ii.

23. Sweet, *Antiquaries*, 314, 316.

24. "Advertisement," in *Atlas geographus*, vol. 4 (1714).

25. *Magna Britannia et Hibernia, antiqua & nova*, 1:v–vi.

26. Sweet, *Antiquaries*, 189–190.

27. *Magna Britannia et Hibernia, antiqua & nova*, 1:i.

28. *Magna Britannia et Hibernia, antiqua & nova*, 1:i.

29. *Magna Britannia et Hibernia, antiqua & nova*, 1:i–ii.

30. *Magna Britannia et Hibernia, antiqua & nova*, 1:i.

31. *Magna Britannia et Hibernia, antiqua & nova*, 1:ii–iv.

32. Barnard, "British History and Irish History," in *The New British History*, ed. Burgess (1999), 201–204.

33. Colley, *Britons* (1992); Armitage, *The Ideological Origins of the British Empire* (2000), 170–171.

34. Colley, *Britons*, 204–236.

35. Armitage, *The Ideological Origins of the British Empire*, 173.

36. Armitage, *The Ideological Origins of the British Empire*, 170–178, esp. 177–178.

37. Purcell, "'Settled in the North of Ireland' or, Where Did Sloane Come From?," in *From Books to Bezoars*, ed. Walker, MacGregor, and Hunter (2012), 24–32.

38. On competing views and critiques of "Britishness" as an ideology in the context of empire, see Armitage, *Ideological Origins of the British Empire*, 178–181, 188–194.

39. See, for example, *Welsh History Review* 25 (2010): 1–115, a special issue on Lhuyd published to mark the tercentenary of his death.

40. Sweet, *Antiquaries*, 310–311.

41. Beavan and McDougall, "The Scottish Book Trade," in *The Cambridge History of the Book in Britain*, vol. 5, ed. Suarez and Turner (2009), 353–365; Benson, "The Irish Trade," in *The Cambridge History of the Book in Britain*, vol. 5, ed. Suarez and Turner, 366–382.

42. Sweet, *Antiquaries*, 325.

43. Sweet, *Antiquaries*, 269.

44. J. Mordaunt Crook, "Britton, John (1771–1857)," *ODNB*.

45. John Britton, "Editor's Preface," in Aubrey, *The Natural History of Wiltshire*, ed. Britton (1847), v–vi.

46. Britton, "Editor's Preface," in Aubrey, *The Natural History of Wiltshire*, ed. Britton, v–vi.

47. Britton, "Editor's Preface," in Aubrey, *The Natural History of Wiltshire*, ed. Britton, v.

48. Britton, "Editor's Preface," in Aubrey, *The Natural History of Wiltshire*, ed. Britton, v.

49. Britton, "Editor's Preface," in Aubrey, *The Natural History of Wiltshire*, ed. Britton, 82–88, quote on 82.

Bibliography

MANUSCRIPT SOURCES

To the extent possible, I have cited archival versions of documents (such as correspondence) that circulated in manuscript in the early modern era, rather than modern print editions. In some cases, letters were accessed via manuscript images and transcriptions available in the Oxford University database Early Modern Letters Online (http://emlo.bodleian.ox.ac.uk), a product of the Cultures of Knowledge collaboration. I have indicated in the notes when letters have been accessed in this way; all letters were accessible as of the date of this writing (2 May 2015).

Bodleian Library

MS Ashmole 1813
MS Ashmole 1814
MS Ashmole 1817
MS Ashmole 1819
MS Ashmole 1820
MS Ashmole 1834
MS Aubrey 1
MS Aubrey 2
MS Aubrey 4
MS Aubrey 5
MS Aubrey 10
MS Aubrey 12
MS Aubrey 13
MS Aubrey 22
MS Ballard 14
MS Ballard 24
MS Ballard 98
MS Don.a.3
MS Tanner 456A
MS Wood 658
MS Wood F. 13

MS Wood F. 29
MS Wood F. 39
MS Wood F. 49
MS Wood F. 51

British Library

Add. MS 4458
Add. MS 78328
Add. MS 78329
Add. MS 78330
Add. MS 78331
Add. MS 78332
Add. MS 78333
Add. MS 78334
Add. MS 78339
Add. MS 78340
Add. MS 78342
Add. MS 78343
Add. MS 78344
Add. MS 78348
Add. MS 78350
Add. MS 78430
Add. MS 78515
Sloane MS 4062

Royal Society Library

The Hooke Folio, MS 847, digital facsimile (http://cell.livesandletters.ac.uk/Hooke/
    Hooke.html)
MS 92
Register Book, vol. 4, 1668–1675
Journal Book Copy, vol. 4
Journal Book Original, vol. 10
Journal Book Original, vol. 11

Printed Primary Sources

Unless otherwise noted, most pre-1800 printed sources were consulted via *Early English Books
Online* and *Eighteenth Century Collections Online*.

Atlas geographus: or, a compleat system of geography, ancient and modern. 5 vols. Vols. 1–4, In the
    Savoy: Printed by John Nutt, 1711–1714. Vol. 5, London: Printed by Eliz. Nutt, for John
    Nicholson, 1717.

Aubrey, John. *Brief Lives, Chiefly of Contemporaries, Set Down by John Aubrey.* Ed. Andrew Clark. Oxford: Clarendon Press, 1898.

Aubrey, John. *Miscellanies.* London: Printed for Edward Castle, 1696.

Aubrey, John. *Monumenta Britannica: or, A Miscellany of British Antiquities.* 2 vols. Ed. John Fowles. Sherborne: Dorset, 1980–1982.

Aubrey, John. *The natural history and antiquities of the county of Surrey.* 5 vols. London: printed for W. Mears and J. Hooke, 1723. Houghton Library, Harvard University.

Aubrey, John. *The Natural History of Wiltshire.* Ed., and elucidated with notes by, John Britton. London: J. B. Nichols and Son for the Wiltshire Topographical Society, 1847.

Aubrey, John. *Three Prose Works.* Ed. John Buchannan-Brown. Fontwell: Centaur Press, 1972.

Aubrey, John. *The Topographical Collections of John Aubrey, F.R.S.* Ed. John Edward Jackson. London: Longman & Co., 1862.

Aylmer, Brabazon. *Proposals for the first volume of the works of the eminently learned Dr. Isaac Barrow.* London: B. Aylmer, 1682.

Bacon, Francis. *New Atlantis and the Great Instauration.* Ed. Jerry Weinberger. Wheeling, Ill.: Harlan Davidson, 1980.

Bacon, Francis. "Of Travaile." In Francis Bacon, *The essayes or counsels, civill and morall,* 100–104. London: Printed by John Haviland for Hanna Barret, 1625.

Bacon, Francis. *Sylva sylvarum: or A naturall historie.* London: Printed by I. Haviland for William Lee, 1627.

Bacon, Francis. *Works.* Vol. 8, ed. James Spedding. Boston: Taggard & Thompson, 1864.

Bale, John, and John Leland. *The laboryouse journey and serche of Iohan Leylande.* London: printed by S. Mierdman for J. Bale, 1549.

Bernard, Edward. *Catalogi manuscriptorum Angliae et Hiberniae.* Oxford: at the Sheldonian Theater, 1697.

Bernard, Edward. *Librorum manuscriptorum academiarum* Oxoniensis & Cantabrigiensis & *celebrium per* Angliam Hiberniamque *bibliothecarum catalogus cum indice alphabetico.* Oxford: s.n., 1694.

Birch, Thomas. *The History of the Royal Society of London.* 4 vols. London: Printed for L. Davis and C. Reymers, 1756–1757; repr. Brussels: Culture et Civilization 1967.

Blome, Richard. *Britannia, or, A geographical description of the kingdoms of England, Scotland, and Ireland.* London: printed by Tho. Roycroft for the undertaker, Richard Blome, 1673.

Blount, Thomas. *The 1675 Thomas Blount Manuscript History of Herefordshire.* Trans. and ed. Norman C. Reeves. Trans. and research Richard Botzum and Catherine Botzum. Hereford: Lapridge, 1997.

Boate, Gerard. *Irelands Naturall History.* Intro. Samuel Hartlib. London: Imprinted for John Wright, 1652.

Britannia reflorescens, in a prospect of the ancient and flourishing state of Great Britain. London: Printed by T. Milbourn, for Christopher Hussey, 1684.

Browne, Thomas. *Notes and Letters on the Natural History of Norfolk.* Intro. and annotated Thomas Southwell. London: Jarrold & Sons, 1902.

Browne, Thomas. *A true and full coppy of that which was most imperfectly and surreptitiously printed before under the name of: Religio medici.* London: Printed for Andrew Crooke, 1643.

Bureau d'adresse et de rencontre. *Another collection of philosophical conferences of the French virtuosi.* Trans. G. Havers and J. Davies. London: printed for Thomas Dring and John Starkey, 1665.

Bureau d'adresse et de rencontre. *A general collection of discourses of the virtuosi of France.* Trans. G. Havers. London: printed for Thomas Dring and John Starkey, 1664.

Camden, William. *The abridgment of Camden's Britannia with the maps of the several shires of England and Wales.* London: Printed by John Bill, 1626.

Camden, William. *Britain, Or a chorographicall description of the most flourishing kingdomes, England, Scotland, and Ireland, and the ilands adioyning.* Trans. Philemon Holland. London: Printed for George Bishop and John Norton, 1610.

Camden, William. *Camden's Britannia, newly translated into English: with large additions and improvements.* London: printed by F. Collins, for A. Swalle and A. & J. Churchil, 1695.

Campbell, J. L., and Derick Thomson. *Edward Lhuyd in the Scottish Highlands 1699–1700.* Oxford: Clarendon Press, 1963.

Carew, Richard. *The survey of Cornwall.* London: Printed by S. S. for John Jaggard, 1602.

A catalogue of the subscribers names to the English Atlas, *now printing at the* Theater *in* Oxford. London: s.n., 1680? Bod MS Wood 658, item 791.

Childrey, Joshua. *Britannia Baconica, or, The natural rarities of England, Scotland, and Wales.* London: printed for the author, and are to be sold by H. E., 1660.

Coles, William. *The art of simpling.* London: printed by J. G. for Nath: Brook, 1656.

Darwin, Charles. *The Variation of Animals and Plants Under Domestication.* 2 vols. London: John Murray, 1868.

Digby, Kenelm. *Observations upon Religio medici.* London: printed by R. C. for Lawrence Chapman and Daniel Frere, 1643.

Dryden, John. *The Poems of John Dryden: Volume One, 1649–1681.* Ed. Paul Hammond. Abingdon: Routledge, 2014.

Dugdale, William. *The antiquities of Warwickshire illustrated.* London: printed by Thomas Warren, 1656.

Dunton, John. *Athenian Mercury.* 19 vols. London: John Dunton, 1691–1697.

Dury, John. *The reformed librarie-keeper with a supplement to the reformed-school.* London: printed by William Du-Gard, and are to bee sold by Rob. LIttleberrie, 1650.

Earle, John. *Micro-cosmographie: or a piece of the world discovered.* 9th ed. London: printed by Thomas Ratcliff and Thomas Daniel for Philip Chetwind, 1669.

Enderbie, Percy. *Cambria triumphans, or, Brittain in its perfect lustre shewing the origen and antiquity of that illustrious nation.* London: printed for Andrew Crooke, 1661.

Evelyn, John. *Diary and Correspondence of John Evelyn, F.R.S.* Ed. William Bray. 4 vols. New ed. London: Henry Colburn, 1850–54.

Evelyn, John. *Elysium Britannicum, or The Royal Gardens.* Ed. John E. Ingram. Philadelphia: University of Pennsylvania Press, 2001.

Evelyn, John. "Of Manuscripts: An Unfinished Treatise." In *Memoirs Illustrative of the Life and Writings of John Evelyn, Esq. F.R.S.,* ed. William Bray. Vol. 2, pt. 1, , 333–348. London: Henry Colburn, Conduit Street, 1818.

Evelyn, John. *Sylva, or, A discourse of forest-trees.* 4 eds. 1st and 2nd eds., London: printed by Jo. Martyn and Ja. Allestry, 1664 and 1670. 3rd ed., London: printed for John Martyn, 1679. 4th ed., London: Printed for Robert Scott, Richard Chiswell, George Sawbridge, and Benj. Tooke, 1706.

Fiennes, Celia. *The Journeys of Celia Fiennes.* Ed. Christopher Morris. Foreword by G. M. Trevelyan. London: Cresset Press, 1947.

For Printing the Manuscripts *of Dr.* WILLIAM HOWELL, *late Chancellour of* Lincoln, *being the following Parts of his* Institution of General History. London: s.n., 1685. Bod MS Wood 658, item 786*.

Goedaert, Jan. *Johannes Goedartius de insectis, in methodum redactus: cum notularum additione. Operâ M. Lister.* London: printed by R. E. for S. Smith, 1685.

Graham, Timothy, and Andrew G. Watson, eds. *The Recovery of the Past in Early Elizabethan England: Documents by John Bale and John Joscelyn from the Circle of Matthew Parker.* Cambridge: Cambridge Bibliographical Society, 1998.

Grattius, Faliscus. *Cynegeticon or, A poem of hunting.* Trans. Christopher Wase. London: printed for Charles Adams, 1654.

Grew, Nehemiah. *Whereas a book entituled, Musaeum Regalis Societatis.* London: s.n., 1680. Bod MS Wood 658, item 794.

Guidott, Thomas. *Propositions touching printing a book entituled, De thermis Britannicis.* London: s.n., 1686?

Gunther, R. T. *Early Science in Oxford.* 14 vols. Oxford: Printed for the subscribers, 1920–1945.

Hartlib, Samuel. *Considerations tending to the happy accomplishment of Englands reformation in church and state.* London: s.n., 1647.

Hartlib, Samuel. *A faithfull and seasonable advice, or, The necessity of a correspondencie for the advancement of the Protestant cause.* London: Printed by John Hammond, 1643.

Hartlib, Samuel. *A further discoverie of the office of publick address for accomodations.* London: s.n., 1648.

Hartlib, Samuel. *The Reformed Virginian Silk-Worm.* London: printed by John Streater for Giles Calvert, 1655.

Hartlib, Samuel, and Gabriel Plattes. *A description of the famous kingdome of Macaria.* London: printed for Francis Constable, 1641.

Hearne, Thomas. *Remarks and Collections of Thomas Hearne.* Vol. 1. Ed. C. E. Doble. Oxford: Oxford Historical Society, 1885.

Heylyn, Peter. *Aerius redivivus: or, the history of the Presbyterians.* London: Printed for Jo. Crosley and sold by Tho. Basset and Chr. Wilkinson, 1670.

Hooke, Robert. *The Diary of Robert Hooke, M.A., M.D., F.R.S., 1672–1680.* Ed. Henry W. Robinson and Walter Adams. London: Taylor & Francis, 1935.

Hooke, Robert. *The posthumous works of Robert Hooke.* Ed. Richard Waller. London: printed by Sam. Smith and Benj. Walford, 1705.

Houghton, John. *A Collection for Improvement of Husbandry and Trade.* 20 vols. London: Published by Randal Taylor, S. Smith, F. Saunders, and W. Hensmen, 1692–1703. Bod Hope Folios 22–23.

Jones, Inigo. *The most notable antiquity of Great Britain vulgarly called Stone-Heng on Salisbury plain.* London: James Flesher for Daniel Pakeman and Laurence Chapman, 1655.

Josten, C. H., ed. *Elias Ashmole, 1617–1692: His Autobiographical and Historical Notes, His Correspondence, and Other Contemporary Sources Relating to His Life and Work.* Oxford: Clarendon Press, 1966.

Keepe, Henry. *By HENRY KEEPE, formerly of New-Inn-Hall in the University of Oxford, gentleman-commoner, and now of the Inner-Temple London, Esq;. Having in the year 1681. published a small treatise, by way of Essay to a more compleat history of Westminster-Abbey.* S.l.: s.i., 1683. Bod MS Wood 658, item 800.

Lambarde, William. *A perambulation of Kent: conteining the description, hystorie, and customes of that shyre.* London: by Henrie Middleton for Ralphe Newberie, 1576.

Leland, John. *The Itinerary of John Leland the Antiquary.* Ed. Thomas Hearne. 9 vols. Oxford: printed at the Theater for Thomas Hearne, 1710–1712.

Lhuyd, Edward. *A compleat translation of the Welsh preface to Mr. Lhuyd's Glossography, or Archeologia Britannica.* London?: s.n., 1710?

Lhuyd, Edward. *A Design of a British Dictionary, Historical and Geographical; With an Essay, Entituled, Archaeologia Britannica: and a Natural History of Wales.* Oxford: s.n., 1695.

Lhuyd, Edward. *Archaeologia Britannica.* Vol. 1, *Glossography.* Oxford: Printed at the Theater for the Author, 1707.

Lhuyd, Edward. *Archaeologia Britannica: an account of the languages, histories and customs of the original inhabitants of Great Britain.* Intro. Anne O'Sullivan and William O'Sullivan. Shannon: Irish University Press, 1971.

Lhuyd, Edward. *Lithophylacii Britannici ichnographia.* London: Ex officina M.C., 1699.

Lhuyd, Edward. *Parochialia: Being a Summary of Answers to "Parochial queries in order to a geographical dictionary, etc., of Wales."* Ed. Rupert H. Morris. 3 vols. London: Cambrian Archaeological Association, 1909–1911.

Lhuyd, Edward. *Parochial Queries in Order to a Geographical Dictionary, a Natural History &c. of Wales.* Oxford?: s.n., 1697.

Magna Britannia et Hibernia, antiqua & nova. 6 vols. Vols. 1–2, London: Printed by Eliz. Nutt, and sold by M. Nutt and J. Morphew, 1720. Vols. 3–6, London: Printed by E. & R. Nutt, and sold by Thomas Cox, 1724–1731. Special Collections, University of Iowa.

McKenzie, Donald F., and Maureen Bell. *A Chronology and Calendar of Documents Relating to the London Book Trade, 1641–1700.* 3 vols. Oxford: Oxford University Press, 2005.

Molyneux, William. *The case of Ireland's being bound by acts of parliament in England, stated.* Dublin: printed by Joseph Ray, 1698.

Molyneux, William. *Whereas there is an accurate account and description of Ireland designed to be made publick in the English Atlas undertaken by Moses Pitt of London.* Dublin: s.n., 1682.

Morison, Robert. *Plantarum historiae universalis Oxoniensis pars tertia.* Oxford: at the Sheldonian Theater, 1699.

Naudé, Gabriel. *Instructions concerning erecting of a library.* Trans. John Evelyn. London: Printed for G. Bedle, T. Collins, and J. Crook, 1661.

Norfolk, Henry Howard, 6th Duke of. *Bibliotheca Norfolciana..* London: printed by Ric. Chiswel by permission of the Royal Society, 1681.

Ogilby, John. *Britannia, volume the first: or, an illustration of the Kingdom of England and dominion of Wales.* London: printed by the author, 1675.

Oldenburg, Henry. *Correspondence of Henry Oldenburg.* Ed. and trans. A. Rupert Hall and Marie Boas Hall. 13 vols. Madison: University of Wisconsin Press, 1965–1986.

Parker, Matthew. "A Preface into the Byble." In *The Holie Bible.* Trans. overseen by Matthew Parker. London: by Richard Iugge, 1568.

Parkinson, John. *Theatrum botanicum.* London: printed by Tho. Cotes, 1640.

Pepys, Samuel. *The Diary of Samuel Pepys.* 11 vols. Ed. Robert Latham and William Matthews. Berkeley: University of California Press, 1970–1983.

Petty, William. *The advice of W. P. to Mr. Hartlib, For the advancement of learning.* London: s.n., 1648.

Pitt, Moses. *Proposals for printing a new atlas.* London: s.n., 1678.

Plot, Robert. *Enquiries to be propounded to the most sincere and intelligent in the cities of London and Westminster, in order to their history of nature, arts, and antiquities.* Oxford: s.n., 1693? Bod Don.a.3, 6–7.

Plot, Robert. *The natural history of Oxford-shire, being an essay toward the natural history of England.* Oxford: Printed at the Theater, 1677.

Plot, Robert. *The natural history of Stafford-shire*. Oxford: printed at the Theater, 1686.

Plot, Robert. *Quaer's to be propounded to the most ingenious of each county in my travels through England*. Oxford: s.n., 1674?

A Proposal about printing a Treatise of algebra, historical and practical. Oxford?: s.n., 1683.

Proposals for printing a book entituled, The history and antiquities of Hertfordshire. Written by Sir Henry Chauncy, Kt, Serjeant at law. London: s.n., 1700. Bod MS Wood 658, item 812.

Proposals for printing of Holwell's book of dialing. London: s.n., 1684. Bod MS Wood 658, item 789.

Proposals for printing Monumenta Britannica, written by Mr. John Aubrey. London: s.n., 1693. Bod MS Wood 658, item 780.

Proposals for the printing of a book of William Leybourn's. London: Printed for John Dunton . . . , 1693.

Ray, John. *A collection of English words, not generally used*. London: printed by H. Bruges for Tho. Burrell, 1674.

Ray, John. *The Correspondence of John Ray*. Ed. E. Lankester. London: Ray Society, 1848.

Ray, John. *Dictionariolum trilingue*. London: printed by Andrew Clark for Thomas Burrel, 1675.

Ray, John. *The Further Correspondence of John Ray*. Ed. R. T. Gunther. London: Ray Society, 1928.

Ray, John. *Miscellaneous discourses concerning the dissolution and changes of the world*. London: printed for Samuel Smith, 1692.

Ray, John. *Philosophical letters between the late learned Mr. Ray and several of his ingenious correspondents, Natives and Foreigners*. London: printed by William and John Innys, 1718.

Ray, John. *Synopsis methodica avium et piscium*. London: for William Innys, 1713.

Ray, John. *Synopsis methodica stirpium Britannicum*. 2nd ed. London: for S. Smith and B. Walford, 1696.

Ray, John. The *wisdom of God manifested in the works of the creation*. London: printed for Samuel Smith, 1691.

Royal Society. *Philosophical transactions*. London, 1665–1678; 1683–1775.

Salmon, William. *Proposals, for printing a compleat English herbal. Written by William Salmon, M.D.* London: s.n., 1710? Bod MS Ashmole 1819, Item 13.

Sammes, Aylett. *Britannia antiqua illustrata*. London: printed by Tho. Roycroft, for the author, 1676.

Sammes, Aylett. *Proposals concerning the printing of a* Chronological History *of England*. London: s.n., 1677. Bod MS Wood 658, item 801

Sibbald, Robert. *Advertisement*. Edinburgh: printed by John Reid, 1682.

Speed, John. *The theatre of the empire of Great Britaine*. London: By William Hall, to be sold by John Sudbury and Georg Humble, 1611.

Speed, John. *England, Wales, Scotland and Ireland described and abridged*. London: J. Dawson to be sold by Georg Humble, 1627.

Shadwell, Thomas. *The virtuoso*. London: printed by T. N. for Henry Herringman, 1676.

Sharpe, Richard, ed. *Roderick O'Flaherty's Letters, 1696–1709*. Dublin: Royal Irish Academy, 2013.

Sprat, Thomas. *The history of the Royal-Society of London, for the improving of natural knowledge*. London: printed by T. R. for J. Martyn, 1667.

Swall, Abel. *Proposals for printing by subscription, Cambden's Britannia, English*. London: s.n., 1693?

Taylor, John. *The carriers cosmographie*. London: Printed by A. G., 1637.

There is a very large Historie of the Church. London: s.n., 1651. Bod MS Wood 658, item 799.

Thimelthorpe, C. *A short inuentory of certayne idle Inuentions*. London: by Thomas Marsh, 1581.

The translation of Homers Works *into English verse being undertaken by* John Ogilby. London: s.n., 1660. Bod MS Wood 658, item 790.

Turner, William. *A compleat history of the most remarkable providences, both of judgment and mercy, which have hapned in this present age*. London: printed for John Dunton, 1697.

University of Oxford. *An advertisement, concerning the printing and publishing of ancient and other usefull books*. Oxford: s.n., 1680. Bod MS Wood 658, item 775.

Wallis, John. *A treatise of algebra, both historical and practical*. London: printed by John Playford, for Richard Davies, 1685.

Wantner, Abel. *To the nobility, clergy, and gentry of the City an County of Gloucester*. London?: s.n., 1685?

Willughby, Francis and John Ray. *De historia piscium* Oxford: at the Sheldonian Theater, 1686. Royal Society copy.

Wood, Anthony à. *Life and Times of Anthony Wood*. 5 vols. Ed. A. Clark. Oxford: Oxford Historical Society, 1891–1900.

Woodward, John. *An essay toward a natural history of the earth . . . with an account of the universal deluge*. London: Printed for Ric. Wilkin, 1695.

Woolley, Hannah. *The accomplish'd lady's delight in preserving, physic, beautifying and cookery*. London: printed for B. Harris, 1675.

Wotton, William. *Reflections upon ancient and modern learning*. London: printed by J. Leake, for Peter Buck, 1697.

SECONDARY SOURCES

Note: Web sites are listed only in the notes.

Addison, Sir William. *The Old Roads of England*. London: B. T. Batsford, 1980.

Albert, William. *The Turnpike Road System in England, 1663–1840*. Cambridge: Cambridge University Press, 1972.

Anderson, Benedict. *Imagined Communities: Reflections on the Origin and Spread of Nationalism*. Rev. ed. London: Verso, 1991.

Andersen, Jennifer, and Elizabeth Sauer. *Books and Readers in Early Modern England: Material Studies*. Philadelphia: University of Pennsylvania Press, 2001.

Andrews, J. H. "Science and Cartography in the Ireland of William and Samuel Molyneux." *Proceedings of the Royal Irish Academy Section C: Archaeology, Celtic Studies, History, Linguistics, Literature* 80C (1980): 231–250.

"Archival Knowledge Cultures in Europe, 1400–1900." Special issue of *Archival Science* 3 (2010): 191–343.

Armitage, David. "Greater Britain: A Useful Category of Historical Analysis?" *American Historical Review* 104 (1999): 427–445.

Armitage, David. *The Ideological Origins of the British Empire*. Cambridge: Cambridge University Press, 2000.

Ashworth, William B., Jr. "The Habsburg Circle." In *Patronage and Institutions: Science, Technology, and Medicine at the European Court, 1500–1700*, ed. Bruce Moran, 137–167. Rochester: Boydell Press, 1991.

Aston, Margaret. "English Ruins and English History: The Dissolution and the Sense of the Past." *Journal of the Warburg and Courtauld Institutes* 36 (1973): 231–255.

Baldwin, Geoff. "The 'Public' as a Rhetorical Community in Early Modern England." In *Communities in Early Modern England: Networks, Place, Rhetoric*, ed. Alexandra Shepard and Phil Withington, 199–215. Manchester: Manchester University Press, 2000.

Barnard, T. C. "British History and Irish History." In *The New British History: Founding a Modern State, 1603–1715*, ed. Glenn Burgess, 201–237. London: I. B. Tauris, 1999.

Baron, Sabrina Alcorn, Elizabeth Walsh, and Susan Scola, eds. *The Reader Revealed*. Washington, D.C.: Folger Shakespeare Library, 2001.

Baron, Sabrina Alcorn, Eric N. Lindquist, and Eleanor F. Shevlin, eds. *Agent of Change: Print Culture Studies after Elizabeth L. Eisenstein*. Amherst: University of Massachusetts Press, 2007.

Barrera-Osorio, Antonio. *Experiencing Nature: The Spanish American Empire and the Early Scientific Revolution*. Austin: University of Texas Press, 2006.

Barrera-Osorio, Antonio. "Local Herbs, Global Medicines: Commerce, Knowledge, and Commodities in Spanish America." In *Merchants and Marvels: Commerce, Science, and Art in Early Modern Europe*, ed. Pamela H. Smith and Paula Findlen, 163–181. New York: Routledge, 2002.

Beal, Peter. *In Praise of Scribes: Manuscripts and Their Makers in Seventeenth-Century England*. Oxford: Clarendon Press, 1998.

Beal, Peter. *Index of English Literary Manuscripts*. 2 vols. London: Mansell, 1980–1997.

Beavan, Ian, and Warren McDougall. "The Scottish Book Trade." In *The Cambridge History of the Book in Britain,* vol. 5, ed. Michael F. Suarez, S.J. and Michael L. Turner, 353–365. Cambridge: Cambridge University Press, 2009.

Bennett, James, ed. *London's Leonardo: The Life and Work of Robert Hooke*. Oxford: Oxford University Press, 2003.

Bennett, Kate. "Editing Aubrey." In *Ma(r)king the Text: The Presentation of Meaning on the Literary Page*, ed. Joe Bray, Miriam Handley, and Anne C. Henry. Aldershot: Ashgate, 2000.

Bennett, Kate. "John Aubrey and the Printed Book." *Huntington Library Quarterly* 76 (2013): 393–411.

Bennett, Kate. "John Aubrey's Collections and the Early Modern Museum." *Bodleian Library Record* 17 (2001): 213–245.

Bennett, Kate." John Aubrey's Oxfordshire Collections: An Edition of Aubrey's Annotations to His Presentation Copy of Robert Plot's *Natural History of Oxford-shire*, Bodleian Library Ashmole 1722." *Oxoniensia* 64 (2000): 59–86.

Bennett, Kate. "Materials Towards a Critical Edition of John Aubrey's *Brief Lives*." D.Phil. thesis, University of Oxford, 1993.

Benson, Charles. "The Irish Trade." In *The Cambridge History of the Book in Britain*, vol. 5, ed. Michael F. Suarez, S.J. and Michael L. Turner, 366–382. Cambridge: Cambridge University Press, 2009.

Berry, Helen M. *Gender, Society, and Print Culture in Late Stuart England: The Cultural World of the Athenian Mercury*. Aldershot: Ashgate, 2003.

Biagioli, Mario. "From Book Censorship to Academic Peer Review." *Emergences: Journal for the Study of Media and Composite Cultures* 12 (2002): 11–45.

Biagioli, Mario. *Galileo, Courtier: The Practice of Science in the Culture of Absolutism*. Chicago: University of Chicago Press, 1993.

Biagioli, Mario. *Galileo's Instruments of Credit: Telescopes, Images, Secrecy*. Chicago: University of Chicago Press, 2006.

Blair, Ann. "Annotating and Indexing Natural Philosophy." In *Books and the Sciences in History*, ed. Marina Frasca-Spada and Nicholas Jardine, 69–89. Cambridge: Cambridge University Press, 2000.

Blair, Ann. "Errata Lists and the Reader as Corrector." In *Agent of Change: Print Culture Studies After Elizabeth L. Eisenstein*. Ed. Sabrina Alcorn Baron, Eric N. Lindquist, and Eleanor F. Shevlin, 21–41. Amherst: University of Massachusetts Press, 2007.

Blair, Ann. "Humanist Methods in Natural Philosophy: The Commonplace Book." *Journal of the History of Ideas* 53 (1992): 541–551.

Blair, Ann. "Note Taking as an Art of Transmission." *Critical Inquiry* 51 (2004): 85–107.

Blair, Ann. "Scientific Readers: An Early Modernist's Perspective." *Isis* 95 (2004): 420–431.

Blair, Ann. *Too Much to Know: Managing Scholarly Information Before the Modern Age*. New Haven, Conn.: Yale University Press, 2010.

Bleichmar, Daniela. "The Geography of Observation: Distance and Visibility in Eighteenth-Century Botanical Travel." In *Histories of Scientific Observation*, ed. Lorraine Daston and Elizabeth Lunbeck, 373–395. Chicago: University of Chicago Press, 2011.

Bots, Hans. *Commercium Litterarium, 1600–1750: La Communication dans la Republique des Lettres*. Amsterdam: APA-Holland University Press, 1994.

Bradshaw, Brendan, and Peter Roberts, eds. *British Consciousness and Identity: The Making of Britain, 1533–1707*. Cambridge: Cambridge University Press, 1998.

Bray, Joe, Miriam Handley, and Anne C. Henry, eds. *Ma(r)king the Text: The Presentation of Meaning on the Literary Page*. Aldershot: Ashgate, 2000.

Brayman Hackel, Heidi. *Reading Material in Early Modern England: Print, Gender, and Literacy*. Cambridge: Cambridge University Press, 2005.

Broadway, Jan. *"No Historie so Meete": Gentry Culture and the Development of Local History in Elizabethan and Early Stuart England*. Manchester: Manchester University Press, 2006.

Broman, Thomas C. "The Habermasian Public Sphere and 'Science in the Enlightenment.'" *History of Science* 36 (1998): 123–149.

Browne, Janet. *Charles Darwin: The Power of Place*. Princeton, N.J.: Princeton University Press, 2002.

Buchanan-Brown, John. "The Books Presented to the Royal Society by John Aubrey, FRS." *Notes and Records of the Royal Society of London* 28 (1974): 167–193.

Buck, Peter. "Seventeenth-Century Political Arithmetic: Civil Strife and Vital Statistics." *Isis* 68 (1977): 67–84.

Burgess, Glenn, ed. *The New British History: Founding a Modern State, 1603–1715*. London: I. B. Tauris, 1999.

Burke, Peter. *A Social History of Knowledge: From Gutenberg to Diderot*. Cambridge: Polity Press, 2000.

Burns, Kathryn. *Into the Archive: Writing and Power in Colonial Peru*. Durham, N.C.: Duke University Press, 2010.

Burton, Antoinette, ed. *Archive Stories: Facts, Fictions, and the Writing of History*. Durham, N.C.: Duke University Press, 2005.

Cameron, W. J. "A Late Seventeenth-Century Scriptorium." *Renaissance and Modern Studies* 7 (1963): 25–52.

Campbell, Mary Baine. *Wonder and Science: Imagining Worlds in Early Modern Europe*. Ithaca, N.Y.: Cornell University Press, 1999.

Cañizares-Esguerra, Jorge. *How to Write the History of the New World: Histories, Epistemologies, and Identities in the Eighteenth-Century Atlantic World.* Stanford, Calif.: Stanford University Press, 2001.

Canny, Nicholas. "Irish Resistance to Empire? 1641, 1690, and 1798." In *An Imperial State at War: Britain from 1689–1815,* ed. Lawrence Stone, 290–302. New York: Routledge, 1994.

Carey, Daniel. "Compiling Nature's History: Travellers and Travel Narratives in the Early Royal Society." *Annals of Science* 54 (1997): 269–292.

Carter, Harry. *A History of the Oxford University Press.* Vol. 1. Oxford: Clarendon Press, 1975.

Cavallo, Guglielmo, and Roger Chartier, eds. *A History of Reading in the West.* Amherst: University of Massachusetts Press, 1997.

Chambers, Douglas. *The Reinvention of the World: English Writing 1650–1750.* London: Arnold, 1996.

Chandler, James, Arnold I. Davidson, and Adrian Johns, eds. "Arts of Transmission." *Critical Inquiry* 31 (2004): 1–255.

Chartier, Roger. *Cultural Uses of Print in Early Modern France.* Trans. Lydia G. Cochrane. Princeton, N.J.: Princeton University Press, 1987.

Chartier, Roger. *The Order of Books.* Trans. Lydia G. Cochrane. Stanford, Calif.: Stanford University Press, 1994.

Chico, Tita. "Gimcrack's Legacy: Sex, Wealth, and the Theater of Experimental Philosophy." *Comparative Drama* 42 (2008): 29–49.

Clapp, Sarah L. C. "The Beginnings of Subscription Publication in the Seventeenth Century." *Modern Philology* 29 (1931): 199–224.

Clapp, Sarah L. C. "The Subscription Enterprises of John Ogilby and Richard Blome." *Modern Philology* 30 (1933): 365–379.

Clark, Meredith Donaldson. "'Now Through You Made Public for Everyone': John Ogilby's *Britannia* (1675), the 1598 Peutinger Map Facsimile and the Shaping of Public Space." In *Making Space Public in Early Modern Europe: Performance, Geography, Privacy,* ed. Angela Vanhaelen and Joseph P. Ward, 127–150. New York: Routledge, 2013.

Claydon, Tony. *Europe and the Making of England, 1660–1760.* New York: Cambridge University Press, 2007.

Clucas, Stephan. "In Search of 'The True Logick': Methodological Eclecticism Among the 'Baconian Reformers.'" In *Samuel Hartlib and Universal Reformation: Studies in Intellectual Communication,* ed. Mark Greengrass, Michael Leslie, and Timothy Raylor, 51–74. Cambridge: Cambridge University Press, 1994.

Clucas, Stephen. "Samuel Hartlib's 'Ephemerides,' 1635–1659, and the Pursuit of Scientific and Philosophical Manuscripts: The Religious Ethos of an Intelligencer." *Seventeenth Century* 6 (1991): 33–55.

Colley, Linda. "Britishness and Otherness: An Argument." *Journal of British Studies* 31 (1992): 309–329.

Colley, Linda. *Britons: Forging the Nation 1707–1837.* New Haven, Conn.: Yale University Press, 1992.

Colley, Linda. *Captives: Britain, Empire, and the World, 1600–1850.* New York: Anchor Books, 2004.

Cook, Harold J. *Matters of Exchange: Commerce, Medicine, and Science in the Dutch Golden Age.* New Haven, Conn.: Yale University Press, 2007.

Cooper, Alix. *Inventing the Indigenous: Local Knowledge and Natural History in Early Modern Europe.* Cambridge: Cambridge University Press, 2007.

Cooper, Alix. "Latin Words, Vernacular Worlds: Language, Nature, and the 'Indigenous' in Early Modern Europe." *East Asian Science, Technology, and Medicine* 26 (2007): 17–39.

Cope, Jackson I. "Evelyn, Boyle, and Dr. Wilkinson's 'Mathematico-Chymico-Mechanical School.'" *Isis* 50 (1959): 30–32.

Cormack, Lesley B. *Charting an Empire: Geography at the English Universities, 1580–1620.* Chicago: University of Chicago Press, 1997.

Cormack, Lesley B. "'Good Fences Make Good Neighbors': Geography as Self-Definition in Early Modern England." *Isis* 82 (1991): 639–661.

Cowan, Brian. *The Social Life of Coffee: The Emergence of the British Coffeehouse.* New Haven, Conn.: Yale University Press, 2005.

Cowan, Brian. "What Was Masculine about the Public Sphere? Gender and the Coffeehouse Milieu in Post-Restoration England." *History Workshop Journal* 51 (2001): 127–157.

Cram, David. "Edward Lhuyd's *Archaeologia Britannica:* Method and Madness in Early Modern Comparative Philology." *Welsh Historical Review* 25 (2010): 75–96.

Dane, Joseph A. *The Myth of Print Culture: Essays on Evidence, Textuality, and Bibliographical Method.* Toronto: University of Toronto Press, 2003.

Darley, Gillian. *John Evelyn: A Biography.* New Haven, Conn.: Yale University Press, 2006.

Daston, Lorraine. "The Ideal and Reality of the Republic of Letters in the Enlightenment." *Science in Context* 4 (1991): 367–386.

Daston, Lorraine. "Marvelous Facts and Miraculous Evidence in Early Modern Europe." *Critical Inquiry* 18 (1991): 93–124.

Daston, Lorraine, and Katharine Park. *Wonders and the Order of Nature, 1150–1750.* New York: Zone Books, 1998.

Daston, Lorraine, and Peter Galison. *Objectivity.* Brooklyn: Zone Books, 2007.

Daston, Lorraine, and Elizabeth Lunbeck, eds. *Histories of Scientific Observation.* Chicago: University of Chicago Press, 2011.

Daston, Lorraine, and Otto H. Sibum, eds. Special issue on "Scientific Personae and their Histories." *Science in Context* 16 (2003): 1–269.

Daybell, James. *The Material Letter in Early Modern England: Manuscript Letters and the Culture and Practices of Letter-Writing, 1512–1635.* Basingstoke, UK: Palgrave-Macmillan, 2012.

Dear, Peter. "Totius in Verba: Rhetoric and Authority in the Early Royal Society." *Isis* 76 (1985): 144–161.

Delbourgo, James. "Collecting Hans Sloane." In *From Books to Bezoars: Sir Hans Sloane and His Collections,* ed. Alison Walker, Arthur MacGregor, and Michael Hunter, 9–23. London: British Library, 2012.

Delbourgo, James. "Listing People." *Isis* 103 (2012): 735–742.

Derrida, Jacques. *Archive Fever: A Freudian Impression.* Trans. Eric Prenowitz. Chicago: University of Chicago Press, 1998.

DiMeo, Michelle. "Openness vs. Secrecy in the Hartlib Circle: Revisiting 'Democratic Baconianism' in Interregnum England." In *Secrets and Knowledge in Medicine and Science, 1500–1800,* ed. Elaine Leong and Alisha Rankin, 105–121. Farnham, Surrey: Ashgate, 2011.

Dolan, Francis. *True Relations: Reading, Literature, and Evidence in Seventeenth-Century England.* Philadelphia: University of Pennsylvania Press, 2013.

Drayton, Richard. *Nature's Government: Science, Imperial Britain, and the 'Improvement' of the World.* New Haven, Conn.: Yale University Press, 2000.

Eamon, William. "Court, Academy, and Printing House: Patronage and Scientific Careers in Late Renaissance Italy." In *Patronage and Institutions: Science, Technology, and Medicine at the European Court, 1500–1700,* ed. Bruce Moran, 25–50. Rochester: Boydell Press, 1991.

Eamon, William. *Science and the Secrets of Nature: Books of Secrets in Medieval and Early Modern Culture*. Princeton, N.J.: Princeton University Press, 1994.

Eddy, Matthew. *The Language of Minerology: John Walker, Chemistry, and the Edinburgh Medical School, 1750–1800*. Farnham: Ashgate, 2008.

Edgerton, David. *The Shock of the Old: Technology and Global History Since 1900*. London: Profile Books, 2006.

Eisenstein, Elizabeth. "A Conversation with Elizabeth L. Eisenstein." In *Agent of Change: Print Culture Studies after Elizabeth L. Eisenstein*, ed. Sabrina Alcorn Baron, Eric N. Lindquist, and Eleanor F. Shevlin, 409–420. Amherst and Boston: University of Massachusetts Press, 2007.

Eisenstein, Elizabeth. *Divine Art, Infernal Machine: The Reception of Printing in the West from First Impressions to the Sense of an Ending*. Philadelphia: University of Pennsylvania Press, 2012.

Eisenstein, Elizabeth. *The Printing Revolution in Early Modern Europe*. Cambridge: Cambridge University Press, 1979.

Eisenstein, Elizabeth. "An Unacknowledged Revolution Revisited." *American Historical Review* 107 (2002): 87–105.

Ellis, Richard. "Some Incidents in the Life of Edward Lhuyd." In *Early Science in Oxford*, vol. 14, ed. Robert Gunther, 1–51. Oxford: Printed for the Subscribers, 1945.

Ellis, Steven G., and Sarah Barber, eds. *Conquest and Union: Fashioning a British State, 1485–1725*. London: Longman, 1995.

Elton, Geoffrey. *The English*. Oxford: Blackwell, 1992.

Emery, F. V. "Edward Lhuyd and Some of His Glamorgan Correspondents." *Transactions of the Honourable Society of Cymmrodorion*, Session 1965: 59–114.

Emery, F. V. *Edward Lhuyd, F.R.S., 1660–1709*. Caerdydd: Gwasg Prifysgol Cymru, 1971.

Emery, F. V. "English Regional Studies from Aubrey to Defoe." *Geographical Journal* 124 (1958): 315–325.

Emery, F. V. "A Map of Edward Lhuyd's *Parochial Queries in Order to a Geographical Dictionary, &c. of Wales* (1696)." *Transactions of the Honourable Society of Cymmrodorion*, Session 1958: 41–53.

Emery, F. V. "A New Reply to Lhuyd's *Parochial Queries* (1696): Puncheston, Pembrokeshire." *National Library of Wales Journal* 10 (1958): 395–402.

Epstein, S. R., and Maarten Prak, eds. *Guilds, Innovation, and the European Economy, 1400–1800*. Cambridge: Cambridge University Press, 2008.

Ezell, Margaret J. M. *Social Authorship and the Advent of Print*. Baltimore, Md.: Johns Hopkins University Press, 1999.

Feather, John. *A History of British Publishing*. 2nd ed. London: Routledge, 2006.

Feingold, Mordechai. "Of Records and Grandeur: The Archive of the Royal Society." In *The Archives of the Scientific Revolution: The Formation and Exchange of Ideas in Seventeenth Century Europe*, ed. Michael Hunter, 171–184. Woodbridge: Boydell Press, 1998.

Feola, Vittoria, and Scott Mandelbrote. "The Learned Press: Geography, Science, and Mathematics." In *History of Oxford University Press, vol. 1: Beginnings to 1780*, ed. Ian Gadd, 309–349. Oxford: Oxford University Press, 2013.

Findlen, Paula. "Economy of Scientific Exchange in Early Modern Italy." In *Patronage and Institutions: Science, Technology, and Medicine at the European Court, 1500–1700*, ed. Bruce Moran, 5–24. Rochester: Boydell Press, 1991.

Findlen, Paula. *Possessing Nature: Museums, Collecting, and Scientific Culture in Early Modern Italy*. Berkeley: University of California Press, 1994.

Findlen, Paula. "Scientific Spectacle in Baroque Rome: Athanasius Kircher and the Roman College Museum." In *Jesuit Science and the Republic of Letters*, ed. Mordechai Feingold, 225–284. Cambridge, Mass.: MIT Press, 2003.

Fox, Adam. "Custom, Memory and the Authority of Writing." In *The Experience of Authority in Early Modern England*, ed. Paul Griffiths, Adam Fox, and Steve Hindle, 89–116. London: Macmillan, 1996.

Fox, Adam. *Oral and Literate Culture in Early Modern England, 1500–1700*. Oxford: Clarendon Press, 2000.

Fox, Adam. "Printed Questionnaires, Research Networks and the Discovery of the British Isles, 1650–1800." *Historical Journal* 53 (2010): 593–621.

Fox, Adam. "Sir William Petty, Ireland, and the Making of a Political Economist, 1653–87." *Economic History Review* 62 (2009): 288–404.

Fox, Adam, and Daniel R. Woolf, eds. *The Spoken Word: Oral Culture in Britain, 1500–1850*. Manchester: Manchester University Press, 2002.

Frank, Robert G., Jr. "John Aubrey, F.R.S., John Lydall, and Science at Commonwealth Oxford." *Notes and Records of the Royal Society of London* 27 (1973): 193–217.

Frasca-Spada, Marina, and Nicholas Jardine, eds. *Books and the Sciences in History*. Cambridge: Cambridge University Press, 2000.

Fyfe, Aileen, and Bernard Lightman, eds. *Science in the Marketplace: Nineteenth-Century Sites and Experiences*. Chicago: University of Chicago Press, 2007.

Gadd, Ian, ed. *History of Oxford University Press, vol. 1: Beginnings to 1780*. Oxford: Oxford University Press, 2013.

Gadd, Ian, and Alexandra Gillespie, eds. *John Stow (1525–1605) and the Making of the English Past*. London: British Library, 2004.

Gaskell, Philip. *A New Introduction to Bibliography*. Newcastle, Del.: Oak Knoll Press, 1995.

Gerhardt, Ernst. "'No quyckar merchaundyce than library bokes': John Bale's Commodification of Manuscript Culture." *Renaissance Quarterly* 55 (2007): 408–433.

Gerhold, Dorian. "Packhorses and Wheeled Vehicles in England, 1550–1800." In *Road Transport in the Horse-Drawn Era*, ed. Dorian Gerhold, 139–164. Aldershot: Scolar Press, 1996.

Gerhold, Dorian, ed. *Road Transport in the Horse-Drawn Era*. Aldershot: Scolar Press, 1996.

Ghobrial, John-Paul. *The Whispers of Cities: Information Flows in Istanbul, London, and Paris in the Age of William Trumbull*. Oxford: Oxford University Press, 2013.

Gillespie, Alexandra. "Stow's 'Owlde' Manuscripts of London Chronicles." In *John Stow (1525–1605) and the Making of the English Past*, ed. Ian Gadd and Alexandra Gillespie, 57–67. London: British Library, 2004.

Gingerich, Owen. "An Early Tradition of an Extended Errata List for Copernicus's 'De Revolutionibus.'" *Journal for the History of Astronomy* 12 (1981): 47–52.

Gitelman, Lisa. *Paper Knowledge: Toward a Media History of Documents*. Durham, N.C.: Duke University Press, 2014.

Goldgar, Anne. *Impolite Learning: Conduct and Community in the Republic of Letters, 1680–1750*. New Haven, Conn.: Yale University Press, 1995.

Goldgar, Anne, and Robert I. Frost. *Institutional Culture in Early Modern Society*. Leiden: Brill, 2004.

Gordon, Andrew. "Overseeing and Overlooking: John Stow and the Surveying of the City." In *John Stow (1525–1605) and the Making of the English Past*, ed. Ian Gadd and Alexandra Gillespie, 81–88. London: British Library, 2004.

Grafton, Anthony. *Commerce with the Classics: Ancient Books and Renaissance Readers.* Ann Arbor: University of Michigan Press, 1997.

Grafton, Anthony. "Kepler as a Reader." *Journal of the History of Ideas* 53 (1992): 561–572.

Grafton, Anthony, and Lisa Jardine. "Studied for Action: How Gabriel Harvey Read His Livy." *Past and Present* 129 (1990): 30–78.

Graham, Timothy. "Matthew Parker's Manuscripts: An Elizabethan Library and Its Use." In *The Cambridge History of Libraries in Britain and Ireland*, ed. Elisabeth Leedham-Green and Teresa Webber, 322–341. Cambridge: Cambridge University Libraries, 2006.

Greengrass, Mark. "Archive Refractions: Hartlib's Papers and the Workings of an Intelligencer." In *Archives of the Scientific Revolution: The Formation and Exchange of Ideas in Seventeenth Century Europe,* ed. Michael Hunter, 35–47. Woodbridge: Boydell Press, 1998.

Greengrass, Mark. "Samuel Hartlib and Scribal Communication." *Acta Comeniana* 12 (1997): 47–62.

Greengrass, Mark, Michael Leslie, and Timothy Raylor, eds. *Samuel Hartlib and Universal Reformation: Studies in Intellectual Communication.* Cambridge: Cambridge University Press, 1994.

Griffiths, Paul, Adam Fox, and Steve Hindle, eds. *The Experience of Authority in Early Modern England.* London: Macmillan, 1996.

Guldi, Jo. *Roads to Power: Britain Invents the Infrastructure State.* Cambridge, Mass.: Harvard University Press, 2012.

Habermas, Jürgen. *The Structural Transformation of the Public Sphere: An Inquiry into a Category of Bourgeois Society.* Trans. Thomas Burger. Cambridge, Mass.: MIT Press, 1991.

Hagstrom, Warren O. *The Scientific Community.* Carbondale: Southern Illinois University Press, 1965.

Hall, David. *Ways of Writing: The Practice and Politics of Text-making in Seventeenth-Century New England.* Philadelphia: University of Pennsylvania Press, 2008.

Hall, Marie Boas. *Henry Oldenburg: Shaping the Royal Society.* Oxford: Oxford University Press, 2002.

Hall, Marie Boas. *The Library and Archives of the Royal Society 1660–1990.* London: Royal Society, 1992.

Hall, Rupert, and Marie Boas Hall. "The Intellectual Origins of the Royal Society: London and Oxford." *Notes and Records of the Royal Society of London* 23 (1968): 157–168.

Harkness, Deborah. *The Jewel House: Elizabethan London and the Scientific Revolution.* New Haven, Conn.: Yale University Press, 2007.

Harkness, Deborah. "Managing an Experimental Household: The Dees of Mortlake and the Practice of Natural Philosophy." *Isis* (1997): 247–262.

Harris, Brice. "Captain Robert Julian, Secretary to the Muses." *English Literary History* 10 (1943): 294–309.

Harris, Frances. "Ireland as a Laboratory: The Archive of Sir William Petty." In *The Archives of the Scientific Revolution: The Formation and Exchange of Ideas in Seventeenth Century Europe,* ed. Michael Hunger, 73–90. Woodbridge: Boydell Press, 1998.

Harris, Frances. *Transformations of Love: The Friendship of John Evelyn and Margaret Godolphin.* Oxford: Oxford University Press, 2003.

Harris, Frances, and Michael Hunter, eds. *John Evelyn and His Milieu.* London: British Library, 2003.

Harris, Michael. "Moses Pitt and Insolvency in the Booktrade in the Late 17th Century." In *Economics of the British Booktrade 1605–1939,* ed. Robin Myers and Michael Harris, 176–208. Cambridge: Chadwyck-Healey, 1985.

Harris, Robert. *Politics and the Rise of the Press: Britain and France, 1620–1800.* London: Routledge, 1996.

Harris, Steven. "Confession-Building, Long-Distance Networks, and the Organization of Jesuit Science." *Early Science and Medicine* 1 (1996): 287–318.

Harris, Steven J. "Networks of Travel, Correspondence, and Exchange." In *The Cambridge History of Early Modern Science*, vol. 3., ed. Katharine Park and Lorraine Daston, 341–362. Cambridge: Cambridge University Press, 2008.

Harris, Tim. *London Crowds in the Reign of Charles II: Propaganda and Politics from the Restoration Until the Exclusion Crisis.* Cambridge: Cambridge University Press, 1987.

Harris, Tim, ed. *Popular Culture in England, c. 1500–1850.* London: Macmillan, 1995.

Head, Randolph C. "Documents, Archives, and Proof Around 1700." *Historical Journal* 56 (2013): 909–930.

Heal, Felicity. "The Idea of Hospitality in Early Modern England." *Past and Present* 102 (1984): 66–93.

Hechter, Michael. *Internal Colonialism: The Celtic Fringe in British National Development, 1536–1966.* Berkeley: University of California Press, 1975.

Helgerson, Richard. *Forms of Nationhood: The Elizabethan Writing of England.* Chicago: University of Chicago Press, 1994.

Hellyer, Marcus. "The Pocket Museum: Edward Lhwyd's *Lythophylacium.*" *Archives of Natural History* 23 (1996): 43–60.

Henderson, Felicity. "Robert Hooke's Archive." *Script and Print* 33 (2009): 92–108.

Henry, John. "The Origins of Modern Science: Henry Oldenburg's Contribution." *British Journal of the History of Science* 21 (1998): 103–110.

Henry, Maura A. "The Making of Elite Culture." In *A Companion to Eighteenth-Century Britain*, ed. H. T. Dickinson, 311–328. Oxford: Blackwell, 2002.

Hey, David. *Packmen, Carriers and Packhorse Roads: Trade and Communications in North Derbyshire and South Yorkshire.* Leicester: Leicester University Press, 1980.

Hill, Christopher. "The Protestant Nation." In *The Collected Essays of Christopher Hill*, vol. 2, 21–36. Amherst: University of Massachusetts Press, 1986.

Hill, Jacqueline. "Ireland Without Union: Molyneux and His Legacy." In *A Union for Empire: Political Thought and the British Union of 1707,* ed. John Robertson, 271–298. Cambridge: Cambridge University Press, 1995.

Hindle, Paul. *Roads and Tracks for Historians.* London: Phillimore, 2001.

Hoffman, George. "The Montaigne Monopoly: Revising the *Essais* Under the French Privilege System." *PMLA* 108 (1993): 308–319.

Hofmann, Theodore, Joan Winterkorn, Frances Harris, and Hilton Kelliher. "John Evelyn's Archive at the British Library." *Book Collector* 44 (1995): 147–209.

Horden, John. "'In the Savoy' John Nutt and His Family." *Publishing History* 24 (1988): 5–26.

Hornblower, Simon, and Anthony Spawforth, eds. *Oxford Classical Dictionary.* 3rd ed. Oxford: Oxford University Press, 1996.

Houghton, Walter E., Jr. "The History of Trades: Its Relation to Seventeenth Century Thought." *Journal of the History of Ideas* 2 (1941): 33–60.

Howard-Hill, T. H. "'Nor Stage, Nor Stationers Stall Can Showe:' The Circulation of Plays in Manuscript in the Early Seventeenth Century." *Book History* 2 (1999): 28–41.

Hsia, Florence. "Mathematical Martyrs, Mandarin Missionaries, and Apostolic Academicians: Telling Institutional Lives." In *Institutional Culture in Early Modern Society*, ed. Anne Goldgar and Robert I. Frost, 3–34. Leiden: Brill, 2004.

Hunt, Arnold. "Sloane as a Collector of Manuscripts." In *From Books to Bezoars: Sir Hans Sloane and His Collections*, ed. Alison Walker, Arthur MacGregor, and Michael Hunter, 190–207. London: British Library, 2012.

Hunter, Andrew, ed. *Thornton and Tully's Scientific Books, Libraries and Collectors*. 4th ed. Aldershot: Ashgate, 2000.

Hunter, Michael. *Editing Early Modern Texts: An Introduction to Principles and Practice*. Basingstoke: Palgrave Macmillan, 2007.

Hunter, Michael, *Establishing the New Sciences: The Experience of the Early Royal Society*. Woodbridge, Suffolk: Boydell Press, 1989.

Hunter, Michael. "Hooke the Natural Philosopher." In *London's Leonardo: The Life and Work of Robert Hooke*, ed. J. A. Bennett, 105–162. Oxford: Oxford University Press, 2003.

Hunter, Michael. "How to Edit a Seventeenth-Century Manuscript: Principles and Practice." *Seventeenth Century* 10 (1995): 277–310.

Hunter, Michael. *John Aubrey and the Realm of Learning*. New York: Science History Publications, 1975.

Hunter, Michael. "Robert Boyle and the Early Royal Society: A Reciprocal Exchange in the Making of Baconian Science." *British Journal for the History of Science* 40 (2007): 1–23.

Hunter, Michael. *The Royal Society and Its Fellows, 1660–1700: The Morphology of an Early Scientific Institution*. 2nd ed. Oxford: British Society for the History of Science, 1994.

Hunter, Michael. *Science and Society in Restoration England*. Cambridge: Cambridge University Press, 1981.

Hunter, Michael, ed. *Archives of the Scientific Revolution: The Formation and Exchange of Ideas in Seventeenth Century Europe*. Woodbridge: Boydell Press, 1998.

Hunter, Michael, and Simon Schaffer, eds. *Robert Hooke: New Studies*. Woodbridge, Suffolk: Boydell Press, 1989.

Iliffe, Rob. "'In the Warehouse': Privacy, Property and Priority in the Early Royal Society." *History of Science* 30 (1992): 29–68.

Iliffe, Rob. "Material Doubts: Hooke, Artisan Culture, and the Exchange of Information in 1670s London." *British Journal for the History of Science* 28 (1995): 285–318.

Impey, Oliver, and Arthur MacGregor, eds. *The Origins of Museums: The Cabinets of Curiosities in Sixteenth- and Seventeenth-Century Europe*. Oxford: Oxford University Press, 1983.

Ingram, John E. "Introduction." In *Elysium Britannicum, or The Royal Gardens*, ed. John E. Ingram, 1–9. Philadelphia: University of Pennsylvania Press, 2001.

Jackson, H. J. *Marginalia: Readers Writing in Books*. New Haven, Conn.: Yale University Press, 2001.

Jagodzinski, Cecile M. *Privacy and Print: Reading and Writing in Seventeenth-Century England*. Charlottesville: University Press of Virginia, 1999.

James, K. A. "'Humbly Dedicated': Petiver and the Audience for Natural History in Early Eighteenth-Century Britain." *Archives of Natural History* 31 (2004): 318–329.

Jardine, Lisa. *Erasmus, Man of Letters: The Construction of Charisma in Print*. Princeton, N.J.: Princeton University Press, 1993.

Jardine, Nicholas, et al., eds. *Cultures of Natural History*. Cambridge: Cambridge University Press, 1996.

Jenkins, Phillip. *The Making of a Ruling Class: The Glamorgan Gentry, 1640–1790*. Cambridge: Cambridge University Press, 1983.

Jenkins, Phillip. "Seventeenth-Century Wales: Definition and Identity." In *British Consciousness and Identity: The Making of Britain, 1533–1707*, ed. Brendan Bradshaw and Peter Roberts, 213–235. Cambridge: Cambridge University Press, 1998.

"John Evelyn in the British Library." *Book Collector* 44 (1995): 147–238.

Johns, Adrian. "Coffeehouses and Print Shops." In *The Cambridge History of Early Modern Science*, vol. 3, ed. Katharine Park and Lorraine Daston, 320–340. Cambridge: Cambridge University Press, 2008.

Johns, Adrian. "How to Acknowledge a Revolution." *American Historical Review* 107 (2002): 106–125.

Johns, Adrian. "Miscellaneous Methods: Authors, Societies and Journals in Early Modern England." *British Journal for the History of Science* 33 (2000): 159–186.

Johns, Adrian. "Natural History as Print Culture." In *Cultures of Natural History*, ed. N. Jardine, J. A. Secord, and E. C. Spary, 106–124. Cambridge: Cambridge University Press, 1996.

Johns, Adrian. *The Nature of the Book: Print and Knowledge in the Making.* Chicago: University of Chicago Press, 1998.

Kassell, Lauren. *Medicine and Magic in Elizabethan England: Simon Forman: Astrologer, Alchemist, and Physician.* Oxford: Clarendon Press, 2005.

Kearney, Hugh. *The British Isles: A History of Four Nations.* Cambridge: Cambridge University Press, 1989.

Kernan, Alvin. *Printing Technology, Letters, and Samuel Johnson.* Princeton, N.J.: Princeton University Press, 1987.

Keynes, Geoffrey. *John Evelyn: A Study in Bibliophily with a Bibliography of His Writings.* 2nd ed. Oxford: Clarendon Press, 1968.

Kidd, Colin. *British Identities Before Nationalism: Ethnicity and Nationhood in the Atlantic World, 1600–1800.* Cambridge: Cambridge University Press, 1999.

Kilburn, Matthew. "The Fell Legacy, 1686–1755." In *History of Oxford University Press, vol. 1: Beginnings to 1780*, ed. Ian Gadd, 107–138. Oxford: Oxford University Press, 2013.

Knights, Mark. *Representation and Misrepresentation in Later Stuart Britain: Partisanship and Political Culture.* Oxford: Oxford University Press, 2006.

Knoppers, Laura Lunger. "Opening the Queen's Closet: Henrietta Maria, Elizabeth Cromwell, and the Politics of Cookery." *Renaissance Quarterly* 60 (2007): 464–499.

Koerner, Lisbet. "Daedalus Hyperboreus: Baltic Natural History and Mineralogy in the Enlightenment." In *The Sciences in Enlightened Europe*, ed. William Clark, Jan Golinski, and Simon Schaffer, 389–422. Chicago: University of Chicago Press, 1999.

Kupperman, Karen Ordahl. "Fear of Hot Climates in the Anglo-American Colonial Experience." *William and Mary Quarterly* 41 (1984): 213–240.

Kusukawa, Sachiko. "The 'Historia Piscium' (1686)." *Notes and Records of the Royal Society of London* 54 (2000): 179–197.

Kusukawa, Sachiko. "Illustrating Nature." In *Books and the Sciences in History*, ed. Marina Frasca-Spada and Nicholas Jardine, 90–113. Cambridge: Cambridge University Press, 2000.

Kusukawa, Sachiko. *Picturing the Book of Nature: Image, Text, and Argument in Sixteenth-Century Human Anatomy and Medical Botany.* Chicago: University of Chicago Press, 2012.

Kusukawa, Sachiko. "The Uses of Pictures in the Formation of Learned Knowledge: The Cases of Leonhard Fuchs and Andreas Vesalius." In *Transmitting Knowledge: Words, Images, and Instruments in Early Modern Europe*, ed. Sachiko Kusukawa and Ian Maclean, 73–96. Oxford: Oxford University Press, 2006.

Larminie, Vivienne. "The Fell Era 1658–1686." In *History of Oxford University Press, vol. 1: Beginnings to 1780*, ed. Ian Gadd, 79–106. Oxford: Oxford University Press, 2013.

Leedham-Green, Elisabeth, and Teresa Webber, eds. *The Cambridge History of Libraries in Britain and Ireland.* Cambridge: Cambridge University Libraries, 2006.

Leong, Elaine, and Alisha Rankin, eds. *Secrets and Knowledge in Medicine and Science, 1500–1800.* Farnham, Surrey: Ashgate, 2011.

Leslie, Michael, and Timothy Raylor, eds. *Culture and Cultivation in Early Modern England: Writing and the Land.* Leicester: Leicester University Press, 1992.

Livingstone, David. *Dealing with Darwin: Place, Politics, and Rhetoric in Religious Engagements with Evolution.* Baltimore, Md.: Johns Hopkins University Press, 2014.

Livingstone, David. "Science, Site and Speech: Scientific Knowledge and the Spaces of Rhetoric." *History of the Human Sciences* 20 (2007): 71–98.

Love, Harold. *The Culture and Commerce of Texts: Scribal Publication in Seventeenth-Century England.* Amherst: University of Massachusetts Press, 1998.

Lowood, Henry E., and Robin E. Rider. "The Scientific Book as a Cultural and Bibliographical Object." In *Thornton and Tully's Scientific Books, Libraries and Collectors,* ed. Andrew Hunter, 1–25. 4th ed. Aldershot: Ashgate, 2000.

Lux, David S., and Harold J. Cook. "Closed Circles or Open Networks? Communicating at a Distance During the Scientific Revolution." *History of Science* 36 (1998): 179–211.

Lynch, William T. *Solomon's Child: Method in the Early Royal Society of London.* Stanford, Calif.: Stanford University Press, 2002.

MacGregor, Arthur. "Edward Lhuyd, Museum Keeper." *Welsh History Review* 25 (2010): 51–74.

MacGregor, Arthur. "The Tradescants as Collectors of Rarities." In *Tradescant's Rarities: Essays on the Foundation of the Ashmolean Museum in 1683,* ed. Arthur MacGregor, 17–23. Oxford: Clarendon Press, 1983.

MacGregor, Arthur, ed. *Tradescant's Rarities: Essays on the Foundation of the Ashmolean Museum in 1683.* Oxford: Clarendon Press, 1983.

Mah, Harold. "Phantasies of the Public Sphere: Rethinking the Habermas of the Historians." *Journal of Modern History* 72 (2000): 153–182.

Mandelbrote, Giles. "John Evelyn and His Books." In *John Evelyn and His Milieu,* ed. Frances Harris and Michael Hunter, 71–94. London: British Library, 2003.

Mann, Alastair J. "'A Mongrel of Early Modern Copyright': Scotland in European Perspective." In *Privilege and Property: Essays on the History of Copyright,* ed. Ronan Deazley, Martin Kretschmer, and Lionel Bently, 51–65. Cambridge: OpenBook Publishers, 2010.

Margócsy, Dániel. *Commercial Visions: Science, Trade, and Visual Culture in the Dutch Golden Age.* Chicago: University of Chicago Press, 2014.

Margócsy, Dániel. "'Refer to Folio and Number': Encyclopedias, the Exchange of Curiosities, and Practices of Identification Before Linnaeus." *Journal of the History of Ideas* 71 (2010): 63–89.

Marotti, Arthur F. *Manuscript, Print, and the English Renaissance Lyric.* Ithaca, N.Y.: Cornell University Press, 1995.

Marotti, Arthur F. "Folger MSS V.a.89 and V.a.345: Reading Lyric Poetry in Manuscript." In *The Reader Revealed,* ed. Sabrina Alcorn, Elizabeth Walsh, and Susan Scola, 45–57. Washington, D.C.: Folger Shakespeare Library, 2001.

Marotti, Arthur F., and Michael D. Bristol, eds. *Print, Manuscript, Performance: The Changing Relations of the Media in Early Modern England.* Columbus: Ohio State University Press, 2000.

McCormick, Ted. "Alchemy in the Political Arithmetic of Sir William Petty (1623–1687)." *Studies in History and Philosophy of Science* 37 (2006): 290–307.

McCormick, Ted. *William Petty and the Ambitions of Political Arithmetic.* Oxford: Oxford University Press, 2010.

McDowell, Paula. *The Women of Grub Street: Press, Politics, and Gender in the London Literary Marketplace, 1678–1730.* Oxford: Clarendon Press, 1998.

McKenzie, Donald. "Speech-Manuscript-Print." *The Library Chronicle of the University of Texas* 20 (1990): 87–109.

McKitterick, David. *Print, Manuscript and the Search for Order, 1450–1830.* Cambridge: Cambridge University Press, 2003.

McRae, Andrew. *God Speed the Plough: The Representation of Agrarian England, 1500–1660.* New York: Cambridge University Press, 1996.

Mendelsohn, J. Andrew. "The World on a Page: Making a General Observation in the Eighteenth Century." In *Histories of Scientific Observation*, ed. Lorraine Daston and Elizabeth Lunbeck, 396–420. Chicago: University of Chicago Press, 2011.

Mendyk, Stan A. E. "Robert Plot: Britain's 'Genial Father of County Natural Histories.'" *Notes and Records of the Royal Society of London* 39 (1985): 159–177.

Mendyk, Stan A. E. *"Speculum Britanniae": Regional Study, Antiquarianism and Science in Britain to 1700.* Toronto: University of Toronto Press, 1989.

Miller, Peter. *Peiresc's Europe: Learning and Virtue in the Seventeenth Century.* New Haven, Conn.: Yale University Press, 2000.

Monson, Craig. "Through a Glass Darkly: Byrd's Verse Service as Reflected in Manuscript Sources." *Musical Quarterly* 67 (1981): 64–81.

Moran, Bruce. *Alchemical World of the German Court: Occult Philosophy and Chemical Medicine in the Circle of Moritz of Hessen, 1572–1632.* Stuttgart: F. Steiner Verlag, 1991.

Moran, Bruce, ed. *Patronage and Institutions: Science, Technology, and Medicine at the European Court, 1500–1700.* Rochester: Boydell Press, 1991.

Mosley, Adam. "Astronomical Books and Courtly Communication." In *Books and the Sciences in History*, ed. Marina Frasca-Spada and Nicholas Jardine, 114–131. Cambridge: Cambridge University Press, 2000.

Mosley, Adam. *Bearing the Heavens: Tycho Brahe and the Astronomical Community of the Late Sixteenth Century.* Cambridge: Cambridge University Press, 2007.

Moss, Ann. *Printed Commonplace-Books and the Structuring of Renaissance Thought.* Oxford: Clarendon Press, 1996.

Moureau, François, ed. *De bonne main: La communication manuscrite au XVIIIᵉ siècle.* Paris: Universitas, 1993.

Myers, Robin, and Michael Harris, eds. *Spreading the Word: The Distribution Networks of Print, 1550–1850.* Detroit: St. Paul's Bibliographies, 1990.

Myers, Robin, Michael Harris, and Giles Mandelbrote, eds. *Owners, Annotators and the Signs of Reading.* London: Oak Knoll Press & British Library, 2005.

Nummedal, Tara, and Paula Findlen, "Words of Nature: Scientific Books in the Seventeenth Century." In *Thornton and Tully's Scientific Books, Libraries and Collectors*, ed. Andrew Hunter, 164–215. 4th ed. Aldershot: Ashgate, 2000.

Ogilvie, Brian W. "Attending to Insects: Francis Willughby and John Ray." *Notes and Records of the Royal Society of London* 66 (2012): 357–372.

Ogilvie, Brian W. "The Many Books of Nature: Renaissance Naturalists and Information Overload." *Journal of the History of Ideas* 64 (2003): 29–40.

Ogilvie, Brian W. *The Science of Describing: Natural History in Renaissance Europe.* Chicago: University of Chicago Press, 2006.

Olwig, Kenneth Robert. *Landscape, Nature, and the Body Politic: From Britain's Renaissance to America's New World.* Madison: University of Wisconsin Press, 2002.

O'Neill, Lindsay. "Dealing with Newsmongers: News, Trust, and Letters in the British World, ca. 1670–1730." *Huntington Library Quarterly* 76 (2013): 215–233.

Osseo-Asare, Abena Dove. *Bitter Roots: The Search for Healing Plants in Africa.* Chicago: University of Chicago Press, 2014.

O'Sullivan, Anne, and William O'Sullivan. "Introduction." In Edward Lhuyd, *Archaeologia Britannica, an Account of the Languages, Histories and Customs of the Original Inhabitants of Great Britain.* Shannon: Irish University Press, 1971.

Ousby, Ian. *The Englishman's England: Taste, Travel, and the Rise of Tourism.* New York: Cambridge University Press, 1990.

Outram, Dorinda. "New Spaces in Natural History." In *Cultures of Natural History*, ed. Nicholas Jardine et al., 249–265. Cambridge: Cambridge University Press, 1996.

Ovenden, Richard. "Catalogue of the Bodleian Library and Other Collections." In *History of the Oxford University Press, vol. 1: Beginnings to 1780*, ed. Ian Gadd, 279–292. Oxford: Oxford University Press, 2013.

Oxford Dictionary of National Biography. Oxford: Oxford University Press, 2004–2008.

Pal, Carol. "Information Factory: Samuel Hartlib and the Creation of Scientific Knowledge." Paper presented at the annual meeting of the History of Science Society, Boston, 2013.

Parry, Graham. "John Evelyn as Hortulan Saint." In *Culture and Cultivation in Early Modern England: Writing and the Land*, ed. Michael Leslie and Timothy Raylor, 130–150. Leicester: Leicester University Press, 1992.

Parry, Graham. *The Trophies of Time: English Antiquarians of the Seventeenth Century.* Oxford: Oxford University Press, 1995.

Peck, Linda Levy. "Luxury and War: Reconsidering Luxury Consumption in Seventeenth-Century England." *Albion* 34 (2002): 1–23.

Peck, Linda Levy. "Uncovering the Arundel Library at the Royal Society: Changing Meanings of Science and the Fate of the Norfolk Donation." *Notes and Records of the Royal Society of London* 52 (1998): 3–24.

Pfister, Ulrich. "Craft Guilds and Technological Change: The Engine Loom in the European Silk Ribbon Industry in the Seventeenth and Eighteenth Centuries." In *Guilds, Innovation, and the European Economy, 1400–1800*, ed. S. R. Epstein and Maarten Prak, 172–198. Cambridge: Cambridge University Press, 2008.

Phillip, Ian. *The Bodleian Library in the Seventeenth and Eighteenth Centuries.* Oxford: Clarendon Press, 1983.

Pincus, Steven. "'Coffee Politicians Does Create': Coffeehouses and Restoration Political Culture." *Journal of Modern History* 67 (1995): 807–834.

Pincus, Steven. *Protestantism and Patriotism: Ideologies and the Making of English Foreign Policy.* Cambridge: Cambridge University Press, 1996.

Pincus, Steven. *1688: The First Modern Revolution.* New Haven, Conn.: Yale University Press, 2009.

Pittock, Murray G. H. *Celtic Identity and the British Image.* Manchester: Manchester University Press, 1999.

Pocock, J. G. A. "British History: A Plea for a New Subject." *Journal of Modern History* 47 (1975): 601–621.

Popper, Nicholas. "From Abbey to Archive: Managing Texts and Records in Early Modern England." *Archival Science* 10 (2010): 249–266.

Powell, Anthony. *John Aubrey and His Friends*. Rev. ed. London: Hogarth Press, 1963.

Pugliano, Valentina. "Botanical Artisans: Apothecaries and the Study of Nature in Venice and London, 1550–1610." D.Phil. diss., Oxford University, 2012.

Pumfrey, Stephen. "Ideas Above His Station: A Social Study of Hooke's Curatorship of Experiments." *History of Science* 29 (1991): 1–44.

Purcell, Mark. " 'Settled in the North of Ireland' or, Where Did Sloane Come From?" In *From Books to Bezoars: Sir Hans Sloane and His Collections*, ed. Alison Walker, Arthur MacGregor, and Michael Hunter, 24–32. London: British Library, 2012.

Rankin, Alisha. "Becoming an Expert Practitioner: Court Experimentalism and the Medical Skills of Anna of Saxony (1532–1585)." *Isis* 98 (2007): 23–53.

Raven, Charles. *John Ray, Naturalist: His Life and Works*. 2nd ed. Cambridge: Cambridge University Press, 1950.

Rees, Eiluned, and Gwyn Walters. "The Dispersion of the Manuscripts of Edward Lhuyd." *Welsh History Review* (1974): 148–178.

Richardson, Brian. *Manuscript Culture in Renaissance Italy*. New York: Cambridge University Press, 2009.

Richardson, Brian. *Printing, Writers, and Readers in Renaissance Italy*. Cambridge: Cambridge University Press, 1999.

Roberts, Brynley F. *Edward Lhuyd: The Making of a Scientist*. Cardiff: University of Wales Press, 1980.

Roberts, Peter. "Tudor Wales, National Identity and the British Inheritance." In *British Consciousness and Identity: The Making of Britain, 1533–1707*, ed. Brendan Bradshaw and Peter Roberts, 8–42. Cambridge: Cambridge University Press, 1998.

Robertson, John. "Union, State and Empire: The Union of 1707 in Its European Setting." In *An Imperial State at War: Britain from 1689–1815*, ed. Lawrence Stone, 237–250. New York: Routledge, 1994.

Robertson, John. *A Union for Empire: Political Thought and the British Union of 1707*. Cambridge: Cambridge University Press, 1995.

Robinson, F. J. G., and P. J. Wallis. *Book Subscription Lists: A Revised Guide*. Newcastle: H. Hill and Son, 1975.

Robinson, Howard. *Britain's Post Office: A History of Development from the Beginnings to the Present Day*. London: Oxford University Press, 1953.

Roos, Anna Marie. "The Art of Science: A 'Rediscovery' of the Lister Copperplates." *Notes and Records of the Royal Society of London* 66 (2012): 19–40.

Roos, Anna Marie. *Web of Nature: Martin Lister (1639–1712), the First Arachnologist*. Leiden: Brill, 2011.

Rupp, Jan C. "The New Science and the Public Sphere in the Premodern Era." *Science in Context* 8 (1995): 487–507.

St. Clair, William. *The Reading Nation in the Romantic Period*. Cambridge: Cambridge University Press, 2004.

Samuel, Raphael. "British Dimensions: 'Four Nations History.'" *History Workshop Journal* 40 (1995): iii–xxii.

Saunders, J. W. "The Stigma of Print: A Note on the Social Bases of Tudor Poetry." *Essays in Criticism* 1 (1951): 139–164.

Schaffer, Simon. "Regeneration: The Body of Natural Philosophers in Restoration England." In *Science Incarnate: Historical Embodiments of Natural Knowledge*, ed. Christopher Lawrence and Steven Shapin, 83–120. Chicago: University of Chicago Press, 1998.

Schiebinger, Londa. *Plants and Empire: Colonial Bioprospecting in the Atlantic World.* Cambridge, Mass.: Harvard University Press, 2004.

Schwartz, Joan M., and Terry Cook. "Archives, Records, and Power: The Making of Modern Memory." *Archival Science* 2 (2002): 1–19.

Schwartz, Joan M., and Terry Cook, eds. Special issue on "Archives, Records, and Power." *Archival Science* 2 (2002): 1–159.

Scott-Warren, Jason. "Reconstructing Manuscript Networks: The Textual Transactions of Sir Stephen Powle." In *Communities in Early Modern England,* ed. Alexandra Shepard and Phil Withington, 18–37. Manchester: Manchester University Press, 2000.

Secord, Anne. "Corresponding Interests: Artisans and Gentlemen in Nineteenth-Century Natural History." *British Journal for the History of Science* 27 (1994): 383–408.

Secord, James. "How Scientific Conversation Became Shop Talk." In *Science in the Marketplace: Nineteenth-Century Sites and Experiences,* ed. Aileen Fyfe and Bernard Lightman, chap. 2. Chicago: University of Chicago Press, 2007.

Secord, James. "Nature's Fancy: Charles Darwin and the Breeding of Pigeons." *Isis* 72 (1981): 162–186.

Secord, James. *Victorian Sensation: The Extraordinary Publication, Reception, and Secret Authorship of* Vestiges of the Natural History of Creation. Chicago: University of Chicago Press, 2000.

Selwood, Jacob. *Diversity and Difference in Early Modern London.* Farnham: Ashgate, 2010.

Shapin, Steven. "Pump and Circumstance: Robert Boyle's Literary Technology." *Social Studies of Science* 14 (1984): 481–520.

Shapin, Steven. *A Social History of Truth: Civility and Science in Seventeenth-Century England.* Chicago: University of Chicago Press, 1994.

Shapin, Steven. "Who Was Robert Hooke?" In *Robert Hooke: New Studies,* ed. Michael Hunter and Simon Schaffer, 253–285. Woodbridge, Suffolk: Boydell Press, 1989.

Shapin, Steven, and Simon Schaffer. *Leviathan and the Air Pump: Hobbes, Boyle, and the Experimental Life.* Princeton, N.J.: Princeton University Press, 1985.

Shapiro, Barbara. *A Culture of Fact: England, 1550–1720.* Ithaca, N.Y.: Cornell University Press, 2000.

Sharpe, Kevin. *Reading Revolutions: The Politics of Reading Early Modern England.* New Haven, Conn.: Yale University Press, 2000.

Shepard, Alexandra, and Phil Withington, eds. *Communities in Early Modern England: Networks, Place, Rhetoric.* Manchester: Manchester University Press, 2000.

Sherman, William. *John Dee.* Amherst: University of Massachusetts Press, 1995.

Sherman, William. *Used Books: Marking Readers in Renaissance England.* Philadelphia: University of Pennsylvania Press, 2008.

Siraisi, Nancy. *Medieval and Early Renaissance Medicine: An Introduction to Knowledge and Practice.* Chicago: University of Chicago Press, 1990.

Slack, Paul. "Government and Information in Seventeenth-Century England." *Past and Present* 184 (2004): 33–68.

Smith, Pamela H., and Paula Findlen, eds. *Merchants and Marvels: Commerce, Science, and Art in Early Modern Europe.* New York: Routledge, 2002.

Snyder, Christopher A. *The Britons.* Oxford: Wiley-Blackwell, 2003.

Soll, Jacob. *The Information Master: Jean-Baptiste Colbert's Secret State Intelligence System.* Ann Arbor: University of Michigan Press, 2009.

Stallybrass, Peter. "Printing for Manuscript." Rosenbach Lectures. University of Pennsylvania, Philadelphia, February 2006.

Steedman, Carolyn. *Dust: The Archive and Cultural History.* New Brunswick, N.J.: Rutgers University Press, 2002.

Stewart, Larry. *The Rise of Public Science: Rhetoric, Technology, and Natural Philosophy in Newtonian Britain, 1660–1750.* Cambridge: Cambridge University Press, 1992.

Stoler, Ann Laura. *Along the Archival Grain: Epistemic Anxieties and Colonial Common Sense.* Princeton, N.J.: Princeton University Press, 2009.

Stone, Lawrence, ed. *An Imperial State at War: Britain from 1689–1815.* New York: Routledge, 1994.

Stroup, Alice. *A Company of Scientists: Botany, Patronage, and Community at the Seventeenth-Century Parisian Royal Academy of Sciences.* Berkeley: University of California Press, 1990.

Suarez, Michael F., S.J., and Michael L. Turner, eds. *The Cambridge History of the Book in Britain.* Vol. 5, *1695–1830.* Cambridge: Cambridge University Press, 2009.

Suggett, Richard, and Eryn White. "Language, Literacy and Aspects of Identity in Early Modern Wales." In *The Spoken Word: Oral Culture in Britain, 1500–1850,* ed. Adam Fox and Daniel Woolf, 52–83. Manchester: Manchester University Press, 2002.

Sullivan, Isabel. "Their 'Own Sweet Country': The Evelyns in Surrey." In *John Evelyn and His Milieu,* ed. Frances Harris and Michael Hunter, 281–292. London: British Library, 2003.

Summit, Jennifer. *Memory's Library: Medieval Books in Early Modern England.* Chicago: University of Chicago Press, 2008.

Sutherland, L. S., and L. G. Mitchell, eds. *The Eighteenth Century.* Vol. 5, *The History of the University of Oxford.* Ed. T. H. Aston. Oxford: Clarendon Press, 1984.

Swan, Claudia. "On the Same Page: Early Modern Collection and Inscription." Paper presented at the annual meeting of the History of Science Society, Chicago, 2014.

Swann, Marjorie. *Curiosities and Texts: The Culture of Collecting in Early Modern England.* Philadelphia: University of Pennsylvania Press, 2001.

Sweet, Rosemary. *Antiquaries: The Discovery of the Past in Eighteenth-Century Britain.* London: Hambledon and London, 2004.

Thirsk, Joan. *Food in Early Modern England.* London: Hambledon Continuum, 2007.

Thirsk, Joan. "Making a Fresh Start: Sixteenth-Century Agriculture and the Classical Inspiration." In *Culture and Cultivation in Early Modern England: Writing and the Land,* ed. Michael Leslie and Timothy Raylor, 15–34. Leicester: Leicester University Press, 1992.

Tylden-Wright, David. *John Aubrey: A Life.* London: HarperCollins, 1991.

van der Krogt, Peter. "Gerhard Mercator and His Cosmography: How the 'Atlas' Became an Atlas." In *A World of Innovation: Cartography in the Time of Gerhard Mercator,* ed. Gerhard Holzer, Valerie Newby, and Petra Svatek, 112–130. Newcastle upon Tyne: Cambridge Scholars Publishing, 2015.

Vanhaelen, Angela, and Joseph P. Ward, eds. *Making Space Public in Early Modern Europe: Performance, Geography, Privacy.* New York: Routledge, 2013.

Vickery, Brian C. *Scientific Communication in History.* Lanham, Md.: Scarecrow Press, 2000.

Walker, Alison, Arthur MacGregor, and Michael Hunter, eds. *From Books to Bezoars: Sir Hans Sloane and His Collections.* London: British Library, 2012.

Wallis, P. J., and Ruth Wallis. *Book Subscription Lists: Extended Supplement to the Revised Guide.* Newcastle upon Tyne: Project for Historical Bibliography, 1996.

Walsham, Alexandra. *The Reformation of the Landscape.* Oxford: Oxford University Press, 2011.

Walters, Gwyn, and Frank Emery. "Edward Lhuyd, Edmund Gibson, and the Printing of Camden's *Britannia*, 1695." *Library*, 5th series, 32 (1977): 109–137.

Watt, Tessa. *Cheap Print and Popular Piety 1550–1640*. Cambridge: Cambridge University Press, 1991.

Watt, Tessa. "Publisher, Pedlar, Pot-Poet: The Changing Character of the Broadside Trade, 1550–1640." In *Spreading the Word: The Distribution Networks of Print, 1550–1850*, ed. R. Myers and M. Harris, 61–82. Detroit: St. Paul's Bibliographies, 1990.

Wear, Andrew. *Health and Healing in Early Modern England: Studies in Social and Intellectual History*. Aldershot: Ashgate, 1998.

Wear, Andrew. *Knowledge and Practice in English Medicine, 1550–1680*. Cambridge: Cambridge University Press, 2000.

Wear, Andrew. "Making Sense of Health and Environment in Early Modern England." In Andrew Wear, *Health and Healing in Early Modern England: Studies in Social and Intellectual History*, 119–147. Aldershot: Ashgate, 1998.

Welch, Martin. "The Foundation of the Ashmolean Museum." In *Tradescant's Rarities: Essays on the Foundation of the Ashmolean Museum in 1683, with a Catalogue of the Surviving Early Collections*, ed. Arthur MacGregor, 40–58. Oxford: Clarendon Press, 1983.

Weld, Kirsten. *Paper Cadavers: The Archives of Dictatorship in Guatemala*. Durham, N.C.: Duke University Press, 2014.

Wellman, Kathleen. *Making Science Social: The Conferences of Theophraste Renaudot*. Norman: University of Oklahoma Press, 2003.

Wennerlind, Carl. *Casualties of Credit: The English Financial Revolution*. Cambridge, Mass.: Harvard University Press, 2011.

Westfall, Richard. *Never at Rest: A Biography of Isaac Newton*. Cambridge: Cambridge University Press, 1983.

Williams, Derek R. *Prying into Every Hole and Corner: Edward Lhuyd in Cornwall in 1700*. Kernow: Dyllansow Truran, 1993.

Williams, Kelsey Jackson. "Training the Virtuoso: John Aubrey's Education and Early Life." *Seventeenth Century* 27 (2012): 157–182.

Williamson, Arthur. "Patterns of British Identity: 'Britain' and Its Rivals in the Sixteenth and Seventeenth Centuries." In *The New British History: Founding a Modern State, 1603–1715*, ed. Glenn Burgess, 138–173. London: I. B. Tauris, 1999.

Withers, Charles W. J. *Geography, Science, and National Identity: Scotland Since 1520*. Cambridge: Cambridge University Press, 2001.

Withers, Charles W. J. "Geography, Science, and National Identity in Early Modern Britain: The Case of Scotland and the Work of Robert Sibbald (1641–1722)." *Annals of Science* 53 (1996): 29–73.

Woolf, Daniel R. "The 'Common Voice': History, Folklore, and Oral Tradition in Early Modern England." *Past and Present* 120 (1988): 26–52.

Woolf, Daniel R. *Reading History in Early Modern England*. Cambridge: Cambridge University Press, 2000.

Woolf, Daniel R. *The Social Circulation of the Past: English Historical Culture, 1500–1730*. Oxford: Oxford University Press, 2003.

Woolf, Daniel R. "Speaking of History: Conversations About the Past in Restoration and Eighteenth-Century England." In *The Spoken Word: Oral Culture in Britain, 1500–1850*, ed. Adam Fox and Daniel Woolf, 119–137. Manchester: Manchester University Press, 2002.

Wormald, Francis, and C. E. Wright, eds. *The English Library Before 1700*. London: Athlone Press, 1958.

Wormald, Jenny. "The Creation of Britain: Multiple Kingdoms or Core and Colonies." *Transactions of the Royal Historical Society* 2 (1992): 175–194.

Woudhuysen, H. R. *Sir Phillip Sydney and the Circulation of Manuscripts 1558–1640*. Oxford: Clarendon Press, 1996.

Wright, C. E. "The Dispersal of the Libraries in the Sixteenth Century." In *The English Library Before 1700*, ed. Francis Wormald and C. E. Wright, 148–175. London: Athlone Press, 1958.

Wright, C. J., ed. *Sir Robert Cotton as Collector: Essays on an Early Stuart Collector and His Legacy*. London: British Library, 1997.

Wrightson, Keith. *Earthly Necessities: Economic Lives in Early Modern Britain*. New Haven, Conn.: Yale University Press, 2000.

Wrightson, Keith. "'Sorts of People' in Tudor and Stuart England." In *The Middling Sort of People: Culture, Society and Politics in England, 1550–1800*, ed. Jonathan Barry and Christopher Brooks, 28–51. London: Macmillan, 1994.

Yale, Elizabeth. "The History of Archives: The State of the Discipline." *Book History* 17 (forthcoming, 2015).

Yale, Elizabeth. "Making Lists: Social and Material Technologies for Seventeenth-Century British Natural History." In *Ways of Making and Knowing: The Material Culture of Empirical Knowledge, 1400–1850*, ed. Pamela H. Smith, Amy Meyers, and Harold Cook, 280–301. Ann Arbor: University of Michigan Press, 2014.

Yale, Elizabeth. "Manuscript Technologies: Correspondence, Collaboration, and the Construction of Natural Knowledge in Early Modern Britain." Ph.D. diss., Harvard University, 2008.

Yeo, Richard. *Encyclopaedic Visions: Scientific Dictionaries and Enlightenment Culture*. Cambridge: Cambridge University Press, 2001.

Yeo, Richard. "Notebooks as Memory Aids: Precepts and Practices in Early Modern England." *Memory Studies* 1 (2008): 115–136.

Yeo, Richard. *Notebooks, English Virtuosi, and Early Modern Science*. Chicago: University of Chicago Press, 2014.

Zappiah, Nat. "Review Essay: Coffeehouses and Culture." *Huntington Library Quarterly* 70 (2007): 671–677.

Zytaruk, Maria. "'Occasional *Specimens*, Not Compleate *Systemes*': John Evelyn's Culture of Collecting." *Bodleian Library Record* 17 (2001): 185–212.

Index

Acknowledgments

This book (and I) have had a long journey through the wilds of academia, and there are many people and institutions I wish to thank: for their good humor, for their critical perusal of one or more of the many texts that have fed into (or become) this book, for their friendship and hospitality, and for their financial support.

My thanks are due above all to Mario Biagioli, whose support and critical feedback has deeply shaped this book. I continue to value his insights as a reader and a mentor, generously offered at every critical juncture, even as our paths have taken us far from Harvard, where this book began. I thank Steven Shapin for his careful, incisive readings of the project, especially for his suggestion that I think about conversation, as well as correspondence, manuscript, and print. Ann Blair provided crucial intellectual guidance, introducing me to the history of the book and reading and supporting this book all through its several stages of life. She is a model of intellectual generosity and critical acuity. I thank her for her continuing support and friendship; I can only hope to pay it forward. I thank Peter Buck for reading and providing astute commentary on multiple drafts, prodding me as I expanded the book into a study not just of nature but of nation as well. I thank Janet Browne, Anne Harrington, Katharine Park, Owen Gingerich, and Heidi Voskuhl for their support and mentorship. Kathleen Coleman and Henrietta Harrison offered their wisdom and perspective on the academic life; I thank them for it. I thank the administrative staff in the history of science department, especially Jude Lajoie, Richard Wright, Michèle Biscoe, and Allie Belser, for doing so expertly and kindly the work that kept the department running during the time I was there.

I made many friends at Harvard who have become academic colleagues. For their friendship and for conversations across the years that have helped me think about the stories I tell in this book, I thank Dániel Margócsy, Josh

Cherniss, Alisha Rankin, Hanna Rose Shell, Phil Loring, Megan Formato, Nasser Zakariya, Melissa Lo, Alex Wellerstein, and Ellen Bales. While conducting archival research at Oxford, I was sustained by the friendship and collegiality of my fellow members of the history of science and medicine reading group: Erica Charters, Valentina Pugliano, Heather Palmer, and Rosemary Wall. I thank Kate Bennett and Michael Hunter for fruitful conversations and correspondence about John Aubrey, John Evelyn, and John Ray. Many thanks to my colleagues at the Derek Bok Center for Teaching and Learning, especially Cassandra Horii and Erin Driver-Linn, who provided a year to think through the broader contemporary relevance of questions related to the material and social realities of communications technologies.

For reading portions of the manuscript and providing feedback, I thank Jonathan Rose, Alex Csiszar, Roxana Popescu, Elise Lipkowitz, and Dániel Margócsy. Much of the material in this book was presented at conferences over the years; I thank fellow presenters and attendees at these panels for their questions and comments, which have helped me to refine my arguments. In particular, I thank Peter Stallybrass for the opportunity to present at the Penn Material Texts Seminar, and I am grateful to the members of the seminar, especially Roger Chartier, for sharing their thoughts. I thank Dan Carey for inviting me to the Heyman Center for the Humanities for the conference "Travel, Science, and the Question of Observation, 1580–1800"; conversations with fellow panelists and attendees helped spark my thinking on the relationship between topography and nation in early modern Britain. I thank Pamela Smith for asking me to contribute a paper on questionnaires to the volume *Ways of Making and Knowing: The Material Culture of Empirical Science, 1400–1850*, and David Sacks for inviting me to present on subscription publication at the "Nature's Publics" conference at McGill in 2010.

Over the years, conversations with Kathryn James, Tony Grafton, Meghan Doherty, Vera Keller, Maria Portuondo, Barbara Naddeo, Aaron Pratt, Florence Hsia, Matthew Stanley, Melinda Baldwin, Paul Needham, Dahlia Porter, Mordechai Feingold, Mary Fissell, Ted McCormick, Masatake Wasa, and Matthew Eddy have informed my thinking on many of the ideas presented in this book. I thank them. Brooke Conti, Sarah Wall-Randell, and Becky Kornegay stepped in with some valuable advice on the title, and Carolyn Lacey, Tegid Roberts, and Radha Nair-Roberts helped with high-speed Welsh translation. My thanks to them.

This book continued to develop during my years at Western Carolina University. I thank my colleagues there, especially Vicki Szabo, David

Dorondo, Alex Macaulay, Andrew Denson, Libby McRae, Nate Kreuter, Kathy Mathews, and Jim Costa. Thanks, especially, to Sloan Despeaux for her hospitality, friendship, and intellectual fellowship. Many thanks to Kathy Orr, the history department administrative assistant, and to Dean Richard Starnes, who always found a way to say yes to requests for support for research and conference travel.

At the University of Iowa, I have been lucky to land at the Center for the Book, with colleagues and students who challenge me every day to think about the history of the book and science in new ways. Timothy Barrett, Matt Brown, Kathleen Tandy, Adam Hooks, Kathleen Kamerick, Teresa Mangum, Katherine Tachau, Eric Gidal, Paul Greenough, and Linda Kerber deserve special thanks.

At the University of Pennsylvania Press, I appreciated the astute editorial guidance of Jerry Singerman: may all authors be so lucky in their editors. Many thanks to all the staff at the press, especially Hannah Blake, Caroline Winschel, managing editor Erica Ginsburg, and copy editor Patricia Coate. I very much appreciated the feedback I received from Sachiko Kusukawa and Eric Ash, who read the book for the press; their comments helped me to deepen my arguments and express them more clearly.

I thank the following institutions and organizations for their generous financial support, without which this project would not have been possible: Harvard University, the Manuscript Society, the American Council of Learned Societies, the Andrew W. Mellon Foundation, and Western Carolina University. Many thanks to the Rare Book School at the University of Virginia for admitting me to the Andrew W. Mellon Fellowship of Scholars in Critical Bibliography, which has given me the space to bring this project to a close and launch the next one.

This project would not have been possible without the expert and professional help of librarians and archivists on both sides of the Atlantic. At Harvard, I am particularly grateful for assistance provided by the staff at Houghton Library. I thank the staff of the Bodleian Library, particularly the Duke Humfrey's Library, and the staff of the British Library, especially the Manuscripts Reading Room, for their expert assistance. Many thanks to Arnold Hunt for tea and conversation at the BL. The staff at the Royal Society Library were most kind and helpful; special thanks there to Felicity Henderson and Rupert Baker. At Western Carolina University, the Interlibrary Loan staff efficiently and good-naturedly tracked down sources I needed; I thank them.

I gratefully acknowledge permission to reprint sections of the book that first appeared as essays in the journals *Book History* and *Studies in History and Philosophy of Biological and Biomedical Sciences*. Many thanks to Jonathan Rose and Marina Frasca-Spada, the editors with whom I worked at each journal. "With Slips and Scraps: How Early Modern Naturalists Invented the Archive," *Book History* 12 (2009): 1–36, formed the basis of Chapter 6 of this book. The arguments of Chapter 4 were first presented in "Marginalia, Commonplaces, and Correspondence: The Scribal Culture of Early Modern Science," *Studies in History and Philosophy of Biological and Biomedical Sciences* 42 (2011): 193–202. I thank the Bodleian Library and the Royal Society Library for permission to reproduce images from manuscripts in their care. Staff members at the Bodleian and the Royal Society kindly assisted with procuring images (and rights to reprint them). At the Bodleian, I thank Tricia Buckingham and Samantha Sherbourne. At the Royal Society, Joanna McManus provided efficient and expert assistance.

I thank my parents, Stephen and Jane Yale, for their love, support, and intellectual curiosity, which have driven me ever onward. This book is dedicated to them. Thanks to my brothers, Andrew, Thomas, and William Yale; to Andrew, especially, for intellectual companionship and moral support. Many thanks to Pamela and Derek Willard, who have welcomed me into their family with love and generosity. My thanks also to Belina Mizrahi, with deep love and gratitude for her friendship. To Nathan, whose love and support make all things possible, more than thanks; all the thanks. To Martha Jane, who inspires in me more joy than she can know every time she plays at work by writing in the margins of her books. And to Teddy: I hope you always race around libraries with the same enthusiasm you do now.